EDITOR

Susheila Nasta is a senior lecturer in English at
Homerton College, Cambridge, and at the
Polytechnic of North London. She is also a
research fellow at the Institute of
Commonwealth Studies, University of
London, where she is working on the
literatures of the Indian diaspora and is a
contributor to postgraduate research
seminars. Recent publications include *Critical
Perspectives on Sam Selvon* (Three Continents
Press, Washington DC, USA, 1989), as well as
a number of articles and monographs on
African and Caribbean literature. She is
founder-editor of *Wasafiri*, a literary journal
which publishes critical and creative writing
from Africa, the Caribbean and South Asia.

Motherlands

Black Women's Writing from Africa, the Caribbean and South Asia

Susheila Nasta, editor

Rutgers University Press
New Brunswick, New Jersey

First published in the United Kingdom by
The Women's Press Limited, 1991
A member of the Namara Group
34 Great Sutton Street, London ECIV 0DX

First published in the United States by
Rutgers University Press, 1992

Library of Congress Cataloguing in Publication Data
Motherlands : black women's writing from Africa, the
  Caribbean and South Asia
  1. Black women. English literature
  2. Nasta, Susheila

ISBN 0-8135-1781-8 (cloth)
ISBN 0-8135-1782-6 (pbk.)

Phototypeset by Intype, London
Printed and bound in Great Britain by
BPCC Hazell Books
Aylesbury, Bucks, England
Member of BPCC Ltd.

To my new baby daughter
Maya
and for Conrad and Susanna

Permissions Acknowledgments

Grateful acknowledgment is given to the following copyright holders and publishers for granting permission to reprint extracts from material in copyright.

Ama Ata Aidoo, *Dilemma of a Ghost* (1965). Longman. © Aidoo. *Anowa* (1970). Longman. © Aidoo. *Our Sister Killjoy* (1977). Longman. © Aidoo; reprinted by permission of the author.
Mariama Ba, *So Long A Letter* (1980). © Heinemann Educational Books 1981; reprinted by permission of the publisher.
Helene Cixous, *The Newly Born Woman* (1986). © Minnesota University Press; reprinted by permission of the publisher.
Anita Desai, *Village by the Sea* (1987). © William Heinemann. *Clear Light of Day* (1980). © William Heinemann; reprinted by permission of the publisher.
Shashi Deshpande, *That Long Silence* (1988). © Virago Press and author; reprinted by permission of the publisher.
Bessie Head, *Maru* (1972). © Heinemann Educational Books. *A Question of Power* (1968). © Heinemann Educational Books.
Ruth Prawer Jhabvala, *Heat and Dust* (1975). © John Murray: reprinted by permission of the publisher.
Jamaica Kincaid, *Annie John* (1985). © Author and Farrar Straus and Giroux. *A Small Place* (1988). © as above.
Julie Kristeva, *Design in Language* (1982). © Blackwell Books; reprinted by permission of the publisher.
Toni Morrison, '*Rootedness*', in *Black Women Writers*, ed. Mari Evans (1984). © Pluto Press; reprinted by permission of the publisher; *Tar Baby* (1981). © Knopf 1981 and author.
Paule Marshall, *Praisesong for the Widow* (1984). © EP Dutton 1984 and author.
Claude McKay, *Banana Bottom* (1933). © Harper 1961; reprinted by permission of the publisher.
Elizabeth Nunez-Harrell, *When Rocks Dance* (1986). Putnam. © author; reprinted by permission of the author's literary representative.
Marlene Nourbese Philip, Lines from 'Discourse on the Logic of Language', in *She Tries Her Tongue: her silence softly breaks* (1989). © Ragweed Press and the author; reprinted by permission of the author.
Jean Rhys, '*Let Them Call it Jazz*' (1927). © Andre Deutsch and the Jean Rhys Estate. *Voyage in the Dark* (1934). © Andre Deutsch and the Jean Rhys Estate; reprinted by permission of the publisher. Attempts have been made to contact the Jean Rhys Estate.
Nawal El Sa'adawi, *Woman at Point Zero* (1983). © Zed Books 1983; reprinted by permission of the publisher.
Olive Senior, *Summer Lightning and Other Stories* (1986). Longman; reprinted by permission of the author and publisher.
Leopold Senghor, *Senghor Prose and Poetry*, trans. John Reed and Clive Wake. © Oxford University Press; reprinted by permission of the publisher.
Nayantara Sahgal, *This Time of Morning* (1965). © Norton 1965. *Rich Like Us* (1985). © William Heinemann.
Sylvia Wynter, *The Hills of Hebron* (1962). © Jonathan Cape and the author; reprinted by permission of the publisher.
While every attempt has been made to trace the copyright holders of the above material, the editor and publishers would be pleased to hear from any interested parties.

Contents

Acknowledgments

The idea for this book was conceived during the period 1986–89 when I taught a course on black women's writing at Portsmouth Polytechnic. I would like especially to thank my students who helped, through seminar discussions and essays, to confirm my belief in the urgent need for a critical anthology linking women's writing from Africa, the Caribbean and South Asia. I would also like to extend sincere thanks to all of the contributors for their encouragement with the project, particularly to Dr Lyn Innes who has always provided a sympathetic ear. My thanks go also to Professor Shula Marks, the Director of London University's Institute of Commonwealth Studies, who kindly provided an institutional base for the research, to Dr Julia Swindell of Homerton College, Cambridge, to Judith Murray, Katherine Bright-Holmes, Jane Bryce-Okunlola and to Ros de Lanerolle who has throughout been an encouraging force. I would also like to thank Marlene Nourbese Philip for allowing an extract from her poem 'Discourse on the Logic of Language' to be used as a preface to this anthology.

Preface

An Extract From
'Discourse on the Logic of Language'

Marlene Nourbese Philip

English
is my mother tongue.
A mother tongue is not
not a foreign lan lan lang
language
l/anguish
    anguish
—a foreign anguish.

English is
my father tongue.
A father tongue is
a foreign language,
therefore English is
a foreign language
not a mother tongue.

What is my mother
tongue
my mammy tongue
my mummy tongue
my momsy tongue
my modder tongue
my ma tongue?

I have no mother
tongue
no mother to tongue
no tongue to mother
to mother
tongue
me

I must therefore be tongue
dumb
dumb-tongued

WHEN IT WAS BORN, THE MOTHER HELD HER NEWBORN CHILD CLOSE: SHE BEGAN THEN TO LICK IT ALL OVER. THE CHILD WHIMPERED A LITTLE, BUT AS THE MOTHER'S TONGUE MOVED FASTER AND STRONGER OVER ITS BODY, IT GREW SILENT – THE MOTHER TURNING IT THIS WAY AND THAT UNDER HER TONGUE, UNTIL SHE HAD TONGUED IT CLEAN OF THE CREAMY WHITE SUBSTANCE COVERING ITS BODY.

Edict I
Every owner of
slaves shall,
wherever possible,
ensure that his
slaves belong to as
many ethno-
linguistic groups as
possible. If they
cannot speak to
each other, they
cannot then foment
rebellion and
revolution.

dub-tongued
damn dumb
tongue
but I have
a dumb tongue
tongue dumb
father tongue
and english is
my mother tongue
is
my father tongue
is a foreign lan lan lang
language
l/anguish
   anguish
a foreign anguish
is english—
another tongue
my mother
    mammy
    mummy
    moder
    mater
    macer
    moder
tongue
mothertongue

tongue mother
tongue me
mothertongue me
mother me
touch me
with the tongue of your
lan lan lang
language
l/anguish
   anguish
english
is a foreign anguish

Edict II
Every slave caught
speaking his
native language
shall be severely
punished. Where
necessary, removal
of the tongue is
recommended. The
offending organ,
when removed,
should be hung on
high in a central
place, so that all
may see and
tremble.

THE MOTHER THEN PUT HER FINGERS INTO HER CHILD'S MOUTH – GENTLY FORCING IT OPEN; SHE TOUCHES HER TONGUE TO THE CHILD'S TONGUE, AND HOLDING THE TINY MOUTH OPEN, SHE BLOWS INTO IT – HARD. SHE WAS BLOWING WORDS – HER WORDS, HER MOTHER'S WORDS, THOSE OF HER MOTHER'S MOTHER, AND ALL THEIR MOTHERS BEFORE – INTO HER DAUGHTER'S MOUTH.

Susheila Nasta

Introduction

As I write this introduction I can hear the sounds of a number of different, contesting and dynamic voices echoing and pointing to the generation of the powerful literary and critical texts represented in this collection. As the poem by Marlene Nourbese Philip which forms the Preface to this anthology makes plain, 'English' for women writers from the Caribbean can be both a 'mothertongue' and a 'foreign language/l/anguish'. Moreover, in a post-colonial context, whether African, Caribbean or South Asian, this language carries with it a whole history of patriarchal myths and symbols whether originally instituted by the colonial power or later by primarily male-dominated movements towards nationalism and independence. Thus, it is 'father tongue' too. Language is both source and womb of creativity, a means of giving birth to new stories, new myths, of telling the stories of women that have previously been silenced; it can also become 'a major site of contest, a revolutionary struggle'.[1]

Colonised nations have frequently been represented by Europeans as 'female' requiring 'paternal governance' by the dominant power.[2] Later, this mythologised femaleness of the nation culture was perpetuated in the works of male writers who created stereotypes of woman: the 'mulatto figure' (often portrayed as an exotic, luscious fruit), or the powerful matriarch in Caribbean literature, 'Mother is Gold' the fertile earth mother in African literature; female goddesses entrapped by tradition and religion in 'Mother India'. Although such female figures were represented as powerful symbolic forces, repositories of culture and creativity, they were essentially silent and silenced by the structures surrounding them. In addition, 'when women began publishing' they faced the problem not only of making visible the varied experience of women in all of these different cultures but also of 'combatting the orthodoxies of colonial and anti-colonial writing'.[3]

In an early story by Jean Rhys, 'Let Them Call It Jazz', (1927) the Caribbean protagonist Selina finds herself, after a relentless series of negative experiences whether with men or the institutions of British racism, locked away in Holloway prison for singing too loud and disturbing the peace. Ironically, it is there that she discovers a soul mate when she hears one of the other prisoners singing the 'Holloway Song', a song that comes to symbolise the spirit of her existence. When she is released, she possesses her own version of the song which she whistles ('I never sing now') at a party. Almost immediately her song is taken from her by a man who 'jazzes' it up and eventually sends her five pounds. When she receives the money (the transaction being a paradigm for the economic exploitation of colonialism and the story of Selina's oppression as a black woman in Britain) she says:

> I read the letter and I could cry. For after all, that song was all I had. I don't belong nowhere really, and I haven't money to buy my way to belonging. . . . Now I've let them play it wrong, and it will go from me like all the other songs. . . . But then I tell myself all this is foolishness. Even if they played it on trumpets, even if they played it just right, like I wanted – no walls would fall so soon. 'So let them call it jazz', . . . and let them play it wrong. That won't make no difference to the song I heard.[4]

The story of Selina who nearly loses her song and then

encounters it translated into another version which she almost doesn't recognise is a familiar one and is perhaps in danger of being re-enacted in some Western critical discourses which appropriate texts by women writers of the 'Third World' in order to elucidate their theories. Whilst, for instance, there are obviously parallels between the experience of women's oppression in previously colonised territories and women's oppression worldwide, there is a danger even in western feminist literary circles (which often have failed to give full critical attention to literary works by black women writers) of being seduced by easy notions of a 'universal feminism'. The post-colonial woman writer is not only involved in making herself heard, in changing the architecture of male-centred ideologies and languages, or in discovering new forms and language to express her experience, she has also to subvert and demythologise indigenous male writings and traditions which seek to label her. An entrapping cycle begins to emerge. In countries with a history of colonialism, women's quest for emancipation, self-identity and fulfilment can be seen to represent a traitorous act, a betrayal not simply of traditional codes of practice and belief but of the wider struggle for liberation and nationalism. Does to be 'feminist' therefore involve a further displacement or reflect an implicit adherence to another form of cultural imperialism?

Both Ama Ata Aidoo in *Our Sister Killjoy* and Jamaica Kincaid in *A Small Place* have pointed in similar ways to the difficulties facing the woman writer who is seeking her own space and language in a previously colonised world:

What positive is there to be, when I cannot give voice to my soul and still have her heard? Since, so far, I have only been able to use a language that enslaved me, and therefore, the messengers of my mind always come shackled?[5]

Or as Kincaid says describing the problematic of an orphaned consciousness:

For isn't it odd that the only language I have in which to

speak of this crime is the language of the criminal who
committed the crime? And what can that really mean? . . .
The language of the criminal can explain and express the
deed only from the criminal's point of view.[6]

Women writers from these areas inhabit a world where
several 'languages' co-exist and a number of complex issues
are involved. It is not only a question of redressing the bal-
ance; the reclamation is more than simply shifting the ground
of a series of oppositions and areas of struggle: whether
male/female, coloniser/native, black/white, feminist/wom-
anist, post-colonial/post-structuralist, Third World/First
World, traditional literary canons/counter-discourses and
forms. Whilst these writers share a history of colonialism,
their writing is born out of different cultural, social and
economic contexts. Strategies for resistance are necessary
which subvert and question the dominant 'father tongue' but
more critical is a need to break through the notion of a
literature of opposition set up by the kinds of dialectics mentioned above and make space for the expression of a 'multiplicity of perspectives' and literary poetics.[7] As Grace Nichols, the Guyanese poet and novelist, once put it, describing
the positive effects of the cross-fertilisation and Creolisation
of cultures and languages that define the syncretic nature of
the Caribbean literary tradition:

I have crossed an ocean
I have lost my tongue
From the root of the old one
A new one has sprung.[8]

The question of new languages and literary forms springing
from old roots is central to the energy emanating from the
development of women's writing in the regions under consideration here.

Furthermore a creative dialogue can exist between 'Third
World' writers and their western audiences. Western feminist
theories current in 'First World' audiences need not simply

appropriate these writings to elucidate their biases but as Rhonda Cobham has shown can 'illuminate' the texts:

> Sometimes African literature by women writers may be read usefully through models derived from Western theories. [Such readings] may also provide modes of perception through which to examine and qualify Western theory.[9]

Thus women readers in the 'First World' are able to re-evaluate the cultural assumptions which inform their own readings. The texts themselves, as a number of the essays in this collection illustrate, frequently dramatise this inter-relationship in their use of language and form. A double discourse is often at work between the cultural values encoded in the text itself and the individual critic's particular cultural baggage.

The idea for this book derived originally from a BA undergraduate course on Black Women's Writing. The course aimed to examine literary and cultural practices in African, Caribbean, South Asian and Afro-American women's writing. Critical attention in the West had recently focused on the work of African-American women writers such as Maya Angelou, Alice Walker, Toni Morrison and others. However, there were/are also many talented women writers in other parts of the world whose voices remain unheard. This continues to be a surprising fact despite the number of parallels that exist and the enormous number of excellent works of fiction and poetry currently in publication. The relative scarcity of critical coverage raises numerous questions concerning cultural practices in mainstream literary reviews and the policies of western publishers which are beyond the scope of this study. But the fact remains that there is relatively little serious critical material readily available for teachers or students to develop their own readings.

My aim in this book therefore is to explore a number of representative texts by women writers from the Caribbean, Africa and South Asia in the light of recent feminist theory and questions of language, culture and consciousness. In compiling this anthology the intention has been to generate a cross-cultural dialogue between critics and writers whether in 'First' or 'Third' worlds, a dialogue that would ideally investigate the cultural specificity of each text and the critical perspective of the contributor. The selection of particular works and writers was left to the preference of individuals and in some cases their choices are perhaps indicative of another 'canonisation' developing in western audiences and readers.

The essays have wider reverberations in the context of those many writers for whom space did not allow discussion and women writers in other post-colonial areas. In addition, there are important correspondences between the works discussed here and the fiction and poetry of Afro-American writers. Several of the essays point to these parallels explicitly and often extend their scope to include figures such as Ruth Prawer Jhabvala, Marjorie Macgoye and the white West Indian creole, Jean Rhys, who might otherwise reside uneasily in a collection which has the work of black women writers as its main theme. Readers may also want to ask why South Asian writing has been described as 'black writing'. The term is being used in its broadest political sense as a means of drawing links, despite important social and cultural differences, between the writings of women of colour who have suffered the effects of a double colonisation brought about by history and male-dominated social and political systems. It is not attempting to neutralise difference or make claims for unity where they are inappropriate. As Audre Lorde once put it:

> Black writers . . . who step outside the pale of what black writers are supposed to be, are [sometimes] condemned to silences in black literary circles that are as total and destructive as any imposed by racism.[10]

Since this book was conceived three years ago, a number of important critical works have begun to appear. In 1981 Lloyd Brown had already published *Women Writers in Black Africa*;

more recently two other studies, *Ngambika: Studies of Women in African Literature* (1986), ed., Carol Boyce Davies and Anne Adams Graves and *Women in African Literature Today* (1987), ed. Eldred Jones, begin to examine a 'feminist' consciousness as opposed to simply putting African women's writing on the world map. Similarly a special issue of *Research in African Literatures* (1988), introduced by Rhonda Cobham, explores issues such as gender and race in terms of critical and creative practice. The very recent publication of *Out of the Kumbla: Caribbean Women and Literature* (1990), ed. Carol Boyce Davies and Elaine Savory Fido is a further important milestone in the development of the debate. Women's writing from South Asia is still frequently under-represented in anthologies of this kind although there have been several critical studies of individual writers. As far as I am aware, this is the *first critical* work to compare and contrast women's writing in English from Africa, the Caribbean and South Asia.

The idea of *motherlands, mothercultures, mothertongues* seemed an appropriate theme for discussion for a number of reasons. Clearly mothers and motherlands have provided a potent symbolic force in the writings of African, Caribbean and Asian women with the need to demythologise the illusion of the colonial 'motherland' or 'mothercountry' and the parallel movement to rediscover, recreate and give birth to the genesis of new forms and new languages of expression. The whole question of 'motherhood' is also a major concern universally in contemporary women's literature and has obvious reverberations in terms of feminist criticism – the relation between mothers and daughters, mothers mirroring and affirming identity or notions of the birth of female identity through transference to text and symbol, is also particularly important within a post-colonial context: the unwritten stories, for instance, that are just beginning to be told as a result of women's struggles to become all that they can be. The title of Jamaican poet Lorna Goodison's award-winning collection of poems suggests this movement. Entitled *I am Becoming My Mother* (1986), the collection points to a central preoccupation in recently published works by other Caribbean, African and Asian writers. They are frequently novels and poems of 'becoming', where the voices of women from all sectors of the society are explored, voices which often link and bridge the oral/literary mode and which frequently use a multiplicity of vision as a means of telling the story of a previously unwritten history and culture.

As Barbara Christian states, in *Black Feminist Criticism*: 'since a woman, never a man, can be a mother, or a daughter, that experience should be hers to tell and since we all come from mothers it is striking that these stories have remained secondary in a world literature'.[11] Also important is the fact that the role of mother, with all that it implies, is universally imposed upon women as their main identity, their *proper* identity above all others. Adrienne Rich emphasises this in a broad discussion of motherhood in *Of Woman Born* in which she shows that whilst the historical reality is that motherhood is women's experience, the institution is frequently under male control. Moreover the potential of women to be mothers often conditions their entire lives.[12]

The mythology of 'motherhood', then, has long been a familiar one in feminist literary debates whether of 'First' or 'Third' worlds; this anthology explores the ramifications of this theme within the context of a burgeoning post-colonial literature and opens up a critical debate *across* cultures which is long overdue.

The book is divided into three sections. The first, 'Breaking the Silence: Stories of Women and Mothers', examines from a variety of perspectives the idea of 'mother-nations', 'motherlands', as encoded in patriarchal and western symbolic systems. It also explores the idea of inter-textuality and the means by which women are discovering strategies to give voice to 'herstory' and redefining the nature of woman as subject. In remapping and writing 'herstory', a new dynamic is created which repositions the reader in relation to the text.

The starting point of the first essay by Elleke Boehmer is the assumption that nationalism is a gendered ideology and the notion of 'motherland' may therefore mean neither 'source' nor 'home' to women. In the iconographies of nationalism, images of mothers have conventionally invited symbols suggestive of primal origins – birth, hearth, home, roots, the umbilical cord of being – as encapsulated by terms such as 'mothertongue', 'mothercountry'. Boehmer explores the extent to which 'the idea of nationhood bears a masculine identity though national ideals may wear a feminine face', and through an analysis of Flora Nwapa's early writing illustrates how the act of writing can be transformative. Nwapa's fiction 'counterbalances in language and character iconography a post-colonial literary patriarchy and a matrifocal nationalism'.

Judie Newman develops the issue of representation in 'The Untold Story and the Retold Story' where she stresses the need in women's writing for a questioning of acculturated models and exemplary representations particularly when the experience of a double marginalisation has intensified the question as to whose story it is. Focusing on Ruth Prawer Jhabvala's *Heat and Dust* and Anita Desai's *Baumgartner's Bombay*, the essay examines the value of inter-textual strategies in relation to unreliable past narrations and illustrates how the re-positioning of texts can offer important 'revisions of canonical' works as in the case of the relationship between Jean Rhys' *Wide Sargasso Sea*, and *Jane Eyre*.

Shirley Chew's 'Searching Voices' also focuses on Asian women's writing and forcefully demonstrates the extent to which women have been trapped in silence between competing and exclusive discourses – whether colonial versions of history or Brahminical. The theories of Gayatri Spivak are used to show how both Anita Desai and Nayantara Sahgal have been creating a new 'textual space' in their fiction, a space which aims to retrieve for women in India 'both ancestral and present-day, a voice and a presence within their motherland'.

The strategy of retrieval and revisioning is further elaborated on in Carolyn Cooper's piece which explores the work of Caribbean writers, Sylvia Wynter, Erna Brodber and Una Marson in relation to Paule Marshall and the Afro-American writer, Toni Morrison. The 'revalorisation of discredited knowledge is a major project of these female-centred fictions' in the 'rewriting of the colonial text that once defined the place of the native – both black and woman – at the margins of history'. And the phenomenon of spirit possession, the high point of worship in many New World, Afro-centric religious communities, provides a compelling cultural metaphor for the recovery of African cultural values in the Diaspora.

Abena Busia's 'Rebellious Women: Fictional Biographies – Nawal Sa'adawi's *Woman at Point Zero* and Mariama Bâ's *So Long a Letter*' addresses the question of constructing women's biography and autobiography as a 'mode of rebellion' and a means of 'liberating history'. The knowing and reconstruction of such stories (however problematic), 'so that others may hear them, is the burden not just of these stories, but of her story itself'.

Finally, Caroline Rooney in ' "Dangerous Knowledge" and the Poetics of Survival' opens up a discussion which is fundamental to the concerns of this collection. Beginning with an exploration of the nature of 'mother*land*' in the context of colonialism and in relation to dominant western constructions, she illustrates the 'critical practice of the appropriation of self-expression' as it is dramatised in Bessie Head's *A Question of Power* and Ama Ata Aidoo's *Our Sister Killjoy*. Rooney shows how critical discourse is in itself 'imperialist' and the literary text is often not seen as speaking for itself. Furthermore it is critical language that serves to homogenise creative discourse in a way that denies each creative text and each literature its own specificity and social and cultural context. The literary strategies with which, in the actual *telling* of the stories, Head and Aidoo resist such appropriations are illustrated; moreover the effects of a 'power-mongering mentality' or ideology are shown to be not solely a matter of argument but an issue of 'real violence and a question of survival'. Both Aidoo and Head (re)claim the right to 'speak their texts' in ways that resist an easy assimilation into another's system: it is a resistance that is also a liberation.

The second section, 'Mother/Daughters/Sisters?' comprises a group of essays which explore the metaphorical significance of a variety of traditional and mythological mother-figures. The question as to how far umbrella terms for a 'universal feminism' and 'sisterhood' are useful in a discussion of texts which are often distinguished by their cultural differences is also raised. The affirming force of the mother/daughter relationship in the creation of literary texts as new motherlands, and/or mothertongues frequently becomes a central preoccupation in many of the writers.

In 'Mothers or Sisters? Identity, Discourse and Audience in the Writing of Ama Ata Aidoo and Mariama Bâ', C L Innes contrasts the portrayal of the 'mothers of Africa', common in the work of Senghor and other male writers such as Ayi Kwei Armah and Kofi Awoonor with Aidoo's challenge to this nostalgic symbol in her plays, short stories and novel *Our Sister Killjoy*. Interestingly in Aidoo's writing, the 'alliances between women of differing generations are more often between mothers and daughters-in-law, than between mothers and their natural daughters'. Furthermore in *Our Sister Killjoy*, in which Aidoo rewrites and reverses Conrad's *Heart of Darkness* as the 'archetypal European novel about Africa', the possibility of a global sisterhood is encountered through Sissie's relationship with Marija who represents 'Mary', the Madonna icon of the European nuclear family. Aidoo presents the possibility of 'feminist separatism' in this novel, but rejects it. Aidoo's dramatisation in her texts of the dangers of 'universal' and neutralising philosophies which seek to view 'African culture as complementary to Western civilization' contrasts with Mariama Bâ's use of language and form in *So Long a Letter*, where Ramatoulaye views the women's movement worldwide as a force which inspires and sustains her. But this optimism in a creative partnership between Africa and Europe is qualified in her second novel, *Scarlet Song*, which ends with a 'violent denial of motherhood' and Mireille's murder of her 'half-caste' son who has no place or motherland.

In 'The Search for Freedom in Indian Women's Writing', Ranjana Ash writes on the cultural and social background to explorations of women's independence in the works of five writers – Kamala Das, Anita Desai, Amrita Pritam, Shashi Deshpande and Nayantara Sahgal. Her essay points to the conflicts experienced between woman's traditional role in the family as mothers, daughters or daughters-in-law (histori-cally represented by the mythic heroines of Sita and Savitri) and the demands made on educated women caught amongst conflicting attitudes towards Gandhian nationalism and the language of western feminism. In "Heaven Lies Beneath Her Feet"?: Mother Figures in Selected Indo-Anglian Novels', Helen Kanitkar examines in more depth the cultural deter-minants that structure the 'desirable role perception' of an Indian wife and mother and the means by which Indian women writers are engaged in demythologisations in their search for self-expression. The analysis of the ways in which Hindu mythological structures have entrapped women by 'sanctioning accepted values and beliefs' bears an interesting relationship to Elleke Boehmer's examination of male-centred mythologies and their function in nationalist politics. As is evident from Ranjana Ash's essay, however, the movement for freedom is frequently hindered by oppressive traditional practices. Although the force of the Mother Goddess is fully recognised in Hindu legend, the potential of wives and mothers is circumscribed.[13] The challenge of women to exist-ing social norms has to be 'accommodated before it turns destructive'. The goddess has more than one face. Like Kali, or the other side of Parvati, ' "this woman . . . the Great Queen imprisoned in the shrine, is going to shake off her chains and her rebellion will be terrible, for she is a direct threat to the society that men have built without her." '

A more positive portrayal of motherhood is presented by Jane Bryce-Okunlola who examines 'Motherhood as a Metaphor for Creativity' in the works of Flora Nwapa, Rebeka Njau and Bessie Head. The preoccupation in these writers with having or being unable to have children becomes a metaphor for the creative process itself; by the very act of writing women repudiate the 'patriarchal appropriation of power over the Word' and 'motherhood becomes a site of struggle, an exploration by women of the last uncolonised territory'. Writing acts as a 'non-violent but effective weapon' in counteracting the dominance of male mythologies in all of the writers; it is engaged not only in formulating '*alternatives*' but in accurately recording what is, in fact, already there'.

The last two essays in this section, ' "The Bloodstream of Our Inheritance": Female Identity and the Caribbean Mothers'-land' and 'Mothertongue Voices in the writing of Olive Senior and Lorna Goodison' present contrasting critical approaches to Caribbean writing. The first by Ann R Morris and Margaret M Dunn draws on the ideas of western feminist theorists common in the US such as Nancy Chodorow in *The Reproduction of Mothering: Psychoanalysis and the Sociology of Gender* (1978), Carol Gilligan and Jean Baker Miller in their analysis of the relationship between mother–daughter–land in the novels of Jamaica Kincaid, Jean Rhys, Paule Marshall and Michelle Cliff. Unlike male identity, 'which develops through early separation from the mother, female identity develops through early and continued *connection with* the mother'. In the works of these writers, the island itself becomes both mother and text. The land and one's mothers are therefore co-joined. 'If a woman is able to claim a connection to both, she is well prepared for the journey toward self-identity', but if she has been denied this 'developmental bond with her own mother, then the ' "mothers'-land" itself may provide a surrogate'.

In contrast, Velma Pollard's piece examines from an insider's perspective the linguistic fabric of mothertongue voices in the poetry of Lorna Goodison and the short stories of Olive Senior. The question as to what actually constitutes 'mothertongue' in a language situation such as the Caribbean where invariably at least one Creole and one European language co-exist in a sub/superordinate relationship with each other demonstrates the complexity of the Jamaican language continuum and the means by which these writers are operating within and across several codes. 'Mothertongue' in this context is shown to be far more than one-dimensional; it is 'language' rather than 'a language' and reminds us both of the versatility of this medium and of the dangers of eclipsing important social and cultural determinants in our reading of women's texts by neat literary paradigms.

The third section, 'Absent and Adopted Mother(land)s', presents a cross-cultural and comparative approach to writers whose main experience has been one of migration or exile from their homelands, an experience of loss which has nevertheless acted as a creative catalyst in their art. 'Family Connections: Mother and Mother Country in the Fiction of Jean Rhys and Jamaica Kincaid' places Rhys as 'literary mother' to many contemporary Caribbean women writers, particularly Jamaica Kincaid. Rhys was both the 'first' to 'create texts dealing with the complex mother-daughter matrix' as well as the 'first . . . to employ modernist narrative strategies, such as dreams and associative thinking', as a strategy of resistance to the dominant culture. The use of alternative forms of consciousness – through dreams, 'madness', or what Carolyn Cooper calls 'zombification' – in order to define new spaces and realities for women is a common technique and is paralleled in the works of Afro-American women writers. The story of Anna Morgan in Jean Rhys' early novel *Voyage in the Dark* (1934), dramatises not only the negative effects of the 'rupture' created by an inadequate mother-daughter bond and its metaphoric implications in terms of the colonial motherland, England, but also demonstrates how these rup-

tures and oppositions form the text's own mode of resistance
to an emotional and cultural schizophrenia. Jamaica Kincaid's
Annie John, written almost 50 years later, relates closely to
Voyage in the Dark, but offers a different narrative response
to the crucial relationship between mothers and daughters,
surrogate mothers and 'colonial motherlands'.

The idea of absent mother(land)s is explored in a different
context in Isabel Carrera Suárez's study of Joan Riley. Riley's
novels are important in their fictionalisation of the experience
of recent West Indian immigrants in Britain. The texts
emphasise the way in which black women are reduced to a
double silence, imposed by race and gender; it is a silence
that involves the reduction of a 'person' to a 'nobody': 'for
where blacks are constructed as that necessary "other" by
white society, black women are left as the only available
"other" to black men'. The quest of these women for a
'unified self' begins therefore with a negative definition; it
has 'as a starting point a double ontological insecurity which,
beyond a merely split self, produces a fragmented personality, torn between multiple demands, suffering multiple
absences'.

In setting out to inscribe into literature the reality of 'the
forgotten or unglamorous section of [her] people',[14] Riley's
work makes visible those aspects of selfhood that were previously silent in her community. 'The . . . absences which
she describes in her characters become one with her writing'
which expresses 'an effort to heal through representation' and
is 'a mothering of oneself into writing, shared with other
women writers in Britain' as well as 'a mothering of each
other into a solid literary community'.

In contrast, Valerie Kibera in 'Adopted Motherlands: The
Fiction of Bessie Head and Marjorie Macgoye' explores how
the experience of being both an outsider (by birth, culture,
upbringing) and an insider (by choice, commitment and
allegiance) shapes the fiction of Head and Macgoye in their
adopted societies. The essay sets up an interesting comparison
between Macgoye, a white woman who has become an inte-

gral part of the Kenyan clan into which she married, and Head in her ambivalent relationship with Botswana.

The theme of self and separation from 'mother/lands' is the central concern of Elaine Savory Fido's cross-cultural discussion of Buchi Emecheta, Bessie Head and Jean Rhys. The absence of 'mother' and/or 'homeland' here is translated into textual spaces which form a new relationship with the adoptive country. 'Exile . . . becomes a space in which hurt can be explored and contained within the creation of fictions, stories which circle the mother's absence and are, at the same time, circled by it.' This cultural dualism empowers all three writers, whose identity rests upon their particularity as well as their commonality, to 'share the difficulty of belonging to spaces in between' at a 'bewitched crossroad', where 'a number of roads meet and strangely, powerfully, deeply intersect'.

The editing of an anthology of this kind always involves the exclusion of some excellent material. I am not going to make a lengthy apologia here but more positively point to the pressing need for further books of this kind. As the focus of this collection has been on fiction subsequent books could place more emphasis on poetry and drama. The wealth of recent publications by contemporary black women writers living in Britain *alone* could form the subject of yet another critical study. Works by writers such as Beryl Gilroy, Jan Shinebourne, Grace Nichols, Merle Collins, Suniti Namjoshi, Ravinder Rhandawa, Leena Dhingra, Agnes Sam, Barbara Burford, Debjani Chatterjee and Jackie Kay, to name but a few, would testify to the observation made in Isabel Carrera Suárez's essay that in working towards the 'recovery/recreation of a history, a culture, a language', women writers living in Britain need to mother each other into a solid literary community which 'discovers/defines itself in its art'.

The groundwork for this has been well under way for several years and is evident from the number of anthologies that have been published which focus on the collective elements of women's experience. *A Dangerous Knowing* (1985), published by Sheba, marked a unique moment in feminist publishing in Britain in its portrayal of the 'sisterhood' of four poets and of the black lesbian experience. *Watchers and Seekers* (1987), (ed.) Rhonda Cobham and Merle Collins features poems and short stories by African, Caribbean and Asian women whose work reflects the 'traditions of orature which are a powerful historical feature of Black creativity'; furthermore these women have a wider range of options than a simple choice between 'bourgeois marriage and spinsterhood' in their exploration of female sexuality.[15] And *Let It Be Told* (1987), edited by the South African writer Lauretta Ngcobo, examines the history of the development of women's writing in Britain as well as providing individual testimonies from a number of the contributors. A parallel movement forms the context of *Right of Way* (1989), which derived originally from the writings of the Asian Women Writers Collective and is edited by Ravinder Randhawa, one of its founder members.

I could go on . . . but I must close by drawing the reader's attention to where this introduction began with the sounds of a number of varied, dynamic and contesting voices which are currently speaking out and defining their plurality by creating a space in which previously marginalised groups can 'name themselves, speak for themselves and participate in defining [their own] terms of interaction'.[16] Moreover, through the painful process of giving birth to new motherlands of culture and experience, the writers have been able to use their 'mothertongue(s)', however problematic, to speak truths. The pain and liberation of the birth rite also forms the background to the editing of this book, which was conceived before my pregnancy and has come to fruition after the arrival of my new baby daughter who carries in her the strands of four cultures.

Susheila Nasta
1991.

Notes

1   Bronwen Levy, 'Women Experiment Down Under: Reading the Difference', *Kunapipi* VII, 1985, Aarhus, p. 170.

2   Kathleen McLuskie and Lyn Innes, 'Women and African Literature', *Wasafiri* 8, 1988, p. 4.

3   *Ibid*.

4   Jean Rhys, 'Let Them Call It Jazz', in *Tigers Are Better Looking*, Penguin, Harmondsworth, 1968, p. 63; this story was first published in 1927.

5   Ama Ata Aidoo, *Our Sister Killjoy*, Longman, Harlow, 1977, p. 112.

6   Jamaica Kincaid, *A Small Place*, Virago, London, 1988, pp. 32–33.

7   'Women and African Literature', p. 4.

8   Grace Nichols, 'Epilogue', *Fat Black Woman's Poems*, Virago, London, 1984.

9   Rhonda Cobham, 'Introduction', *Research in African Literatures*, Texas, p. 141.

10   'Audre Lorde' in *Black Women Writers at Work*, ed. Claudia Tate, Oldcastle, Herts, p. 101.

11   Barbara Christian, *Black Feminist Criticism*, Pergamon, New York, 1986, p. 212.

12   Adrienne Rich, *Of Woman Born*, Bantam, New York, 1976, p. 33.

13   Anita Desai in 'A Secret Connivance', *Times Literary Supplement*, 14–20 September 1990, p. 972, illustrates the degree to which the deification of Indian women acts as a form of imprisonment in the society.

14   Joan Riley, Introductory notes to *Waiting in the Twilight*, The Women's Press, London, 1987.

15   Rhonda Cobham, 'Foreword' and 'Introduction' to *Watchers and Seekers*, ed. Merle Collins and Rhonda Cobham, The Women's Press, London, 1987, pp. 1, 5.

16   Nancy Hardstock, 'Rethinking Modernism: Minority *vs* Majority Theories', *Cultural Critique* 7, 1987, p. 189.

Breaking the Silence:
New Stories of Women and Mothers

Elleke Boehmer

**Stories of Women and Mothers:
Gender and Nationalism in
the Early Fiction of Flora Nwapa**

She is there at the beginning of the lives of individuals and of nations. In various nationalist mythologies and, more recently, in the matriarchal yearnings of dispossessed women seeking their own place in nations and in history, mother figures cradle their children in comforting and capacious laps. (Before her recent troubles), Winnie Mandela was given the title 'Mother of the Nation'.

The West Indian poet and historian, Edward Kamau Brathwaite, has addressed his home island of Barbados as mother, the matrix of his connection with the past, the source of meaning and identity.[1] Nuruddin Farah has commented that referring to a nation as a father- (rather than as a mother-) land is to him an absurd idea.[2] Many male writers from Africa – Camara Laye, Kofi Awoonor and Wole Soyinka among them – speaking from various historical and geographical perspectives, have seen the image writ larger: Africa, the continent whole and full-bellied, is both the beloved land and mother. In 1988, when making a call to Africans to stand together not on the basis of colour but on that of Africanness, Jesse Jackson adopted this grand trope, urging that African people everywhere 'identify with Africa as . . . mother continent.' His conviction was that 'the blood that unites us is stronger than the water that divides us',[3] a metaphor knitting together images of common womb and origin, and of shared birth-ground.

Although they perhaps hold different sentiments and ideals, the figure of the common African mother is one to which African women and women of African origin have also made obeisance. Buchi Emecheta, the London-based Nigerian novelist, for example, is of the opinion that 'the white female intellectual may still have to come to the womb of Mother Africa to re-learn how to be a woman.'[4] For the Zimbabwean poet and former guerrilla fighter, Freedom Nyamubaya, to speak of the free Zimbabwean nation is to speak of the motherland. The concepts are so closely associated that Nyamubaya bestows upon the concept of freedom the same honorific title: 'mother freedom'.[5] Aneb Kgotsile, poet and activist, speaking from an Afro-American perspective, observes: 'Mother Africa is of great importance . . . Through our study of African history the motherland was unearthed to us and we reclaimed Africa.'[6] In her recent novel, *The Temple of My Familiar*, Alice Walker also sings threnodies over the destruction of the ancient matriarchal worship of Africa: history in Walker's representation achieves meaning in so far as her characters become either avatars or acolytes of the composite, omnibenevolent 'Africa/Mother/ Goddess'.[7]

But to what sort of mother image is it that women writers appeal when they speak in this way? Is their gaze fixed longingly on the same object as their male counterparts? Does the icon represent for them a more or less direct transposition within the forms of language of male-dominated nationalism and, if so, what does this transfer mean for their own strategies of self-retrieval? Do nationalist vocabularies not implicate women in certain paradoxes of identity and affiliation? Such questions point to the main concern of this essay, which will explore what an investment in the doctrines and symbolism of a typically 'masculine' nationalism entails – firstly for women's politics of identity and then also for women's writing.[8]

The dilemma is that where male nationalists have claimed, won and ruled the 'motherland', this same motherland may not signify 'home' and 'source' to women. To 'Third World' women and women of colour these concerns speak with particular urgency, not only because of their need to resist the triple oppression or marginalisation that the effects of colonialism, gender and a male-dominated language create, but also because their own tactics of self-representation are often usefully adopted from the older and more established nationalist politics of 'their men'.

Mariamma Bâ once said that:

> We [women] no longer accept the nostalgic praise to the African mother whom, in his anxiety, man confuses with Mother Africa.[9]

Though she was here keeping hold of the image of Mother Africa, Bâ shows herself to be uncomfortable about the male glorification of African women as national and continental mothers. Lauretta Ngcobo addresses this discomfort when she observes:

> Africa holds two contradictory views of woman – the idealised, if not the idolised mother, and the female reality of woman as wife.[10]

These two quotations can be set alongside a comment made by Virginia Woolf on the subject of nationalism and women. In her anti-patriarchal pacifist manifesto *Three Guineas*, Woolf is moved to assert that 'in fact, as a woman, I have no country. As a woman I want no country.'[11]

Because men have drawn up, defined and directed national boundaries and national affairs, Woolf suggests, women cannot legitimately lay claim either to a national territory or to their own national mythology and history. Thus, the lap of the Mother Nation may not be as soft and capacious for women as it is for men.

Despite professed ideals, nationalisms do not address all individuals equally: significant distinctions and discriminations are made along gendered (and also class and racial) lines. Such distinctions are not mere decoration; on the contrary, nationalism relies heavily on gendered languages to imagine itself.[12] Gender informs nationalism and nationalism in its turn consolidates and legitimates itself through a variety of gendered structures and shapes which, either as ideologies or as political movements, are clearly tagged: the idea of nationhood bears a masculine identity though national ideals may wear a feminine face.[13]

The gender specifics of nationalism are clearly illustrated in the iconographies held dear by nations. In the literature, rhetoric and pageantry of nations, as in nationalist politics and political structures, it is a male figure who is cast as the author and subject of the nation – as faithful soldier, citizen-hero or statesman. In the national family drama that has the achievement of selfhood as its denouement, it is he who is chief actor and hero; the mother figure in this drama may be his mentor, fetish or talisman, but advice and example are taken from a heritage of fathers. Typically, then, the male role in the nationalist scenario may be characterised as metonymic. Male figures are brothers and equals, or fathers and sons and thus rivals; but in both cases their roles are specific and contiguous with one another. The 'female', in contrast, puts in an appearance chiefly in a metaphoric or symbolic role. She is the strength or virtue of the nation incarnate, its fecund first matriarch, but it is a role which excludes her from the sphere of public national life. Figures of mothers of the nation are everywhere emblazoned but the presence of women in the nation is officially marginalised and generally ignored.[14]

I will attempt to ground these contentions a little more firmly. Two mutually reinforcing cases can be made for the relationship between patriarchy and nationalism. The first identifies in both a unitary, monologic vision, a tendency to authorise homogenising perceptions and social structures and to suppress plurality.[15] Nationalism, like patriarchy, favours singleness – one identity, one growth pattern, one birth and blood for all. Though this interpretation relies a little uncomfortably on ideas of immanence, the claim is therefore that nationalism, like patriarchy, will promote specifically unitary or 'one-eyed' forms of consciousness.

The second case is based on more historical grounds. The emergence of nationalism was characterised by a co-operation between patriarchies in the nation-state and in the household, a development that coincided with the rise of the bourgeoisie and the emergence of the middle-class family unit within it.[16] Nationalism, then, found in existing social patterns the models for hierarchical authority and control.

The interleaving of gender and nationalism was clearly demonstrated in the national movements which arose in Europe's former colonies, shaped by the history of intersecting patriarchies that was part of colonialism. At all points in the long process of decolonisation and national reconstitution, male power elites were operative, their authority having been already endorsed and blessed by earlier colonial and indigenous patriarchies.[17] With a dominant male presence rooted in the state, it was predictable that a gender bias would persist in neo-colonial nationalisms well beyond the time of independence. Whether in literature or in law, the national subject was in most cases either implicitly or explicitly designated as male. Despite the promises of national freedom, women were therefore excluded from full national participation on an equal footing with men. Even where women, as in Algeria or Zimbabwe, fought for freedom alongside men, national consciousness was composed by male leaders. Mother Africa may have been declared free, but the mothers of Africa remained manifestly oppressed.

Little resistance to such processes of patrimonial designation could be expected from within the ranks of the newly empowered. In the Manichean allegory that typified the colonial power struggle,[18] dominant, 'true' power – that of the coloniser – had been characterised as rational, disciplined, assertive, masculine; while inertia, weakness, the disorderly, was represented as feminine. Where nationalists were committed to rebuild their shattered self-esteem, to 'selving', images signifying autonomy, force, will – and, by implication, masculinity – would be avidly promoted.[19] So the new rulers might portray themselves as a rising strength, as self-determining, as powerful – and also as patriarchal and/or as one another's brothers. Thus, though seeking to step out of inherited allegorical roles, they would try as far as possible to avoid 'negative' – that is feminine – meanings. Underlying gendered values remained intact.

At the level of national symbolism, colonial images of the land or nation as invincible protectress or progenitress were assimilated to local conventions of respect for the earth or for mothers, ensuring that national leaders granted some sort of compensatory iconic recognition to the 'mothers of the nation' while at the same time vouching for the cultural integrity of the whole national entity. Observe once again however that it is the sons who are the authors of meaning: whether of 'tradition', or of present social realities; whether of their own self-image as national representatives or of the women they would presume to represent.[20]

So the glad achievement of nationhood presented women with a conundrum. For women such selving, with its emphasis on the male personality, only confirmed a lack of self, their difference from national wholeness. This alienation represented, and still represents, an especially serious problem for the new nationalisms of the South or 'Third World'. For where, in nationalist rhetoric, as in the official discourse of the state, masculine identity is normative, and where the female is addressed in the main as idealised bearer of nationalist sons, woman as such, in herself, has no valuable place.

But, if nationalism does not see women as nationals, then a woman seeking to claim a place or identity in any field of national activity faces multiple perils of self-contradiction.

Literature as a medium of self-expression offers a representative case. In African nationalism, especially that of the immediately pre- and post-independence periods, writing was an important source of national myth-making and dreaming. For a writer to be nationalist, was to be that much more a worthy writer, as well as that much more a loyal nationalist. It was also, by implication, to be that much more male. The circle of mutually reinforcing identities shut – and still shuts – women out.

A woman might choose to crack this ring of identity by attempting to repossess matriarchal myths. For some women the reclaimed myth of an age-old, long-suffering Afrika – Walker's Africa/Goddess/Mother, for example – might continue to hold out much promise of communion and liberation. Yet how are such myths, such apparently redemptive symbols, to be separated from those which continue to shore up patriarchal desire and a system of gendered national authority? To compound these difficulties, the idealisation and possible fetishisation of single mother figures bears an uncanny resemblance to the monolithic aspects of male-centred nationalism. Subscribing to the unitary icon threatens to defeat the women's objective of affirming their own particular mode of being. Given that men have monopolised the field of nationalist identity and self-image, women may thus have to evolve other strategies of selving – perhaps less unitary; perhaps more dispersed and multifarious. It is not only that the patriarchal sources which inform nationalist images must in some way be confronted. It is also necessary to explore forms of women's self-representation that would counterpose inherited symbolic languages of gender. Here, despite existing traditions of male authorship, writing holds out fruitful possibilities of redress.

If African literature in the past has constituted a nationalist and patriarchal preserve, then, simply by writing, women may begin directly to challenge the male prerogative. In writing, women express their own reality and so question received notions of national character and experience. But writing is also more than this. To write is not only to speak for one's place in the world. It is also to *make* one's own place or narrative, to tell the story of oneself, to create an identity. It is in effect to deploy what might be called a typically nationalist strategy. As Simon Gikandi has put it:

> To write is to claim a text of one's own; textuality is an instrument of territorial possession; because the other confers on us an identity that alienates us from ourselves, narrative is crucial to the discovery of our selfhood.[21]

This idea of self-creation through narrative connects with the Kristevan concept of excess in writing. Kristeva observes, à propos of Barthes's criticism, that writing is 'transformative', operating through the displacement of what is already signi-fied, bringing forth the not-yet-imagined and the transgres-sive.[22] Through writing, then, through claiming a text – or a narrative territory – women sign into and at the same time subvert a nationalist narrative that excluded them as negativity, as corporeal and unclean.

Possibilities for the disruption and/or transformation of a patriarchal nationalist text can be seen to operate in two main ways in women's writing: the 'textual' and the (broadly) 'temporal/territorial'. The first occurs through the medium of the text, in the substance of the writing, and involves, quite simply, interrupting the language of official nationalist discourse and literature with a women's vocality. Nation-hood is so bound up in textuality, in 'definitive' histories and official languages and mythologies, that to compose a substantially different kind of text, using vernacular forms that are part of people's experience, is already to challenge normative discourses of nationhood.

Yet because national identity rests on received images of national history and topography, the second method of trans-formation is as important. It involves changing the subjects that dominated the nationalist text. Where women tell of their own experience, they map their own geography, scry their own history and so, necessarily, contest official representations of a nationalist reality. They implicitly challenge the nation's definition of itself through territorial claims, through the reclamation of the past and the canonisation of heroes.

Both these methods obviously correspond closely to techniques of literary subversion in which women writers have long been engaged. Yet where African literary narratives, like those of the fifties and the sixties, depend on nationalist ideas and themes – and so on gendered interpretations of social reality – such methods will have particular relevance.

The second part of this essay will demonstrate how such techniques could work in practice in a discussion of two early novels by Flora Nwapa, *Efuru* (1966) and *Idu* (1970). Published during the first decade of Nigerian independence, a time featuring robust and cocksure, if also embattled nationalisms, Nwapa's novels represent the first narrative appearance from a woman on the broader African literary stage. This in itself was a significant voicing, yet added to this was Nwapa's specific focus on women's community and colloquy in Igbo culture.

Flora Nwapa

Like Elechi Amadi or Nkem Nwankwo, her male counterparts of the first post-independence decade, Flora Nwapa has written 'after Achebe', both chronologically and in terms of literary influence. Nwapa's narratives, like Amadi's and Achebe's, remember and recreate the Igbo village past in the colonial period. Period generalisations, however, tend to obscure the significant differences that exist between Nwapa and her male cohorts.

Her writing is situated outside of conventional male narrative history; she chooses to engage neither with the manly adventures and public displays of patriarchal authority described by male writers from her community nor with the narrative conventions of their accounts. Instead she concentrates, and at length, on what was incidental or simply contextual to male action – domestic matters, politics of intimacy.

In both *Efuru* and *Idu*, Nwapa's interest is in the routines and rituals of everyday life specifically within women's compounds. Women press into Nwapa's narrative as speakers, actors, decision-makers, brokers of opinion and market prices and unofficial jurors in their communities. But Nwapa's specific intervention as a writer goes beyond her interest in women subjects. What also distinguishes her writing from others in the 'Igbo school' are the ways in which she has used choric language to enable and to empower her representation, creating the effect of a women's verbal presence within her text,[23] while bringing home her subject matter by evoking the vocality of women's everyday existence.

Though it may have attracted a certain amount of negative comment,[24] the apparent lack of conventional novelistic complexity in *Efuru* and *Idu*, I would argue, far from being a deficiency, instead clears the space for the elaboration of another kind of narrative entirely – a highly verbalised collective women's biography – 'transsubjective, anonymous', transgressive,[25] a narrative method which bears comparison with Zora Neale Hurston's recreation of porch-side comment and of gossip on the road.[26]

The precise contribution represented by Nwapa's writing can perhaps be more clearly demonstrated when set in contrast on the one side with a historical narrative by Elechi Amadi, and on the other with an anthropological account of a Nigerian Igbo community by a woman researcher, Ifi Amadiume. In his novel *The Great Ponds*, written in 1969,[27] Elechi Amadi has depicted the life of an Igbo village as strongly determined by the forces of war, rumour and disease. Over war and rumour, it soon becomes clear, men hold undisputed sway; of disease, the gods decide, but they, like the village leaders, are all male. As with Achebe's writing, *The Great Ponds* is not uncritical of the 'masculine' social values which may contribute to and exacerbate community crises. Yet, unlike in Achebe, no locus of value is suggested which might form the rallying point of a new order: the male characters represent different types and degrees of manliness, but their actual position of authority is not called into question. It is thus quite within the terms laid down by the novel that the women in the community form a completely marginal and passive group. Their existence is affirmed by male subjects – they are desired, taken in marriage, captured as booty in male wars and are heard speaking when spoken to. For the rest, they are ignored.

Superficially this arrangement would seem hardly to differ from conventional gender divisions of power and cultural space. Upon closer scrutiny, however, it would appear that in Amadi the gender separation is perhaps more pronounced. The physical distance of the gender groups and their extreme social and political non-equivalence both suggest that they may well be independently reproduced and regulated. It is this view of a society radically split by gender that allows Amadi in *The Great Ponds* to represent the male side of Igbo life as though it were not only normative and authoritative, but self-sufficient and entire.

Yet, the writer's individual bias aside, it does not necessarily follow that this sort of exclusivity is the sign of a lack of power or self-determination on the part of women. It may just as well be the case that the distance between genders signifies and allows an autonomy and also a social validity for women. The women possess jurisdiction and authority over an area of village life which, though separate, is only *apparently* marginal; women conduct the business of their lives convinced of the validity of their activity.

Contrary to appearances, then, the representations of writers such as Amadi and Achebe, rather than defining the whole compass of the Igbo world, describe only one section of it. That another independent sphere of social existence exists is intimated only once, and then very briefly, in the Amadi text. It does, however, represent a significant break in the narrative when, in confrontational tones reminiscent of some of Nwapa's speakers, a senior wife, though nameless, comments on the folly of the protracted war and its goals:

> Why can't men take advice? . . . They think they are wise but they are as foolish as a baby in arms. Look at all the suffering of the past month. What good will that pond [the site of the contention] do us? (p. 72)[28]

Ifi Amadiume offers a corroborative perspective on the self-reliance of Igbo women, and on one of the chief conditions of that self-reliance – what might be called the mutual exclusivity of gender groups. In her study *Male Daughters, Female Husbands*, she shows that women obtain a great deal of power in Igbo – and specifically Nnobi – society because of the separation of gender from sex roles.[29] Amadiume does not always deal satisfactorily with the continuing predominance of *de facto* patriarchal authority in the community, and the status commanded by the roles of son and husband. Yet she does present evidence not simply for the existence of a clearly demarcated women's 'sphere' (which in itself says relatively little), but also for the independence and self-coherence of women's lives within that 'sphere'. She indicates that in precolonial times political and economic roles, as well as compound space and village ground, were divided according to the conventional sex dualities, with family units being matricentric. She argues, however, that these socially constructed dualities were mediated by the cross-gender roles available to women. Women were thus granted a range of powers with the appeal to Idemili, the water goddess, as offering the highest sanction of their authority.

It is the autonomous women's world delineated by Amadiume which Nwapa embodies in *Efuru* and *Idu*: Nwapa thus extends the boundaries of the African novel to include the women's side of the compound, a domain of village life which writers like Amadi have neglected for reasons not only of patriarchal lack of interest but also perhaps (a fact not given sufficient attention) of ignorance. Nwapa refracts a women's presence into her text through creating the conceit of women representing themselves in voice. Dialogue dominates in both novels, especially in *Idu*, as numbers of partly curious, partly phatic and frequently anonymous women's voices meet, interact with and interpellate one another. This vocality, rambling and seemingly unstoppable, pulls against the confinements of the women's lives – their market rivalries, their anxieties about husbands, families and children. Therefore, if, as Nwapa portrays it, though not always overtly, male values in the society remain normative,[30] women's talk can be interpreted not only as a way of life but as a mode of self-making. The impression of the fullness and autonomy of women's lives which Nwapa creates must remain partially qualified by their acquiescence in patriarchal views and values. Yet, at the same time, in their discourse, even as they speak, not only do the village women share their woes and confirm female bonds, they also transpose their lives into a medium which they control. The reader is made privy to the women representing and so, in effect, re-creating their lives in speech. The narrative result is that most of the (non-discursive) action in *Idu* and *Efuru* happens offstage and is more or less incidental to the 'spoken' text. Nwapa's writing is thus a decisive vindication of that congenital fault of garrulousness often attributed to 'the sex' (for example, in *The Great Ponds* pp. 23, 42 and 45). As Idu bemusedly observes: 'You know women's conversation never ends.' (p. 97)

How does this method of verbal self-representation work in practice? *Efuru* and *Idu* unfold as conversations; both are loosely chronological and markedly lacking in the temporal framework of conventional narrative. *Efuru* begins at the time that the heroine marries Adizua without parental consent: 'one moonlit night' they make plans; the next Nkwo (market) day she moves to his house (p. 7). With this information in hand the gossip-mongers can have their say, and, sure enough, by the second page of the novel speculations are afoot regarding Efuru's movements. These form the first soundings of that hum of conjecture that will run throughout the novel, commenting on Efuru's fortunes, her barrenness, her second marriage, her second barrenness. Against the background of this flow, trade seasons, other moonlit nights, gestation periods come and go with their accustomed regularity, but have significance in the conversational narrative largely as arbitrary starting points for new fragments of chatter. In *Idu* the verbal presence of the community would seem to be even more pervasive. Of the novel's 22 chapters, 14 including the first begin in mid-dialogue, and then usually à propos of events mentioned in some earlier conversation, the dialogue thus propagating itself across the pages of the novel.

The social setting Nwapa has chosen for her novels enables this self-generating orality. In each, the women occupy a self-enclosed, stable domestic domain – custom and environment are known to all the speakers and few characters are unfamiliar. Where these may be physically gestured at or taken as understood, reference to external objects or to habitual activity is elided or abbreviated. From the non-Igbo reader's point of view, this is emphasised when in both novels Igbo words and concepts are left unexplained and cannot always be elucidated by context – *ganashi, obo, nsala* soup. Within the community, the meanings of such words would not require elucidation. The insularity of the community is also suggested by the frequent repetitiveness of the conversation: comments are echoed, opinions reiterated, events retold, and it would appear that the point of talking is often simply the interaction, confirming contact, and not an exchange of information. Or as Uzoechi in *Idu* says, 'Sometimes, after discussing something, I like to come back to it and talk it over again' (p. 29).

So much is action a function of what is spoken that, especially in *Idu*, 'plot' developments take place off-stage as the conversation passes. At one moment in *Idu*, for example, Adiewere and Idu think of sending their new wife away; within a few paragraphs it is said that 'Adiewere had already sent her away' (pp. 43, 44). In chapter 13 of *Efuru*, Eneberi, Efuru's husband, expresses interest in taking a new wife; in the next chapter, during a chat between his mother and her friends, we learn that she (the mother) has a new daughter-in-law (p. 195). Thus a particular state of affairs may change into its opposite after a few pages, almost in the course of a few fragments of dialogue: here Idu observes that market is bad, there that it is good (pp. 45 and 47, 121 and 131). With dialogue constituting the main action and medium of community life, narrated or conversational time predominates over chronological time. Gossips summarise changes that have taken place over a span of years while also running through community opinion of those changes. One of the clearest examples of this occurs in *Efuru* when the heroine hears of her husband's desertion through overhearing gossip at market (p. 54–55).[31]

Though Nwapa's dialogic approach appears as the dominant feature of her narrative, its prominence should not detract from that other important aspect of her writing which in fact enables the vocality of her style – her focus on women's affairs. Nwapa's women represent themselves in voice, yet their spirit of pride and self-reliance is manifested also in the relative diversity of their quotidian activity.[32]

Efuru and *Idu* document in some detail women's customs, business preoccupations and worries: certain sections, in particular the chapter on childbirth in *Efuru* (chapter 2), read like extracts from an almanac of women's simples. Through recreating a sense of the fullness of Igbo women's lives during the time of colonisation, Nwapa thus begins to chart out the neglected gender dimension in the grand narrative of nationalist historical literature as told by male writers. She questions, if only implicitly, the gender-bound space-time co-ordinates of that narrative. More specifically even than this, however, she delivers her riposte to a male-dominated nationalist tradition and its iconography of womanhood by making available for her women characters roles and symbols of identity which diverge from the mother stereotype. Nwapa's women characters are concerned about bearing children and being good mothers, yet their lives are not defined solely through their maternal function. Especially in *Efuru* Nwapa delineates the 'clearly expressed female principle' in Igbo life where 'fecundity [is] important, not entire'.[33]

Efuru opens with the heroine marrying without parental consent, defiant and unafraid. Later, when her husband proves unworthy, she leaves, just as defiant. Though her action is more problematic, *Idu* ends with the heroine willing her own death so as to join her husband: she resolves that the relationship provided by the marriage was more important to her than bearing children. Both heroines are admittedly exceptional figures, yet it is important to note that they are not unique. Characters like the older woman, Ajanupu, in *Efuru* and Ojiugo in *Idu* exemplify comparable qualities of decisiveness, outspokenness and self-sufficiency.

In Igbo society, as Amadiume shows, it is in trade as much as in marriage and childbirth that women obtain power. Accordingly, both novels focus on marketing as the chief dynamic of women's lives and the means whereby they obtain status.[34] Attracted by the lure of a good business reputation, women like Idu and Efuru structure their lives around market days and keep out a vigilant eye for profit. In this way, as well as through sheer audacity and hard labour, they develop the trading prowess for which the community respects them. Two important qualifications should perhaps be made here. One, that the economic abilities shown by Nwapa's women characters are compromised in her later writing when, in a capitalist cash system, marketing heroines turn exploitative and conspicuously consumerist. And two, that, even while women command power through economic means, patriarchal law is never challenged, even in matters of trade.[35]

It is therefore only when women take on spiritual power, thus discarding their sex roles, that they are able to enter a sphere where male authority has little effect. Nwapa's Woman of the Lake deity in *Idu* and especially *Efuru* bears a strong resemblance to the water goddess, Idemili, described by Amadiume. In Amadiume's account, women wield considerable power as the worshippers and representatives of this water spirit: ritual elites develop from groups who worship her; successful market women are seen to be blessed by her.[36] So too, in Nwapa, Uhamiri, the Woman of the Lake, is held in high regard, as are her followers. At the end of *Efuru*, the heroine is chosen to represent the deity in recognition of her status in the community. As infertility is a necessary condition of the goddess' chosen followers, Uhamiri's intercession gives Efuru's barrenness new meaning – in a way, makes it fruitful.

Where Amadi recognised only male deities, Nwapa thus puts the community's shrines in order, setting the female goddess back in her rightful place. This readjustment reflects on what I have argued is the more general effect of her writing – that of counterbalancing both in language and in character iconography a post-colonial literary patriarchy and a matrifocal nationalism. In the crucial decade of the sixties, Nwapa in *Idu* and *Efuru* re-angled the perspective set by male writing, showing where and in what ways women wield verbal and actual power. If nationalism has typically been embodied in patriarchal formations and fraternal bonding, and involves the exclusion of women from public political life, then Nwapa, in choosing not to engage with 'big' national themes, dealt with the exclusion first by reproducing it – by situating her narratives in another place entirely – and then by making of that occlusion a richness. By allowing a women's discourse apparently to articulate itself in her writing, she elaborates the text of national experience. Yet even more importantly than this perhaps, Nwapa also uncovers the practical, lived reality of motherhood – she digs into the muddy, grainy underside of nationalism's privileged icon. The mothers of Africa, Nwapa shows, also have voices, anger, rival aspirations, their own lives. Most of all, they are as much the subjects of communal history as their nationalist sons.

Notes

1   See Edward Kamau Brathwaite, *Mother Poem*, Oxford University Press, Oxford, 1977. The other two parts of the trilogy, as their titles suggest, are also relevant: *Sun Poem* (1982) and *X/Self* (1986), also published by OUP.

2   Nuruddin Farah, 'A Combining of Gifts: An Interview', *Third World Quarterly* 11.3, (July 1989), p. 180.

3   *West Africa* 3729, (January 16–22 1989), pp. 59–60.

4   Buchi Emecheta, *New Society*, 4 September 1984; quoted by Kathleen McLuskie and C L Innes in 'Women in African Literature', *Wasafiri* 8, (January 1988), p. 4.

5   Freedom TV Nyamubaya, *On the Road Again*, Zimbabwe Publishing House, Harare, 1986, pp. 3–4, 10–11.

6   *West Africa* 3721, December 12–18 1988, p. 2324. The Afro-American critic, Barbara Christian, has also projected an expression of nationalist sentiment on to her interpretation of images of Afro-American and African motherhood in Alice Walker and Buchi Emecheta. Stressing the importance of the institution of African motherhood for cultural regeneration, she observes: 'Motherhood provides an insight into the preciousness, the value of life, which is the cornerstone of the value of freedom.' Barbara Christian, *Black Feminist Criticism: Perspectives on Black Women Writers*, Pergamon, Oxford, 1987, p. 247.

7   Alice Walker, *The Temple of my Familiar*, The Women's Press, London, 1989. The quotation is from p. 63, but the remythologising continues throughout.

8   As will later be more fully described, the idea is that writing involves the creation and assertion of identity.

9   Quoted in *Unheard Words*, ed. Mineke Schipper, trans. Barbara Potter Fasting, Allison & Busby, London, 1985, p. 50.

10   Lauretta Ngcobo, 'The African Woman Writer', *A Double Colonisation: Colonial and Post-Colonial Women's Writing*, eds. Kirsten Holst Petersen and Anna Rutherford, Dangeroo, Oxford, 1986, p. 81.

11   Virginia Woolf, *Three Guineas*, The Hogarth Press, London, 1986, p. 125.

12   The concept of the imagined or invented nation is advanced by Benedict Anderson in his compact and well-known book on the subject, *Imagining Nations*, Verso, London, 1983.

13 For reasons of brevity, these statements must here remain at the level of assertion. However, for a compelling argument that 'gender is implicated in the conception and construction of power' and so also of politics, see Joan W Scott, 'Gender: A Useful Category of Historical Analysis', *American Historical Review* 91, (1986), pp. 1053–1075.

14 In African novels and poems of the forties, fifties and sixties, especially, writers cast themselves or their heroes as sons singing in praise of the African Mother. Or, in the case of Irish nationalism, a rhetoric of martyrdom encourages son-sacrifice to the Mother who is the land and the Church. See Richard Kearney, *Myth and Motherland*, Field Day Theatre Company, Belfast, 1984.

15 These assertions are influenced by Mikhail Bakhtin's theories of polyphony. Bakhtin has spoken of the coincidence of unisonance and patriarchal motifs in national 'epic' art forms. Mikhail Bakhtin, 'Epic and Novel', *The Dialogic Imagination*, ed. Michael Holquist, trans. Caryl Emerson and Michael Holquist, University of Texas, Austin, 1986, pp. 3–40 and especially pp. 13–15.

16 See Philip Corrigan and Derek Sayer, *The Great Arch: English State Formation as Cultural Revolution*, Blackwell, Oxford, 1985, pp. 1–13, for a discussion of the familial affinities of nation-states.

17 For evidence of the intersection of colonial and indigenous patriarchies, a wide range of work might be cited. With reference to Africa, see, for example, Marjorie Mbilinyi, 'Runaway Wives in Colonial Tanganika: Forced Labour and Forced Marriage in Rungwe District 1919–1961', *The International Journal for the Sociology of Law* 16.1 (February 1988), pp. 1–29; Christine Obbo, 'Sexuality and Economic Domination in Uganda', *Woman – Nation-State*, eds. Nira Yuval Davis and Floya Anthias, Macmillan, London, 1989, pp. 79–91; and Terence Ranger's discussion of the transference of kingly motifs in the colonial appointment and interpellation of chiefs in 'The Invention of Tradition in Colonial Africa', *The Invention of Tradition*, Eric Hobsbawm and Terence Ranger, Cambridge University Press, Cambridge, 1983, pp. 211–262.

18 See Abdul R JanMohammed's reading of the Fanonist concept in his essay 'The Economy of Manichean Allegory: The Function of Racial Difference in Colonialist Literature', *'Race', Writing and Difference*, ed. Henry Louis Gates Jr, University of Chicago, Chicago, 1986, pp. 78–106.

19 Consider, for example, the dominant characterisation of the

alienated, self-hating colonised in Frantz Fanon, *Black Skin, White Masks*, trans. CL Markmann, Paladin, London, 1970; or Jean-Paul Sartre, *Black Orpheus*, trans. SW Allen, Presence Africaine, Paris, 1976.

20 To take the words of Simone de Beauvoir somewhat out of context, replacing her term 'world' with that of 'nation':

> Representation of the [nation], like the [nation] itself, is the work of men; they describe it from their own point of view, which they confuse with absolute truth.

Simone de Beauvoir, *The Second Sex*, Penguin, Harmondsworth, 1979, p. 175.

21 Simon Gikandi, 'The Politics and Poetics of National Formation: Recent African Writing', conference paper, ACLALS Conference, Canterbury, 24–31 August 1989, pp. 1–20.

22 Julia Kristeva, *Desire in Language*, Basil Blackwell Ltd, Oxford, 1987: in particular the essay, 'How Does One Speak to Literature?' pp. 92–123.

23 See Bernth Lindfors, 'Introduction', in *Critical Perspectives on Chinua Achebe*, eds. Bernth Lindfors and CL Innes, Heinemann, London, 1979, pp. 5–6, for further comment on the 'School of Achebe'.

24 For criticism of Nwapa's narrative approach see James Booth, *Writers and Politics in Nigeria*, Hodder and Stoughton, London, 1981, pp. 80–81; Eustace Palmer, review, 'Elechi Amadi, *The Concubine* and Flora Nwapa, *Efuru*', *ALT* 1 (1969), pp. 56–58; Adiola A James, review, '*Idu*, Flora Nwapa', *ALT* 5 (1971), pp. 150–153; Kirsten Holst Petersen, 'Unpopular Opinions: Some African Woman Writers', *A Double Colonisation* 112–113; Oladele Taiwo, *Female Novelists of Modern Africa*, Macmillan, London, 1984, p. 47.

25 See Kristeva pp. 104–106.

26 Zora Neale Hurston, *Their Eyes Were Watching God*, Virago, London, 1987.

27 Elechi Amadi, *The Great Ponds*, Heinemann, London, 1982.

28 Similarly, Carole Boyce Davies finds in the Chielo-Ezinma episode in *Things Fall Apart* the traces of a 'suppressed larger story'. Carole Boyce Davies, 'Motherhood in the Works of Male and Female Igbo Writers: Achebe, Emecheta, Nwapa and Nzekwu', *Ngambika: Studies of Women in African Literature*, eds. Carole Boyce

Davis and Anne Adams Graves, Africa World Press, New York, 1986, pp. 241–256.

29 Ifi Amadiume, *Male Daughters, Female Husbands: Gender and Sex in an African Society*, Zed, London, 1987.

30 Thus we find Nwapa's central women characters submitting to the rule of callow husbands and to the circumcision knife and, in every case, taking responsibility for barrenness. See *Efuru* pp. 53, 55, 63; *Idu* p. 91.

31 Refer also to p. 209 for a similar example.

32 As Amadiume's account suggests, Nwapa could have gone even further in representing the range of roles and social positions open to women. In the event, we assume, inherited novelistic conventions, a colonial education, patriarchal strictures, any one or all of these, continue to set limits on her narrative.

33 Boyce Davies pp. 243, 249; Amadiume p. 29.

34 *Idu* p. 29; *Efuru* p. 125.

35 The buying expedition in *Efuru* pp. 140–141 is a representative incident.

36 Amadiume, pp. 42, 53–55, 102–103.

Judie Newman

The Untold Story and the Retold Story: Intertextuality in Post-Colonial Women's Fiction

Post-colonial writers frequently embark upon writing with a self-conscious project to revise the ideological assumptions created by Euro-centric domination of their culture, and to undermine and delegitimise the centrality of that of the West. Political and literary rewritings therefore go hand in hand, as the post-colonial novelist revises the fictions of influential predecessors in order to deconstruct conventional images of the colonial situation.

The need to question acculturated models and exemplary representations is particularly acute for women writers whose double marginalisation brings into sharp focus the question: whose story is it? Women write with an informed awareness that stories condition their readers and influence future events and, in order to lay claim to their own stories, to take possession of their own realities, women writers may employ intertextual strategies, repositioning the text in relation to its point of origin, or offering revisions of canonical texts.

Jean Rhys' *Wide Sargasso Sea*, a retelling of *Jane Eyre* that supplies the untold story of the first Mrs Rochester, comes appropriately from both a female and a post-colonial pen.

The intertextual strategy does, however, raise problems of a theoretical nature. Rewritings may give the impression that post-colonial culture can *only* rework, that it has no creativity of its own, and is fundamentally dependent for its materials on the colonising culture.

Wide Sargasso Sea, for example, chooses not to tell the story of Tia, the heroine's black friend, and only partly tells the story of Christophine, her black nurse. For all its revisionings, the tale remains that of the white slave-owner's daughter. Rhys nevertheless adroitly counters the charge of parasitism on an 'original' by historically positioning her novel before *Jane Eyre*. *Wide Sargasso Sea* is a 'post-dated prequel'[1] not a sequel, and therefore enjoins future readers to envisage Victorian Britain as parasitic on its colonies, just as Brontë's heroine depends on both a colonial inheritance and the warning example of her predecessor, in the negotiation of her own independence. A reader-centred model of reading practice therefore substitutes for a paradigm based on literary history. Readers do not 'begin at the beginning', reading from origins, and a reading of *Wide Sargasso Sea* first, and as a frame for *Jane Eyre* is possible, and even desirable.

Intertextuality is achronological and anachronistic, inviting us to consider (in David Lodge's phrase) the influence of TS Eliot on Shakespeare. In consequence, however, it may be objected that it plays fast and loose with material history, textualising events in order to revise their meanings in a cavalier fashion, opening the doors once more to mythic readings of the 'madwoman in the attic' variety.[2]

In *The Rape of Shavi*, Buchi Emecheta's interweaving of a Biafran war allegory with a fable narrated in the manner of George Bernard Shaw risks neo-Tarzanism in its Shavian temporal and geographical dislocation. Underlying both the objection of parasitism and that of ahistoricism lies the difficulty implicit in any counter-discourse, the danger of using the terms of the dominant social language in order to attack that language and its assumptions, as 'the contesters discover that the authority they sought to undermine is reinforced by the very fact of its having been chosen, as dominant discourse, for opposition.'[3]

Rewritings, counter-texts, run the risk of slippage from oppositional to surreptitiously collusive positions. A symptomatic reading of two contemporary Indian novels reveals alternative narrative strategies which respond to these problems: Ruth Prawer Jhabvala's *Heat and Dust*, which focuses on retold stories, in relation to the role of the reader; and Anita Desai's *Baumgartner's Bombay*, in which the connections between silence and repetition are altogether bleaker in their historicity.[4]

Heat and Dust presents two stories: that of Olivia and her Nawab, set more or less contemporaneously with *A Passage to India* in 1923; and that of the narrator who retraces Olivia's steps 50 years later and to some extent re-enacts her story. The two plots are intercut – 'spliced' in Jhabvala's filmic metaphor – in order to compare Imperial and independent Indias, past and present, and to interrogate the relative merits of each. Olivia's story has been silenced, declared a 'forbidden topic' (p. 2) by her own generation, and is rediscovered by the narrator through letters, which extend into 'belles lettres' – literature – as the narrator retells Olivia's story in her own words. Behind these two stories there lurks a third. Richard Cronin has demonstrated the presence of a specific set of revisionings in *Heat and Dust* which act to repoliticise EM Forster's liberal humanist creed of the primacy of personal relations over divisive political ideologies.[5]

As Cronin points out, Forster visited India in 1921, to spend six months as private secretary to the Maharajah of Dewas, and published an account of his experiences in *The Hill of Devi* (1953). Harry, in *Heat and Dust*, is a thinly disguised Forster – an English homosexual who loathes the British in India and idealises the Indian princely state as the antithesis of the Imperial world, a place where personal relationships are all, and friendship transcends politics. In the 1983 edition of *The Hill of Devi*, however, it was revealed that Forster had edited the letters which form the basis of his account, in order to conceal his own 'untold story', a sexual relationship with a boy, whose services were procured and paid for by the Maharajah. The boy subsequently boasted in public of going to bed with Forster. Cronin is surely right to suggest that the Maharajah tempted his secretary into an open display of homosexual behaviour in order both to control Forster and to humiliate the British.

Jhabvala sets up a precisely parallel situation in Khatm, where Harry is similarly prized by the Nawab as 'a very improper Englishman' (p. 43):

> . . . a living exemplar of all the possibilities of Englishness that the British in India would rather deny existed. His patronage of Harry is a delicate racial affront. Racial hatred is the motive of much of his behaviour.[6]

Jhabvala's new twist on the old tale is to introduce Olivia as a second victim of the Nawab's revenge. While Harry is aware of the Nawab's darker side (displayed annually in a murderous religious riot), Olivia remains in a state of naiveté. She rejects the possibility that the Nawab orchestrates the riot, in highly Forsterian terms:

> She felt it was *she* who knew the Nawab, not they. To them he was just a person they had to deal with officially, an Indian ruler, but to her he was – yes, a friend. (p. 70)

Despite mounting evidence of the Nawab's dacoities, extortion and political machinations, Olivia persists in reading the situation in personal terms: 'People can still be friends, can't they, even if it is India.' (p. 103) The setting for her response is doubly ironic – Harry's room, hung with Indian miniatures depicting erotic pleasures. Outside lies the town, 'a miserable stretch of broken roofs, and beyond that the barren land: but why look that far?' (p. 103) Quite overtly, Jhabvala frames Olivia's creed of friendship in such a way as to emphasise the riches of the princes, the poverty of their subjects, and her own almost wilful blindness. Olivia is happy to remain in an eroticised miniature world which excludes wider political perspectives.

Eventually her affair with the Nawab culminates in a messy abortion, discovery and flight. To the British, Olivia has simply been destroyed by a scheming Indian: 'No one ever doubted that the Nawab had used Olivia as a means of revenge' (p. 170). Jhabvala provides some basis to this charge in the scene of Olivia's seduction, in a grove. Immediately beforehand, the Nawab glorifies friendship as a transcendent virtue: our friends on earth are those we sat close to in Paradise. Within the grove, however, a band of dacoits are waiting, also 'friends', with whom the Nawab collaborates in extortion. He comments that 'I suppose you think they are bad men. You must have heard many stories' (p. 133) and counters with a story of his own, that of Amanullah Khan, his ancestor, who lived for booty just like the dacoits. For the Nawab, Amanullah Khan is an object of envy, able to fight his enemies openly, via direct challenge rather than plots and intrigue. He describes how Amanullah Khan, under pretence of friendship, entertained his enemy to a feast, only to trap him in his tent and stab him to death. It is hardly a heroic image of direct and open challenge, and a distinctly odd prelude to the seduction. The suspicion lingers that the Nawab seduces Olivia partly to shut her mouth, to prevent her carrying tales to the British. Rather than emphasising passion or love, the seduction is set in a context which suggests revenge, under cover of affection. Olivia's story therefore revises the personal, liberal views of Forster, to insist on the political consequences of Imperial domination, and to make the point that a relation of dominance cannot be converted into an image of friendship or love: it must be destructive.

The Nawab's story ends with a description of Khan's tent, on which the bloodstains are still fresh 'as if it had happened yesterday' (p. 137). This image points to the inherent awkwardness of intertextual revisioning. Repoliticisation may amount to demonisation; the overhaul of Forsterian liberalism may turn the clock back, to Indian horror stories, rather than forward, to acknowledge the real implications of Imperialism. Olivia is last seen through the eyes of Harry, as she arrives, pale, dishevelled and in native dress, at the Nawab's palace:

> She reminded him of a print he had seen called *Mrs Secombe in Flight from the Mutineers*. Mrs Secombe was also in native dress and in a state of great agitation, with her hair awry and smears of dirt on her face: naturally, since she was flying for her life from the mutineers at Sikrora to the safety of the British Residency at Lucknow. Olivia was also in flight – but, as Harry pointed out, in the opposite direction. (p. 172)

Superficially, therefore, the novel appears to reinforce the notion that revisionary retelling courts anachronism. The counter-discourse, aimed at revising apolitical liberalism, has merely crossed over into an earlier demonic discourse of India, the 'Mutiny' horror story.[7] Mrs Saunders, another English woman abroad, offers an action replay of this stereotypical image of India as sexuality linked to destruction. She is discovered in a room furnished with scenes from the Mutiny, fully dressed despite illness, since she considers that the sight of her gaunt chest may inflame the servants' passions: '"You hear a lot of stories," Mrs Saunders said' (p. 119). Neither Olivia nor the reader is treated to the full horror story of what happened to the Somerset lady in Muzzafarbad when her servant was ironing her underwear: the story is too predictable to need an ending. Mrs Saunders simply completes it with the phrase, 'They've got only one thought in their heads and that's to you-know-what with a white woman' (p. 119).

All the British display a similar tendency to textualise India, to transform the Other into a set of codes and discourses which can be recuperated into their own system of cultural recognition. Olivia is regaled at various points by 'interminable anecdotes about things that had happened in

Kabul or Multan' (p. 15), by Dr Saunders' stock of racist tales (p. 120), by Major Minnies' account of 'a devilish clever Hindu moneylender in Patna' (p. 16), and by a veritable anthology of anecdotes about suttee. The latter 'were drawn not so much from personal experience as from a rich storehouse of memories that went back several generations' (pp. 57–8), it being, of course, the function of hegemonic discourse endlessly to replicate itself.

In addition, such stories have material consequences. Harry (unwittingly explaining his own fear of being poisoned by the palace food) passes on the tale of a chorus girl, mistress of a former Nawab, who flees the palace after his death, in terror that the Begum will poison her. She is under the spell of 'some tale she had heard' (p. 151) involving poisoned wedding clothes sent to an unwanted bride, the fatal garments having supposedly been prepared by an old woman still resident in Khatm. So afraid is she of a repetition of these past events that she flees in her nightclothes. The imagistic link to Olivia, who flees in the opposite direction in native dress, reinforces the suggestion that fictions may function to coercive effect. No threat was necessary on the Begum's part: the mere existence of the story was enough to put the girl to flight. Jhabvala's recovery of Olivia's story poses the question of how such revisionings can avoid repropagating an original demonic discourse.

Jhabvala's solution is to frame Olivia's story within the tale of her successor in such a way as to lay bare the structure of revisionary processes by focusing upon the role of the Reader. Her procedure invites comparison with Wilson Harris' project for a fiction that seeks through complex rehearsal and repetition continually to consume its own biases.[8]

Most readers have tended to privilege Olivia's story over the narrator's, an emphasis fostered by the narrator: 'India always changes people, and I have been no exception. But this is not my story, it is Olivia's as far as I can follow it' (p. 2).[9] Unfortunately this very nearly turns out to be true.

The narrator is in grave danger of being swamped by Olivia's story. In the opening pages of the novel India is glossed by an English missionary as a horror story: as a veteran of famines, a Hindu–Muslim riot, and a smallpox epidemic; he declares that 'Wherever you look it's the same story' (p. 4). 'Paper-white, vaporous', the missionary resembles a ghost, but a 'ghost with backbone' (p. 6), comparable to Olivia, now firmly 'ghosting' the narrator's story.

The narrator is unnamed, but as Douglas Rivers is her paternal grandfather, may be assumed to be 'Miss Rivers'. The lack of a name suggests a weakened identity, and invites comparison with another unnamed narrator in women's fiction, the heroine of Daphne du Maurier's *Rebecca*, also a plain Englishwoman, transplanted in exotic circumstances, and overshadowed by a more glamorous, artistic predecessor, whose life ended in erotic disaster. *Rebecca* takes its plot from *Jane Eyre*, whose heroine narrowly avoided becoming Jane Rivers in a passionless marriage to a missionary, St John Rivers, in India.

In contrast to Olivia, the narrator seems extremely uncertain of her sexual identity. Flat-chested, and so tall that she has to wear men's sandals with her trousers, she is pursued in the streets by urchins, shouting '*hijra*' (eunuch) – indeed she is drawn to the spectacle of eunuchs dancing (p. 10), enacting a sad parody of womanly gestures and dress. For the narrator, therefore, Olivia offers an idealised 'feminine' alter ego: 'She was everything I'm not' (p. 7). Her own lack of sexual confidence appears to explain her extreme passivity to Chid, an English would-be holy man, to whose sexual demands she accedes despite feeling neither respect for his Tantric beliefs, nor any attraction to his body. She admits: 'I have never had such a feeling of being used' (p. 65). Much as the Nawab used Olivia, so Chid uses the narrator, in an explicit image of impersonal sexual exploitation.

The narrator, however, does not seem to have learned from the past. Like the other British protagonists she approaches India through framing fictions: 'All those memoirs and letters I've read, all those prints I've seen' (p. 2). She appears to have no other purpose but to follow in Olivia's footsteps, proceeding directly to Satipur, and seeking to enact a repetition of Olivia's amours, substituting the arms of Inder Lal for those of the Nawab.

Critics have tended to suggest that Miss Rivers is an unreliable narrator, piecing Olivia's story together from the letters, Harry's memories and other sources, and inevitably having to fill in the gaps of the story with her own imaginings. But rather than Miss Rivers rewriting Olivia's story to her own ends (as Jhabvala revises Forster's) it is arguable that it is Olivia who very nearly succeeds in scripting the narrator's life for her. The narrator is, at least initially, passive to the discourses which 'write' her.

She is, for example, much more eager to protect Olivia's letters from Chid's pawing than to safeguard her own body. (She locks up the letters, when Chid covers them with dirty fingermarks.) Later Chid himself sends the narrator letters, which she keeps together with Olivia's. The contrast between them is instructive. Chid's letters are 'absolutely impersonal' (p. 94), beginning not with a personal salutation but with 'Jai Shiva Shankar!' (Long live Lord Shiva!), a general greeting which could be used when writing to anyone; and their philosophical content makes them eminently suitable for public consumption – the narrator reads them aloud to Inder Lal. Since Chid's spiritual quest has involved a complete renunciation of personal relations, including his name, his own history and all personal attributes, his letters form a living example of the total revision of the Forsterian creed. They do not, however, avoid continuing the demonic image of India; their few factual sentences always report being 'cheated and robbed' (p. 94). In contrast Olivia's letters, are 'intensely personal' (p. 94), written on her own elegant stationery, unlike Chid's 'impersonal post office forms' (p. 94). Unsurprisingly perhaps, Olivia's letters, 50 years old, look 'as if they had been written yesterday' (p. 95), whereas Chid's appear to have been travelling long distances, absorbing smells and stains along the way. The two sets of letters visibly contrast the hothouse anachronism of the personal with a larger, time-stained vision of India, and draw attention to the danger of the narrator's apparent closeness to Olivia. She is in fact more vulnerable to a past script than to present reality. Her personal life is so empty that it is easily filled with an engrossing, emotional tale like Olivia's. Making a wish at a shrine, the narrator describes herself as 'too lacking in essentials for me to fill up the gaps with any one request.' (p. 127)

A variety of echoes, repetitions and parallels suggest that the narrator's story hovers between two possibilities – the reassertion of a past story, as Olivia influences the narrator, or its revision in the present.[10]

Inder Lal, the narrator's lover, has like the Nawab a wife with mental problems, a dominating mother, and a public life marked by plots and intrigue – in his case within the petty sphere of office politics – and, like the Nawab, he impregnates his white mistress. These juxtapositions invite the reader to compare past and present, and to assess their relative merits. In addition, the comparative method establishes the lack of any fixed yardstick or norm, colonial or independent, by which to measure events. Which figure gains in each comparison? Does the parallel between the Nawab and Inder Lal raise Inder Lal to princely status? Or does it cut the Nawab down to size? Is the Begum a sinister and powerful matriarch? Or merely a meddlesome mother? Is the Nawab's wife a mysterious madwoman, hidden from view like the first Mrs Rochester? Or is she simply the victim of an unfortunate marriage, as Inder Lal's young wife Ritu so obviously is? By splicing her two stories Jhabvala highlights the role of the reader's imagination, capable of magnifying or diminishing the characters.

The juxtapositions also suggest a foreshadowing to the readers who themselves must undergo the process of scripting and revising, wondering whether the narrator will follow Olivia's example, and anticipating what will happen in the one plot from the parallel events of the other. In some respects, therefore, the reader becomes a shadow to the narrator. As narrator, Miss Rivers tells the story, using her diary, letters and personal research. Yet, as the reader of Olivia's letters who then projects herself into the scene, she is extremely close to *the reader*, and exemplifies the perils and rewards of imaginative reading. Similarly, since Olivia wrote the letters she is to some extent telling her own story; yet, throughout the novel, it is only the narrator who knows the whole story. The reader is almost as ignorant as Olivia, and advances towards knowledge at much the same pace, hand in hand with Olivia. The roles of reader and narrator therefore crisscross in order to keep posing the question: whose story is it? Who is in control – an independent narrator or a colonial one? In broader terms, to what extent is any reader controlled by a story? How much do any readers actually create that story for themselves?

As readers, for example, we first learn that the narrator made love in the grove with Inder Lal, then in the ensuing scene that Olivia consummated her affair with the Nawab in the same place. In the time of reading, the narrator's seduction precedes Olivia's; in the time of history, of course, it follows. Does the narrator follow Olivia's example, deliberately setting out to imitate her? Or, in intertextual anachronism, does Olivia follow the narrator's example – since, after all, it is the narrator who imagines the seduction scene for the reader, inventing some or all of its particulars from her own preceding experience.

This proleptic technique also forces the reader to read one story through another, in a continual process of revision. We learn, for example, that the narrator is pregnant. She speculates as to whether Maji's ancestors (midwives) 'attended Olivia' (p. 138). The obvious supposition is that Olivia also became pregnant and had a baby – not, as we later learn, an abortion. Some expectations are fulfilled. Mrs Saunders' gloomy bungalow is similarly musty in 1973, and her horror stories of Indians as sex-mad robbers are repeated almost verbatim on her verandah by an English tourist, who recites a litany of disasters from sexual molestation in Fatehpur Sikri to pickpockets in Goa, with ringworm and dysentery to boot.

As this repetition suggests, the narrator is not an exceptional case – one neurotic Englishwoman mesmerised by the past. Her position is generalised by the examples of other characters who are scripted by past stories. Douglas Rivers, now essentially a bureaucrat, yearns for the days of heroic activity in India. He is compared to 'a boy who read adventure stories and had dedicated himself to live up to their code of courage and honour' (p. 40). He particularly enjoys mooning over the 'dead heroes' (p. 107) of the Mutiny in the Christian graveyard. By dint of frequent re-readings the inscribed epitaphs become increasingly familiar and even, after the rainy season, fresher, so that 'the lettering stood out clearer' (p. 153), as clear as Olivia's letters 50 years later. Ironically Olivia's own favourite epitaph is one which memorialises a Lt Edwards as 'a kind and indulgent Father but most conspicuous in the endearing character of Husband' (p. 105). Douglas, however, is so busy imitating past heroes that he neglects Olivia and loses the opportunity to feature as a character in the Lt Edwards' mould. The Nawab's exploits with the dacoits, the source of his eventual ruin, are also pale imitations of the tales he has heard of Amanullah Khan, in which he tends to take refuge whenever he is feeling frustrated. Throughout the novel, therefore, Jhabvala elicits a self-conscious awareness of the potentially destructive power of past 'letters', and the urgent need to foster resistant readings. The British cemetery is contrasted with the suttee stones with their crudely inscribed figures: although the vigorous Indian widows of the novel, led by Maji, express respect for those commemorated thus, their reverence does not extend to following the example of the past. Significantly, the shrine of the last '*sati*' (in 1923) looks 'as age-old as the others' (p. 55), firmly consigned to a past with which the present has broken.

The slate, however, cannot be wiped altogether clean. When Chid annuls his personal story, he is eventually destroyed, both mentally and physically. The narrator herself drifts towards anonymity and passivity, but learns her lesson at the emblematic location of the suttee stones. She discovers a beggar woman, dying on a mound of refuse. After some token efforts to arrange medical treatment, she simply gives up and later speaks of the beggar to Maji 'with the same indifference as everyone else' (p. 113). Maji, however, reacts with force: '"Leelavati? Her time has come?" Leelavati! The beggar woman had a name! Suddenly the whole thing became urgent again' (p. 113). When Maji finds Leelavati, by the suttee stones, she at once settles down to tell the narrator the story of Leelavati's life. With a name and a story (unlike, as yet, the narrator) Leelavati is humanised once more, and her death in Maji's arms becomes meaningful, even joyful: 'Suddenly the old woman smiled, her toothless mouth opened with the same bliss of recognition as a baby's' (p. 114). Anonymous extinction is transformed by story into an image of rebirth, pointing the way towards the narrator's subsequent decision, abetted by Maji, to avoid a re-enactment of Olivia's abortion, and therefore to make a decisive break with the past.[11]

At the close of the novel the narrator follows Olivia's path to the hills, but names her destination only as 'X'; no other reader will be able to follow in *her* footsteps, as she followed in Olivia's. She also confronts the profound dissimilarity between herself and Olivia, recognising herself as an interloper, when she introduces for the first time an account of the designated reader of Olivia's letters, their first recipient, Olivia's sister Marcia. Marcia had insisted that she and Olivia were alike: 'She claimed she could understand Olivia completely' (p. 179). Though Harry is merely sceptical, the Nawab rejects the resemblance without a moment's hesitation: 'The idea seemed to strike him as simultaneously ludicrous and horrifying' (p. 179). Now Miss Rivers recognises that she cannot project herself into Olivia, any more than Marcia could. She acknowledges that the letters from 'X', which are 'short and quite unrevealing' (p. 178), no longer provide a script for her, and that Olivia is beyond the reach of her imagination: 'I still cannot imagine what she thought about all those years, or how she became' (p. 180). Whereas Harry had written Olivia off in a stereotypical image (Mrs Secombe) the narrator allows the full mystery of her later years to persist. She tells one more story, as originally narrated by the Nawab, of the final words of a hanged dacoit. At the last moment the dacoit had turned to the hangman to ask 'Are you a—?' (p. 178) but did not live to finish his phrase. The Nawab completes it for him ('chamar' – an enquiry about caste) but the narrator refuses to do the same for Olivia. Her life is not rounded off in an exemplary story but is left with its gaps and omissions, as the narrator takes possession of her own story and moves towards an as yet invisible and unscripted future.

Jhabvala thus refuses to establish a hierarchy of discourses, as between plot and subplot, 'frame' and 'tale', which might definitively establish the 'truth' of events. Rather than espousing a mimetic, representational aesthetic, in which a narrator can be reliable or unreliable, *Heat and Dust* insists upon textuality as productive of meaning, while simultaneously refusing to constitute itself as hegemonic.

Baumgartner's Bombay also begins with a cache of letters, here immediately associated with crime, the murder of Baumgartner, a Jew, by a young German, many years after Baumgartner's escape from Nazi Germany.

As the recurrent image of the racetrack suggests ('the circular track that began in Berlin and ended here in Bombay', p. 194), Baumgartner's story comes full circle, and his trajectory is marked by repetition. After being dispossessed as a Jew in Germany, narrowly avoiding the camps, Baumgartner is seized in India as a German, and imprisoned in a British internment camp. When global war gives way to Independence struggles, his Muslim business partner is dispossessed in his turn by Hindus, and flees east. Later, the

death of his Hindu employer sees Baumgartner once more
booted out, into an independent India which has little use for
Europeans. It is hardly surprising therefore that he comes to
see life as a meaningless series of repetitions, as if 'In India,
Europe repeats itself, the first time as tragedy, the second as
farce' (Salman Rushdie).

Before the war Baumgartner had existed less in a real
Berlin than in a redolently textual realm, in which nursery
rhymes and fairy stories yield to Goethe, *Der Gute Kamerad*,
the Torah, pastoral poetry, the *Kaiserbuch*, and Rabindranath
Tagore. Isolated in this bookish world, Baumgartner's
beloved Mutti refuses to read the reality of Nazi Germany
(despite the word 'Jude' having been painted in bold red
letters on her windows) and dismisses the idea of escape to
India as 'diese Märchen' (p. 55) – a fairy tale. Indeed, in
moving East, Baumgartner appears at first to have merely
traded Hansel and Gretel for Aladdin. In his letters home he
edits out the less enchanting aspects of India, and revels
in exotic tales of elephant hunts, tiger shoots and fabulous
banquets (p. 99).

When Mutti's letters cease, however, Baumgartner, disen-
chanted by the recognition that all the 'polite letters' in the
world could not prevent atrocity, that those who read Goethe
can also run camps, adopts a tactic of silence, distancing
himself as far as possible from the plot of history. His passivity none the less eventually exposes him to the horrors of
re-enactment. The German hippy murders Baumgartner for
money, because *he* has not received a letter (read – money
order) from his 'dear mummy' (p. 16).

Baumgartner is killed by an alter ego as immersed in tales
as he himself once was, though of a less comforting variety.
The German's repetitive traveller's tales (a recital of Indian
horror stories involving cannibalism, ritual sacrifice, whole-
sale slaughter, leprosy, flagellation, excess both erotic and
narcotic, and even, farcically, a yeti) which eventually culmi-
nate in the horror of Baumgartner's death, provide a familiar
image of revision as demonisation. The novel's title, with its

echoes of travelogue or guidebook (*Fodor's Beijing*[12]) is doubly ironic, at the expense of both generic and textual assumptions and at Baumgartner's own pose of detached observer.

It is another series of texts, however – the postcards discovered by Baumgartner's body – which explain his condition. 'Strangely empty, repetitive and cryptic' (p. 164), they merely repeat the same phrases: 'Are you well? I am well. I have enough. Have you enough?' These letters cannot be glossed or decoded; they appear to say nothing. The explanation, indicated by the number on each card, is that they were sent by Mutti from a concentration camp. They thus offer an emblematic opposition between endless reprise and an untold story, repeated horrors and a paralysed silence – which cannot in the end itself avoid repetition. Baumgartner is frozen in the horror of Mutti's untold story. He cannot move on, and can therefore only repeat. In themselves the letters have no content. (The rules permitted inmates to say very little.[13]) But their material reality is crushingly significant, a witness to the worst horrors of modern history.

Importantly, it was a similar cache of real letters, passed to Desai, which triggered the novel. Desai remarked that, 'Perhaps because they had been so empty they teased my mind. I had to supply the missing history to them.'[14] Their story could not be allowed to pass into oblivion as Baumgartner does. His death is presented as an unravelling text, as the letters fall from him, 'Impossible to capture, to hold, to read them, make sense of them' (p. 216), and he passes into 'the thick black ink of oblivion, of *Nacht und Nebel*.' (p. 216)

When, therefore, Desai rewrites Forster, the effect is tellingly different, a movement away from textual freedom and back towards history. In a reprise of the 'Marabar' incident in *A Passage to India*, Baumgartner enters a cave, where he hears *not* a repetitive echo (Forster's 'ou-boum') but absolute silence. Neither symbolic nor transcendent, Desai's cave is fully historicised. In the internment camp, Baumgartner had tried to occupy his mind by watching ants entering a crevice, a 'dark cave' (p. 119), only to be repelled by:

. . . their silence, their tedium, the endless repetition of forms and actions that blurred and turned into an endless labour of human forms – bent, driven into caves from which they did not re-emerge. *Nacht und Nebel* (p. 119)

The German phrase repeats the term applied to Nazi prisoners destined for death, for disappearance into 'Night and Fog', whether in forced labour, deportation, or extermination blocks.[15] When Baumgartner squeezes into the narrow crevice of the actual cave he has a moment of panic, but unlike Forster's heroines he overcomes what are merely imaginary terrors. Within, he finds blackness, silence and a total absence of explanatory text: 'No voice, no song, not even a dim inscription' (p. 189). Some things are forever lost to history; the shrine in the cave is unnamed, unexplained.

Desai, however, will not expand precise historical horror into totalising negativity. Refusing any easy vision of nothingness, Baumgartner leaves Forster firmly behind him and makes a rapid exit from the cave: 'Baumgartner would not have its no' (p. 190). Without minimising the repeated horrors of the past, Desai emphasises the need not to be complicit with the forces which would erase historical truth, reducing events to myth or silence. Where Jhabvala's Miss Rivers attempted to close the gap in time between Europe and India, erasing the distance traversed by the letters, and almost succeeding in anachronistically re-enacting Olivia, Desai recognises that only a sense of the historical violence which originally crossed that gap can supply its meaning. Imagination baulks at filling in the silences in Mutti's letters. For some stories there can be no revisions.

Notes

1   The phrase is Susan Gubar's and is quoted in Elizabeth R Baer, 'The Sisterhood of Jane Eyre and Antoinette Cosway', in *The Voyage In: Fictions of Female Development*, ed. Elizabeth Abel, Marianne Hirsch and Elizabeth Langland, University Press of New England, Hanover and London, 1983, p. 132.

2   Sandra Gilbert and Susan Gubar, *The Madwoman in the Attic: The Woman Writer and the Nineteenth-Century Literary Imagination*, Yale University Press, London, 1979.

3   Richard Terdiman, *Discourse/Counter-Discourse. The Theory and Practice of Symbolic Resistance in Nineteenth Century France*, Cornell University Press, Ithaca, 1985, p. 65.

4   Page references which follow quotations in parenthesis are to the following editions: Ruth Prawer Jhabvala, *Heat and Dust*, John Murray, London, 1975; and Anita Desai, *Baumgartner's Bombay*, Heinemann, London, 1988.

5   Richard Cronin, '*The Hill of Devi* and *Heat and Dust*', *Essays in Criticism* 36 (1986), pp. 142–159.

6   Cronin, p. 157.

7   For a discussion of the enduring life of 'Mutiny' stories see Patrick Brantlinger, *Rule of Darkness: British Literature and Imperialism 1830–1914*, Cornell University Press, Ithaca, 1988, chapter 7. Several readers have envisaged Jhabvala as propagating a 'demonic' view of India and of continuing the traditions of colonial British novelists, e.g. David Rubin, *After the Raj: British Novels of India Since 1947*, University Press of New England, Hanover and London, 1986, p. 70 and chapter 4, *passim*.

8   Wilson Harris, 'Adversarial Contexts and Creativity', *New Left Review* 154 (November/December 1985), pp. 124–128.

9   Ralph J Crane, 'Ruth Prawer Jhabvala: A Checklist of Primary and Secondary Sources', *Journal of Commonwealth Literature* XX, 1, (1985), p. 200. See also NS Pradhan, 'The Problem of Focus in Jhabvala's *Heat and Dust*', *Indian Literary Review* 1, 1 (1978), pp. 15–20.

10   For a full account of such parallels see Yasmine Gooneratne, *Silence, Exile and Cunning: The Fiction of Ruth Prawer Jhabvala*, Orient Longman, Hyderabad, 1983.

11   Shirley Chew comments perceptively on this incident as evidence of the narrator's development. Shirley Chew, 'Fictions of Princely States and Empire', *Ariel* 17 (1986), pp. 103–117.

12   Paul West, 'The Man Who Didn't Belong', *New York Times Book Review*, 9 April 1989, p. 3.

13   Konnilyn G Feig, *Hitler's Death Camps*, Holmes and Meier, London, 1981, p. 52. The rules for correspondents in Dachau limited postcards to ten lines of legible prose.

14 Andrew Robinson, 'Out of Custody', *The Observer*, 3 July 1988, p. 42.

15 Feig notes that a block at Ravensbrück, the women's camp, was known as 'Nacht und Nebel'.

Shirley Chew

Searching Voices: Anita Desai's *Clear Light of Day* and Nayantara Sahgal's *Rich Like Us*

In 'The Rani of Sirmur: An Essay in Reading the Archives',[1] the documents which Gayatri Chakravorty Spivak uses to exemplify the imperialist production of a 'true' history of India relate to the second decade of the nineteenth century when the East India Company's territorial ambitions on the northern frontiers of Hindustan brought the British into conflict with the Gurkhas of Nepal. During the Anglo-Gurkha War (October 1814 to February 1816), and until the treaty between the two parties was ratified in March 1817, national prestige together with more practical interests required the British, in so far as the small princely states dispersed among the Simla Hills were concerned, 'to acquaint the people who they are subject to . . . ' (p. 254) One way of asserting paramountcy was through political and military intervention, leading eventually to outright annexation. Another was the fabrication of a narrative which inscribes the 'native' throughout as 'self-consolidating other'. Spivak's examples range from the communications of soldiers and administrators to those of policy-makers in London. But whether it was Captain Birch, assistant agent, earnestly advocating that the country should be 'properly informed of . . . our existence' (p. 254); or Major–General Sir David Ochterlony appropriating for the British the 'right' to possess or dispose of the territory of the Indian rulers at will; or the Board of Control loftily desiring that, thousands of miles away in India, their 'orders . . . may be implicitly obeyed' (p. 256), these imperialist constructions of master and native show a remarkable consistency, determining thereby 'the absence of a text that can "answer one back" ' (p. 251).

Central to Spivak's essay is the attempt on the part of the Company's officials to construct the Rani of Sirmur as the object of political instrumentality. Out to secure their eastern frontier against Nepal, the Company proceeded against Sirmur along familiar lines, that is deposing the old Rajah on the grounds he was 'barbaric and dissolute' and installing in his place his son, a minor king. The guardianship of the young Rajah having devolved upon the Rani, she did not seem to the British, however, to fulfil that trust seriously. Instead it was understood that she wished to be a *sati*, to perform widow-sacrifice. Whether that was in fact the case, or whether the government agent with whom she was consulting had mistaken her intention, will never be known, for while the archives contain official petitions that 'every means of influence and persuasion should be employed to induce the Ranee to forgoe her supposed determination' (p. 269), no clue as to her ensuing fate can be found. It is possible that she was dissuaded from sacrificing herself by the pressures which the Company brought to bear upon her; and equally possible that she did perform widow-sacrifice but her action, being both an embarrassment and a rebuff to the British, went conveniently unrecorded. What is certain, Spivak argues, is that once the Rani was thought to have intentions of being a *sati*, then, as *sati*, she became the object of competing discourses, Brahminical and colonial:

For the female 'subject', a sanctioned self-immolation within Hindu patriarchal discourse, even as it takes away the effect of 'fall' attached to an unsanctioned suicide, brings praise for the act of choice on another register. By the inexorable ideological production of the sexed subject, such a death can be understood by the female subject as an *exceptional* signifier of her own desire, exceeding the general rule of a widow's conduct. The self-immolation of widows was not invariable ritual prescription. *If however, the widow does decide thus to exceed the letter of ritual,* to turn back is a transgression for which a particular type of penance is prescribed. When before the era of abolition, a petty British police officer was obliged to be present at each widow-sacrifice to ascertain its 'legality', to be dissuaded by him after a decision was, by contrast, a mark of real free choice, a choice of freedom. (pp. 268–269)

The above passage establishes the equivocal basis of woman's 'freedom', both as constructed by Brahminical discourse ('her own desire') and colonial discourse ('a mark of free choice').[2] Given that a decisive attempt by the Rani to release herself from her appointed role under British rule, and be a *sati*, merely left her caught between 'patriarchal subject-formation and imperialist object-constitution', it follows that silence and invisibility were inevitable. As if echoing the Rani's plight, Spivak's closing paragraphs run repeatedly towards absence: 'the Rani is not in any of these things', 'there is no "real Rani" to be found' (pp. 270–271).

The archives are a closed book and 'the lost self of the colonies' cannot be restored following the planned 'epistemic violence' of the imperialist project. Spivak's reading of the story of colonialism has been criticised for being restrictive and self-defeating.[3] Equally, it may be argued that, in her pursuit of the Rani, the ground she has traversed, not in geographical terms alone but in deconstructing the archives, opens up for review a textual space which in recent years has been staked out and explored in the works of Indian women novelists writing in English. Each distinct in itself, novels such as Anita Desai's *Clear Light of Day* and Nayantara

Sahgal's *Rich Like Us*, as I shall go on to show, share a number of significant characteristics at the basis of which is the writers' compulsion to understand and thereby determine their position as women and as writers in modern Indian society. One of these characteristics, given that the archives are a closed book, is a serious and passionate commitment to the task of reconstructing the past, and with the view to retrieving for women, both ancestral and present-day, a voice and a presence within their motherland. A second and related characteristic, given that 'the lost self of the colonies' cannot be redeemed, is an informing sense in their writing of the paradoxical nature of the task, with the result that the text becomes the site of struggle, of voices in conflict, and a 'self' continually pitted against its multiple and shifting realities.

> It is history which provides us with evidence that things
> have changed. And if they have changed in the past, they
> do not have to stay as they are now.[4]

In *Clear Light of Day*,[5] as the two sisters, Bim and Tara, look back upon their childhood and youth, and the events surrounding India's arrival at independence, a question which troubles their memories and appraisal of their present lives is to what extent things have changed for them in the two decades or so following 1947. Merely to visit the family house in Old Delhi, it seems to Tara, is to be steeped once more in the dullness and boredom of a time 'when father and mother were alive, always ill or playing cards or at the club, always *away*, always leaving us out, leaving us behind . . . ' (p. 156) Yet this is a past which she cannot relinquish and which Bim has shored up in defiance of that terrible summer when, against the background of Partition and widespread violence, a series of domestic crises overtook the family.

First, the deaths of their parents within a few months of each other; then their elder brother Raja's illness, exacerbated by his worries over the fate of their Muslim neighbour, Hyder Ali; Tara's swift courtship and marriage; Aunt Mira's fatal attacks of chronic alcoholism; and lastly, Raja's departure for Hyderabad. As the crises thickened, it fell to Bim to assume the responsibilities of housekeeper, nurse, parent and partner in her father's insurance firm. But, with Raja drawn close to her again as in childhood, their relationship at least seemed to be safe from destruction. Afterwards, Raja having deserted her, only the house and its ghosts remain, and not unlike a ghost himself, her younger brother Baba, silent, pale and captive to the plangent strains of music from the 1940s which he churns out of his His Master's Voice gramophone: 'Don't Fence Me In', 'I'm Dreaming of a White Christmas' . . . Desai has a remarkable gift for making local details luminous with significance and it is not only a family history that is figured forth in the personal and symbolic hauntings in *Clear Light of Day* but a world of which the Das family was a part, full of yearning and violence, lost yet refusing to be forgotten, demanding to be remade.

Stirred by old memories, other questions presented themselves to the Das sisters – 'Do you know anyone who would . . . really prefer to return to childhood?' (p. 4) and 'What did we really *see*?' (p. 148) – until they find themselves launched upon a process of retrieval and revisioning which is both theme and action in the novel. What they begin to *see* is twofold: first, their common inheritance so that an episode as casual as Tara's meeting with her 'childhood snail' is, at a more permanent level, a shared recovery:

> Bim watched her sister in surprise and amazement. Was Tara, grown woman, mother of grown daughters, still child enough to play with a snail? Would she go down on her knees to scoop it up on a leaf and watch it draw its albuminous trail, lift its tiny antennae, gaze about it with protruding eyes and then the instant before the leaf dipped and it slid downwards, draw itself into its pale pod? (p. 2)

Couched in precise and detailed language, Bim's train of

thought is nothing like Tara's ecstatic outburst yet, in its distinctive manner, it serves to underline her own participation in the eternal mystery of the snail. Second, since the play of light and shade must fall differently even upon the points of intersection within a common inheritance, the revisioning process brings into relief their divergent responses to the past. An example is their contrasting attitudes upon being reminded of the occasion when they were attacked by bees in the Lodi Gardens. Although she was badly stung, the incident, as far as Bim is concerned, is a faded memory whereas it has stayed with Tara through the years, a vivid and barbed reminder of her cowardly flight:

> 'You still remember that?' Bim asked. 'I had quite forgotten.'
> Tara opened her mouth to say something more – now that she had brought it out in the open, even if only under cover of darkness she wanted to pursue it to its end. She wanted to ask for forgiveness and understanding, not simply forgetfulness and incomprehension. But neither Bim nor Bakul was interested. (p. 150)

As in the example cited above, important exchanges between the sisters, together with their solitary reveries, often take place in the dark of evening or in shuttered rooms, and as one or the other of them searches out her innermost feelings and thoughts, *seeing* in this novel is intimately bound up with the play and application of voice, whether in directly rendered speech or narrated monologue.[6] When Tara tries to describe some of her motivations in marrying Bakul, such as her despair over the stagnant quality of life at home and her desire to be above all things a mother, it is the continually shifting registers of her voice, at once honest, timid, complacent, naive, sensible, astute, as she works her way towards the right words, which bring to light, for Bim as well as the reader, her many-faceted personality and the coherence of her life.

In comparison, Bim's attempts at self-scrutiny are deliberated rather than instinctive, an unearthing rather than impetuous flights. It is not her voice in conversation therefore – sharp, mocking, hostile – which the reader is drawn into but her mental responses as, in the seclusion of her own room or in the dark, they beat and steer a path to understanding. The climactic moment to such wrestlings occurs when a business letter arrives from the insurance office, thereby adding to the oppression of visitors, the heat and an uneasy conscience. Bim's anger breaks but, as she rounds on Baba this time, so it becomes evident even to herself that there is a large element of self-indulgence and self-deception behind her assumption of responsibility for the family:

> All these years she had felt herself to be the centre – she had watched them all circling in the air, then returning, landing like birds, folding up their wings and letting down their legs till they touched solid ground. Solid ground. That was what the house had been – the lawn, the rose walk, the guava trees, the verandah: Bim's domain. (p. 153)

Faced at this point with her own inadequacies and the realisation that her siblings, even the passive Baba, have centres of being independent of herself, Bim comes close to the psychological state which unsettled Aunt Mira towards the end of her life. But her resources being more extensive than her aunt's, she is better equipped to 'draw the tattered shreds of her mind together and plait them into a composed and concentrated whole'. For moral support, there are the words of the austere emperor Aurangzeb, speaking out of a deeper weariness than her own: 'Strange that I came with nothing into the world, and now go away with this stupendous caravan of sin!' (p. 167). For guidance as to her best course of action, there are the strengths rooted in her working life as a teacher, 'the keeping to a schedule, the following of a timetable, the application of the mind to facts, figures, rules and analyses' (p. 169). Thus her judgment coming to the fore in her assessment of Raja's poetry, she sees at last that the work consists of youthful imitations, less good than in her hero-worship of her older brother she had imagined them to be and less bad than in her disillusionment she had insisted they were. As for the offending letter which he wrote in his capacity as her landlord, the only solution is to destroy it and 'to pretend it had never been written' (p. 169). Finally disburdened, Bim finds her voice is 'flying, buoyant' (p. 175), as next day she sends Tara and her family off to Hyderabad with many messages to Raja: 'Tell him I'm – I'm waiting for him – I want him to come – I want to see him' (p. 176).

In *Clear Light of Day*, the task of recovering the past and, with it, the knowledge that holds chaos at bay is painstakingly and sensitively pursued. At its close, after the disruptions caused by Tara's visit, after the shared memories and proffered reconciliations, Bim for a brief moment catches sight of a new pattern and significance to her life. Appropriately, such being the sureness of conception behind Desai's art, this illumination rises out of an act of listening, first to Mulk's song and then the guru's, both brilliantly actualised in the narrative.

. . . Bim was suddenly overcome with the memory of reading, in Raja's well-thumbed copy of Eliot's *Four Quartets*, the line:

Time the destroyer is time the preserver.

Its meaning seemed to fall out of the dark sky and settle upon her like a cloak, or like a great pair of feathered wings. She huddled in its comfort, its solace. She saw before her eyes how one ancient school of music contained both Mulk, still an immature disciple, and his aged, exhausted guru with all the disillusionments and defeats of his long experience. With her inner eye she saw how her own house and its particular history linked and contained her as well as her whole family with all their separate histories and experiences – not binding them within some dead and airless cell but giving them the soil in which to send down their roots, and food to make them grow and

spread, reach out to new experiences and darkness. That
soil contained all time, past and future, in it. It was dark
with time, rich with time. It was where her deepest self
lived, and the deepest selves of her sister and brothers and
all those who shared that time with her. (p. 188)

The language here is nicely judged, holding together and yet
making distinct 'her own house' and 'its particular history',
'her whole family' and 'their separate histories', 'her deepest
self' and 'the deepest selves of her sister and brothers'. It is
alive with poetic suggestion, the rich soundings of a technique in which motifs, once announced, are repeated,
developed and transformed, like the variations tirelessly elaborated by the singers upon the *raga*,[7] or the figures in *Four
Quartets* that vanish only to 'emerge/in another pattern &
recreated &/reconciled/redeemed'.[8] It waxes with visionary
power as family history is remade in transcendental terms
that find their correspondences in the performances of the
singers, Iqbal's verses and Eliot's poetic sequence.

Time the destroyer is time the preserver – to the aesthetic
symbols commingled at the close of *Clear Light of Day*, and
which reach back to antiquity through layers of the history
of the Indian sub-continent, one further image of poise, paradox and completeness can perhaps be added, and that is the
figure of Shiva-Nataraja. The inscription is less adventitious
than it may seem because, first, the idea of dance is central
to the cosmogony of Hindu belief, and all nature, as well as
all forms of artistic creation are the effects of Shiva's divine
energy;[9] second, it is shadowed forth in various ways in the
novel: for example in the absurd imitations of Krishna's
dances which Mulk's sisters attempt, in the very movement,
at once fluid and controlled, of Desai's prose and, most teas-
ingly, the attitude that Baba strikes, asleep,

lying on his side, one leg stretched out and the other
slightly bent at the knee as if he were running, half-flying
through the sky, one hand folded under his chin and the

other uncurled beside it, palm upwards and fingers curved in – a finely composed piece of sculpture in white. (p. 40)

Why then should the phrase with which the sisters take leave of each other – 'Nothing's over, ever' – sound so despairing even as it sets out to console? Is it because, despite the healing powers of time, and the regenerative powers of memory, there is no way of stilling entirely the first pangs of experience and knowledge? Is it because, beneath the lyrical quality of Desai's prose, there persist unmuffled the deep notes of disillusionment in the lives she is representing? Is it because the visionary ending of the novel can only encompass without resolving the violence that lies unredeemable at its core, and which is embodied in the tragic figure of Aunt Mira?

Where in the totalising systems of Indian and European culture does she fit? Married at 12, widowed at 15, an inauspicious creature, a household drudge, a cast-off, a nursemaid, an alcoholic – had she not aged prematurely 'her brothers-in-law would have put the widow to a different use' (p. 108); had circumstances permitted, they might have forced her to burn on her husband's funeral pyre. That is Miramasi's history, neatly epitomised in the one good sari she possesses and wore once as a bridal garment and then as a shroud. Within a narrative centreing upon identity and self-realisation, she is an object constructed and used by others. She has no voice to sing as the guru does, like one 'who had come, at the end of his journey, within sighting distance of death', no means of gathering her fragments of life into 'a composed and concentrated whole' (p. 167). Miramasi haunts Bim's memory, unquiet like her ghost, and her story will continue to be, has to be, rewritten. For herself when alive, however, there was only madness, and regression into the childishness which, in her early years, she was given so very little opportunity to enjoy.

But what was the use, oh what was the use of anything

any more? The past was finished, and when I thought of the future I saw only as far ahead as a lawyer for Rose and hands for the beggar. (p. 58)[10]

On 26 June 1975, Indira Gandhi declared a state of emergency in India, a ruling which was not lifted until March 1977. Nayantara Sahgal's novel *Rich Like Us* is an enquiry into the condition of the country almost 30 years after independence and the tendencies inhering which have conduced to the erosion of its democratic principles and practices, and to the assumption of authoritarian rule.

The burden of the enquiry is carried by one of the novel's two alternating narratives, Sonali's first-person account of the crisis which has overtaken her and her country. A believer in the liberal ideal of history as progress and, until arbitrarily sacked in July 1975, a dedicated member of the Indian civil service, it is to this organ that she first turns in her search for explanations.

> Once upon a time we had thought of the civil service as 'we' and politicians as 'they', two different sides of the coin. 'We' were bound by more than a discipline. We partook of a mystique. Our job was to stay free of the political circus. We were successors to the ICS, the 'steel frame' the British had ruled India with, but with more on our hands since independence than the steel frame had had in two hundred years. And we had a new tradition to create, our own independent worth to prove. (p. 28)

These days, however, the integrity of the profession has been undermined, with civil servants 'playing politics' for all they are worth or caught up in 'a conspiracy of silence'. Too often its members are connected by caste, community, and background, speak a language that scarcely rises above the level of family gossip, and are insulated by their complacency against the bitter contradictions of modern India. In brief, 'as the civil service elite we were closer than a class. We were a club, and we knew we would survive . . . ' (p. 29)

'Club', 'elite', 'mystique' – Sonali's words hark back with disturbing anachronism to Kipling's stories about the ICS and suggest in part the nature of the malaise. The 'steel frame', taken over more or less intact, has stood but to what extent has it also operated as a constraining factor in the creation of 'a new tradition'? What common ground can possibly exist between this privileged minority and the 'appalling images' her memory throws up of the victims of greed, cruelty and injustice – the bride burnt to death by her in-laws because their demands for dowry have not been satisfied; the untouchable relegated to the far end of the classroom, away from the other children; shaven-headed little girls, child widows, scavenging for food? Prompted by questions such as these, it seems to Sonali that she must venture further back into the past and further afield than the 'prize Gangetic plain' for possible answers.

The discovery of a manuscript belonging to her paternal grandfather is pivotal to Sonali's enquiry. Reproduced in full in chapter 11, midway in the novel, it parallels her own narrative in that, for the grandfather also, the act of writing constituted a search for answers; moreover, written in 1915, and looking back towards the previous century, it puts Sonali in touch with an epoch which saw the making of British India and with world events which were to have important repercussions on the sub-continent; finally, based on painful memories of the ritual sacrifice of the writer's mother in the wake of the natural disasters which beset their princely state in 1905, it is the means by which the *sati* is inscribed into Sonali's narrative.

> When I got to the river bank where we had cremated my father a new pyre was blazing where the old one had been. I saw her fling her arms wildly in the air, then wrap them about her breasts before she subsided like a wax doll into the flames. (p. 145)

This terrifying image lies at the core of the grandfather's text. Framing it, however, are more familiar associations, such as the exchange between his own father, a lawyer, and Mr Timmons, the British Resident, on the government's handling of the practice of *sati* as an example of the equivocations with which the workings of British law are hedged. To the Indian, fired with reformist zeal, simply to promulgate a law abolishing *sati* was not good enough since, 70 years or so after Bentinck's famous Regulation 17, widow-burning continued to recur. What was needed to root out the custom was moral fervour, a quality lacking among the British in India who, while they claimed to be on a civilising mission, resorted instead to expediency in dealing with *sati* as with other issues.

Despite the note of friendly mockery, for clearly the sparring partners shared a tacit understanding of the rules of their debate, British administration stands accused in the light of this retrospective account. So, too, does Hindu society. Indeed, as the text goes on to detail, the economic and psychological circumstances surrounding this particular ritual sacrifice bear a strong resemblance to those which, according to Ashis Nandy, attended the 'popularisation' of *sati* in Bengal in the early decades of the nineteenth-century.[11] First the drought, and then famine, were both taken as a sign that 'we are cursed' for having deviated from traditional ways. A scapegoat being required, a local clairvoyant singled out the westernised lawyer as being mysteriously doomed. And when the prediction came true, for the community to countenance the sacrifice of the lawyer's widow, an action which for self-interested reasons would have the support of the dead man's relatives, was tantamount to demonstrating renewed allegiance in traditional beliefs.

A curious feature of the manuscript text is that it treads a precarious line between the writer's open adherence to progressive views and his instinctive leanings towards more rooted habits of mind, 'the subterranean layers of ourselves we cannot escape'. This is especially true with regards to his recollections of his mother. 'The Hindu wife is a Hindu wife and can be nothing else . . . It is only looking back that I see her as a person, not the personification of an image' (p. 143). Even so, the 'person' recalled here is constructed through a series of stereotype images – the devout wife, the tireless housekeeper, a figure of modest bearing and good sense, a child of nature who, without the help of formal education, managed 'to span centuries of progress in her lifetime', a widow silent and ghostlike, a *sati*.[12] Only for one moment does she come fully alive and that occurs when she is heard rather than seen. As the relatives gathered and the funeral ceremonies got underway, 'What shall we do?' she asked of her son, a question which may be said to hover between helplessness and decision-making, desperation and resource-fulness, the weighing of choices and a weight of resignation. For him, she sought the assistance of the law. For herself, there was only silence.

> It was left to Mr Timmons to try to find out why my mother had committed *sati*. My uncle told him she had insisted on it as part of a bargain that would ensure my inheritance and, even before I came into it, my education abroad. I have no reason to believe he spoke the truth, for how could she have imagined I would begin a new life in a new world with that knowledge locked in me? How could I arise a phoenix from her ashes, and did she not join me to those who killed her, or at least make me the reason why she died? But of course it is a lie. She who had embraced my father's world and his ideas was too offensive a reminder of them. (p. 151)

There is no reason why the uncle's words should be believed. At the same time, the self-centred protestations of the writer fail to convince entirely, being a strange mixture of disin-genuousness (he *was* enabled by her death to begin a new life) and real contrition (he was part of the law which had failed to provide for her and the patriarchal society which sanctioned such a death). Finally, the likelihood cannot be ruled out that, stranded between two worlds, she took the course dictated by her pieties.

As might be expected of a westernised Indian, a secular Hindu and a student of Marxism, Sonali's attitude to myth is negative. Watteau's *L'Embarquement pour l'île de Cythere* had struck her as being interesting only because its subject and style, 'aristocrats dressed up and romping around pretending to be peasants, living in a little dream world' (p. 204), went out with the French Revolution. Similarly, in the Hindu myth, Sita's ordeals by fire, banishment and immurement are no more than an exemplification of society's arbitrary power which commits women to the funeral pyre and then glosses murder as self-sacrifice. It is not ancient myths and their timeless authority which Sonali feels she needs as a chronicler of contemporary Indian society and politics, but new images that will speak in dynamic fashion for the present age. Predominant among these must be the voice of her great-grandmother for, although briefly heard, 'What shall we do?' carries a distinctive resonance that springs from its applicability to the situation in 1975 as in 1905. It connects across the decades dead ancestor and living woman, and associating in Sonali's mind with other examples of resistance and engagement which she has witnessed – the boy in Connaught Place unlawfully arrested and fighting desperately all the way to the police van, the armless beggar, 'slipping and slithering from his tormentor's grasp' (p. 152) – it suggests broad lines of continuity as well as the possibility of change.

'But it's questions we're all hanging on to, not answers' (p. 236), and far from being authoritative, Sonali's views, such as those on accepted myths, are subject to corroboration and contradiction throughout *Rich Like Us*. The impetus of debate is sustained, first, by a structure of two alternating narratives, incorporating in each case the same characters but placed in different contexts and situations; and second, by the inclusion of an outsider such as Rose as one of the central characters.[13] Thus, to turn to the third-person narrative, which focuses in the main on Rose's memories, is to find not only India's fight for freedom recaptured with intelligence and ungrudging sympathy, but also the Sita story continually

tested against the particulars of daily living until it becomes
revitalised as a parable for modern times.

> . . . how voluntary are voluntary deaths, and was it bliss
> hereafter or earthly hell that drove *satis* to climb their
> husbands' funeral pyres and be burned alive? Why would
> a lovely princess cry out for the earth to swallow her if
> life hadn't become a wilderness? (p. 75)

Bearing in mind his family's history, it does not surprise that
the plight of the heroine of the famous epic should loom
large in the consciousness of Sonali's father Keshav; nor, the
time being the 1930s, that as an Indian working for the
British and simultaneously committed to *satyagraha*, he
should persistently have 'second thoughts' about his own
position, both in relation to colonial authority and traditional
beliefs. Far more important for Rose is that Keshav's
questions, like Sita's dilemmas, project the vacillations and
uncertainties which she herself inhabits – an English-woman
married to an Indian, marginalised in England on account of
her working-class background but in India part of the British
Raj, installed as a wife in a Hindu household yet an intruder,
arrived in India, in Cythera, and still never to arrive. It is a
condition of 'two-ness' that she likens to being 'on a see-saw
going up and down and that's enough to drive one crazy if
it goes on and on' (p. 67). Thankfully there are occasions
when some prospect of equilibrium is conceivable.

One of these, significantly located in a chapter that flanks
the manuscript account of the *sati*, was precipitated by Ram's
other wife Mona and her attempted suicide by fire. It marked
the climax of domestic tensions brought about by living
together, at Ram's insistence, as a 'Hindu Undivided Family'
in the family house in Lahore. Looking back, Rose perceives
that she as much as Ram was to blame since, ensnared in the
ambiguities of a situation in which each woman was both
aggressor and victim, her one wish concerning Mona was,
'If only she'd be dead, dead, dead . . . ' (p. 97) And yet,
when she came upon Mona sitting cross-legged in front of

her prayer table, 'her eyes closed, a band of flame advancing up her cotton sari, consuming it soundlessly', it was not a victim crushed by hate whom she rescued but a woman caught up in a rigorous exercise of her will and determined to meet unendurable conditions by transforming 'a curse of dying' into 'the discipline of dying'. Rose had seen, mirrored in Sita's sufferings in exile, the constraints she lived under after her arrival in India: 'Her spirit came alive in the night to other spirits long before the walls of these rooms, before the city, endlessly before, until she heard the cries of newborn twins in a forest hermitage.' (p. 74) It would seem, however, that Mona, whose recitations from the Ramayana used to insinuate their way into the hubbub of Rose's cocktail parties, had been more receptive to what may be read as the spirit of defiance in Sita's actions. In the conclusion of the *Uttara-Kanda*, the Supplement to the Ramayana, not only did the heroine refuse to plead her cause with Rama the second time round but, when she spoke, it was to appeal to another authority: 'If in truth unto my husband I have proved a faithful wife,/Mother Earth! relieve thy Sita from the burden of this life!'[14]

The domestic incident is one example of Sahgal's deftness and assurance in juxtaposing the momentous and the contingent, myth and living experience. To gauge its impact, the historical context of August 1942, within which the incident occurred, has to be taken into account.

> Here is the *mantra*, a short one, that I give you. You may imprint it on your hearts and let every breath of yours give expression to it. The *mantra* is: 'Do or die'. We shall either free India or die in the attempt . . . (p. 126)

With Gandhi's call for self-sacrifice as a weapon in India's struggle against the British, the Quit India movement gathered to a head. While nationalist activities spread across the country, so the spirit of the old freedom-fighter Lalaji shook the house in Lahore. British goods were thrown out, prayer meetings were 'patterned after the Mahatma's' (p. 127), and all who came to the house were caught up in a collective will so strong as to make no distinction between Hindu and Muslim, rich and poor, Lalaji's friends and Rose. It was against such a background that Mona staged her private insurrection against patriarchal oppression and, by her action, and in the light of *satyagraha*, the Sita story is remade as underlining women's capacity, even under society's pressures, to choose a way to truth. 'How voluntary are voluntary deaths . . . ?' Framed in that way, the ambivalence of the 'how' in the question is crucial, opening up a space between a speculative 'bliss hereafter' and a far too real 'earthly hell' within which women can lay claim to some measure of power as reinterpreters of stories and of their destinies.

It was, Rose recognises, an extraordinary time in which myth, history and daily life continually impinged on each other, each becoming transformed as a result of their coincidence. Faced now with the emergency, and problems closer to home – Ram paralysed after a stroke, and Dev her stepson increasingly insolent as he gains favour under the authoritarian regime – she, like Sonali, must review the past in search of answers to the present. Not that Rose can always be sure about these for, to judge by Ram's high-handed conduct throughout their relationship, Dev's bullying ways, and the difficulties she must now face to secure her lawful share of her husband's property, it would seem that patriarchal structures and, therefore, social and economic inequalities, are still well entrenched some 30 years after independence.[15] Besides, once right, answers have the habit of losing their relevance with time. Far more important for her, as for Sonali, are the images which her memory calls up of ordinary persons and their courage. Prominent among them is Mona, of course, whose example in refusing to be passive or accepting, 'fate or no fate', whose voice, 'Rose-ji, get up and deal with my son, your son now', are sharp spurs to new resolution in Rose even at the very last moment of her life – 'She was on her knees in the act of getting up when a cloth came down over her head, arms pinned hers down and she heard a thick satisfied grunt as she lost consciousness' (p. 249).

Sahgal's tough intelligence and her grasp of history ensures that *Rich Like Us* offers no easy answers. But in that image of Rose about to re-engage in action, the two narratives are drawn together; and with Sonali at the close of the novel immersed in writing her history of Mogul power and Shiva-ji's resistance in the period from 1650 to 1750, together they return the reader to the question which has underpinned the novel: 'What can we do?' The words of Sonali's great-grandmother ring true still, repeated throughout the century and in the various voices of women who, against a colonial history and a cultural memory which have colluded in determining their absence, continue to struggle to reclaim the past and, with it, a sense of their lost self and motherland.

Notes

1 Gayatri Chakravorty Spivak, 'The Rani of Sirmur: An Essay in Reading the Archives', in *History and Theory*, vol. 24, 1985, pp. 247–72. Page references included in the text are to this article. Also in Francis Barker, Peter Hulme, Margaret Iversen and Diana Loxley (eds.), *Europe and its Others: Proceedings of the Essex Conference on the Sociology of Literature*, vol. 1, University of Sussex, Colchester, 1984, pp. 128–151.

2 See also Spivak, 'Can the Subaltern Speak?', in Larry Grossberg and Cary Nelson (eds.), *Marxist Interpretations of Literature and Culture: Limits, Frontiers, Boundaries*, University of Illinois Press, Urbana, 1987, pp. 271–313; and Lata Mani, 'The Production of an Official Discourse on *Sati* in early Nineteenth-century Bengal', in Barker, *et al* (eds.), *Europe and its Others*, pp. 107–127.

3 Benita Parry, 'Problems in Current Theories of Colonial Discourse', *The Oxford Literary Review*, vol. 9, 1987, pp. 27–58.

4 'Introduction: The Story So Far', in Catherine Belsey and Jane Moore (eds.), *The Feminist Reader: Essays in Gender and the Politics of Literary Criticism*, Macmillan, London, 1989, p. 3.

5 Anita Desai, *Clear Light of Day*, Penguin, Harmondsworth, 1980. All page references included in the text are to this edition.

6   'The narrated monologue is a choice medium for revealing a fictional mind suspended in an instant present, between a remembered past and an anticipated future.' For a useful account of this technique, see Dorrit Cohn, *Transparent Minds: Narrative Modes for Presenting Consciousness in Fiction*, Princeton University Press, Princeton, 1978.

7   See Ananda Coomaraswamy, *The Dance of Shiva*, Asia Publishing House, Bombay, 1948, pp. 105–106: 'The *raga* may be best defined as a melody-mould or the ground plan of a song. It is this ground plan which the master first of all communicates to the pupil; and to sing is to improvise upon the theme thus defined . . . Psychologically the word *raga*, meaning colouring or passion, suggests to Indian ears the idea of mood; that is to say that precisely as in ancient Greece, the musical mode has definite *ethos*. It is not the purpose of the song to repeat the confusion of life, but to express and arouse particular passions of body and soul in man and nature. Each may be appropriately sung, and some are associated with particular seasons or have definite magic effects.'

8   Christopher Ricks, *TS Eliot and Prejudice*, Faber and Faber Ltd, London, 1988, p. 238.

9   See Coomaraswamy, pp. 94–5: 'In the night of Brahma, Nature is inert, and cannot dance till Shiva wills it: He rises from His rapture, and dancing sends through inert matter pulsing waves of awakening sound, and lo! matter also dances, appearing as a glory round about Him. Dancing, He sustains its manifold phenomena. In the fullness of time, still dancing, He destroys all forms and names by fire and gives new rest.'

10   Nayantara Sahgal, *Rich Like Us* (first published in 1985), Sceptre, London, 1987. All page references included in the text are to this edition.

11   Ashis Nandy, 'Sati: A Nineteenth Century Tale of Women, Violence and Protest', in VC Joshi (ed.), *Rammohun Roy and the Process of Modernization in India*, Vikas Publishing House, Delhi, 1975, pp. 168–194.

12   On the imprisoning hold Indian mythology has exerted over women, see also Anita Desai, 'A Secret Connivance', *Times Literary Supplement*, no. 4563, 1990, p. 972: 'She [the Indian woman] is called by several names – Sita, Draupadi, Durga, Parvati, Lakshmi, and so on. In each myth, she plays the role of the loyal wife, unswerving in her devotion to her lord. She is meek, docile, trust-

ing, faithful and forgiving. Even when spirited and brave, she adheres to the archetype: willing to go through fire and water, dishonour and disgrace for his sake.'

13   On her reasons for using locale and characters other than Indian, see Nayantara Sahgal, 'The Schizophrenic Imagination', *Wasafiri*, no. 11, 1990, p. 20.

14   Romesh C Dutt (trans.), *The Ramayana and the Mahabharata*, JM Dent, London, 1955, p. 152. Meena Alexander's 'Outcaste Power: Ritual Displacement and Virile Maternity in Indian Women Writers', *The Journal of Commonwealth Literature*, vol. XXIV, no. 1, 1989, also examines this conclusion to the epic as well as Gandhi's dubious control over female sexuality.

15   For an account of the contradictions in the position of women during the nationalist struggle in the 1930s and 1940s, and after independence, see Joanna Liddle and Rama Joshi, *Daughters of Independence: Gender, Caste and Class in India*, Zed Books, London, 1986.

Carolyn Cooper

'Something Ancestral Recaptured': Spirit Possession as Trope in Selected Feminist Fictions of the African Diaspora

Spirit possession, that ecstatic moment of displacement central to the religious practices of Africans in the diaspora, literally embodies the transmission of cultural values across the Middle Passage. As metaphor spirit possession doubly signifies both the dislocation and rearticulation of Afro-centric culture in the Americas; divine possession mirrors its subversive other – zombification[1] – that diabolical ownership of the enslaved in the material world. The ubiquitous tales of flying Africans miraculously shedding the weight of slavery to reclaim the freedom of African space testify to the authority of metaphors of transport in Afro-American/Caribbean iconography. Possessed of divinity, the believer dares to make that liberating leap from fact and history into myth and metaphor.

The countervailing tropes of Euro-centric cultural imperialism that redefine such movements of transcendence as savage/demonic/demented are encoded in 'universalising' mythologies that have been systematically diminished in the subversive fictions of black feminist writers. When, for example, in Paule Marshall's *Praisesong for the Widow* the ten-year-old Avey innocently asks her Great-aunt Cuney "'But how come [the Ibos] didn't drown?'" as they walked on water away from American slavery, the painfully studied response – a counter-question – is more eloquent than any disquisition on cultural relativism: "'Did it say Jesus drowned when he went walking on the water in that Sunday School book your momma always sends with you?'"[2] Mythic polarities of Bound Native/Free Imperialist Wanderer; Female Landscape/Male Explorer are thus deconstructed in the particularising language of culture-specific fictions.

Una Marson's unpublished 1938 play, *Pocomania*,[3] Sylvia Wynter's 1962 novel, *The Hills of Hebron* and Erna Brodber's 1988 novel, *Myal*,[4] taken together constitute a multi-form Jamaican/Caribbean rewriting of the colonial text that once defined the place of the native – both black and woman – at the margins of history. Toni Morrison's *Tar Baby* (1981) and Paule Marshall's *Praisesong for the Widow* (1984) are Afro-American versions of that reconstructive tale of dispersal, loss and redemptive flight. In these novels the Caribbean becomes the locus of (re)possession; recuperation of identity is accomplished by reappropriating devalued folk wisdom – that body of subterranean knowledge that is often associated with the silenced language of women and the 'primitiveness' of orally transmitted knowledge. 'Discredited knowledge' in Toni Morrison's words:

We are very practical people, very down-to-earth, even shrewd people. But within that practicality we also accepted what I suppose could be called superstition and magic, which is another way of knowing things. But to blend those two worlds together at the same time was enhancing, not limiting. And some of those things were 'discredited knowledge' that Black people had; discredited only because Black people were discredited therefore what they *knew* was 'discredited'. And also because the press toward upward social mobility would mean to get as far away from that kind of knowledge as possible.[5]

The revalorisation of 'discredited knowledge' is a major project of these female-centred fictions.

In Una Marson's *Pocomania*, set in a small village in colonial Jamaica, the ideological lines are firmly drawn: the upright piety of middle-class Baptist respectability versus the spontaneity of the Afro-centric religious practices of the peasantry. In the starry-eyed view of the play's main character, Stella, spirit possession represents the fascinating freedom of the peasantry from the boring constraints of her rigid little world. In an exchange with Sister Kate, the leader of the Pocomania group, who has a much more practical view of social class and the boundaries it defines, Stella confesses her ambivalence:

> Sister Kate: You like hear de drum dem Miss Stella?
> Stella: I don't know whether I like them or not. They frighten me a little but they certainly fascinate me.
> Sister Kate: Fascinate, Miss Stella? Dem is more wonderful dan dat! Troo de drum de spirit speak – de Lawd Himself speak to de soul of him people.[6]

Sister Kate's mild reprimand, with its benevolent dismissal of the young woman's *naiveté*, puts Stella firmly in her place. In a later exchange with Sister Mart and Brother Kendal, Sister Kate expands on her clear cut view of the dynamics of respectability and commonness:

> Sister Kate: I don't kip wid respectable ladies like she fe come to de meeting. Dem can't understand it. It is not possible to be respectable and common at de same time.
> Sister Mart: But we not common, we is destant.
> Kendal: We is quite destant.
> Sister Kate: Yes, destant in de eyes of de Lawd but not in de eyes of de worl! I don't care what de people wid larning say, dere will always be de common people and de better class people. I know I like to stay in common set, for den I can spress meself widouten noting happen.
> Kendal: An you know I want hagree wid you Sister Kate.

Sometimes I see some respectable people jes' wid look like a hungry dawg in dem eyes. All dem feeling hab to hide because dem is respectable.

Sister Kate: Tek dem upper classes if dem come to de meeting and shout and sing dem will be sick, but eben dough some ob fe we people is tear wid de debil dey get up nex day so go long bout dem business . . . But I maintains people fe kip to dem own station in life. (p. 18)

Stella temporarily strays from her own station, and has to be pulled back to respectability when she suffers a 'collapse' after attending the nine-night[7] ceremony for the now deceased Sister Kate, which degenerates into a brawl. Like Claude McKay's Bita Plant who is similarly fascinated by the peasant world beyond the ordered way of her adoptive parents, Stella is drawn to the edge of the void and rescued before she becomes possessed. McKay's ambiguous representation of Bita's moment at the boundary evokes both the dread and ecstasy:

In the midst of them Bita seemed to be mesmerized by the common fetish spirit. It was a stranger, stronger thing than that of the Great Revival. Those bodies poised straight in religious ecstasy and dancing vertically up and down, while others transformed themselves into curious whirling shapes, seemed filled with an ancient nearly-forgotten spirit, something ancestral recaptured in the emotional fervour, evoking in her memories of pictures of savage rites, tribal dancing with splendid swaying plumes, and the brandishing of the supple-jacks struck her symbolic of raised and clashing triumphant spears.

The scene was terrible but attracting and moving like a realistic creation of some of the most wonderful of the Annancy tales with which her father delighted and frightened her when she was a child. Magnetized by the spell of it Bita was drawn nearer and nearer into the inner circle until with a shriek she fell down. A mighty shout went up and the leading woman shot out prancing around Bita with uplifted twirling supple-jack, but a man rushed in and snatched her away before she could strike.[8]

A man rescues Stella similarly, but he, unlike Bita's rescuer, is not a Jubban (named for that healing plant of Afro-Jamaican folk medicine). David, Stella's knight in shining armour, is properly respectable, with no embarassing connections with the folk. Indeed, when he sets out secretly to follow Stella to the meeting from which he will rescue her, he takes off his jacket and pulls on an old felt hat. He has to assume a disguise in order to penetrate the underworld in much the same way that Len, of Trevor Rhone's *Old Story Time*,[9] must appropriate an alien identity to cover his dealings in obeah.

Una Marson's play is remarkable for its sophisticated handling of Jamaican Creole; its dramatic deployment of Afro-Jamaican religious ritual as theatrical device; and for its foregrounding of gender in the conflict of cultural values on which the play is structured. For what Stella struggles against is not simply the burdens of a generalised respectability, but more the gender-specific weight of appropriate behaviour for an upright young woman in colonial Jamaica. As she mockingly tells David: 'I can tell from the puzzled look on your face all these weeks. You have been saying to yourself, "I can't understand why Stella, a nice, educated, middle class girl is so attracted to an obnoxious cult" . . . Has it ever occurred to you that I feel trapped, bound and imprisoned in this dull house and this boring village?' (p. 46)

Sylvia Wynter's novel, *The Hills of Hebron*, focuses not on the ideological anxieties of the middle-class – its cultural ambivalence – but on the dynamics of power and powerlessness among the members of the congregation of the New Believers, a religious organisation rooted in the peasantry. Though they carefully distance themselves from the mad grandeur of spirit-possessed Pukkumina cultists, the New Believers are heirs to a common legacy of Afro-centric beliefs and practices: the dispossession and then the visionary flight from the city:

> The instinct for survival was as strong in them as in their slave ancestors. Some weight of memory in their blood carried the ghosts of dark millions who had perished, coffined in the holds of ships, so that some could live to breed more slaves; and they, after their freedom had been won, survived the rootless years. They survived the loss of gods and devils that were their own, of familiar trees and hills and huts and spears and cooking pots, of their own land in which to see some image of themselves. And their descendants, the New Believers, survived the exodus from Cockpit Centre, the passage through the wilderness and up to the hills of Hebron, where Prophet Moses had promised them those things that had been lost in their trespass across the seas, across the centuries.[10]

The novel is largely about the failure of leadership of the womanising Prophet Moses, whose mock-messianic career ends in ritual suicide. He allows himself to be stoned to death by the Believers in a grand gesture of self-sacrifice. But it is the female characters who come to assume a central role in the unfolding drama. For not only is Miss Gatha, the Prophet's widow, an inciting force, beating the despondent Believers into a renewed confidence in themselves, but Rose, the victim of Miss Gatha's righteous malice and her son's lust, becomes the symbol of silenced woman, dispossessed of voice, identity and will:

> Rose looked away from the hills and the morning. She wanted to reply to Obadiah, to try to explain. But when she saw the hard mouth and violent eyes that demanded answers from her, her mind became a wide and empty space. She had grown up in the midst of long silences, and words came with difficulty to her. (p. 23)

In the terms of Erna Brodber's *Myal*, Rose is 'zombified', her spirit and body possessed by forces beyond her control.

Her crime is to have been raped and impregnated by a man whose identity she will not reveal. Her husband Obadiah, who has taken a vow of sexual abstinence as a mark of his piety, is enraged by her refusal to exonerate him. The curse that he cries down upon her foreshadows Ella's fate in *Myal*: "'Rose Brown, the Lord make thy thigh to rot, thy belly to swell. And the woman shall say Amen!'" (p. 37)

In *Myal*, the ambiguities of spirit possession/zombification are developed in the novel's parallel plots which centre on the dis/possessed women, Ella and Anita. The stories of both women illustrate that appropriation of consciousness and destruction of will which are both defined in the world of the novel as the process of zombification or spirit thievery. It is Reverend Smith who most clearly elaborates the problem:

> Taken their knowledge of their original and natural world away from them and left them empty shells – duppies, zombies, living deads capable only of receiving orders from someone else and carrying them out. (p. 107)

The accreted negative connotations of the word 'zombie' – in English – thus encode the acculturation/zombification process itself. Maureen Warner-Lewis, in a carefully speculative note to her study *The Nkuyu: Spirit Messengers of the Kumina* traces the etymology of the appellation 'King Zambi Ampungo', used by Miss Queenie, the leader of a Kumina *bands*** in Kingston, whom she interviewed. Warner-Lewis incorporates into her reading of the designation the research findings of Joseph Moore, whose unpublished 1953 Ph.D. thesis, 'Religion of Jamaican Negroes – a study of Afro-Jamaican Acculturation', is a major resource:

> Moore . . . mentions the recognition of sky – and earth-bound deities in the Kumina, some of whom possess devotees. Chief among the sky gods is King Zombie or Oto who never manifests his presence at Kumina through

---

* A *bands* – the form appears plural but is singular – 'is [a] Kumina group held together by an internal hierarchical organisation' (Maureen Warner-Lewis, 1979).

possession . . . He is clearly identical with 'King Zambi Ampungo' whom Miss Queenie named as God and whom she, like Kongo descendants in Jamaica and Trinidad, associates with thunder and rain. So that Moore's 'King Zombie', it seems to me, is none other than *Nzambi* – 'Supreme God' in the Kikongo language. Under the influence of English the Bantu word-initial pre-consonantal syllabic nasals are dropped so that *Nzambi* becomes Zambi.[11]

Warner-Lewis 'see[s] a close phonological similarity between "Zambi" and "zombie" and consider[s] it a strong possibility that the Kumina use of the term "zombie" is a semantic extension of "Zambi", for "a zombie is a god or ancestor who was once possessed by a god or another ancestral zombie, or a living being who has been possessed by one of these". (Moore, *op. cit.*, p. 34)'[12]

Miss Queenie gives a graphic description of myal, the antidote to obeah/zombification, which suggests the potency of this form of spirit possession:

Myal is de ting dey call a spirit where you' head 'pin
roun' an you drop an' you 'kin pupalick[13] 'pon you neck
you see?
Dat a myal spirit.
Dat a bongo myal spirit
which all de hol' African dem –
de dead African dem dem come roun' an' dem lick you all
a' you' headside
an' ride you 'pon you' neck an' you drop.
You see?
Dat dere mean to say myal hol' you now.[14]

In Brodber's novel, the powerful grip of obeah – the debilitating obverse of therapeutic myal, is imaged most dramatically, and ironically, in the attempted theft of Anita's spirit by Mass Levi, a deacon in the Baptist church. Mass Levi, suddenly become impotent, appropriates the spirit of the young girl in order to regain sexual potency: a particularly perverse manifestation of the sexual exploitation of woman.

The Kumina Queen, Miss Gatha (in collaboration with the Baptist minister, Simpson; the necromancer, Ole African and somewhat surprisingly, the English wife of the white Jamaican Methodist minister, Brassington) draws the malevolent possessing spirit from. ᵗʰe girl on to her own person.

Brodber's quiet shaping of this act of exorcism focuses on the intimate, human scale of this potentially sensationalist complex of circumstances. The spirit's power is manifest, but it is its containment (the healing) and the ordinariness of faith in the spirit world that is Brodber's point. This is not a lurid voodoo tale. Comparison with Elizabeth Nunez-Harrell's melodramatic *When Rocks Dance*, set in colonial Trinidad, which similarly deals in obeah, immediately clarifies the differences between the point of view of the *voyeur* and that of the sympathetic insider: the subtlety of Brodber's narrative art is underscored. Nunez-Harrell:

> He jumped behind a tree to hide from her, irritated at the same time by his childish fear. She was no more than the old woman with young hands and legs whom he saw everyday selling chataigne from a smoke-blackened tin can. Yet when he saw her searching him out through the liquid-silver rain, his heart froze. The peace, the calm he brought with him through the rain from his house, left him entirely. Images he despised because they filled him with shame for the ignorance of his people flooded his imagination: women dressed in white; half-naked men jumping in a frenzy to the wild beat of drums; their babbling cries, foaming mouths, stinking sweat, clothes torn to shreds, bodies writhing on the ground in the dirt, and blood, the blood of their wretched cock, their sacrifice. Images, filling him not only with revulsion but with fear too, for more than once he witnessed them 'catching the spirit,' transformed into beings he could not recognize as human.[15]

And Brodber:

> Fainting was one thing. They could fan her and rub her

up with smelling salts. And they did. But what to do when the child's face changed to that of an old woman and she began in her stupor to moan and groan like Miss Gatha and her companions at the tabernacle? Where Miss Gatha herself had fallen on the ground; where they had pinned her dress between her legs; where she was thrashing, boxing and kicking and screaming what seemed like 'Let me go'; where her face changed to that of a beautiful fifteen-year-old and back again to that of a woman of Miss Gatha's sixty-odd years and back again and back again until she was silent, her limbs quiet and she was fifteen years old. In the tabernacle there was no consternation at these changes. There, there was instead joy: 'Amen', 'Thank the Lord', 'Telephone from earth to heaven, telephone'. The water mother, full in white, lifted the whistle from her belt and with its cord still joined to her waistband, moved it to her lips and blew one long, sharp report. All jumping, singing, drumming and groaning ceased and everyone including water mother herself, froze. She blew again, said softly 'It is finished' and with that all took what they had and left Miss Gatha's form with its fifteen-year-old face on the ground. (p. 73)

There *is* a voodoo doll in Brodber's fiction – 'what Levi doing with dolly baby? When she looked closer and saw the circle etched round her head-cup, the knife marks where her legs meet and the bright nail through her neck, she knew . . . that this was a very serious matter' (p. 75) – but its significance in the total architecture of the novel is not only that it is a literal artefact in the practice of obeah; rather, like the crumbling fertility doll that Baba mockingly carves for Nellie in *Jane and Louisa Will Soon Come Home* (Brodber's earlier novel), it becomes an icon of the zombification of diminished woman who is robbed of her possibilities: the alabaster baby. This is Ella's story, as well as Anita's. In Brodber's subtly shaded rural world, the reader focuses less on the 'strangeness' of events and more on their import for characters who

fully believe in a cosmology where the natural and the supernatural, the demonic and the divine regularly consort. For
example, the novel opens with a thunderstorm (echoes of the
'thunder and rain' of King Zombie), that is clearly connected
in the eyes of Mass Cyrus, the Myal man, with the psychological trauma of the young woman, Ella, whom he is called
upon to heal:

> 'What a bam-bam when that grey mass of muck comes
> out of this little Miss Ella lying down so stiff and straight,
> this little cat choked on foreign, this alabaster baby, ship-
> ped on a banana boat and here to short-circuit the whole
> of creation.' (p. 4)

Ella is 'choked on foreign', but her stifling began much earlier
in her alienation from the reverse racist, black world of childhood. Like her mother and her grandparents, she is displaced:
'. . . long face, thin lip, pointed nose souls in a round face,
thick lip, big eye country!' (p. 8) Appropriately, 'big eye'
has associations with 'red eye' and 'long eye', metaphors in
Jamaican folk culture for envy and greed; the evil eye. Ella,
envied and thus excluded from ordinariness, becomes invisible. Persecuting schoolmates and cynical teachers alike,
simply look through her: '"That child is odd. No fight at
all. Suppose the colour will carry her through." And they
were more than a little vexed at that and built up resentment
against her. For it was true' (p. 10).

Not surprisingly, it is in the world of books and the
imagination that Ella is able to escape to an illusory sense of
wholeness: 'When they brought out the maps and showed
Europe, it rose from the paper in three dimensions, grew
big, came right down to her seat and allowed her to walk
on it, feel its snow, invited her to look deep down into its
fjords and dykes. She met people who looked like her'
(p. 11). This is the marvellous world of Alice in Wonderland,
a resonant motif that is there in *Jane and Louisa Will Soon
Come Home*. Ella, Nellie's near-white Other, is doubly imprisoned in a *kumbla*[16] of race and gender. In the racist, imperial

terms of the Kipling poem she recites with such feeling, Ella becomes '[h]alf devil and half child' – 'the white man's burden'. But she is also the black community's burden. For it is the community that has deformed her; she has been zombified by spirit thieves.

Her debilitating marriage to the white American with the Anglo-Saxon sounding name, Selwyn Langley, whose family are 'chemists, manufacturers of herbal medicines and today doctors and travelling medical lecturers' (p. 42), introduces Ella to the respectable other side of the world of alternative medicine and folk practices in which she has been reared, and which has failed her. Her attempts to dredge up that alienating past are potentially therapeutic. But Langley alchemically transforms her richly textured world into the flatness of minstrelsy. His play, *Caribbean Days and Nights*, based on her remembered childhood, is the 'biggest coon show ever' (p. 80). Another form of spirit possession: 'He intended to immortalize it into film. He was a man on the make, a man of success who could not now be stopped: Ella's spirit and with it that of Grove Town would be locked into celluloid for the world to see for ages on end' (p. 92). Entrapped in Langley's *kumbla*, Ella learns the bitter truth that '[m]arriage have teeth' (p. 52). The unseasonal fertility of Langley's threateningly luxuriant celluloid landscape mocks Ella's impotence. Unable to become pregnant, unable to understand her place in Langley's onanistic schema, she suffers a collapse of will, swelling up in a fiction of her own fabrication.

It is the return to the Caribbean after her breakdown that is therapeutic. There at home the psychological problem of the phantom pregnancy which conventional medicine could not accurately diagnose, let alone treat, is fully understood in the superior science of folk medicine:

Willie: It has a head but does not nod.
Mother Hen: Hair but it does not brush it.
Dan: Throat but it does not drink.

Willie: Arms but it does not lift.
Mother Hen: Legs but it does not kick.
Dan: It is a doll. (p. 92)

An important sub-text in the novel is the role of colonial
school textbooks in the zombification of children. Mr Dan,
redeemed by Brodber's subversive fiction from the perversi-
ties of just such a colonial reading book for Caribbean
children, defines the problem thus:

> 'My people have been separated from themselves, White
> Hen, by several means, one of them being the printed
> word and the ideas it carries . . . Our people are now
> beginning to see how it and they themselves, have been
> used against us. Now, White Hen, now, we have people
> who can and are willing to correct images from the inside,
> destroy what should be destroyed, replace it with what it
> should be replaced with and put us back together, give us
> back ourselves to chart our course to go where we want
> to go.' (pp. 109–110)

Brodber deconstructs the message of the problem reading
book, which offers a political model of the colonial ideal of
zombification. The animals on the farm who revolt against
the complacent tyranny of Mr Joe – a clear parable of the
political upheavals in post-emancipation Jamaica – are forced
to return to the dubious security of the plantation because
of their lack of ownership of property and the means of
production. They do not have the capacity to function independently of its reassuring certainties. In Brodber's rewriting
of that pervasive colonial myth, the animals Willie, Dan and
Percy become Ole African, Rev Simpson, Mass Cyrus, and
it is they who help to exorcise the ghost of Langley – to
draw the duppy off Ella.

   She returns to Grove Town to teach, as part of her own
therapy, and revolts against the ideology of the textbooks
she is constrained to use. So she asks Reverend Simpson/Dan:
'"Is that what I am to teach these children, Reverend Simp-

son? That most of the world is made up of zombies who cannot think for themselves or take care of themselves but must be taken care of by Mr Joe and Benjie? Must my voice tell that to children who trust me?"' (p. 107) Simpson's response prefigures his more elaborate statement as Mr Dan, cited above: '"You have a quarrel with the writer. He wrote, you think without an awareness of certain things. But does he force you to teach without this awareness? Need your voice say what his says?"' (p. 107)

The novel ends with the assurance that '[t]hat little gal's gonna break it up and build it back again' (p. 111). But it is Mother Hen, Miss Gatha, the Kumina Queen who sums up, in rhyme, the collective, visionary certainty of transformed political/ideological relations:

'Different rhymes for different times
Different styles for different climes
Someday them rogues in Whitehall
Be forced to change their tune.' (p. 111)

And even if Whitehall doesn't change its tune, the Stellas, Roses and Ellas of the Caribbean, resisting zombification, will truly repossess themselves. Something ancestral recaptured.

In Toni Morrison's *Tar Baby* the theme of zombification recurs. Jadine Childs, the Tar Baby of the novel's title, is a woman who 'has forgotten her ancient properties'.[17] Like Ella, the alabaster baby of Brodber's novel, Jadine is adopted by whites and educated out of her skin. She becomes a cultural orphan cut off from the black community. The fate of her love match with the 'homeboy', Son, is thus predictable: a protracted playing with the despised other and then a rapid retreat to the security of the pampering Frenchman whom she had self-protectively feared to marry because he might have wanted not her but a generic black woman.

It is Son who reduces the complicated affair to the stark simplicity of folk tale:

'Once upon a time there was a farmer – a white farmer . . .'

'Quit! Leave me *alone!*'

'And he had this bullshit bullshit bullshit farm. And a rabbit. A rabbit came along and ate a couple of his . . . ow . . . cabbages.'

'You better kill me. Because if you don't, when you're through, I'm going to kill you.'

'Just a few cabbages, you know what I mean?'

'I am going to kill you. *Kill* you.'

'So he got this great idea about how to get him. How to, to trap . . . this rabbit. And you know what he did? He made him a tar baby. He made it, you hear me? He made it!' (p. 270)

This tale of seduction, entrapment and cultural death prefigures a collision of values between the stuck-up Tar Baby and the Rabbit who is stuck on her – despite his superior knowledge:

Each was pulling the other away from the maw of hell – its very ridge top. Each knew the world as it was meant or ought to be. One had a past, the other a future and each one bore the culture to save the race in his hands. Mama-spoiled black man, will you mature with me? Culture-bearing black woman, whose culture are you bearing? (p. 269)

The outcome of the conflict is more enigmatic than Son's attempted dismissal of this constructed black/white woman would allow. The Uncle Remus story is itself inconclusive: "'Did the fox eat the rabbit?" asked the little boy to whom the story had been told. "Dat's all de fur de tale goes," replied the old man. "He mout, en den again he moutent. Some say Jedge B'ar come long en loosed 'im – some say he didn't."'[18]

Morrison's retelling of 'The Wonderful Tar-Baby Story' exposes the paradoxes of 'success' for blacks in America, a theme that is also developed in Marshall's *Praisesong for the*

Widow. For Jadine, the racial history of enslavement and deprivation is the entrapping past from which she wishes to extricate herself:

> 'I can't let you hurt me again. You stay in that medieval slave basket if you want to. You will stay there by yourself. Don't ask me to do it with you. I won't. There is nothing any of us can do about the past but make our own lives better, that's all I've been trying to help you do. That is the only revenge, for us to get over. Way over.' (p. 271)

But Son doesn't want to 'get over'. His hometown Eloe – the past he carries around in his head – is a mythic space that shelters him from the many aliases he is forced to assume.

Jadine's abortive attempt to share Son's rural, down-home space is frustrated by the spirits of the insistent night women who possess her dreams, forcing her to confront her vulnerability and her doubts about what she has surrendered in the passage to success:

> New York was not her home after all. . . . She thought it could be a shelter for her because there the night women could be beaten, reduced to shadows and confined to the brier patch where they belonged. But she could not beat them alone. There were no shelters anyway; it was adolescent to think that there were. Every orphan knew that and knew also that mothers, however beautiful, were not fair. No matter what you did, the diaspora mothers with pumping breasts would impugn your character. And an African woman, with a single glance from eyes that had burned away their own lashes, could discredit your elements. (p. 288)

Son had tauntingly assumed that the price of Jadine's success was sexual: ' "Dick. That you had to suck, I mean to get all that gold and be in the movies. Or was it pussy? I guess for models it's more pussy than cock" ' (p. 120). But the price of success is not a literal giving up of the body; it is a magical surrender of the soul that primitives rightly fear will be appropriated by the camera: the model refashioned in the image of the photographer.

Like Aunt Cuney, whose haunting presence forces the Widow to abandon the persona of tourist and go native, the night women come in dream to offer Jadine an alternative identity. But she is unable to make the leap of possession. In Eloe she becomes a bored tourist snapping pictures that Son himself will later acknowledge as accurately diminished versions of his history. Jadine refigures Son's past, forcing him to abandon something essential in himself. Thus, if the story of *Tar Baby* is Jadine's failure to find home and the lost mother whose death she experiences as betrayal, it is equally the story of Brer Rabbit, the black man fatally attracted to white America's model black woman.

The mesmerised Son cannot at first effect the rescue that Therese had wished for Jadine: "'He's a horseman come down here to get her'" (p. 107). He is not yet the divine horseman who will mount the living, riding the ritual of possession. Jadine will remember him as 'the man who fucked like a star' (p. 292). But that will not be enough. The black man as stud is himself in need of rescue. Not the rescue that Jadine proposes – a degree, a profession (perhaps law) and mis-education into otherness. Morrison begins and ends the novel with Son in flight, a seemingly circular movement of entrapment. But the second flight so cunningly engineered by Therese is a heroic, headlong lickety-split climb to the waiting horsemen and freedom from the spell of the Tar Baby.

Tar Baby is also the story of Margarèt Lenore whose physical abuse of her infant son is an extreme expression of the frustrated rage of the alienated wife and mother. Like Ella, who was ostracised because of her privileged light skin, Margaret, 'a principal beauty of Maine' (p. 54) must bear the burden of her 'astonishing good looks' (p. 82). Her later acts of self-punishing abuse are the obverse of a pathological need to please. She revolts against the greedy intimacies of mothering; the child's demanding need for constant security mirrors

Margaret's own need for protection. Her husband's distant innocence of his family's grief is an act of complicity which Margaret finally forces him to acknowledge. Morrison's subtle portrayal of this ageing white woman underscores the limits of a too-easy sisterhood. However much Margaret may be a victim in a sisterhood of suffering, she is a privileged victim sharing the class and race prejudices of her husband in relation to her black female servants, Ondine and Jadine. Like Maydene Brassington, the busybody Englishwoman of Brodber's *Myal* who is pulled into the circle of compassion that surrounds Ella yet is nevertheless shrouded in strangeness, Margaret Lenore is ambiguously placed.

Paule Marshall's *Praisesong for the Widow* charts the liberating journey of Avey Johnson from a state of zombification – haunted by the spirit of her dead husband whose drive for success had alienated them both from the nurturing rituals of their early marriage:

> . . . something in those small rites, an ethos they held in common, had reached back beyond her life and beyond Jay's to join them to the vast unknown lineage that had made their being possible. And this link, these connections, heard in the music and in the praisesongs of a Sunday: ' . . . *I bathed in the Euphrates when dawns were/young* . . . ' had both protected them and put them in possession of a kind of power . . . (p. 137)

Images of Jerome Johnson as a man possessed speaking in the voice of another parody that other possession,[19] evoking the psychic displacement and cultural amnesia that mark the path of upward mobility from Brooklyn to White Plains:

> There was something even more disquieting which she slowly became aware of over the years. On occasion, glancing at him, she would surprise what almost looked like the vague, pale outline of another face superimposed on his, as in a double exposure. It was the most fleeting

> of impressions, something imagined rather than seen, and she always promptly dismissed it (p. 131)

and

> Worse, during the same period, he began speaking in a way at times she found hard to recognize. The voice was clearly his, but the tone, and more important, the things he said were so unlike him they might have come from someone (perhaps the stranger she thought she spied now and again) who had slipped in when he wasn't looking and taken up residency behind his dark skin. (p. 131)

This discomfiting sensation of double exposure is reflected in Avey's inability to recognise herself in the mirror: an image of the deconstructed self. To be a successful middle-class black person aspiring to 'whiteness' is literally to lose touch with sensory reality. The living dead borne along without will. The cruise ship on which Avey travels to the Caribbean signifies the seductive power of The American Dream: integration within definite limits. A ghostly invisibility:

> She idly scanned her fellow diners. As usual, even those who sat directly facing her at the nearby tables somehow gave the impression of having their backs turned to her and her companions. It had to do with the expression in their eyes, which seemed to pass cleanly through them whenever they glanced across, and even, ironically, with the quick strained smiles some of them occasionally flashed their way. (p. 47)

Like Jadine's Paris, the Versailles Room, the cruise ship's most formal dining room, epitomises the envied elegance of Euro-American culture. But Marion, Avey's politicised daughter who is always quoting Gwendolyn Brooks, vainly tries to show her mother the perverse other side of that rapacious splendour:

> 'Versailles . . . ' Marion had echoed despairingly when Avey Johnson had made mention once of the name. 'Do

you know how many treaties were signed there, in that infamous Hall of Mirrors, divvying up India, the West Indies, the world? Versailles' – repeating it with a hopeless shake of her head. (p. 47)

The cruise ship as slave ship bearing its deadened cargo across the Middle Passage images the imperial authority and techno-logical grandeur of neo-colonial America imposing its frigid alienness on the Caribbean seascape. Like Son, Avey must jump ship in order to remember her ancient properties. When she abandons the liner for the seemingly frail boat that will carry her to Carriacou and the Ceremony of the Big Drum she surrenders her sense of awe at the technological might of her (American) nation[20]: 'And on a group tour of the bridge that first trip she had seen the huge Ferranti computer that monitored operations on board. Her group had stood awe-struck and reverent before the console with its array of key-boards, switches and closed-circuit television screens' (p. 15). What will replace that hi-tech display will be the much older technology of orally transmitted knowledge – the weighted sound of the drum resonating over time:

And the single, dark, plangent note this produced, like that from the deep bowing of a cello, sounded like the distil-lation of a thousand sorrow songs. For an instant the power of it brought the singing and dancing to a halt – or so it appeared. The theme of separation and loss the note embodied, the unacknowledged longing it conveyed summed up feelings that were beyond words, feelings and a host of subliminal memories that over the years had proven more durable and trustworthy than the history with its trauma and pain out of which they had come. After centuries of forgetfulness and even denial, they refused to go away. The note was a lamentation that could hardly have come from the rum keg of a drum. Its source had to be the heart, the bruised still-bleeding innermost chamber of the collective heart. (pp. 244–245)

It is to this point of recognition that Aunt Cuney's forceful ministrations lead. Carriacou, like the Tatem Island of Avey's youth, is a place of ritual where extraordinary people walk on water and unsettled spirits claim their bodies. Aunt Cuney's grandmother, for whom Avey is named, and who passes on the story of the flying Ibos (or Igbos), expresses her alienation from her literal-minded community in terms of a mind/body divorce; a liberating 'madness':

> The way my gran' tol' it (other folks in Tatem said it wasn't so and that she was crazy but she never paid 'em no mind) 'cording to her they just kept on walking like the water was solid ground. Left the white folks standin' back here with they mouth hung open and they taken off down the river on foot. Stepping . . . They sounded like they was having such a good time my gran' declared she just picked herself up and took off after 'em. In her mind. Her body she always usta say might be in Tatem but her mind, her mind was long gone with the Ibos . . . ' (p. 39)

It is this same kind of madness that Avey is accused of by her travelling companions when she is forced to abandon ship as a result of her Aunt's insistent struggle to reclaim her for the night women. The pale mink stole that falls in their physical struggle is reminiscent of the superb sealskin coat given to Jadine by the Frenchman, a symbol of the material luxury promised in exchange for cultural amnesia.

In all of these feminist fictions of the African diaspora the central characters are challenged, however unwillingly, to reappropriate the 'discredited knowledge' of their collective history. The need of these women to remember their 'ancient properties' forces them, with varying degrees of success, to confront the contradictions of acculturation in societies where 'the press toward upward social mobility' represses Afrocentric cultural norms.[21] The writers employ strategies of oracy – praisesong, animal tale, religious ritual – to transmit their versions of this collective history that is so often absent from the written histories of their adoptive nations. The body of the text may be grounded in Western literary forms, but the mind and its metaphors, possessed of the spirit, are long gone with the Ibos.

Notes

1 'Zombie': 'cf. Kongo *Zumbi*, fetish. In the kumona cult: an ancestral spirit.' *Dictionary of Jamaican English*. The apparent pejoration of 'zombie' seems to be itself evidence of the displacement of cultural values in the African diaspora. See, for example, the OED definition: 'In the West Indies, a corpse said to be revived by witchcraft.' The more general popular usage of zombie as 'living dead' has clearly negative connotations of enslavement. For a literary treatment of the topic see Maximilien Laroche, 'The Myth of the Zombi' in Rowland Smith, ed. *Exile and Tradition – Studies in African and Caribbean Literature*, Longman & Dalhousie Univ. Press, London, 1976, 44–61. For a popularised/ scientific account of zombification in Haiti see Wade Davis, *The Serpent and the Rainbow*, (first published in 1985), Warner, New York, 1987.

2 Paule Marshall, *Praisesong for the Widow*, EP Dutton, New York, 1984, p. 40. Subsequent references cited in text.

3 'Pocomania': 'origin obscure: the present established form is due to false hispanising of a probably African form which may be *po-* (unidentified) + *kumona*, of which dances wildly performed under possession by "ancestral spirits", and induced catalepsy, are the prominent features.' *Dictionary of Jamaican English*. Note the scholarly scepticism of the quotation marks.

4 'Myal': 'cf. Hausa *maye*, 1. Sorcerer, wizard; 2. Intoxication; Return. (All of these senses are present in the Jamaican use of the word.) . . . In recent use in AFRICAN and similar cults: formal possession by the spirit of a dead ancestor, and the dance done under possession.' *Dictionary of Jamaican English*. Myal is the complement of obeah which is defined thus in the *Dictionary of Jamaican English*: '. . . the derivation is prob multiple – cf Efik *ubio*, "a thing or mixture of things, put in the ground, as a charm to cause sickness or death" (OED); also the base of Twi *ɔ-bayifó*, witch, wizard, sorcerer . . . The practice of malignant magic as widely known in Jamaica. Its origins are African; in practice it has never been clearly distinguished from MYAL: though the latter was supposedly cura-

tive of the ills caused by the former, both have shared the same methods to a great extent (MYAL with some admixture of elements derived from Christianity).' An alternative etymology for myal – which admits moral ambivalence – is provided by the linguist Hazel Carter in personal communication with Maureen Warner-Lewis, March 1985: '*mayal* < *Mayaala*, Kikongo, "person/thing exercising control."' In 'Masks of the Devil: Caribbean Images of Perverse Energy,' unpublished conference paper, U.W.I., St. Augustine, 1991, Warner-Lewis argues that the universe is governed by opposing energy flows, one, which is creative/sustaining ('good'), the other, destructive/negating ('evil'). The myal/obeah dichotomy seems to have its genesis in an Afro-centric cosmology where good and evil, though distinguishable, are derived from a common energy source. Thus, for example, in the novel *Myal*, booklearning, which functions in part as an agency of colonial zombification/obeah, becomes in Brodber's own fictive practice the medium of psychic reintegration.

5 Toni Morrison, 'Rootedness: The Ancestor as Foundation', in Mari Evans, ed. *Black Women Writers* (first published in 1984), Pluto Press, London, 1985, p. 342.

6 Una Marson, *Pocomania*, unpublished manuscript, Institute of Jamaica, p. 16; subsequent references cited in text. At least two versions of the manuscript exist.

7 'Nine-night': 'the celebration that concludes the nine-day period of funeral activities: there are singing, dancing, games, story-telling, ring-play, etc.' *Dictionary of Jamaican English*.

8 Claude McKay, *Banana Bottom*, (first published in 1933), Harper, New York, 1961, p. 250.

9 Trevor Rhone, *Old Story Time*, Longman, Harlow, 1986.

10 Sylvia Wynter, *The Hills of Hebron* (first published in 1962), Longman, London, 1984, p. 51.

11 Maureen Warner-Lewis, *The Nkuyu: Spirit Messengers of the Kumina*, Savacou Publications, Kingston, Jamaica, 1977, p. 79.

12 *Ibid*.

13 "kin pupalick': 'do a somersault'. *Dictionary of Jamaican English*.

14 Maureen Warner-Lewis, pp. 59–60.

15 Elizabeth Nuncz-Harrell, *When Rocks Dance*, Putnam, New York, 1986, p. 243.

16 kumbla/coobla/calabash is used in that novel as an image of entrapment in subterfuge. For an extended discussion see my essay

'Afro-Jamaican Folk Elements in Brodber's *Jane and Louisa Will Soon Come Home*', New Beacon, London, 1980, in a recent collection on Caribbean women and literature which employs the metaphor of the kumbla in its title: Carole Boyce Davies and Elaine Savory Fido, eds., *Out of the Kumbla*, Africa World Press, Trenton, New Jersey, 1990, pp. 279–288.

17   Toni Morrison, *Tar Baby*, Alfred A Knopf, New York, 1981, p. 305. Subsequent references cited in text. Jadine is thus described by Therese, the half-blind/visionary island woman whose 'voice was a calamitous whisper coming out of the darkness' (p. 305) to warn her surrogate son of Jadine's fatal charms.

18   Joel Chandler Harris, *Uncle Remus*, Appleton-Century-Crofts, Inc., New York, 1880, p. 11.

19   In states of possession the possessed often speaks in the clearly recognisable voice of others. Consider the shifts in voice and bearing of Miss Gatha/Anita in *Myal*.

20   For an African reading of the novel see Abena Busia, 'What is Your Nation?: Reconnecting Africa and her Diaspora' in Cheryl A Wall, ed., *Changing Our Own Words*, Rutgers University Press, New Brunswick, 1989, pp. 196–211.

21   Less obviously so of the main female characters in Wynter's *The Hills of Hebron*. But Miss Gatha's total investment of her resources in her son's education in town, and his eventual betrayal of the community's belief in him (and his acquired book-learning) are yet other manifestations of the theme of colonial mis-education and zombification.

Abena P. A. Busia

Rebellious Women: Fictional Biographies – Nawal el Sa'adawi's *Woman at Point Zero* and Mariama Bâ's *So Long a Letter*★

The two novels I have chosen to discuss here both raise and address the question of the possibility of constructing women's biography and autobiography as a mode of rebellion and as liberating history. By being novels in which the intention of the fiction is the subject of narrating history itself, both *So Long a Letter*[1] and *Woman at Point Zero*[2] raise the question of the difficulty of enacting and inscribing women's rebellion. And it is the nature of the narrative artifice, the ways in which the stories are told, which serves as a commentary on their supposed realities and thus on ours, as black women without official voice of recognised history. My choice of words is deliberate: the question is not one of having no voice of history, so much as having no *official* voice of *recognised* history.

The structures of *Woman at Point Zero* and *So Long a Letter* are in and of themselves educations on the significance of

★ This essay is a transcript of a paper delivered at the 1987 annual convention of the African Studies Association, Denver, on a panel entitled 'Rebellious Women/Women's Resistance: Biographical Approaches'. The papers on the panel discussed the problematics of uncovering and reconstructing women's histories, from the point of view of literature, history and political science.

narration as the control of the meaning of one's own life. The novels explore the ways in which women realise the shape of their lives, and the inter-relation between this realisation and the nature of their stories, thus demonstrating recognition of the context in which their voices must be heard. In the company of such writers as Simone Schwarz-Bart and Alice Walker, Bâ and Sa'adawi are aware that for women, the ability to inhabit their own stories, and to become the subject of their own histories can be of itself an act or gesture of rebellion. Thus Ramatoulaye in *So Long a Letter*, at the central critical moment of her story says, 'This time I shall speak out, my voice has known thirty years of silence, thirty years of harassment, it burst out.' (157) And the opening words of the central defiant autobiographical narrative of *Woman at Point Zero* are: 'Let me speak, do not interrupt me.'

At first glance there would seem to be very little in common between these two texts, the one by Bâ about a middle-class Senegalese teacher, looking back after widowhood in the relative comfort of money, status and children, to reflect upon the meaning of her sometimes happy and often turbulent life; the other by Sa'adawi, about a dispossessed Egyptian prostitute on death row, after a life of degradation, on the eve of being executed for the murder of a pimp, who says of herself: 'Only my make-up, my hair and my expensive shoes were "upper class". With my secondary school certificate and suppressed desires I belonged to the "middle class". By birth I was lower class' (p. 12).

Yet these two women have much in common, and the most striking parallel between them is not that they are both about Islamic African women, but that despite the seeming distance between the two fictional heroines, they both speak out of enclosed spaces; the desire to speak is first generated out of confinement, and then enabled by the presence, literal or spiritual, of another woman.

To begin with Firdaus: I would first like to emphasise how the mode of presentation frames her autobiography. This work is a fictional autobiography, represented as biography, by a fictional narrator, based on a real–life encounter between the author, Sa'adawi, and the real woman bearing the same name as the fictional heroine, Firdaus. That is, the text itself has three concentric frames.

The central chapter, chapter 2 of the text, is essentially a dramatic monologue in which Firdaus, a woman dispossessed in every sphere of her life and, as I said, on the verge of being dispossessed of that very life, speaks her story. She chooses to do this by enclosing in her circumscribed space that narrator who is to take her story beyond the prison walls. The story is itself framed therefore by chapters 1 and 3, by the words of the narrator of her story, who tells in chapter 1 of her desire to hear Firdaus and of the struggle she had in order to see her, and in chapter 3 of the impact of Firdaus' story upon her.

Now, this narrator bears a great resemblance to, but for the purposes of interpretation, should not be confused with, the named author Nawal el Sa'adawi. She prefaces, but does not encapsulate the entire novelistic artifice in a third and outer frame consisting of the author's preface in which, she as a doctor, speaks of her own research (published as *Women and Neuroses in Egypt*). This research was undertaken in the Quantir women's prison, during the course of which she encountered the real woman Firdaus who was later executed, from whose life the fictional Firdaus was created, 'to give her life after she had died', in this particular form. I stress the matter of form, because Sa'adawi is very well known for her controversial non-fiction. We therefore need to take seriously her decision to tell Firdaus' story in the form of a novel. It is that choice of form, and the way she shapes her text, which is the subject of my enquiry.

The nature of the narrative itself is important – a dramatic monologue full of breaks and sudden transitions, deliberate echoes and repetitions, spoken as a last will and testament to a 'free' stranger who is held equally captive for the duration of its telling.

One of the images that reverberates throughout the text is the succession of eyes which makes it clear that for Firdaus the order of life is a succession of dispossessions, in a world where power is masculine, and access to power a masculinisation.

Her story is one of loss and alienation, a story of separations in a world where very desire or gesture of trust is betrayed; where the hope which lies in women like the mother disappears, only to be replaced by men who violate; where eyes in which Firdaus remembers her person being drowned in love, are sooner or later always replaced by eyes which clinically dissect her body as a sexual commodity. Quite unlike Ramatoulaye, at no point in her life does Firdaus find a mirror image of herself. Instead, after a series of flights, from her uncle, from her husband, fom her lover who turns into her first pimp and even from her first madam, she has a series of 'veils' lifted from her eyes, as she puts it; a series of visions which reveal to her a path to apparent power and control.

However, the imprisoned Firdaus has no doubts at all about who it is that has taught her the limits of her life, and the near impossibility of reclaiming any power and control over the meaning of that life. Though Firdaus speaks her life as if its end were a triumph and a liberation, she never leaves the place of her incarceration for a literal earthly liberation. At the end of the text she moves out only to die. It is a willing departure for, as she puts it at the start of her narrative, and repeats at the end, 'This journey to a place unknown to everybody on this earth fills me with me pride. All my life I have been searching for something that would fill me with pride, make me feel superior to everyone including kings, princes, and rulers.' I need hardly emphasise the point that her 'everyone' is a male collective – kings, princes and rulers.

Both of these novels deal with access to language as the primary metaphor for access to control of life, a control which includes most specifically (to greater or lesser degree), access to control over one's economic destiny, one's body and one's sexuality. It is important to note that for *both* the prostitute – who is likely to structure her story as one of economics bound up with control over one's body and sexuality – and the widow – who is not likely to do so – the two are inextricably intertwined.

The first time Firdaus learns that her body can earn her money, and that she alone can control her response, is represented as almost orgasmic: 'The sudden contact [with the ten pound note] sent a strange tautness through my body, an inner contraction as though something had jumped inside me and shaken my body with a violence which was almost painful.' (p. 65) She controls something which, in her experience, has only hitherto been in the power of men. And her first response to this moment is to do something which also she had only ever seen done by men, and which certainly men had never permitted her to do, and that is the very simple act of choosing and eating her own food in peace. The power present in that act of choice and autonomy lifts a second veil: for her, food, sex and her first ten pound note become inter-related and identified with the sacrilegious thrill of male pleasure. For a time this liberates Firdaus; she becomes a successful prostitute. But we should look closely at the manner in which her story unfolds.

In brief Firdaus becomes a successful prostitute until the day when a man's words, claiming that she is not a 'respectable' woman, penetrate her heart. She returns to the 'legitimate' work force, becoming a secretary, and even falls in love and joins a radical labour movement. But her experience of 'legitimate' life teaches her that:

Now there was no more room for illusions. A successful prostitute was better than a misled saint. All women are victims of deception. Men impose deception on women and punish them for being deceived, force them down to the lowest level and punish them for falling so low, bind them in marriage and then chastise them with menial service for life, or insults, or blows. Now I realized that the least deluded of all women was the prostitute. That marriage was the system built on the most cruel suffering for women (p 86).

So she returns to prostitution, but this time with an even more high-class elite clientele. And true to the metaphor of the veils, she learns that even the show of respectability which had driven her into legitimate work can be bought.

But how is the whole question of respectability framed? In her first incarnation as a prostitute, when she talks about how her life had changed and how she took pleasure in having her own apartment and so on, she builds on the one great achievement of her life as she sees it, 'her high school certificate with honours', she says:

> I had developed a liking for culture, ever since I had started to go to school and had learned to read, but especially during this last period, since I could now buy books. I had a large library in my apartment, and it was here that I spent most of my free time. On the walls I had hung some good paintings, and right in the middle was my secondary school certificate surrounded by an expensive frame. I never received anyone in the library. It was a very special room reserved for me alone. My bedroom was where I received guests (p 69).

So we have this inversion, the library as the sacred space, and the bedroom as the public space. And significantly, it is the journalist who wants to talk to her, who then insults and wounds her, teaching her she is not respected and precipitating her return to 'legitimate' life. So when she later returns to an even more exclusive prostitution, she buys that respectability by getting her name in the newspapers:

> All women are prostitutes of one kind or another. Because I was intelligent I preferred to be a free prostitute, rather than an enslaved wife. Every time I gave my body I charged the highest price . . . Everybody has a price, and every profession is a paid salary. The more respectable the

profession, the higher the salary, and a person's price goes up as he climbs the social ladder. One day, when I donated some money to a charitable association, the newspapers published pictures of me and sang my praises as the model of a citizen with a sense of civic responsibility. And so from then on, whenever I needed a dose of honor or fame, I had only to draw some money from the bank (p. 91).

But we have seen a different attitude to newspapers and to those whose honour or fame they promote at the beginning of her story, in that first paragraph which begins 'Let me speak. Do not interrupt me.' She concludes that opening with the words:

Each time I picked up a newspaper and found the picture of a man who was one of them, I would spit on it. I knew I was only spitting on a piece of newspaper which I needed for covering the kitchen shelves. Nevertheless I spat, and then left the spit where it was to dry (p. 11).

Thus when we see her at the high point of her 'liberated' life, we need to ask ourselves why is it that these same newspapers become the symbol of her achievement. If we look at Firdaus' story again we see that at the heart of the story, each seeming liberation is presented as a kind of masculinisation. The first instance we have already seen: her moment of economic independence is simultaneously the moment she identifies the connection between sex, money and food, and the sense of power which stems from entering the male preserve.

We then see this moment, when her successful self possesses the same space as those successful men whose images she begins by spitting upon.

And finally we have the murder of that usurping pimp from whom she would not take one more act of theft, nor one more act of violence. As Firdaus' narrative opens she is incarcerated for killing this man who had had no business encroaching on her life. He realised she had become independently successful as an elite prostitute, and he moved in to capitalise on her success. He threatened and beat her until she agreed to give him a share of her income; but one day she killed him because he would not even let her leave her home:

> I caught hold of the latch door to open it, but he lifted his arm up in the air and slapped me. I raised my hand even higher than he had done, and brought it down violently on his face. He started to reach for the knife he carried in his pocket, but my hand was quicker than his. I raised the knife and buried it deep in his neck and then thrust it deep into his chest, pulled it out of his chest and plunged it deep into his belly. I stuck the knife into almost every part of his body. I was astonished to find how easily my hand moved as I thrust the knife into his flesh, and pulled it out almost without effort (p. 95).

When she relives this moment later on, she makes very clear the emphasis on thrust and penetration; at this moment, therefore, she usurps the man's role – she beats him, takes his knife and repeatedly plunges it in and pulls it out of his flesh. She ends her story with the repetition of the opening paragraph about her superior journey, and of her enactment of her defence of the violation of death, emphasising that it is a liberation from a desire to live what she considers the lies and exploitation of the patriarchal bureaucratic state. It is her truth that the ability to see through the lies that form our social and political lives makes her fearsome; but is also why she must die. I am left trying to resolve a paradox, about words spoken, words written and empowerment. A paradox which will perhaps be a little more clear if I say a few words about *So Long a Letter*.

As I said, the situations of the two women are parallel. Both are contemporary Muslim women living in patriarchal cultures whose religious tenets and social conventions serve to keep them subject. Both are confined – one on death row, the other in the ritual confinement of mourning, and in that ritual confinement Ramatoulaye tackles the same questions as does Firdaus in prison: the meaning of marriage, the question of choice, questions of sex and sexuality, of economic viability and, in all of this, the place of women and family in the modern state. But, whereas Firdaus dies, Ramatoulaye herself is 'reborn', as if she 'had emerged into the light after a long journey through a dark, narrow tunnel'. Ramatoulaye's ability to write an autobiography seems to leave her free to do more than simply die a defiant death. Both women claim their stories, and become the centre of their own narratives, and these things bind them both.

But none the less there are differences between the two works. Far from being literally and spiritually orphaned, as is Firdaus, Ramatoulaye constructs her story as familial. She begins as estranged widow and ends as embraced mother. She moves from an externally based definition of self, legally constructed in relation to an absent man – the dead husband, to a self-definition, voluntarily articulated in relation to her children as separate individuals without reference to this absent father. She therefore begins her self-meditation as a specific response to words from the other as self – her childhood friend Aissatou – of whom she says, 'I've related at one go your story as well as mine' (p. 65). And though this is a letter that is not sent, Aissatou is not a mesmerised listener, even in spirit, but a sympathetic one who has faced similar situations but made different choices which need to be addressed.

Like Firdaus, Ramatoulaye's journal represents a refusal to be silenced. But where Firdaus gives us a meditation on the community which leaves her literally imprisoned, Ramatoulaye gives us a meditation on the self which liberates her to join the community. For her the triumphant moment of speech is the moment of self-discovery when she speaks defiantly to her brother-in-law in her refusal of marriage. In that moment she makes it very clear that part of her defiance is directed against the sexual and economic violation of herself and other women which is at the heart of his proposal. Here Bâ emphasises the single heroine who can both speak and inscribe her own text. A rebellious, articulating self becomes a speaking and inscribing self. But what of Firdaus?

Firdaus teaches us that words are lies and that social structures perpetuate lies about women. Furthermore, printed words are a form of masculine empowerment which allow no room for the words of women. Firdaus narrates, but does not inscribe her own story. In fact, I am haunted by the vision of her at the beginning of her story, hunched over the pen and paper she has requested for hours on end, without moving. The warder could not tell whether she was writing a letter or something else, or not writing anything at all. And, although she says at the end 'I am speaking the truth without difficulty', it is a truth learnt from the penetrating thrust of a man's knife, a truth which proves deadly. She can speak, but not write, and her speech exposes the limits of that masculinist venture sanctioned by writing – empowering for the male, a useless certificate for the lower-class female. Though she speaks her story, she still dies, spitting on those newspapers, and it is someone else who inscribes her story. What she has is her story, trapped within prison walls, with no way out except to hand it on through speech to an equally, though temporarily, entrapped listener. Firdaus' act of creation is to generate a self-text, to order her life into meaning through spoken autobiography in her final moments, as a last will and testament.

Whether or not we consider these two stories as contradictory or in tandem depends in part, I think, on our readings of the role of the silent listener. Is there a difference between the 'let me speak do not interrupt me', with which Firdaus begins her address to the narrator to whom she is talking, and 'I have received your letter, by way of reply', the opening words of so long a *So Long a Letter*? Unlike Sa'adawi, who keeps the speaker and the narrator structurally separated, Bâ makes them one and the same person. I believe that, on one level, the two writers are making the same point – that for a survival to be not only spiritual but literal, we need control over our private and communal lives, and over our spoken and our written words. Otherwise we become limited to accepting the thrust of the knife as our only option, and spat-upon words as our only legitimacy. We therefore need Firdaus' courage, as well as Ramatoulaye's ability to challenge the patriarchal order of discourse, in order to breach that confinement. It is not, as both these writers make clear, an easy task: the creative process of autobiography and biography depend upon the question of access to transferable speech.

Ramatoulaye does not mail the letter, but she does keep in communion with Aissatou and, at the end of her confinement, she prepares to welcome her into her home. But what of Firdaus? Her story is, in a way, a closure: she makes sense of her life and goes out to die. But her text does not.

In this case, the transferal of Firdaus' story has to be a shared activity; the responsibility for transferring Firdaus' story out of its confinement is placed upon her middle-class narrator, from whom she is separated at the start. Does the narrator remain separate? Or must she, to receive Firdaus' heritage, become identified at the end? Does the 'other' remain 'other', or does she become 'self', as in the case of Aissatou and Ramatoulaye? The tropes of power are masculine, but where does this place Firdaus' oral account? A further complication exists in the obvious class difference between Firdaus and her inscriber. Firdaus cannot control the mode of the 'dissemination' of her story and this sets up serious reverberations in the text, such as whether or not her death is a necessary sacrifice for the germination of another kind of story. But then in knowing and reconstructing our stories, however problematic, to tell them so that others may hear them, we have the burden not just of these stories, but of *herstory* itself.

Notes

1　Mariama Bâ *Une fi Langue Leftre* trs. *So Long a Letter*, Heinemann, London, 1981. All citations given in the text are to this edition.

2　Nawal el Sa'adawi, *Woman at Point Zero*, Zed Press, London, 1983. All citations given in the text are to this edition.

Caroline Rooney

'Dangerous Knowledge' and the Poetics of Survival: A Reading of *Our Sister Killjoy* and *A Question of Power*

I

Mother*land*

The OED definition of 'motherland' is: 'native country'.[1] 'Mother' then functions as a substitute for 'native' and a trope for 'of origin'. It seems then that one could alternatively use the term 'fatherland' which is defined as: 'one's native land'. However, there is obviously an assymetry. Fatherland is marked by ownership – 'one's' – whereas motherland is, in comparison, 'no one's'. 'Motherland' can also be placed next to 'mothercountry', defined as: 'country in relation to its colonies'. '-land' therefore pertains to the native, while '-country' to the colonial relation, which suggests that motherland/native country is only country in terms of terrain, whereas mothercountry, as country-country and not country-land, is a proper country, a territory.

In terms of the above, the motherland can be situated in relation to colonial history, where it would signify (a) country belonging to no one, so open to adoption by the colonising country as its other land. It serves thus as both the 'other', as woman and nature are other to man, and as an other, an additional resource, yet more nature/land to be acted upon and made to serve. Furthermore, in post-colonial times, this model of the land can be said to continue to be operative in much of the western ideologies and practices of development, in so far as it is used to justify them. Vandana Shiva writes: 'The dichotomised ontology of man dominating woman and nature generates maldevelopment because it makes the colonising male the agent and model of development.'[2] Development is maldevelopment in that the land is destructively treated as merely an exploitable resource, while other forms of development and knowledge, the local and ecological, are not recognised.

In terms of dominant western constructions, an instance of which is indicated above, 'motherland' is constituted as an originally dispossessed or subjectless state.[3] The silent paradox is that the supposedly original state or place of origin is always primarily a place of exile or lost origins. What this erasure of originality ensures is the naturalisation of the construction of motherland as no one's, as it forecloses the self-originating capacities of what goes by the name of motherland.

But there are other stories, other versions.

*Mother*land, Other Lands

Motherland, as no one's land, can be taken to signify a different relation to the land, for instance, a non-appropriative one. It could be a case of everyone's land; or, a case of being subject to the land or nature, an acknowledgment of a certain vital dependency. Then again, Motherland may not be that which would-be only 'one's' land. For instance, Cheik Anta Diop has argued that western history cannot lay claim to matriarchal origins, whereas African history does have a precedent for this in a material and, not necessarily a mythical sense.[4]

Mother-soil

It can be argued that it is in Aeschylus' *Eumenides* that the foreclosure of matriarchal originality is portrayed, a foreclosure that legitimises matricide. Apollo excuses Orestes his matricide on the grounds that the father is the sole parent or origin, while the mother is but the 'soil' for his 'seed'.[5] In other words, she is but the passive medium of creation. I put it in this way because I want to make the following connection or leap: literature can also be spoken of as a medium of creation, one whose own creative originality is critically appropriated.

II

Generally speaking, critical discourse can be regarded as a colonising or imperialist discourse: one which annexes its textual object in order to perpetuate itself, institutionalise itself and its attendant ideological assumptions, be they derived from the discipline or the particular critic in question. As an index of this, it can be noted that critics are in the habit of expressing themselves in a rhetoric of colonialist or imperialist metaphors. For example, in a fairly recent anthology on African literature, we are told that literature is 'field', that African literature is a 'developing field'. One critic speaks of a 'tremendous blossoming' and another of 'a new crop of the same'.[6]

It can further be noted that a western/northern critical appropriation of an African text involves the subjection of not only the particular text but its 'world' or cultural and historical context to the homogenising standards and interests of the so-called 'first' world. This homogenising or equalising operation is more than a matter of a failure to recognise cultural specificity; it is also a matter of a cultural failure to recognise global inequalities of power.

The predicament of the critical appropriation or foreclosure of what can be termed the originality of an other, is one that

I will dramatise in my (hypocritical critical) reading of Ama Ata Aidoo's *Our Sister Killjoy* and Bessie Head's *A Question of Power*.[7]

At this point it should perhaps be emphasised that my reading comes from, and so, departs from a Euro-American scene of letters in which literature can be said to have been deprived of its estate.[8] Such a point of departure constitutes a slight elaboration of the critical hypocrisy referred to above, which I will leave for you or others to elaborate further. What I would add is that since my concerns involve the legitimacy of a creative cognizance – that of the literary text – I write in the assumption that, firstly, as I inform and transform the texts in my readings of them, they may inform and transform my readings; and that, secondly, my concerns may not only be my concerns:

> The students had simply become humiliated little boys shoved around by an hysterical white woman who never saw black people as people but as objects of permanent idiocy (*QP*, p. 76)

> The academic-pseudo-intellectual version is even more dangerous, who in the face of a reality that is more tangible than the massive walls of slave forts standing along our beaches, still talks of universal truth, universal art, universal literature . . . (*OSK*, p. 6)

I will represent a reading of the texts.

III

Katherine Frank, in her reading of *OSK*, writes: '[at the] heart of this rich literary stew and binding all its ingredients together is the figure of Sissie.'[9] This is hard to swallow, for what is at the 'heart' of this text is the story of a heart transplant, that of an African coloured man's heart into the body of a white man's, and, in my reading, what Sissie most revolts against is the European assimilation of that which is or those who are African, of what belongs in and to Africa.

Euro-assimilation

One aspect of the dangerous knowledge referred to in my title is the imposition or adoption of a foreign – in this case, European – thought pattern which, at the expense of the subject's own mind, renders him/her mindless. In the opening section of OSK we are given this portrait of a 'nigger who is a moderate' who can 'regurgitate only what he has learnt from his bosses' (p. 6) and from this regurgitation of 'his master's voice' we move on to encounter Sammy who 'sings for his supper' by parroting Europe's flattering self-image:

> Perhaps he had been invited to the dinner to sing of the wonders of Europe?
> He spoke their language well . . . (p. 9)

Food becomes what is taken in, in the act of being taken in, welcomed into the fold/duped. Eating is not simply eating but an ideological matter of consuming so that one is assimilated into and assimilates a certain would-be global order, say, one of multinational capitalist consumerism; 'More saliva rushed into her mouth every time he spoke./She did not enjoy the food . . . ' (p. 9). Perhaps Sissie refuses, instinctively, the paternalistic hospitality of her benefactors because she will not incur the debt of a lip-service because the real debt . . . but this is to rush on ahead.

I have been considering the opening section of the novel, entitled 'Into a Bad Dream', which leads up to entry into Europe. The next section, dealing with Sissie's experiences in Germany, is entitled 'The Plums'. The sequential inference is that 'The Plums' and the plums referred to constitute a 'Bad Dream' and I will briefly indicate how this may be so.

With reference to 'The Plums' in general, Sissie finds herself in a lotus-eater's land of ease and plenty. This is indicated especially by the glut of food she and her fellow vacation-workers are plied with: 'Sissie and her companions were required to be there, eating, laughing, singing, sleeping and eating. Above all eating' (p. 35). In other words, my words, they are to comply with a certain mythological representation of Europe as a place of utopian plenitude, where nothing is lacking and all desires may be satiated. With reference to the plums in particular, they are the gift of Marija, a young German *hausfrau* who is eager to befriend Sissie. In microcosmic terms, it is possible that the plums partially reflect Sissie's seduction into complicity with the myth of Europe's fulfilment of every desire. When Marija kisses Sissie, 'As one does from a bad dream, Sissie impulsively shook herself free' (p. 64). It is here that the bad dream is explicitly mentioned and realised.

The narrative of this section of the book is somewhat split between a narrating subject or consciousness and the story of Sissie.[10] One might say that Sissie is presented as a passive object in another's system, a vulnerable sleepwalker in a foreign or unreal landscape. Sissie stays in an ex-castle, cut off from its past, from history; it is like a stage-set for romance, as it is said in the text, for European-style puppy-love. 'That was a game. A game in which she became so absorbed, she forgot who she was . . . In her imagination she was one of these black boys in one of those involvements with white girls from Europe' (p. 61). The bad dream is the dream is forgetfulness. After Marija's attempted seduction and Sissie's awakening from the 'bad dream' it is asked: 'And now where was she? How did she get there? What strings, pulled by whom, drew her into those pinelands where not so long ago human beings stoked their own funeral pyres with other human beings, where now a young Aryan housewife kisses a young black woman . . . ' (p. 64).

It is more than a question of a self that forgets itself; it is also a question of historical and cultural self-forgetfulness and oblivion. It is this history – of Europe, of Africa – that the narrating consciousness or conscience cannot forget. While Sissie is, to an extent, in danger of being caught up in or made to play out the myth/dream of endless consumption, or the satiation of every appetite, desire or taste, an ironic commentary inserts an historical and political frame of reference. What the utopian 'everything' lacks is this mapping which amounts to an awareness of lack and loss. Among other things, we are reminded of the black diaspora of people lured to Europe in the hope of fulfilling their dreams only to be worn down and broken (pp. 20–23). And we are told of the home countries left behind, to waste away in neglect (pp. 32, 34), and of the depleting effects of neo-imperialism (pp. 56–58). German history too is unearthed before our eyes:

> They wonder if, should they
> Stop cultivating the little pine trees, would
> Something else,
> Sown there,
> Many years ago,
> In
> Those Bavarian woods
> SPROUT? (p. 37)

So many skeletons in the cupboard/rich soil. As for Marija, behind the facades of her little family and new, done-up home, Sissie discovers loneliness and unhappiness (p. 65), and sees in such unhappy or lacking lives a key to those Europeans who stray in search of the foreign and foreign lands. In this respect, the colonising enterprise is not just an expression of heartless greed, but an expression of an emptiness or loss of heart at the heart, the supposed source or centre, motivating quests for rejuvenation and reassurance – elsewhere.

Sissie leaves Germany for England where the opium this time is the degree: the bribe or enticement, the study award. In Germany, Sissie becomes, as a non-German-speaking African, an exotic cultural artefact without context, a kind of fetishised commodity (see, e.g. p. 43). In the text as a whole, the predicament of the African, or 'black other', being treated as just the inert research material for the inspection and use of the European savant is generalised. Funded education turns out to be imperialist appropriation:

> For a few pennies now and a
> Doctoral degree later,
> Tell us about
> Your people
> Your history
> Your mind
> Your mind
> Your mind (pp. 86–7).

Earlier it is said:

> You cannot achieve the
> Moribund objectives of a
> Dangerous education by using
> living forces (p. 39).

Words such as these are given a graphic reality when we are presented with this case of a heart-transplant from an African corpse into a Dying White Man. Allegorical reverberations suggest themselves, but now I do not want to turn this incident purely into a symbol. For, it seems, what we have here is the actuality of that symbolic realm of knowledge – its de-symbolisation, or a realisation of what the symbolic forgets. Kunle, a character in the text, reads this heart-transplant as a heartening symbol of the transgression of apartheid ideology: black and white in one. But, it is Kunle whom Our Sister Killjoy takes issue with: for her the use of an African heart implanted into a dying white man, to eke out his life, for the glory of science, cannot be so dangerously allegorised.

The next and last section of the text, 'A Love Letter', explicitly and intimately addresses the problem of Euro-assimilation. A reading of it here is perhaps unnecessary, or would be presumptuous.

Strange Invasions

> The only way to end up a cultural
> Vulture
> Is to feed on carrion all the way (*OSK,* p. 39).

> What did they gain the power people, while they lived off
> other people's souls like vultures? (*QP*, p. 19)

In *A Question of Power*, what is specifically dramatised is not
the assimilation but the invasion of the would-be other subject, an invasion by foreign or inexplicable powers, by name,
Sello and Dan. The 'bad dream' is here a living nightmare
of a mind and body without borders, compelled to think or
experience the ideological abuses, dogmatic cant, and so on,
of others:

> Someone had turned on a record inside her head (p. 45)

> People's souls walked right into her (p. 104)

> [B]efore she awoke she had seen two large, familiar black
> hands move towards her head. They had opened her skull.
> He'd bent his mouth towards the cavity and talked right
> into the exposed area. His harsh, grating voice was unintel-
> ligible. It just said: 'Rrrrrrraaaaa' (p. 177)

What does this mean?

But this is not the question, as I will later indicate. In
the meantime, I will confine myself to just one possible
approach.

There is the question of madness and magic. Imagine, for
a moment, if *QP* were compelled to repeat 'originally' the
chapter of Freud's *Totem and Taboo*, entitled 'Animism,
Magic and the Omnipotence of Thoughts'.[11] Freud says of
animism, the doctrine of souls or spiritual beings, that: 'Originally souls were pictured as very similar to persons . . .'
(*TT*, p. 76) and Bessie Head's Elizabeth is preoccupied with,
and occupied by, 'large, looming soul personalities' (*QP*,
p. 57). Freud goes on to identify the principle of animistic
thinking as 'the omnipotence of thoughts' and writes:

> Since distance is of no importance in thinking – since what
> lies furthest apart both in time and space can without diffi-
> culty be comprehended in a single act of consciousness –
> so, too, the world of magic has a telepathic disregard for
> spatial distance and treats past situations as though they
> were present. (*TT*, p. 85)

This can be juxtaposed with: 'her [Elizabeth's] head simply
filled out into a large horizon', (p. 22). Then, the presence
of the past is a phenomenon of Elizabeth's infernal journey.
Furthermore, as far as she is concerned, people enter her
with telepathic disrespect (e.g. pp. 57, 192). The question is
though: whose 'telepathic disregard'? (Already things are
going 'off-beam'.) Quickly then, Freud goes on to link the
animistic mode of thought with neurotic regression to a belief
in psychic reality, which would be to see Elizabeth, in Freudian terms, as neurotic, at least. But there is something askew
or unhinged about this analysis for, in short, Elizabeth is not
the agent but the receiver of an omnipotence of thought:
'Things I'd never have thought of get to dominate my mind
and create neurotic fears . . . They just move in . . . ' (*QP*,
p. 192). Whose thoughts then? Dan's? Sello's? Freud's?
Analysts'?

The Imitation Compulsion: The Power of Language (1)

The compulsion to repeat that I am referring to here is related
to the notion of the 'analysand' (the one analysed, in the most
general sense, by the 'analyst') who is compelled to repeat
not her/him-self but the 'truth' of the analyst as the subject
of knowledge. In other words a *self*-sacrifice, one of the
power to originate, is required to authenticate the analyst,
who is not then himself the suspect origin of his truth. An
instance, rather than an analogy, of this would be the text
that 'originally repeats' what the critic wants it to. In *A
Question of Power* it is said: 'It was as though he [Sello] had
thought out the whole story ahead of meeting her . . . '
(p. 29), such being a repeated allegation in this text.[12]

As has already been indicated, OSK and QP can be said to show, respectively, something of a compulsion to imitate or repeat the truths of a dominant order or powers. Moreover, this language of power is presented as the power of language to inflict concrete harm. What is shown is that destructive abstractions are not merely abstractions but a matter of real violence and so a question of survival. We are shown what would be, from one perspective, the waste products of the machines of power and progress, and, from another, the unburied historical debts:

> They had still, sad, fire-washed faces . . . It was the expression of people who had been killed and killed and killed again in one cause after another for the liberation of mankind. (QP, p. 31)

> Beautiful Black Bodies
> Changed into elephant-grey corpses,
> Littered all over the Western world . . . (OSK, p. 62)

This must be remembered, recorded, despite what 'they' say:

> They say that after all, literature, art, culture, all information is universal. So we must hurry to lose our identity quickly in order to join the great family of man.
> My Dear, isn't that truly crazy? (OSK, p. 21)

Truly crazy. One reason I have called on Freud, pioneer of the science of psychoanalysis, to give evidence has been simultaneously to invoke and problematise a diagnosis of madness with regard to Elizabeth/Head's text.[13] In a manner of speaking, the madness, the 'omnipotence of thought', belongs to Freud's theory. Generally speaking, it can be said that the construction of this animistic mode of thought, as opposed to other possible elaborations, is a fiction of the rational mind's own devising, but in order that it not appear as such, this self-reflexive fabrication or self-confusion is inadmissible. The given properties of animistic thought – self-reflexivity, belief in its own reality – are those owed to the self-negations of its rational determination. Moreover, constructed in this way, it is only the rational, normal, mind, as the one which can truly know, that can read it. The reason that I have provided this basic, no doubt primitive, resumé is to indicate a tyranny of thought that is at the expense of its own creative powers and, more than this, at the expense of the legitimacy of other self-determining capacities and creative modes of thought.

The above prefaces what I want to consider now, namely, not only the violent realisations of a constructed truth, but the violence of the construction of its realisation, or coming into being, particularly as it is shown in *A Question of Power*.

Dan, who in everyday life is a cattle millionaire and locally prominent African Nationalist, is indicated as being the 'master of psychology behind witchcraft' (p. 21). In African society, the practice of psychic tyranny or terrorism can go by the name of witchcraft; but it is comparable to what goes on in other societies, with particular reference to QP, it is comparable to the powers of intimidation of white racist South African society.[14]

Elizabeth experiences directly in herself the operations of an evil 'master-minding' by the soul personalities of Dan and others. She becomes the appropriated medium in which the rudiments of philosophies, ideologies, mythologies, religions, and so on, are concretely and painfully experienced:

> Torture . . . Once the record was turned on in her head it just went on and on in the same groove. It was so powerful and insistent that it had the effect of killing the beauty of the living world . . . (p. 116)

Carolyn Merchant, writing on the ideological transformation of mother nature from nurturing source to inert, exploitable resource says: 'One does not readily slay a mother, dig her entrails or mutilate her body.'[15] But, in words to this effect, this is what does happen in QP, especially if Elizabeth is seen as that medium/'soil-for-the-seed-of-the-father'.

'He [Dan] thought you might not fall in with his plans.

> That's why he took you on, to remould you in his own image . . . I'm sorry it was so painful'. (p. 200)

Elizabeth might be said to be the brutally invaded and dispossessed 'medium' or resource, where or out of which tyrannical powers construct or enact their truths and compete for authority or dominance, at her expense, at the expense of her active inclusion in the process and at the expense of crediting her with a soul or subject reality of her own. She becomes the contested site for a contestation of authority. For instance, it is said: 'There seemed to be a mutual agreement in the beginning that an examination of inner hells was to end all hells forever. Elizabeth was their pivot' (p. 12). While Elizabeth may be said to be the subjected or oppressed site where meanings are constructed, she is also the subjectless or effaced host of a parasitic deconstruction: 'I [Sello] saw a way of taking away his [Dan's] power through you' (p. 199). Sello uses her as instrument or medium to stage and expose the truth of Dan as a truth based on self-image – in Dan's regard, a matter of possession of the phallus and black skin. However, this deconstruction of Dan's power and authority entails Sello's further displacement of Elizabeth, a woman and a Coloured, as he occupies the already displaced place of the feminine and non-African (pp. 11, 24).[16] In short, he is not only where she would 'be', but his undoing of the subject, 'Dan', leaves her with no possible subject position of her own:

> [S]he had no distinct personality apart from Sello (p. 32)

> How had she fallen so low. It was a state below animal, below living . . . (p. 14)

> The two men were conducting . . . a fierce struggle over her nearly dead body . . . (p. 187)

Elizabeth, as 'an open territory easily invaded by devils' (p. 192), is in danger of repeating only what possesses her: 'a person eventually becomes the replica of the inner demons he battles with' (pp. 149–50). So there is the need for reminding, re-minding. Elizabeth says: 'I imagine my face contorted with greed and hatred . . . And in this darkness of the soul you will one day walk up to me and remind me of my nobility' (p. 85). And I would say, the texts themselves record so as to remind, and to this postscript add Head's own: '[I]f I recorded the evil and the same story was about to happen . . . I would read *A Question of Power* and it would save me from such suffering.'[17]

Wording and Warding Off: The Power of Language (2)

What I wish to talk of now is the writing, the writing which resists resolution or closure, that is, of a writing which resists critical mastery and appropriation. I want to show how this writing turns the problem of language not just into an articulation of the problem but into a certain creative power.

In Aidoo's text the problem is '*this* language' (p. 112). While this language, as opposed to another language, might be said to be English, it is with respect to the issue of writing in one's mother tongue or also a question of this English as opposed to another usage or formulation of this English, among other languages. I will briefly follow Aidoo's/Sissie's comments on this matter.

Firstly, this language is a problem since: 'So far, I have only been able to use a language that enslaved me, and therefore, the messengers of my mind always come shackled?' (p. 112) This language colonises but we are told of another possibility: 'the language of love . . . It is beyond Akan or Ewe, English or French' (p. 113). Say, this language is beyond language, yet a language; beyond yet in language. '[A]ll that I was saying about language', *osk* continues, 'is that I wish that you and I could share our hopes, our fears and our fantasies, without feeling inhibited because we suspect someone is listening' (p. 115). This seemingly imperceptible language is one that is to be uninterceptable – but what language, I, in the act of intercepting, would ask – cannot be 'ciphered' off, re-routed, interfered with in this way? 'That is why', *osk* continues, 'above all, we have to have our secret language . . . we must create this language. We are too old a people not to. We can. We must. So we shall make love with words and not fear of being overheard' (p. 116). This intimate correspondence, this beyond/in language is, I would like to suggest, a matter of a creative language – a we-must-create language – that is 'African', in its necessity at least, whether it appears in an African language or in the English one . . . It is this language that would resist 'colonisation' and I will now concentrate on what could be called a 'poetics of resistance'. In other words, I will look at some aspects of the writing which resist critical interception at the same time as they enable the text to speak (for) itself, as that which can know (for) itself.

Arlene Elder writes: 'The first section of the book [OSK] . . . is connected to "The Plums" by three pages containing one word each: Where, When, How . . . These words are the equivalent of the narrator saying something like: Now I will tell you where Sissie went, when she returned and how her time in England progressed . . . '[18] I don't think the words work like that, primarily. While I would say that the words serve to mark the importance of a 'cognitive mapping'[19] *itself*, their effect, perhaps purpose, is to check any explicatory intervention. What the words do is to arrest the flow of the narrative; what they constitute is a quite deliberate pacing of the narrative – Where [PAUSE] When [PAUSE] How [PAUSE] – so that we-readers cannot rush on ahead to our 'dazzling', perhaps, 'conclusions'. Elder also says that the words serve as a 'bridge' and as such a lapse in 'the oral quality of the narrative'. But they are not a convenient way of stepping over some rift – they mark a rift, say, between our habits of prose-reading and this specific text whose writing will itself dictate its where, its when and its how. We are to submit to the moment of its telling, and this, far from being a matter of suspension of the 'oral quality', is a matter of oratorical performance.

Throughout the text, Aidoo's rhythmic control of the narrative induces us to submit to the moment of its telling so that we read as she writes, that is, not only temporally speaking, but in terms of the way she writes. Apart from this control of the pace of the narrative – something that can be termed a 'spoken writing' – Aidoo unpredictably interrupts or intercepts her own text with columns of poetic commentary. The commentary is perhaps a cross-section of the narrative at a particular point so that we not only read 'across', sequentially, but 'down'. In a way, this self-intervention pre-empts other interventions. A cross-section is by definition 'ironic', showing the simultaneity of different layers of meaning. A critical reading is ironic in so far as it perceives a meaning (for a privileged or particular audience) in addition to the seeming or surface meaning. Aidoo's commentaries are ironic in this sense as well as in another way, that is, in the adoption of another's point of view or tone for the sake of ridicule or derision. That is, they perform a function of criticism – in the first sense given, that of delivering an 'inner' meaning for a privileged or certain audience – but more than this they also serve to ridicule the would-be critic in terms of an ironic adoption of a point of view or tone. This point of view or tone that is adopted is precisely that of the critic/educator/subject of knowledge. For example:

> And what shall it profit a native that
> He should have
> Systems to give
> A boy
> A girl
> Two
> Three names or
> More? (p. 26)

The tone or point of view are obviously not those of the writer but of the coloniser or 'civilising' missionary or Dr Intellectual Whoever.

However, not all the commentaries are ironic or satirical:

> Wherever they are and from whatever causes

My God,
Black people still
Die
So
Uselessly! (p. 108)

The shifts in tone and point of view, posing questions of who is or is not speaking, have the effect of making overall generalisations difficult. While some may be unsure of how to take what is being said, the writer is already (giving a) reading between her own lines.

I want to pick up on something mentioned briefly above – the use of irony for a 'privileged' audience, in this case, not an elitist academic one, but, say, one with an understanding of the blindspots of such an audience. Aidoo could be said to specify or delimit her audience from within the text,[20] another means of resisting interception. For instance, in 'The Plums' the dramatic confrontation is between an African woman and a European audience, particularly as represented by Marija as would-be interrogator of Sissie. The text moves on to address an audience of 'gone-to's' and, in particular, Kunle, where the narrator writes as Kunle's mother addressing her truant son. The audience is then specified still further, in a sense, in 'A Love Letter' which addresses a friend/ 'brother'/lover. Finally, in the concluding section, the text becomes, in a way, self-addressed: 'Sissie wondered whether she had spoken aloud to herself' (p. 124). Part of the effect of indicating who is being addressed is to indicate who has the 'right to reply'.

I would now like to point to aspects of Aidoo's writing, and Head's, that are difficult to speak about, in other language, in that they already achieve a saying of the unsayable.

. . . a strange company/ of women – no not women . . . these were/ wingless, black, utterly loathsome . . . / They are creatures of no race I ever saw; no land / Could breed them and not bear the curse of God and man. (*The Eumenides*, QP p. 149)

Then he turned and showed Elizabeth a small, round, deep opening in the earth from which her soul had emerged. It was a black, shapeless mass with wings. (p. 43)

. . . these were / wingless, black, utterly loathsome

'The horror. The horror.' [He dies][22]

She wondered why they never told the truth of their travels . . . (*OSK*, p. 89)

[N]one of mankind's godlike figureheads recorded seeing what she saw on this nightmare soul-journey. (*QP*, p. 35)

There is this discursive haunting of the discursive field of histories of domination and exploitation. Aidoo speaks of this 'inner logic' (p. 39) and Head of this 'soul-reality' (e.g. p. 38). It can be said that Aidoo/the narrator writes out the internal logic, the unconfessed or surreptitiously elided vested interests of western or westernised authorities, experts, powers, and she records the silent debts. For instance, it is shown that the benevolent hospitality of foreign hosts functions as a kind of bribe, while the actual debt is to the countries exploited by these 'benefactors' whose people suffer or die as a result. In *QP*, it can be said that Head/the narrator writes out the soul reality of mankind's or society's would-be leaders and saviours in terms of a brutality and deprivation that is at the expense of creative powers and the subjectivity and lives of others.

In *QP* and *OSK*, there is what can be termed a *shocking truth*. It is not just that cruelties and obscenities are recorded. What is shocking, or astounding, or exhilarating, is the saying of these things. The repetition or parody of what is not said involves not only the exposure of the unsaid craziness of said truths and dominant powers, but, through a parodic insinuation, the assumption of a foreclosed or withheld site of creativity. However, since it is a case of a parody of what has not or never been said, it is not a case of mimicry but one of original repetition or representation.

Through inhabiting the elisions of a naturalising and rationalising discourse, QP and OSK produce a fracture or open up a space for the elaboration of different cartographies:[22] non-naturalising, poetic and political, non-abstracting, concrete. It can further be claimed that, in certain respects, these texts suspend a rhetoric of literal or natural truths. The monstrous abuses that Elizabeth is physically subject to do not literally take place. In OSK, the foreign hosts, powers, financial and scientific masterminds, and so on, do not literally eat or live off African corpses. These things do not literally happen, but they do happen; they are more than just metaphoric situations.

The reality of ghoulish, diabolical powers? Of modern cannibals? This is of course precisely that which the 'enlightened' rational mind could not be enlightened by, could not both assimilate and remain itself. In its fearful self-defence, it would call such manifestations the hallucinations or disturbances of a mystic or superstitious imagination or of a paranoid one.

> As Elizabeth watched, brown-suit's face slowly changed to the shape of an owl. He said: 'Oh no, I'm not a monkey. I'm a wise old owl.'
> She jerked upright in bed. What was this? (p. 48)

Elizabeth underscores the difficulty of explaining or translating what she has seen and learnt: 'She couldn't even begin to say: "Well, you know Sello, don't you? He isn't all he seems to be . . . "' (p. 57) And Sissie insists on a credibility in her own terms: 'So please do not say that what I felt after you left was part of my . . . How did you describe it? "Anti-western neurosis?" Maybe. Though . . . *I am convinced . . . It is there* in the artificial heat in the room which dried my skin and filled my sleep with nightmares' (my emphases; p. 119). These things cannot be spoken *about*, that is, they can neither be abstracted nor literalised, though they can be expressed, in a particular manner of speaking.

In Totem and Taboo (TT), Freud notes that the remnants of animism are to be found in art, both having in common some belief in the reality of wishes, thoughts, fantasies.[24] What Freud sees as a literalisation can be seen as a reflection of a literal-minded, even 'illiterate' reading, one which fails to read or recognise the medium or the sign – that which signifies. In other readings,[25] animism is not a case of the literal identification of the spiritual with the natural but of reading nature as *signifying* vital powers. Apart from seeing nature as creative, this is a creative way of conceptualising nature. That is, animism may be considered, or renewed, as a creative mode of knowledge (as opposed to art being considered as a primitive one).

Earlier, I drew attention to Aidoo's narratorial/oratorical pre-emption of critical interventions and would now like to briefly indicate a similar effect, though produced by different strategies or means, in Head's work.

In Head's text, she/Elizabeth, as victim and escapee of privileged exclusions, refuses to privilege and exclude. This results in a process of infinite differentiation. For instance, the white racist doctor whom she strongly dissociates herself from, is none the less: 'also a magnificent human being with a kind heart' (p. 185). And Dan, her tormentor, is still 'one of the greatest teachers she'd worked with' (p. 202). I would add that this is not an exercise in liberal tolerance. It is rather a case of acknowledging that truths are not 'equal-but-separate', but, instead, complexly contradictory in themselves: they hold true only in so far as they are capable of losing their hold. Head's shifting text can be said to be constantly and *unpredictably* revising itself. For instance, terms such as 'African' and 'soul' are re-worked throughout in such a way as to introduce uncertainty into habitual readings and simultaneously show that fixtures of the past, history, can be expressed quite differently.[25]

Head herself dramatises the will-to-interpret within her own text. She questions herself: she retains the power of questioning and also submits herself to it. She both under-scores the inexplicability of the experience – that is, the impossibility of the attempt to transcribe it further – and at once demonstrates that the process of writing, or writing up, is simultaneously one of speculative interpretation. Some citations may serve to indicate these two aspects:

> [H]er mind dwelt entirely at this intangible level of shifting images and strange arguments . . . Why was everything so pointed? The wild-eyed Medusa was expressing the surface reality . . . (p. 38)

> How did it all happen here, in so unsuspecting a climate, these silent tortured, universal questions of power and love, of loss and sacrifice? What did all those dead bodies mean? She was startled to hear Sello say quite clearly: 'If you did not like anything, I destroyed it . . . I destroyed it all.'
>
>   It couldn't be that simply put. (p. 98)

Perhaps, with those words, I should stop.

III

And Motherlands?

'How did it all happen here . . . ?'

And I would ask: (where or what is this) here? The happening 'here' of the text is not simply or directly Motabeng, Botswana. I would suggest that 'here' is to an extent initially a crossroads of dispossession or rather un-belonging. On this map South Africa is here too: 'the evils overcoming her were beginning to sound like South Africa from which she had fled . . . ' (p. 57). Elizabeth responds to various 'unburied' appeals for empathy (pp. 16–17, 47) and identifies with all who suffer 'racial hatreds and oppressions of all kinds' (p. 53). The landscape of exile or ostracism may be said to be a hybrid one, and so may the landscape of 'recovery'. In a certain respect, Elizabeth recovers herself, her mental peace and social being, through her participation in the collective project of the vegetable garden in which people of different races and different places are involved.

Some might want to set up an opposition between Head's advocacy of a 'universal brotherhood of man' and Aidoo's resistance to the dissolution of (African) identity in any such brotherhood. However, in Aidoo's book, 'universal' pertains to the pseudo-universal: a universality that is European, and so on, and so not universal. In Head's book, 'universal' pertains not to the all, but the not-all, say, sons and daughters of the soil, ordinary people (p. 206). If one speaks of inclusion in a universal brotherhood, the question is: of whom in whom? Mass participation in a multinational capitalist brotherhood is obviously not at all the same as or translatable into mass participation in the communities of subsistence economies. The two texts taken together serve to articulate this discrepancy, this remarkable inequality.

In *QP*, the 'snake' in the otherwise promising vegetable garden venture is Camilla, 'Rattle-tongue', who is determined to aid with her superior-foreign-textbook-knowledge. She threatens to recuperate the space in which the local students, including Elizabeth, may find out amongst and for themselves, and in doing so recover their own powers of discovery or their creative and practical capacities for learning/knowing . . . otherwise (pp. 74–7, 82–3). What is at stake is the transformation of 'no one's land' – land of original exile, or expropriated originality – into a land that is owned by no one but is instead a shared space with potential for self-determination. In Head's work, social transformations occur, new worlds are created or begin in the most local circumstances, having the potential to ripple out or catch on from there, as a process distinct from the impositions of would-be omnipotent forces. Head's/Elizabeth's vision of a 'new dawn and a new world' (p. 205) is originally, locally an African one:

'Africa isn't rising. It's up already. It depends on where one places the stress. I place it on the soul. If it's basically right there, then other things fall into place. That's my struggle, and that's black power, but it's a power that belongs to all of mankind and in which all of mankind can share.' (p. 135)

In its search for a genuine homecoming, African literature will truly reflect the universal struggle for a world which truly belongs to us all.[26]

With regard to this essay – how did it all happen here? – the question of the relation of African literature to an international scene (of letters) is perhaps obliquely raised. I have not been arguing for a return of these texts to their 'countries of origin' to safeguard their purity. Nor have I been pressing for the importation of foreign critical theories with the proviso of their adaptation to the homegrown. Rather, I have sought to indicate that these texts form in themselves sophisticated critiques, and so may serve to interrogate that which would interrogate them, however indirectly or 'in passing'.[27] In short, what these texts discover for themselves, in the first instance, may have wider applications, and challenging implications with regard to what and how others know. It is a question of their capacity to effect transformations not only in themselves but in the texts of others. Obviously, I am not simply arguing for a re-location of centres of authority, but a case for acknowledging and legitimising equal rights of address and self-determination. It *is* a question of power. While it may be said that the texts under consideration refer to what can be called motherlands, what remains at stake is the objectification of a 'motherland' in terms of what who–defines–it needs or seeks.

In OSK, it can be seen that the 'have–all' western countries lack in themselves what might be termed 'motherlands'. This old/new lack or loss[28] is perennially noted by western critics critical of aspects of their culture.

Read in a certain way, QP, with its not so magical power displays, might ironically hold a mirror up to those quests from the west for spiritual rejuvenation or for the would-be recovery of a last spiritual earth mother which ignore the subject realities of others. Head's 'emphasis on the soul' can be said to be an emphatically secular and not supernatural one (pp. 205–6). In her terms, spiritual matters pertain to ethical matters – questions of compassion, equality, fellow-love – and to creative, life-enhancing powers. These ethical and creative issues, though the terms may yet be inadequate, have crucial bearings on sociopolitical realities and aspirations. The vegetable garden in QP is obviously not a metaphysically spiritual health farm, nor a metaphor for an unearthly paradise.

In OSK, the urging of 'prodigal' sons and daughters to return home is not for the sake of the salvation of their souls, at least not directly nor in those terms; it is for the sake of the material, social and cultural needs of the lands and mothers they have left behind in pursuit of their individual ambitions. What is needed is the expertise of these educated sons and daughters to bring a beneficial modernisation for the sake of a recovery of the land – a restoring it to strength – as opposed to modern re-appropriations and depletions of it (pp. 120–1, 129–30). Praise for mothers from a distance is not enough. It is a question of landings, homecomings, coming down to earth, locally and practically, with the aspiration of creating new societies, a shared world.

Or so I surmise, in making a point; for I myself would not like to say what an objectification of these motherlands might be or mean. I will, finally, begin again. Say, then, motherland is the place of the subject: where the subject finds herself or achieves her identification with a 'place'. The conclusions of Aidoo's and Head's texts are instructive in these respects.

In OSK, Sissie does not in the end send the letter she has been writing. Her ex-lover, ex-compatriot and the ex-mothercountry, England, are only nominally the addressee and place of address of the love letter, text-letter, which is more profoundly addressed to Africa: 'Sissie woke up. She had been completely absorbed [in writing the letter] . . . Sure enough, there was Africa' (p. 133). Arriving back in Africa, there is no need to send a/the letter: 'There was no need to mail it . . . [S]he was back in Africa' (p. 133). And, when she addresses herself, it is also Africa she addresses: ' "Oh Africa . . ." Sissie wondered whether she had spoken aloud to herself . . . [I]n Africa . . . She had fallen from the beginning into the warm embrace of a brotherhood of man . . . she placed one soft hand over her land. It was a gesture of belonging' (*QP*, last page).

Both texts end with returns to and identifications with Africa. I say they end here, but these endings are also the places from which the narratives begin as narratives: they are written from the place they are heading towards.[29] Among the lessons that can be drawn from this is that the event of the story is a writing up, already a self-cognitive process, a writing that is a reading. This process of writing up is one that validates the textually originating conclusions.[30] And, as the texts end where they have begun, they prompt the re-telling of the telling of the stories, or remain: 'what is to be read.'[31]

This literary textual economy of recyclement, in which the text becomes legend ever to be re-told, is not necessarily or only an African one.[32] Yet, as these texts are about addressing oneself to and from Africa, it is this message that will continually be repeated, whatever else may be interposed.

Notes

1 *The Concise Oxford Dictionary*, seventh edition.

2 Vandana Ṣhiva, *Staying Alive: Women, Ecology and Development*, Zed Books, London, 1988, p. 41.

3 There are certain dangers in an unexamined use of the term 'motherland', and in the yoking together of 'mother' and 'land', in that such constructions may serve to support patriarchal and imperialist epistemologies and teleologies. It can further be noted that 'motherland' is constituted as not only subjectless but apolitical. I have offered only an illustration and not an archaeology of this predicament.

4 Cheikh Anta Diop, *The Cultural Unity of Negro Africa: The*

Domains of Patriarchy and Matriarchy in Classical Antiquity (first published in 1959), Présence Africaine, Paris, 1962.

5   Aeschylus, *The Eumenides* in *The Oresteian Trilogy*, trans. Philip Vellacott, Penguin, Harmondsworth, 1974, p. 169. All further references in the text are to this work.

6   These citations are taken from *Women in African Literature Today*, eds. Eldred Duromisi Jones, Eustace Palmer and Marjorie Jones, Africa World Press, James Currey, London, 1987 (hereafter *WALT*). It is not my intention to single out individual authors or to discredit the essays from which the citations come.

7   Ama Ata Aidoo, *Our Sister Killjoy: or Reflections from a Black-eyed Squint* (first published in 1977), Longman, Harlow, 1982 (hereafter *OSK*. Bessie Head, *A Question of Power* (first published in 1974), Heinemann, London, 1985 (hereafter *QP*). All further references in the text are to these works.

8   With respect to this essay, I refer not only to a critical appropriation, but to the displacement of literature in a post-structuralist context. That is, the self-displacing moves of post-structuralism, such as the erasure of textual authority and the dissolution of the classical text of knowledge into the generalised fictionality of all texts, may be said to displace literature, in the specificity of that denomination, still further. This is not to repudiate the use and usefulness of such strategies, but to foreground problematic side-effects.

9   Katherine Frank, 'Women Without Men: The Feminist Novel in Africa' in *WALT*, p. 29.

10   The commentaries of the narrator can be seen in terms of a retrospective knowledge or in terms of Sissie's unexpressed thoughts. In *QP* there is also a split between the narrator and self as object, the one written of, though it is less demarcated.

11   Sigmund Freud, *Totem and Taboo* in *The Standard Edition of the Complete Works*, trans. James Strachey, Hogarth Press, London, 1958 (hereafter *TT*). All further references in the text are to this work.

12   The same is said of Dan (p. 103), and the story of her mother's life is said to be an 'imposition' on her own (p. 16).

13   It can be said that while for Freud animism is a property of primitive cultures that becomes individual madness in modern civilisation, Head reverses this, showing such 'madness' to be attributable to the constructions of civilisation. She not only reverses the

animism-madness/civilised mind opposition, but transforms or renews an animistic mode of thought in terms of a creative one, as I will indicate.

14 I will later argue that the 'setting' of the book involves a super-imposition of South African realities. It can be noted that while Dan is comparable to white racists, he also sometimes speaks a gangster rhetoric of the townships. The point is also made in the novel that barbaric practices and the mis-use of power is no one's special preserve, neither that of white or black despots (pp. 134–135).

15 Carolyn Merchant, *The Death of Nature: Women, Ecology and the Scientific Revolution*, Harper & Row, New York, as quoted by Shiva, p. 17.

16 Elizabeth can be said to be doubly doubly (sic) displaced. As a Coloured, she is displaced from being African and 'non-African'. As a woman, she is displaced from being the phallocentric subject and the undoing of this subject. Moreover, being classified as Coloured disqualifies her from being not only totally African, but white as well. See, also, Gayatri Chakravorty Spivak, 'Displacement and the Discourse of Women' in *Displacement: Derrida and After*, Indiana University Press, Bloomington, 1983. It is also possible to read Dan and Sello in terms of the internalisation of racial stereotypes.

17 Bessie Head, letter to Charles Ponnuthurai Sarvan, 25 April 1980. As quoted by Sarvan, 'Bessie Head: *A Question of Power* and Identity' in *WALT*, p. 87.

18 Arlene Elder, 'Ama Ata Aidoo and the Oral Tradition: A Paradox of Form and Substance' in *WALT*, p. 13.

19 See Frederic Jameson, 'The Cultural Logic of Capital' in *New Left Review* 146 (July–August, 1984), p. 84. Jameson speaks of the importance of a 'cognitive mapping', and I have re-used the phrase in this essay. While Jameson uses the term with reference to a post-modernist culture, this is not inappropriate to the European setting of *OSK*, nor to the scattering of an African diaspora.

20 This specificity of address is especially explicit in her poetry, where poems are dedicated and addressed to particular people.

21 Joseph Conrad, *Heart of Darkness*, JM Dent, London, 1974, p. 149.

22 See Jean Fisher, 'Other Cartographies', *Third Text* 6 (Spring, 1989). My references to 'unburied debts' have, to an extent, this essay as a sub-text.

23   Freud speaks of art in terms of wish-fulfilment in his essay, 'Creative Writers and Day-Dreaming'.

24   For other readings see John S Mbiti, *African Religions and Philosophy*, (first published in 1969), Heinemann, London, 1980, p. 57; Emmanuel Obiechina, *Culture, Tradition and Society in the West African Novel*, African Studies Series 14, CUP, Cambridge, 1975, p. 43. There is also Birago Diop's poem 'Souffles' in his story 'Sarzent the Madman'. *Diverse Voices* ed. Harriet Devine Jonip, Harvester-Wheatsheaf, 1991.

25   See my essay, 'Are We in the Company of Feminists? A Preface for Bessie Head and Ama Ata Aidoo' in *Diverse Voices*, Harvester, Brighton, 1991.

26   Ngugi wa Thiong'o, 'From the Corridors of Silence' in *Weekend Guardian* (21–22 October 1989), p. 4.

27   Head's text may be said to interrogate Freud in passing; Aidoo's text reads the consumerist culture and educational scene that would consume or decipher the African Other.

28   This lack may be seen as endemic, from the beginnings of western history, or it may be seen as one instituted by the scientific rationalism of the enlightenment, or as a symptom of late capitalist society as expressed in the depthlessness and placelessness of postmodern culture.

29   My point here is not that the plots are circular, but that the stories begin with the completion of a story yet to be written up.

30   It might also be claimed, with special reference to the texts in question, that the writing begins from the foreclosed originality of the subjects in question.

31   The subtext of this pertains to the etymology of 'legend': *legenda*, Latin, translated as 'what is to be read'.

32   I might have spoken of the re-discovery, from a European site, of a literature that has not lost its 'estate', or line of authority. This would not be to suggest that African literature is a naturally or purely creative other, since the issue is one of a literature that has a cultural legitimacy as a form of knowing (otherwise). Nor would it be to suggest that African literature is a long-lost European literature, in so far as this question of a literary estate relates to specific social and historical conditions.

Mothers/Daughters/Sisters?

C L Innes

Mothers or Sisters? Identity, Discourse and Audience in the Writing of Ama Ata Aidoo and Mariama Bâ

The nostalgic songs dedicated to African mothers which express the anxieties of men concerning Mother Africa are no longer enough for us. The Black woman in African literature must be given the dimension that her role in the liberation struggles next to men has proven to be hers, the dimension which coincides with her proven contribution to the economic development of our country. (Mariama Bâ)[1]

Mariama Bâ refers here to the Francophone African poetry associated with the *Négritude* school, whose headmaster and chief representative was Léopold Sédar Senghor, president of Senegal from 1960 till 1980. Originating in the works and pronouncements of a group of black students and intellectuals in Paris in the late thirties and early forties, a group which included the Martiniquan poet and politician Aimé Césaire and Guyanan poet Léon Damas as well as Senghor himself, the poetry and philosophy of *Négritude* asserted pride in 'blackness' in the face of French contempt. In Senghor's essays and poetry, the emphasis is particularly on the affirmation of traditional African culture and values expressed in poems which recall a pastoral and idyllic childhood and a noble heritage.

As Clive Wake remarks, Senghor shared with others of his generation the situation of being 'an African who is in almost every sense of the word a Frenchman'.[2] The French colonial policy of assimilation created an elite in West Africa who, like Senghor, were educated from the age of six entirely in French to become part of the French cultural and political system. Senghor eventually became a French citizen, a teacher in the French university system, Senegal's deputy to the French Constituent Assembly (in 1945), and a member of the French Academy (in 1969). For Senghor, *Négritude* or '*Africanité*' is not a negation of European civilisation, but is complementary – the African restores and affirms his own identity in order to contribute to a 'universal' civilisation. Thus for Senghor, there is no contradiction in drawing upon European philosophers such as Marx, Sartre and Teilhard de Chardin in order to advocate 'African socialism' or to declare that '*Négritude* is a humanism', nor in his use of the elegant and eloquent French typical of his poetry and prose, for the 'universal civilisation' he envisages will be a synthesis of European, African and, presumably, Asian values and qualities. Again and again, Senghor has argued that cultural liberation must precede political liberation, and that the acknowledgment of the existence of African culture will be followed by acknowledgment of the right to self-government.

Written in the early forties, while still in 'exile' in France, Senghor's first collections of poems recall the Africa of his childhood with nostalgia and longing, in a style which evokes the African *griot* – the traditional oral poet – and ceremonial traditions, but which is also strongly influenced by the French poet, Paul Claudel. He dramatises himself as the prodigal son, as the ambassador of his people, as the child and lover, longing for the maternal warmth and sensual embrace of Africa. From his 1945 collection, *Chants d'Ombre*, the poem

'Black Woman' epitomises that convergence of mistress, mother and land which becomes the focus of the poet's nostalgia and desire:

Naked woman, black woman
  Clothed with your colour which is life, with your form
  which is beauty!
In your shadow I have grown up; the gentleness of your
  hands was laid over my eyes
And now, high up on the sun-baked pass, at the heart of
  summer, at the heart of noon, I come upon you, my
  Promised Land,
And your beauty strikes me to the heart like the flash of
  an eagle.

Naked woman, black woman
Firm-fleshed ripe fruit, sombre raptures of black wine,
  mouth making lyrical my mouth
Savannah stretching to clear horizons, savannah shudder-
  ing beneath the East Wind's eager caresses
Carved tom-tom, taut tom-tom, muttering under the Con-
  queror's fingers
Your solemn contralto voice is the spiritual song of the
  Beloved.[3]

But although his emotional allegiance will be primarily to his African mother, to 'the Kingdom of Childhood', Senghor also acknowledges that he is the child of two cultures, that he is 'a cultural half-caste'; his sisters and his mothers 'who cradled my nights' are African *and* European:

To have to choose! deliciously torn between these two
  friendly hands
  . . . A kiss from Soukeina! . . . these two antagonistic
  worlds
When the pain . . . ah! I cannot tell now which is my sister
  and
  which is my foster-sister

Of the two who cradled my nights with their dreamt-of
   tenderness,
   with their mingled hands
When the pain . . . a kiss from you Isabella! . . . between
   those two
   hands
That I want to make one again in my own warm hand.[4]

Writers from Anglophone Africa, such as Achebe, Soyinka,
and Mphahlele, representing a new generation some 20 years
later, expressed their scepticism about *Négritude*, and Achebe
provides a wicked parody of those 'nostalgic songs' in Cool
Max's 'Dance-offering to the Earth-Mother', in *A Man of the
People*:

I will return home to her – many centuries have I
   wandered –
And I will make my offering at the feet of my lovely
   mother:
I will rebuild her house, the holy places they raped and
   plundered,
And I will make it fine with black wood, bronzes and
   terra-cotta.[5]

Nevertheless, Mariama Bâ's characterisation of literature
which expresses 'the anxieties of men concerning Mother
Africa' is also applicable to much Anglophone literature,
including fiction by Ama Ata Aidoo's well-known Ghanaian
compatriots, Kofi Awoonor and Ayi Kwei Armah. Kofi
Awoonor's hero in *This Earth, My Brother . . .* [6] is haunted
by the memory of his dead girl cousin, Dede, whom the
imagery of the novel links to the mythical Mammy Water,
and who is also a symbol of the Ghanaian nation born 103
years after the signing of the Bonds by African rulers which
recognised British jurisdiction on the Gold Coast. Armah's
second novel *Fragments*[7] begins and ends with the reflections
and memories of Nana, the grandmother of the novel's protagonist, Baako. She speaks for the wisdom and conscious-

ness of ancestral Ghana, untouched by European materialism and individualism, but now ignored and belittled by all. In Armah's fifth novel, *The Healers*,[8] the main woman character, Araba Jesiwa, is first healed psychologically by the male guru, Damfo, whereupon she is able to find her 'true' fulfilment as a mother. Almost destroyed physically and psychologically again by the murderers of her son, she becomes a symbol of fragmented Africa, whom the men must carry around, care for and heal; she is both their burden and their hope for salvation. Asked in a 1986 interview what she thought of Armah's portrayal of women, Aidoo responded:

> He is like any of the male African writers. They can only portray women the way they perceive them . . . Armah's female characters are very much out there to act as foils to his male heroes. For me, the quintessential female character is this old woman in *The Healers*. She is so articulate and clear, but what does he do? He encases her in this orthopedic contraption which symbolically and literally immobilises her completely. For me that is very symbolic. If they are up and about, they are servicing men; if they are clear, they are lying prone.[9]

From her earliest work, and well before Armah's first fiction had been published, Aidoo has challenged the nostalgic image of 'African mother' as symbol with a series of mothers whose characters and roles as well as their very plurality prevent them from being seen either symbolically or nostalgically.

Her play, *The Dilemma of a Ghost*, first performed in 1964, makes motherhood a central issue, concerning three generations of women – Nana, the grandmother; Esi Kom, the mother; and Monka, the sister of a young Ghanaian man named Ato – he has just returned from America, after marrying Eulalie, an Afro-American. It is a cast very closely paralleled in Armah's novel *Fragments*, published four years later, although Armah's Afro-American outsider is a mistress rather than a wife. Unlike the frail, blind and unheard Nana of Armah's novel, however, Aidoo's grandmother is lively, imperious and very much at the centre of her family's life. And although she speaks as a member of the older generation, unable or unwilling to countenance change, she is also a 'character' in her own right and in all senses of the word. The impetus to symbolise comes not from the author or audience, but from Eulalie, the Afro-American wife, who seeks a lost homeland and a lost mother in Africa. The contrast between Eulalie's imagined caricature of her African 'homeland' and the actuality is central to this tragi-comic play.

The other central dilemma, which remains largely unresolved in Aidoo's earliest published work, is the choice between motherhood and childlessness, a dilemma shadowed in the debate between the two village women who act as a kind of secondary chorus, one of whom is burdened with the care of her many children and the other who is barren and longs for children. For them, and for Ato's family, the fact that Eulalie and Ato have *chosen* to remain childless is incomprehensible. It is a choice which, as in Armah's *Fragments*, is linked to materialism and western individualism as opposed to commitment to family and community, and to the view of marriage as a continuation of romance rather than as the continuation of family. It is interesting that Eulalie is less certain about this choice than her Ghanaian husband is. When she worries whether 'it won't matter at all', it is he who declares that they will 'create a paradise, with or without children', and insists:

> I love you, Eulalie, and that's what matters. Your own sweet self should be OK for any guy. And how can a first born child be difficult to please? Children, who wants them? In fact, they will make me jealous. I couldn't bear seeing you love someone else better than you do me. Not yet, darling, and not even my own children.[10]

The play ends abruptly and unexpectedly with a kind of reconciliation between Eulalie and her mother-in-law, in league against Ato after he has struck her for 'shaming' him in front of his family. Although this reconciliation seems imposed and is not altogether convincing, it nevertheless foreshadows a number of mother/daughter-in-law alliances in Aidoo's short stories, and also the failure of alliances between men and women of the younger generation for whom pregnancy or childbirth all too often bring disruption. Thus in an early story, 'Certain Winds from the South',[11] a northern Ghanaian mother is left to tell her daughter-in-law that the son has decided he must go south to earn money for his wife and new born child, and she remembers her own sorrow at the departure of her husband over 20 years previously to join the British army. In two stories, 'A Gift from Somewhere', and 'No Sweetness Here', a child for whom the mother bears special affection is the cause of marital anger and dissent. The husband in 'Two Sisters' is unfaithful to his wife because he finds her pregnant body repulsive. 'Something to Talk About on the Way to the Funeral' recounts the story of a mother who takes in the girl her son impregnates and deserts, and of the relationship between the two women: 'Some people said they were like mother and daughter. Others that they were like sisters. Still even more others said they were like friends.' 'The Message' humourously reveals the cultural distance between a rural grandmother and her urban granddaughter, but at the same time celebrates the grandmother's heroic journey to the city and her unwavering determination to do what is right for her grandchild – a journey that ends triumphantly with the discovery that the granddaughter has given birth to twins and that all are well. In this story, the husband appears only as the sender of a telegram; there is no further thought of him in either the grandmother's or the storyteller's mind.

Yet it is interesting to note that the alliances between women of differing generations are more often between mothers and daughters-in-law, than between mothers and their natural daughters. Between the latter friction is often the norm. Yaaba, the unruly young girl in the story 'The Late Bud', desperately longs for signs of affection from her

mother, and is painfuly beaten by her. Monka, the daughter
in *The Dilemma of a Ghost*, resents the fact that all family
resources have gone towards her brother's education while
she has had to leave school early, and she rebels against the
norms of 'feminine' behaviour. We are told:

> But if Esi Kom bears a daughter
> And the daughter finds no good man
> Shall we say it is Esi Kom's fate in childbirth,
> Or shall we say it is her daughter's trouble?
> Is not Monka the sauciest girl
> Born here for many years?
> Has she not the hardest mouth in this town? (pp. 16–17)

Monka is the prototype for the title character in Aidoo's
second play, *Anowa*, who is condemned by her elders for
'behaving as though she were the heroine in a story.'[12] In
both plays, the older women are seen (at first sight anyway)
as conservative supporters of a tradition which restricts the
roles of women and limits their choices. Anowa's mother,
Badua, laments her daughter's refusal to marry a suitor
approved by her parents, and resists the father's suggestion
that she might be a priestess who would have 'glory and
dignity', because a priestess is 'not an ordinary human being'.
Badua declares:

> I want my child
> To be a human woman
> Marry a man,
> Tend a farm
> And be happy to see her
> Peppers and her onions grow.
> A woman like her
> Should bear children,
> Many children,
> So she can afford to have
> One or two die.
> Should she not take

Her place at meetings
Amongst the men and women of the clan?
And sit on my chair when
I am gone? And a captainship in the army
Should not be beyond her
When the time is ripe. (pp. 12–13)

It is worth noting that Badua's concept of a normal 'human' life for a woman differs from the future a traditional European mother might have envisioned for her daughter 100 years ago, a future which was unlikely to have included a captainship in the army or a place at meetings amongst the men and women of the clan. But such positions for women are earned through fulfilling accepted roles, of which being a wife and mother are primary. Such roles also assume a stable, agrarian way of life, and a closely knit extended family which will provide support for the old and weak.

Anowa's assertion of her own choice of marriage partner entails other unforeseen choices and assertions, beginning with the rejection by and of her mother, and thus of a place in her own community. Her refusal to be subservient as a daughter is in character with her refusal to be subservient as a wife, and although it is clear that she is physically and intellectually more adventurous than Kofi, her husband, and that this is what at first attracts him to her, these very same characteristics alienate him once he has become relatively wealthy (thanks to her assistance).

In this play, Aidoo links Anowa's movement away from the restrictions of her mother's culture (or her motherculture) with the increasing impact of British colonisation (the play opens in 1874, the year that the British marched into the royal capital, Kumasi), a movement which is emphasised visually by the contrast between the opening scenes of village life and the closing scene in Kofi's sumptuous house, with its mixture of heavy Victorian furniture, animal skin rugs, and the self-glorifying portrait of Kofi Ako flanked by pictures of Queen Victoria and of the crow which is the totem bird of Kofi's clan.

In rebelling against her mother, Anowa finds that she has asserted her freedom only to lose it. Kofi cannot accept her as a comrade and equal; he wants a wife who will endorse his status, and who will bear him children. For Anowa, hierarchies of gender and class are clearly linked: she identifies with the slaves that Kofi has bought despite her bitter disapproval, and seeks desperately to disassociate herself from the privileged and ostentatious life that their labour brings for Kofi. Her determination to be true to herself and her principles, her vision, results in her becoming an outcast, rejected by her own family and branded as a witch by her husband, before he too casts her out. The ending of the play is a deeply pessimistic one, for in speaking out and telling the truth – that it is her husband rather than she who is infertile – she destroys him, the man for whom she gave up everything. The message seems to be that 'man cannot bear very much reality', and that women must either flatter their men and deny their own integrity; or speak out and destroy both themselves and those they love.

The dilemma of the woman who has views of her own, and the determination not to disassociate the personal and the political become the central concerns of Aidoo's novel, *Our Sister Killjoy: or Reflections from Black-eyed Squint.*[13] In this experimental novel, form and technique are linked explicitly, rather than implicitly, through the use of traditional forms (as in her earlier fiction), with the problem of exploring and expressing those concerns, so that the questions of personal and communal welfare are tied to the problem of writing and speaking in and through 'the master discourse'. The mode and message of the novel are encapsulated in the opening four pages of the novel, where typographical lay-out is used to emphasise first the simple and uncomplicated optimism and determination of the narrator to see that 'Things are working out/to their dazzling solution' (one phrase to each page), despite the accumulation of clutter given five lines on the third page. Her desire to see through that 'dazzling solution' is met with the frustrating block of verbiage taking up over half the fourth page, the discourse of the coloniser parroted by African 'liberals' and academics:

> What is frustrating though, in arguing with a nigger who is a 'moderate' is that since the interests he is so busy defending are not even his own, he can regurgitate only what he has learnt from his bosses for you. Like:
>
> The need for law and order;
>
> The gravest problem facing mankind being hunger, disease, and ignorance;
>
> ....
>
> .... The academic–pseudo–intellectual version is even more dangerous, who in the face of a reality that is more tangible than the massive walls of the slave forts standing along our beaches, still talks of universal truth, universal art, universal literature and the Gross National Product. (p. 6)

This first section, titled 'Into a Bad Dream', ends with Sissie's arrival in Germany and her first real encounter with a European language as an *alien* language, when she overhears a mother affirm to her child, **'Ja, das Schwarze Mädchen'** (p. 12). The bold type used in the text and the free verse meditation which follows it emphasise not only that all languages are built upon difference, as Saussure maintained, but that the differences which structure each language are culture specific. Here, the differences which matter are of colour and gender, and hearing herself named as different, Sissie finds that she has become irretrievably caught up in the language of that culture, which notices differences of colour.

Thus, in seeking to change 'the way things are', Aidoo, and her protagonist Sissie, must also challenge the way things are described, including the forms and language in which they have been described. Her experimental technique revises the form and conventions of the novel as they have been handed down from British writers and, more specifically,

rewrites and reverses Conrad's *Heart of Darkness*, as the archetypal European novel 'about' Africa. Conrad's male European narrator, Marlowe, recounting what he has learned
from an earlier journey to the Congo, the heart of darkness,
is challenged by Aidoo's female African narrator, Sissie,
reflecting in the light of 'knowledge gained since' on her
youthful journey to Europe, and specifically to Bavaria, the
heart of whiteness – with its associations of Christmas trees,
Hitler and unspeakable horrors, such as the laboratories
where 'experiments were done on herb, animal and man.'
(p. 44) But for Sissie, the deepest understanding of 'the
horror' at the very heart of whiteness comes from her
encounter with Marija, the fair 'Intended' whose loneliness
is both a consequence of and a clue to the interrelated
seduction and exploitation of others. Marija's home is a
shrine to sensuality and materialism with its expensive furniture, its well-stocked refrigerator, the 'funereal elegance' of
its white-walled cave-like bedroom, with a dressing table
packed with an array of perfumes and lotions: 'Fragile
weapons for a ferocious war. There they stood, tall and
elegant with slender necks and copious bottoms, their tops
glittering golden over bodies that exuded delicate femaleness
in their pastel delicacy' (p. 63).

The terrible irony is that this shrine to sensuality, this
marital chamber, is empty – the husband/father (perhaps
rather too significantly named Adolf) is always absent, working day and night in the factory to pay for and furnish their
home. Trapped in the identity of wife and mother, roles
which are empty masks, Marija seeks out 'black' people –
the Indians in the shop and then Sissie – as safe repositories
for her thwarted affection and need for community and even
learning. For Sissie, Marija's case is exemplary; through her
situation she understands that colonisation is born of need,
the desperation of those 'whose only distinction in life was
that at least they were better than the Natives . . . '

But there are other, related lessons to be learned from this
episode. In a novel concerned with exploring the connected

problems of finding an audience and of finding alliances so that the writer might help construct a freer and stronger Africa (as well as a freer and stronger self),[14] the notion of a 'global sisterhood', an alliance of women throughout the world to overturn patriarchal power is a possibility to be considered. Indeed, Aidoo contributed a piece 'On Being A Woman' to a volume titled *Sisterhood is Global*, edited by American feminist Robin Morgan, in 1983. But if the name given to husband and son – Adolf – is a reminder of European assertions of male and racial superiority, the name Marija epitomises a feminine type which is specific to and claimed by all European nations (pp. 24–25). It is significant that Sissie has been given the name Mary, and has rejected it as a name belonging to European culture, social structures and institutions:

> 'My name? My name is Sissie. But they used to call me Mary too. In school.'
>
> ....
>
> 'Vai?'
>
> 'I come from a Christian family. It is the name they gave me when they baptised me. It is also good for school and work and being a lady.' (p. 24)

A name 'good for school and work and being a lady', Mary/ Marija is also 'good' for 'a young mother pushing her baby in a pram'; thus Marija and the whole episode is introduced. Like the madonna of western iconography, Marija is forever tied to her son, while her husband is a husband only in name. She is the virginal mother, the icon of the European nuclear family, and her femininity and identity derive from that role. In rejecting the name, Sissie has rejected this western concept of femininity – very pale and pastel as she sees it – a female identity derived solely from motherhood, sexuality and the centrality of the nuclear family – and has asserted an identity as comrade, which nevertheless acknowledges gender and a wider, African concept of family.

'Zo vas is zis name, "Sissie" '?

'Oh, it is just a beautiful way they call "Sister" by people who like you very much. Especially if there are not many girl babies in the family . . . one of the very few ways where an original concept from our old ways has been given expression successfully in English.' (p. 28)

In an essay on 'The Feminist Novel in Africa', Katherine Frank has placed *Our Sister Killjoy* among a group of novels by African women writers which urge women to 'spurn patriarchy in all its guises and create a safe, sane, supportive world of women: a world of mothers and daughters, sisters, and friends.' This ideology, Frank declares, 'amounts to feminist separatism, though only obliquely in Aidoo's *Our Sister Killjoy* do we find the logical outcome of this ideology: lesbianism.'[15] While it is accurate to describe Aidoo's novel as 'spurning patriarchy in all its guises', it seems to me that Aidoo explores the possibility of feminist separatism and rejects it. The apparent safety and sanity, the cosy world of female friendship offered by Marija, is seen as deceptive, in part because it is based on need and emotional deprivation rather than genuine recognition of equality, and in part because the female relationships all too readily take on the patterns and structures of heterosexual relationships in both cultures. Marija seeks to seduce the black woman, offering her the same mixture of mothering (through constant feeding) and sexuality she offers her husband; Sissie has had fantasies about a relationship with Marija in which she (Sissie) was the man: 'In her imagination she was one of these black boys in one of these involvements with white girls in Europe,' (p. 61) and she recognises with dismay the brief sadistic pleasure she experiences in being able to hurt Marija when she is about to leave Germany:

'It hit her like a stone, the knowledge that there is pleasure in hurting. A strong three-dimensional pleasure, an exclusive masculine delight that is exhilarating beyond all

measure. And this too is God's gift to man? She wondered.' (p. 76)

As the reader can understand at this point, the fact that Sissie
experiences this 'delight' signifies that it is not 'exclusively
masculine', but 'God's gift' to whomever is in a position of
power, whether emotional or economic.[16]

The structure and plot of the novel reinforce Sissie's rejection of 'female separatism', and of a global sisterhood which
ignores differences of race and culture, for she goes from
Marija to join her boyfriend and his friends in London. Here,
the question of language also takes on a different emphasis.
Sissie's lack of any but the most basic German words, and
Marija's broken English, have allowed the two women to
escape to a certain extent from the power of the 'master
discourse' which precedes 'The Plums' section and upon
which Sissie meditates soon after her meeting with Marija
who associates Sissie with the English-speaking and dark-
skinned Indians she also liked so very much:

A common heritage. A
Dubious bargain that left us
Plundered of
Our gold
Our tongue
Our life – while our
Dead fingers clutch
English – a
Doubtful weapon fashioned
Elsewhere to give might to a
Soul that is already fled. (pp. 28–29)

Without a common language, however dubious its connotations, Marija and Sissie must rely largely on feeling and
intuition, and on symbolic offerings such as the plums to
communicate. At a time in the early seventies when some
western feminists were arguing that 'the oppressor's language' could be by-passed, and that female intuition and

'body-language' might be a truer means of communication, Ama Ata Aidoo suggests feelings and intuition without conceptual language may be also dubious and deceptive. While European languages may be used to deceive, and while they also inescapably carry their own cultural perceptions of difference in terms of colour and gender, the *can* be used, and are used powerfully by Sissie/Ama Ata to speak truths.

In the third section of the novel, 'From Our Sister Killjoy', Sissie uses English to speak and debate political truths. The central debate, over the significance of Dr Christian Barnard's transplant of an African heart into a European body (here the heart of darkness literally enters the white man!), and the insistence that scientific knowledge and discourse is universal and value-free, sets Sissie on one side and her male compatriots on the other. It is sadly fitting that Kunle, who is unable to see anything but universal good in the story of the transplant, is killed in the crash of his powerful car, that western technological status symbol, and his family is robbed of all compensation from the insurance company which interprets the fine print to its own advantage.

The fourth and final section, 'A Love Letter', seeks to use English for personal communication, which cannot be divorced from sexual politics nor from the consequences of colonialism which reinforce divisions of class, race and gender, while at the same time providing the 'dubious weapon' with which those divisions must be overcome. The problem of language is raised in the very first sentence:

My Precious Something,
　　First of all, there is this language. This language.

Like his male friends, Sissie's 'precious something' (the phrase highlights the inadequacy of English to name male/female relationships which do not fit into the traditional and socially approved ones of husband, father or brother) draws upon scientific analogies to allow optimism, and rejects Sissie's political analogies which are too 'serious' and 'negative'. But, Sissie rejoins,

How can I help being serious? Eh, My Love, what positive is there to be, when I cannot give voice to my soul and still have her heard? Since so far, I have only been able to use a language which enslaved me, and therefore, the messengers of my mind always come shackled? (p. 112)

Our Sister Killjoy ends with a letter which is not sent, because Sissie realises that its original purpose – reconciliation with her ex-lover – cannot be achieved, and that, anyway, is no longer the point. The writing, the act of attempting communication, has been a process of self-understanding, which has cleared her mind of 'the ticky-tacky' and prepared her for her return to Africa, a return in which she can rejoice – and where she can speak aloud and not care what the person in the next seat thinks. Mariama Bâ's *So Long A letter*,[17] published three years later, takes further the device of a personal letter which is also primarily a process of self-understanding, where writing allows the female narrator to envisage a new and independent beginning. At first sight, the two novels seem, as Katherine Frank argues, to belong to similar categories and to embody a similar feminist perspective, rejecting patriarchal structures and the need for relationships with males. There are, however, significant differences between them, differences which relate to the interconnected attitudes toward audience and language.

Whereas Sissie's letter is addressed to her male lover, who is also her antagonist, and seeks to persuade him, and to meet his attitudes and arguments head-on, Ramatoulaye's letter is addressed to her female friend, Aissatou, who has also undergone and proudly survived the same experience of being confronted by the fact that her husband has taken a second wife. As Katherine Frank points out, Ramatoulaye is writing to her dearest friend and thus celebrating the strength and depth of female friendship which endures long after marital bonds have been disrupted, and at the same time writing to the self that she is struggling to become.[18] The letter is also a kind of internal monologue, a diary of the memories and reflections, of the 'stock-taking' or *mirasse*, which according to Islamic culture should be undertaken upon the death of a relative.[19] Within Ramatoulaye's long letter is set, like a jewel, Aissatou's shorter letter, which in its form and imagery of stripping bare ('*dépouillement*') crystallises the attitude of independence and firm self-assurance which Ramatoulaye's monologue brings her to:

> I am stripping myself of your love, your name. Clothed in my dignity, the only worthy garment, I go my way. (p. 32)

In addressing her letter to a female audience whose experience mirrors her own, Ramatoulaye seeks to confirm, to recognise her own feelings and understandings. Speaking to and for her 'soul mate', the problem of communication is not an issue; in contrast to the deliberately fragmented and disruptive technique chosen by Aidoo, Mariama Bâ's narrative letter flows on, eloquently, and seemingly without pause. Nor is 'this language' ever seen to be problematic. Nowhere does Ramatoulaye raise the difficulty of speaking in a colonial language, or complain of the imposition of alien concepts. This has to do in part with the nature of the struggle that Ramatoulaye undergoes, which is not a confrontation with European attitudes parroted by privileged male Ghanaians, but a struggle with traditional attitudes, interpreted to their own benefit by Senegalese men. In rejecting the polygamous marriage authorised by Islamic tradition, Aissatou and Ramatoulaye implicitly and sometimes explicitly affirm a western view of romance as the basis of marriage. Moreover, the harsh picture painted of the machinations of mothers-in-law, of the demands of extended families, of the sacrifice expected of wives and mothers, of the irresponsibility of husbands within this traditional context, all imply a movement toward the concept of the nuclear family from which Sissie flees. Towards the very end of her letter, Ramatoulaye writes of her sense of a global sisterhood or woman's movement which inspires and encourages her:

I am not indifferent to the irreversible currents of women's liberation that are lashing the world. This commotion that is shaking up every aspect of our lives reveals and illustrates our abilities.

My heart rejoices each time a woman emerges from the shadows. I know that the field of gains is unstable, the retention of conquests difficult: social constraints are ever present and male egoism resists.

Instruments for some, baits for others, respected or despised, often muzzled, all women have almost the same fate, which religions or unjust legislation have sealed. (p. 88)

Ramatoulaye, as Mariama Bâ herself did, continues to find sustenance in her Islamic faith; she seeks to reform it rather than reject it. At the same time she shares with Léopold Senghor, promulgator of *Négritude* and autocratic president of her country for some 20 years, a reverence for the French language and French culture. Nowhere does she question the French education she and Aissatou were 'privileged' to receive; there seems to be no irony in her presentation of the white French teacher who 'loved' them both:

To lift us out of the bog of tradition, superstition and custom, to make us appreciate a multitude of civilizations without renouncing our own, to raise our vision of the world, cultivate our personalities, strengthen our qualities, to make up for our inadequacies, to develop *universal* [my emphasis] moral values in us: these were the aims of our admirable headmistress. (pp. 15–16)

Presumably these too are the aims of Ramatoulaye in her chosen profession as teacher. Aidoo's keen awareness of the gap between such hand-me-down phrases and the stark realities of poverty and inequality which affect the majority of her countrymen and women, her rejection of talk of 'universal truth, universal art, universal literature', her use of a variety of voices recalling local oral traditions, all contrast sharply with Mariama Bâ's vision explicitly endorsed by Ramatoulaye's monologue, and implicitly endorsed by the style and language of this novel. *So Long A Letter*, like Oyono's *Une Vie de boy*,[20] brilliantly adapts the epistolary or diary novel to its African subject without questioning the form.

Ramatoulaye's concern for her personal dignity, her closing vision of the meeting between herself and Aissatou, uniting African custom and western feminism, can be seen in the context of the cultural nationalism espoused by President Senghor, a concern for establishing the dignity and worth of African culture as complementary to western civilisation, and as taking precedence to eradicating inequalities of wealth and power. Aidoo's analysis is closer to that of another Francophone writer, Frantz Fanon, whose Marxist analysis of colonialism emphasied the ways in which cultural discourse and institutions were used to reinforce colonial power. Despite her disillusion with Nkrumah as a leader, she shares his more radical socialist ideology that political liberation and cultural liberation must proceed hand in hand.

However, Mariama Bâ's second novel, *Scarlet Song*,[21] not quite completed at the time of her death in 1981, gives her a choice of subject and perspective which involves a far from compliant view of Senegal's governing ideology between 1960 and 1980. The romance between the beautiful blond French girl, Mireille, daughter of a French diplomat, and the Senegalese student, Ousmane, who comes from one of the poorer suburbs of Dakar, is often portrayed in terms reminiscent of those in which Senghor idealised the relationship between African and French cultures. It is a romance founded in their common love of philosophy and in their common attraction to each other's external good looks, a romance which attempts to ignore the differences in class, original language, family loyalties, fundamental religious and cultural values. Above all, it is the *image* of the other which each clings to and which nurtures their romance from a distance, and those images signify a convergence of the two individuals and the ideas of the worlds they belong to. Ousmane's photograph, treasured by Mireille and treated with contempt by her father as 'this object', shows him with 'the finely chiselled features, the bared chest, the red shirt, the blue sky, the black rock, the sun that shone out of his eyes' – a composite image which 'fires her love' (p. 26). To Ousmane's parents, Mireille's image is an object of veneration, an icon of the glamour associated with western culture, an insubstantial ideal seemingly beyond the reach of Africans: they assume she is a film star. Like Senghor's 'black woman', Ousmane's image embodies the idea of a place; Mireille's image embodies the idea of a culture.

But the attempt to marry the two worlds, to transfer Mireille and her culture to Ousmane's home is disastrous. In the 'unreal worlds' of the universities of Dakar and Paris, or in the isolation of their own rooms, the romance can be imagined and can thrive; in the actual surroundings of Ousmane's family compound, amid the poverty and the culture born of poverty, amid the traditions nurtured by Islam, Mireille is 'out of place'. As a result, when Mireille and Ousmane return to Dakar, she is cut off from all community. Once her son is born, Mireille becomes a lonely and desperate figure, in many ways like Marija of *Our Sister Killjoy*, increasingly isolated from her husband, and shut away in her perfectly kept apartment with its expensive French decor. Ousmane turns to *Négritude* to justify his taking a second, Senegalese wife, declaring that his callous treatment of Mireille is necessary if he is to assert his African identity.

So Long a Letter ended with Ramatoulaye's affirmation of her identity as a mother, an identity which is stronger and more firmly rooted than that of wife. *Scarlet Song* ends with a violent denial of motherhood, when Mireille goes mad and murders her baby son because as 'a half-caste' he has no place. Rejected by both families, Mireille and her son find they have no motherland. In her second novel, Mariama Bâ has moved away from Senghor's optimistic declaration that 'we are all cultural half-castes' and his vision of a 'universal' culture which will be a partnership between Europe and Africa. Like Ama Ata Aidoo she has become a 'black-eyed squint', peering sceptically at the ways in which ruling ideologies are used by men to deceive themselves as well as others in order to justify the fulfilment of their own desires.

Notes

1   Cited in Hans Zell, Carol Bundy and Virginia Coulon, eds. *A New Reader's Guide to African Literature*, Holmes & Meier, New York, 1983, p. 358.

2   John Reed and Clive Wake, eds. *Senghor: Prose and Poetry*, Oxford Universiy Press, London, 1965, p. 2.

3   Translated by John Reed and Clive Wake, *Senghor: Prose and Poetry*, p. 105.

4   From 'For Koras and Balafong', *Senghor: Prose and Poetry*, p. 110.

5   Chinua Achebe, *A Man of the People*, Heinemann, London, 1966, p. 91.

6   Kofi Awoonor, *This Earth, My Brother . . .* , Heinemann, London, 1972.

7   Ayi Kwei Armah, *Fragments*, Heinemann, London, 1970.

8   Ayi Kwei Armah, *The Healers*, Heinemann, London, 1978.

9   *Wasafiri* 6/7 (1987), p. 27.

10   *The Dilemma of a Ghost*, Longman, London, 1965, p. 4. Further page references in the text are to this edition.

11   All stories referred to in this essay are published in *No Sweetness Here*, Longman, London, 1979. (First published in 1970.) Further page references in the text are to this edition.

12   *Anowa*, Longman, London, 1970, p. 64. Further references in the text are to this edition.

13   Ama Ata Aidoo, *Our Sister Killjoy: or Reflections from a Black-eyed Squint*, Longman, London, 1977. References in the text are to this edition.

14   In the 1986 interview cited above, Aidoo declared, 'I wish, of course, that Africa would be free and strong and organised and constructive, etc. That is basic to my commitment as a writer. That is a basic and consistent part of my vision. I keep seeing different

dimensions of it, different interpretations come through my writing.' *Wasafiri* 6/7, p. 25.

15   Katherine Frank, 'Women Without Men: The Feminist Novel in Africa', *African Literature Today* no. 15, James Currey, London, 1987, p. 15.

16   Doris Lessing's first novel, *The Grass Is Singing*, and a number of her stories set in Africa, also explore this issue of the victim who seeks to victimise.

17   Mariama Bâ, *So Long a Letter*, translated by Modupe Bode-Thomas, Virago, London, 1982. First published in French by Les Nouvelles Editions Africaines, Paris, 1980.

18   Katherine Frank, ALT 15, p. 18.

19   For a further discussion of the importance of this concept in Bâ's novels see Mbye B Cham, 'Contemporary Society and the Female Imagination: A Study of the Novels of Mariama Bâ', *African Literature Today* 15 (1987), pp. 89–101.

20   Oyono, *Une Vie de boy*, Juillard, Paris, 1956.

21   Mariama Bâ, *Scarlet Song*, translated by Dorothy S Blair, Longman, Harlow, 1986. First published by Les Nouvelles Editions Africaines, Paris in 1981 as *Un chant écarlate*.

Ranjana Ash

The Search for Freedom in Indian Women's Writing

I

This essay explores the meaning of freedom for women in modern India as developed in the various works of five major Indian writers – Kamala Das, Anita Desai, Shashi Deshpande, Amrita Pritam and Nayantara Sahgal. While some of these writers, like Desai for instance, are not necessarily associated with explicitly feminist issues, in the same way as, for example, Ashapurna Devi, Ismat Chughtai or Krishna Sobti, their work does present interesting variations on the theme of women's freedom and is intrinsically linked to their conception of the motherland – to their own sense of being Indian.

As Indian society has been modernised and industrialisation and urbanisation have developed rapidly, and interchange of ideas in a global sense has increased, it is difficult to isolate the concept of women's freedom from western models. Nevertheless, there is considerable prejudice towards the westernised woman and women's fiction, no less than men's, has tended to equate the liberated woman with frivolous and trivial stereotypes of which just one is the westernised college girl.[1] On a more serious level there is fear of what is described in leftwing circles as 'cultural imperialism' – the imposition of cultural moves enabled by access to pornography and satellite television and other ways of seeing and thinking that will be profitable to those seeking new forms of domination. Such fears are accentuated by the prejudicial treatment of Indian and other Asian cultures in Britain and the West. And the responses of the writers studied here, not uniform or in agreement over many issues, reveal a common commitment in trying to maintain their cultural identity, their relationship to the motherland.

The concept of the motherland became a highly charged metaphor for aesthetic and political rhetoric during India's freedom struggle against British rule from the second half of the nineteenth century until 1947, the year of Indian independence. *Bharatmata*, Mother India, bound in chains waiting for her children to free her, became a popular figure in the literature, music and art of the period. As the freedom struggle was extended to include programmes of economic and social reform, nationalism and the emancipation of women began to be linked.[2] Women like Sarojini Naidu (1879–1949) were nationalist leaders and also pioneers of the women's movement. Naidu, who used to write romantic poetry in English in her younger days and was highly regarded by Edwardian aesthetes, wrote of Mother India lying in darkness, until she could be led into the dawn of progress by her sons and daughters.[3]

Naidu's facile optimism had begun to fade by the 1940s and 1950s when the oldest of the five writers under discussion began to publish, yet the spirit of nationalism which informed her work lingers on in their writing. Educated and knowledgeable about current feminist ideas, they are also conscious of their own roots and cultural identity – viewing women's freedom not as a uniform entity but as a plurality shaped and modified by diverse religious, linguistic and historical factors – and they perceive the changes taking place in women's lives from their own particular 'motherland' perspective.

Pritam, Desai and Sahgal lived through the horrors of Partition, the division of old India into the new states of Pakistan and a truncated India, which was a necessary condition of the negotiated settlement with Britain. They are sensitive therefore to the diversity and fusions of Indian culture composed of various cultural strands – Sanskritic and Perso-Muslim in north India. Das and Deshpande are from different regions of southern India. Das uses her part of the Dravidian inheritance in Indian civilisation for her works, which evoke her Kerala home. Deshpande's view combines Indian classicism with modern feminism.

They are older women born before 1940. They have lived in India during four decades of Indian independence and witnessed many changes in the lives of Indian women. There has been great effort by successive governments to introduce reform in women's position in such fields as marriage, divorce, inheritance, equal pay and abortion rights. The women's movement is undergoing radical changes as a new generation of active younger women, concerned about breaking the middle-class mould of feminism, forge links with women from the peasantry and the working class. Women's studies, in which feminist readings of literature and history by Indian women academics predominate, are also proliferating,[4] and there are echoes of this new discourse in the writings under consideration. However, the works of fiction and poetry discussed here are important primarily because the writers are a group of women who combine their sense of being part of Indian civilisation with their unique creative vision.

This essay does not attempt to present a comprehensive survey of the writings of the five authors. Rather, it selects a few books from their oeuvre, in order to illuminate issues related to women's search for freedom in contemporary India.

II

Amrita Pritam (born in 1919) is one of India's leading writers in Panjabi. Her poetry has been translated into several European languages, although few of her twelve important collections has been rendered into English.[5] She is also a prolific writer of short fiction, mainly novellas and short stories. A public figure, she was nominated to the upper house of the Indian Parliament and is a frequent delegate to international gatherings on peace, Third World literature and democratic rights. Born into a Sikh family in west Punjab, now a part of Pakistan, she experienced personally the trauma of being a refugee at the time of Partition when she had to leave her home in Lahore and settle in Delhi. Many of her poems and fiction describe the horrors inflicted on women during the communal riots, and the savagery that accompanied the mass uprooting of people and the transfer of population. Her love poems embody a characteristic of Indian literature – the linkage of physical love with a transcendental and spiritual dimension. Best known is 'To Waris Shah', which invokes the memory of the Muslim Sufi poet of the Punjab who wrote *Heer Ranjha*, a love story which is also a metaphor for the soul that seeks union with the divine. A rebel and fighter for women's freedom in her personal life, as vividly portrayed in her much-read autobiography,[6] her poetic persona's attitude can be summed up in one of her early poems, 'Not Today':

I always do the right thing/But not today,
I always do what people ask/But not today . . .[7]

Nayantara Sahgal (born in 1927) is a political novelist who writes in English. Educated in India and the USA Sahgal knows and understands western cultures but her interest lies in India's past and present political struggles and conflicts, especially as they affect civil liberties. The niece of Jawaharlal Nehru (1889–1964), Free India's first prime minister, and daughter of Vijayalakshmi Pandit, one of India's foremost

women politicians, Sahgal is *au fait* with the intricacies of
India's politics. While most of her novels are about women
from the upper middle-class, their lives are directly or
indirectly connected with struggle and controversy. *Storm in
Chandigarh* (1969) deals with women trapped in unhappy
marriages in a town shaken by industrial unrest. The heroine
of *A Situation in New Delhi* (1977) is a minister in the Indian
government whose comfortable life and love affair with an
English journalist is shattered by the death of her son, a
Maoist, during the Naxalite uprising in India in the late 1960s
and early 1970s. *Rich Like Us* (1985) is set in Delhi during
the Emergency (1975–1977) when the then prime minister,
Mrs Indira Gandhi, Sahgal's cousin, suspended many parts
of the Indian constitution and various civil rights and ruled
by decree. Sahgal's most recent novels have turned away
from women's lives into the field of political events under the
Raj. *Plans for Departure* (1986) is about English and European
people in India around the First World War though the main
woman character is a Danish suffragette. *Mistaken Identity*
(1989) concerns a political conspiracy against the British in
the early 1930s and is written from the viewpoint of a man
rather than that of the liberated mother who runs off with a
Communist agitator after a lifetime in *purdah* (behind the
veil).

Though Anita Desai (born in 1937) is not completely
Indian – her mother was a German – she was born and
brought up in India. Her father was a Bengali and she was
educated in Delhi. She writes in English, though she is familiar with several European languages and literatures which
she introduces into her novels, along with Urdu poetry. Her
work is not generally associated with the theme of women's
freedom, especially in novels like her first, *Cry the Peacock*
(1963), with its emotionally disturbed heroine who seeks
freedom from her older and unloving husband by pushing
him off the terrace! *In Custody* (1984) is about the declining
fortunes of Urdu poetry in Delhi; *Baumgartner's Bombay*
(1988) examines the world of a Jewish refugee from central

Europe fleeing from Hitler's persecution. However, in her best book, *Clear Light of Day* (1980) which was short-listed for the Booker Prize, she has created one of the most spirited and original of liberated women in contemporary Indian-English fiction. Bimala Das or Bim, as she is called, represents a free woman who, although encumbered by many domestic responsibilities, as will be seen in the subsequent discussion, has also freed herself from acquisitive desires.

Kamala Das (born in 1934) is an important Indian-English poet. She burst on to the scene in the early 1960s with her highly personal, almost autobiographical poems written in a new idiom she describes as 'half English, half Indian'.[8] She is from the Nair community of Kerala in south-western India and she writes her fiction in her native Malayalam. She, like Pritam, is a rebel and her candid autobiography,[9] translated by her from the Malayalam, reveals her own search for freedom and strategies of resistance. Her output is small – three main collections of which only one is available. She has written more fiction but little has been translated. One of her best short stories has recently been included in a new collection of Indian women's stories.[10]

Shashi Deshpande, also from south India, writes in English. She is the most overtly feminist of the five writers. Three of her novels, *The Dark Holds No Terrors* (1980), *Roots and Shadows* (1983) and *That Long Silence* (1988) are regarded as having made a significant contribution to modern feminist Indian writing. The daughter of a Sanskrit savant, she is well versed in Hindu and Buddhist thought as well as holding degrees in economics and law. Her feminism combines an awareness of classical Indian values derived from Sanskrit and Pali works with contemporary women's needs.

III

The discussion covers three main areas: the development of women's self-awareness and identity; women's search for freedom in the family; and, finally, the question of women's relationship to their 'motherlands' and the resolution of problems and conflicts which this relationship generates.

Women traditionally, at least since the Code of Manu compiled some time in the first two centuries AD, have been viewed not as individuals in their own right but as related to male members of the family:

> She can do nothing independently even in her own house. In childhood subject to her father, in youth to her husband, and when her husband is dead to her sons, she should never enjoy independence.[11]

The most important aspect of freedom demonstrated in the novels and verse discussed here therefore concerns women as individuals in their own right. The woman's self, her awareness of who she is and what she can do had been changing throughout the nineteenth century, affected by innovations in education and social reforms such as the abolition of *sati* (the practice of women burning themselves on the funeral pyre where the bodies of their husbands were being cremated). The nationalist movement also helped to bring women out of the *zenana* (the secluded parts of the house intended for women) beautifully described by Rabindranath Tagore (1861–1941), India's most famous writer, in his novel, *The Home and the World* (1916).

The freedom struggle received new power and impetus under the leadership of MK Gandhi, popularly called Mahatma Gandhi (1869–1948). His call to the masses of India brought thousands of men and women on to the streets in demonstrations, boycotts and other forms of non-violent non-co-operation with British rule. While the women's movement today is in many respects critical of Gandhi's views of woman's special capacity for suffering and their unique gift for the role of motherhood, and of his puritanical attitude towards chastity, Gandhi's insistence on the fundamental equality of men and women, and of the role women could play in passive resistance against the colonial government, were decisive in radicalising women's sense of self-identity.[12]

Sahgal's first and second novels deal with the influence of Gandhi's message and the actual participation of women in the freedom struggle in the 1920s and later. Maya Shivpal, in *A Time to be Happy* (1958), married to an Anglicised civil servant, is introduced as a colourless woman whose only role in life is to wear expensive saris and jewellery and attend official dinner parties. On meeting the nationalist narrator she decides to learn spinning in order to teach it to village women as part of the Gandhian programme of rural reconstruction. She sheds her silks and golden ornaments for the homespun cloth Gandhi advocated and, more importantly, develops a sense of her own needs. While the love that develops between her and the nationalist cannot be allowed to continue, its very emergence in her is a major step in her movement towards self-affirmation.[13]

The underlying spirit of *This Time of Morning* (1965) is the optimism of the early 1950s which coloured people's attitudes in the first phase of national development immediately after independence. Addressing a women's college, a veteran Gandhian tells the students:

> Real reform starts with your mental approach. The laws of your country may tell you (that) you are equal to men in every way. You may be given the opportunity to acquire a further education . . . But all this can be of no avail if you have not liberated yourselves from the attitudes that have traditionally bound you.[14]

Rashmi, the daughter of another Gandhian leader, is unhappy with her husband though the novel does not specify any special grievance beyond their incompatibility. It is through becoming aware of the kind of person she is that she recognises the flaw in her marriage.

> A part of her had married a man, loved him, given herself to the task of making a home, and suffered the wilderness

that only two mismatched people could create. But there was a self that had stood free from all this, the unsurrendered core of her, the waiting, watching guardian spirit that belonged to no man.[15]

Amrita Pritam, whose poem 'Not Today' with its note of defiance has already been quoted (see p. 155), uses the horrors of Partition to convey a new dimension to women's self-awareness. Her famous novella, translated from the Panjabi as *The Skeleton* (1973), is the story of a Hindu village girl abducted by a young Muslim from a neighbouring village because of a family vendetta. Pooro tries to escape, does meet her parents only to discover that according to Hindu tradition she has become an outcast because of her abduction. She will not be able to marry the man to whom she is engaged nor will her parents be accepted within their community. Pooro is forced to return to her captor who is shown by Pritam as a man with his own sense of honour. He does not violate her, has her converted to Islam and marries her. She is now Hamida, a person whose own suffering has enlarged her self-identity. She can help others irrespective of their ethnic, religious or social position. She has a son, adopts another, the child of a raped woman. When after Partition the governments of India and Pakistan arrange for the rescue of abducted women on either side of the border and she has an opportunity of returning to her native village she declines. Affirming her unity with all women in their suffering and joy she says:

> Whether one is a Hindu girl or a Mohammedan one, whoever reaches her destination, carries along my soul also.[16]

Kamala Das' poetic persona asserts herself in the poem 'An Introduction'. Her native language is Malayalam, her mother is Balamani Amma, an award-winning Malayalam poet and her entire family, as Das describes in her autobiography, were devoted Gandhians.[17] For a daughter from such a family to write poetry in English was an act of defiant self-assertion.

> . . . Don't write in English, they said,
> English is not your mother-tongue. Why not leave
> Me alone, critics, friends, visiting cousins . . .
> Why not let me speak in
> Any language I like? The language I speak
> Becomes mine, its distortions, its queernesses
> All mine, mine alone.[18]

It is again a defiant self that tries to escape an unhappy marriage by seeking a lover. It does not, however, raise her self esteem.

> . . . It is I who drink lonely
> Drinks at twelve midnight, in hotels of strange towns,
> It is I who laugh, it is I who make love
> And then feel shame . . . [19]

In Deshpande's important treatment of what one might call Indian 'feminism' in her novel, *Roots and Shadows* (1983), she shows that the self is not a simple construct: Indu struggles to be free, escaping from the joint family and not coming back for a decade, hating the traditional ways and wanting to create a new identity for herself, after discovering that she has not understood the real nature of the self. A theme to be developed in a more philosophical vein in her most recent novel, *That Long Silence* (1988), Deshpande has already begun to qualify a simplistic desire for the self to be freed of all restraints, of family duties and obligations. In the earlier book Indu learns from an old uncle, who gently chides her: if the entire world is composed of interdependent parts, why should Indu feel that she is a totally free agent? *Roots and Shadows* is a many-layered novel in which traditional and modern ways are both set against each other and shown to be interlinked, and in which the concept of freedom is qualified: no one can be wholly free.[20]

What Indu realises in the Deshpande novel is pursued further by Bim in Desai's *Clear Light of Day*. While still at school she knows, if not who she is, then what she wants to do. Arguing with her younger sister about the folly of getting married before one has finished one's education, like the Misra girls who live near them, Bim declares with passion:

> I shall work – I shall do things . . . I shall earn my own living – and look after Miramasi and Baba and – be independent. There'll be so many things to do – when we are grown up – when all this is over . . . [21]

Bim has realised that, in the Indian context where the idea of family responsibility is ingrained from childhood and forms an integral part of the ethical precepts of all Indian religions, there can be no freedom for the individual outside of the larger units that help one to define oneself.

IV

The search for freedom within the family can be set in context by the three aspects of women's lives as set down in the Code of Manu – as daughters, wives and mothers. The most elementary demand for freedom in the parental home is the right to education and thus access to work and economic independence. Nita Narang in Sahgal's *This Time of Morning* (1965) makes just such a simple plea to postpone the dreaded prospect of marrying one of the men whose families have started bombarding her parents with proposals of marriage. Nita's father is a wealthy society doctor so she has no economic reason to seek employment, the only motive recognised by middle-class parents. She has got her BA degree – the necessary educational qualification in Nita's upper middle-class social group. What more can she want, asks her mother. Nita cannot tell her how bored she is with the kind of life the mother leads with her coffee-drinking, canasta-playing set. Instead, as soon as she receives an offer of a job – as the social secretary of a charismatic politician – she is thrilled. This is the beginning of her liberation: she falls in love with the politician despite the risk of ruining her reputation (she has already become engaged to be married); it is a risk worth taking because she has had the chance of doing what she has really wanted – to *initiate* her own relationship.[22]

The freedom Sarita wants in Deshpande's *The Dark Holds no Terrors* (1980) is to go to Bombay to study medicine. She might be able to browbeat her father into agreeing but the mother with whom she has a tense relationship is adamant. They do not have the money to pay for her medical education *and* to provide her with a dowry. Sarita wins in the end but at a cost – the relationship with the family is snapped. She qualifies as a doctor, becomes a successful paediatrician and does not return to her parental home until long after the mother is dead.[23]

Desai presents the problem in a more complex way in her second novel, *Voices in the City* (1965). Amla, an artist, gets work as a commercial illustrator in Calcutta. She should feel glad because her older sister, Monisha, did not have such freedom and was married off to a pompous, insensitive bureaucrat. Her aunt, Lila Chatterjee, who belongs to an earlier generation of feminists, gets irritated by Amla's lack of interest in her work or any desire to pursue her art seriously. Lila keeps reminding Amla that she is fortunate to belong to the 'free generation'. Lila had wanted to be a doctor but instead had to become first a nurse and then a social worker. Amla has all the freedom but no zest, no spirit. She cannot tell her aunt the thoughts that trouble her – her infatuation with a much older man, her concern for her married sister who is obviously unhappy and, above all, a growing realisation that the work she does might be serving negative social forces and not helping people.[24]

The question raised in Desai's exploration of Amla's situation – freedom, but for what? – is brought to the fore by Sonali, a senior civil servant in Sahgal's *Rich Like Us*. She has not paid attention to the curtailment of civil liberties, the police brutality exercised against demonstrating students, until she is personally involved. As joint secretary at the Ministry of Industry she must grant applications to industrialists for new economic ventures. Because she is not satisfied with a particular proposal and rejects it she is summarily dismissed from her post and transferred to a junior position outside of Delhi. The entrepreneurs who had sought the application are in secret discussions with powerful politicians and are furious with Sonali's interference. It is only at this point, humiliated and angry, that Sonali begins examining her so-called career. She, like her peers, has been blind to the realities of India. Cocooned in a safe world, cut off from what is really taking place under the Emergency, Sonali has to expose the self-deception in her existence. She decides to resign from the civil service to take up, at a reduced salary, the position of a history researcher, which will enable her to regain some links with her country's past so as to understand its present condition.[25]

The second area within the family which women find restricts their freedom concerns the relationship with the husband. Because the world the five writers depict is generally that of upper middle-class women the usual constraints, such as the tyranny of the mother-in-law and other members of the husband's family or the onerous burden of domestic chores, are absent. These women have ample leisure thanks to domestic servants, plenty of space in their well-appointed homes and the freedom of physical mobility, which allows escape – shopping sprees, island retreats, going abroad – as marital tension increases.

Yet there are barriers to their freedom. The very upper middle-class which affords them material comforts also makes demands on the way they should behave and pre-scribes their roles. Simrit, in Sahgal's *The Day in Shadow* (1971), has had a happy marriage. Her husband is a successful businessman. She likes to write and enjoys being a mother. Then things change. The husband's entrepreneurial skills take him into bigger ventures with foreign partners. The house is periodically refurbished with more expensive objects. Simrit, who loves permanence even in the things around her, begins to resent the steady accumulation of material goods in their lives. Then she realises that her husband is involved in the international arms trade. She asks for a respite from her role as wife: she can no longer 'follow the goals Som had set for himself, and the inability seemed to be spreading through her veins, affecting the very womb of her desires . . . '[26] Som's fury provokes him into manipulating a cunning divorce settlement which is financially disastrous for Simrit. Yet it is through this very difficult ordeal that she finds new courage and is able to continue with her writing and contemplate a future with a sincere and idealistic political activist.

For Pritam freedom from an unhappy marriage encompassed getting a divorce and living with those she chose to love, as she writes with great honesty and poignancy in her autobiography. Pritam, in her love poetry, seeks freedom to love as she chooses, even if the love she cherishes turns out to be a transient experience. If it is physical desire, so be it, as she expresses in 'Heat of Fire':[27]

> If I warm my hands at the fire of lust
> I know I will blacken them
> But I know I shall be warm.
> And perhaps the day will come
> When someone with blackened hands
> Will be able to shake conventions.

The love poetry of Kamala Das presents a very different world from that of Pritam. Pritam treats of love in its mediaeval Indian setting in which physical, heterosexual love and divine love were intimately connected. Her verse, even when concerned with the transience of the relationship, expresses a sense of joy and even exuberance. For Das there is the occasional moment of happiness but the search for freedom through love outside of marriage does not work. Her autobiographical, 'confessional' type of poetry reveals the woman who, as the poetic voice in the great majority of her verse, seeks love to prove something to the selfish, possessive husband persona. In 'The Old Playhouse' the husband 'planned to tame a swallow, to hold her . . . so that she would forget . . . her nature, the urge to fly.' The wife could only cower beneath his 'monstrous ego' and become a dwarf.[28] But she recovers her spirit. In 'I Shall Some Day' she vows that she will leave the cocoon the husband has built around her:

I shall some day take
Wings, fly around, as often petals,
Do when free in air.[29]

She does but the flight drops into the mire. Her metaphors for the love she needs become harsh for she can find only lust. The names of the poems are revealing – 'Convicts', 'The Freaks', 'Prisoner' – for the search is tarnished. She sought love but finds nothing more than 'skin's lazy hungers' and the heart 'an empty cistern' filling itself 'through coiling snakes of silence'.[30] Fulfilment and contentment will have to be found elsewhere than, in her own words, the 'adultery I too tried for a short while'.[31] Unlike Pritam, who finds in the very act of physical union some sort of transcendence, Das feels the stern puritanism of her Gandhian family and considers this kind of escape sinful. 'We have spent our youth in gentle sinning' nailed to soft beds.[32] She has to turn to another part of the motherland's inheritance – to her ethnic culture, her roots in Malabar, for a resolution.

The last part of the search for freedom within the family is related to the figure and role of the mother. It is here that the women writers under discussion reveal certain traditional attitudes. There is first of all the profound love of children in most of the younger women depicted in the fiction. The ones who seem estranged from their offspring are the older mothers. Sarita's mother in Deshpande's novel, *The Dark Holds No Terrors*, nursing a suspicion that Sarita was responsible for the accidental death of her younger brother, is not prepared to let her daughter know that she is dying of cancer. Nanda Kaul with a brood of children, grandchildren and even a great-grandchild, in Desai's novel, *Fire on the Mountain* (1977), has to admit when she faces up to her self-deception, that the children were 'all alien to her nature. She neither understood nor loved them.'[33] They are the exceptions because in the majority the love of children is quite marked. Sahgal's character, Simrit in *The Day in Shadow*, despite a financially crippling divorce, takes custody of her several – the number remains unspecified – children and enjoys being with them. In another of her novels, *Storm in Chandigarh*, Saroj, though married to a jealous husband who threatens her with violence periodically, has enjoyed her two earlier pregnancies and derives great satisfaction from the child she is carrying in her womb.[34] Pritam landed herself in what could have been a law suit over her joyous evocation of bearing a child, because the mother in her poem was visualised as the mother of Guru Nanak, the founder of the Sikh religion. And the interesting and elaborately formed poem, 'Nine Dreams and the Annunciation', describes both the saint's mother's awareness, through her visions, that she is carrying a very special child in her womb; and the human, earthy reminders of the physical sensations of pregnancy.[35]

Traditional attitudes of pity for the barren woman find expression in Pritam's short story, 'Stench of Kerosene'[36] and Desai's novel, *Voices in the City*. Guleri, a peasant woman, and Monisha, an educated modern woman, both kill themselves by immolation because they are barren.[37]

Child-bearing is not seen as an impediment to freedom. The need for abortion, now legalised in India, scarcely figures in these works. Sahgal provides a single instance of a back street abortion.[38] Desai's character Sita, in *Where Shall We Go This Summer*, does not want her fifth pregnancy. Yet, instead of getting an abortion, she behaves in a strange manner, running off to an island retreat because, as she explains to her husband, she wants to keep the child in her womb for ever, not to kill it.[39] She is persuaded by the husband to return to 'normal' and have the baby delivered in hospital.[40] Sita's little act of defiance – telling her husband that she *could* go against his wishes – is over.

The only writer who treats the theme of abortion seriously is Deshpande. She introduces it in a story included in her very first collection. 'The Death of a Child' shows a married woman feeling trapped when she is pregnant for the third time in less than four years. The husband agrees to an abortion, which now can be performed safely in Indian hospitals. At the end she comes home without a child but can hear a ghost whimpering and is overcome with grief.[41] Ten years on in her most recent novel, *That Long Silence*, she returns to the subject. Jaya has an abortion without telling her husband and then forgets all about it. The memory of it does not recur until the marriage is facing a crisis, when Jaya remembers with distress how she has betrayed her husband.[42] She has now to examine her life as a wife and mother and find a new formulation of her responsibility to husband and children. This, for her, is the heart of freedom.

V

In the final section of this essay we will return to the figure of the motherland and its vital significance. Mother India emerges in the connections, linkages and allusions the writers employ as a device to resolve some of the problematic situations their women characters face in their search for freedom. It is not, of course, Mother India in either the popular nineteenth-century sense of a semi-divine figure, nor a political abstraction defined as India, for these writers cannot be described as simple nationalists. Rather, the motherland provides an anchor for the writers; it provides perspectives on India's complex past; its religious and philosophical contributions and the ethical precepts of sacred texts and popular mythology.

Three aspects of the motherland will be considered in the works of these writers: ideas of love, ideas of the ethical life, and a positive awareness of the force of Indian civilisation.

One of the striking features of much of the work is the natural way in which physical love between a man and a woman is treated. Excluding Das, with her sense of sin when her poetic persona seeks love outside of marriage, the others accept love relationships with a singular absence of guilt. This is remarkable in view of the intrusion of puritanism into middle-class Indian attitudes since the nineteenth century. Victorianism, missionary work, the various reformist movements within Hinduism that did not approve of sexuality being associated with religion and, since the First World War, the puritanism of Gandhian views with their emphasis on chastity, self-control and abstinence have distorted a natural or a culturally accepted view of sexual love found in an earlier period in which men and women were partners in love. Tamil Sangam poetry reveals such a delightful equality.[43]

Love in mediaeval India found expression in so many cultural forms – the love of Radha and Krishna celebrated in poetry, song and dance, the erotic sculpture of the temples of Konarak and Khajuraho and the use of the love metaphor for mystical expressions of Vaishnav and Sufi poets. The boundaries between physical, sexual love and divine love became blurred. There were also the populist, dissenting movements expressing their religious devotion through *bhakti* and new expressions of love. Women saint-poets of that period are being removed from the margins of history where they had been placed as unreal objects of veneration. Feminist readings today are discovering a new world of rebellion and early women's liberation in these women's verse.[44]

Amrita Pritam's poetry expresses some of the many strands of love as found in Indian cultures – tribal fertility rites, devotional love, ecstasy and the easy natural love of the classical Tamil poems.[45] It finds an echo in the natural way in which so many of the women characters find pleasure in their physical relations with men instead of the guilt and remorse they are saddled with in most treatments of relationship outside marriage in Indian literature.

For Sahgal's women – Rashmi, Nita, Simrit, Devi, to name but some – the experience is both an act of self-assertion and emotional satisfaction.[46] Indu's brief sexual encounter with her cousin, Naren, in Deshpande's *Roots and Shadows*, has more complex motives than self-affirmation, related as it is to her intense love for her husband. A natural experience without any 'lingering feelings' to make her 'uncomfortable' with her detached cousin will be liberating, not emotionally upsetting.[47]

India's ancient philosophies and ethical precepts are frequently invoked by these women in their art. Desai and Deshpande use the *Bhagavadgita (The Song Celestial)* which is the most accessible of Hindu sacred works. It is part of the epic *Mahabharata* and is a dialogue between the warrior-prince, Arjuna, and Krishna, his deity, who is also acting as his charioteer. At the heart of the *Gita* and of much of Hindu ethics lies the notion of *dharma*, which can be loosely translated as doing one's rightful duty, appropriate to one's role in life, but in a selfless way. The excerpts used by Desai in *Voices in the City* describe the man of wisdom who is free from attachment, fear and anger. Monisha, the barren and unhappy wife who reads the *Gita* perhaps to ease her mind, fails to learn from its message for she takes her own life.

For Deshpande the very last part of the Gita, 'Do as you desire' is meaningful for the resolution of the crisis in Jaya's life in *That Long Silence*. For years she and her husband, Mohan, have lived in reasonable harmony. Now he is in trouble and fears for his job. She should support and encourage him but she cannot because of a lifetime of evading serious issues. She sees herself as Gandhari, another figure from the *Mahabharata*, who bandaged her eyes to be as handicapped as her husband, a blind king. Jaya has been blinkered in her refusal to examine her own life or her marriage. The *Gita* phrase is interpreted as an expression of human free will. God Krishna tells Arjuna what the right *dharma* is for a warrior but it is up to Arjuna to do as he desires – obey his *dharma* or violate it. For Jaya too there must be a search for her *dharma* and then to follow it: to be a true partner, listening, speaking and understanding that she and Mohan are combined in their mutual *dharma*.[48]

The third connection with the motherland and women's search for freedom is linked to the significance of being part of India's history, or of being connected to a coherent cultural past. It is not simply an impersonal awareness but one closely associated with the family and ancestors.

This is the meaning her ancestral home has for the poetic persona in Das' verse. Defeated in her search for happiness and fulfilment through love, she returns to her matrilineal home in Kerala, the home of her maternal ancestors: grandmothers, great-grandmothers and those who came before. Some of Das' best poems express this longing to recapture the love and happiness and dignity she had found in the *tarwad*, the Nair matrilineal family house. In 'Blood' she describes the stories of past glories narrated to her by her great-grandmother. 'My Grandmother's House', probably her most famous poem, is a nostalgic memory of a house 'where once I received love', but which has now withdrawn into silence and where the snakes are among the books in the great library.[49]

Similarly Bim in Desai's *Clear Light of Day* discovers it as she listens to a recital of classical north Indian music. She has found her freedom by undertaking all her responsibilities to her family and pursuing her studies to become a history lecturer. She has had disappointments, such as the departure from the family home of her brother. But listening to the music she feels an intimacy with the soil and the people who have inhabited the land of Delhi:

> . . . That soil contained all time, past and future in it . . .
> It was where her deepest self lived, and the deepest selves
> of her sister and brothers and all those who shared that
> time with her.[50]

Sonali in Sahgal's *Rich Like Us* has had to fight through her moral blindness in the highest ranks of the bureaucracy and regain her integrity and freedom by resigning. She is now a history researcher. But even as she reads about the greatness of India's attainments in the seventeenth century she realises that she is still a young woman 'alive, with my own century stretched out before me, waiting to be lived'.[51]

Notes

1 See the treatment in women's fiction in Tamil in CS Lakshmi, *The Face Behind the Mask*, Vikas, Delhi, 1984.

2 Kumari Jayawardena, *Feminism and Nationalism in the Third World*, Zed Books, London, 1986, pp. 73–108.

3 Sarojini Naidu, 'To India', *The Golden Threshold*, Heinemann, London, 1905.

4 See *Manushi: A Journal about Women and Society* (founded in 1979); Madhu Kishwar and Ruth Vanita, eds., *In Search of Anwers: Indian Women's Voices from Manushi*, Zed Books, London, 1984; Stree Shakti Sanghatana, *We Were Making History*, Kali for Women, Delhi, 1989; Lola Chatterji, ed., *Woman/Image/Text*, Trianka Publications, Delhi, 1986; Kumkum Sangari and Sudesh Vaid, eds., *Recasting Women*, Kali for Women, Delhi, 1989.

5 See Amrita Pritam, *Black Rose* (English versions of the Punjabi), translated by Charles Brasch, Nagmani Pubs, Delhi, n.d.; *Existence and other Poems* (English versions of the Punjabi), translated by Mahendra Kulasrestha, Nagmani Pubs, Delhi, 1967; *Selected Poems*, ed. Khushwant Singh, Bharatiya Jnanpith Publications, Delhi, 1982.

6 Amrita Pritam, *Life and Times* (translated from the Panjabi, *Rasidi Ticket*), Vikas Publishing, Delhi, 1989.

7 *Black Rose*, p. 25.

8 Kamala Das, 'An Introduction', *The Old Playhouse and other Poems*, Sangam Books, London, 1986, p. 26.

9 Kamala Das, *My Story* (translated from the Malayalam by the author), Sterling Pubs, Delhi, 1988.

10 Kamala Das, 'Summer Vacation', in Lakshmi Holmstrom, ed., *The Inner Courtyard: Stories by Indian Women*, Virago, London, 1990.

11 AL Basham, *The Wonder That Was India* (translated from the Sanskrit by AL Basham), Fontana, London, 1971, p. 182.

12 See excerpts from Mahatma Gandhi's own works, *All Men Are Brothers*, Unesco, 1959, pp. 160–167; for a critique see Jayawardena, pp. 95–97.

13 Nayantara Sahgal, *A Time to be Happy*, Knopf, New York, 1958, pp. 32–46, 67–71.

14 Nayantara Sahgal, *This Time of Morning*, Norton, New York, 1965, p. 211.

15 Nayantara Sahgal, *This Time of Morning*, p. 125.

16 Amrita Pritam, *The Skeleton* (translated from the Panjabi *Pinjar* by Khushwant Singh), Orient Paperbacks, Delhi, 1973, p. 92.

17 Kamala Das, *My Story*, pp. 13–14.

18 Kamala Das, 'An Introduction', p. 26.

19 Kamala Das, 'An Introduction', p. 27.

20 Shashi Deshpande, *Roots and Shadows*, Orient Longmans, Bombay, 1983, p. 15.

21 Anita Desai, *Clear Light of Day*, Penguin Books, Harmondsworth, 1980, pp. 140–141.

22 Nayantara Sahgal, *A Time to be Happy*, pp. 113, 150–51, 222–223.

23 Shashi Deshpande, *The Dark Holds No Terrors*, Vikas, Delhi, 1980, pp. 130–131.

24 Anita Desai, *Voices in the City*, Orient Paperbacks, Delhi, 1965, pp. 145–146, 157–158, 173–175.

25 Nayantara Sahgal, *Rich Like Us*, Heinemann, London, 1985, pp. 24–25.

26 Nayantara Sahgal, *The Day in Shadow*, Vikas, Delhi, 1971, p. 90.

27 Amrita Pritam, *Black Rose*, p. 24.

28 Kamala Das, *The Old Playhouse and other Poems*, p. 1.

29 Kamala Das, *ibid.*, p. 48.

30 Kamala Das, 'The Freaks', *ibid.* p. 11.

31 Kamala Das, *My Story*, pp. 182–184.

32 Kamala Das, 'The Descendants', *The Old Playhouse*, p. 33.

33 Anita Desai, *Fire on the Mountain*, Penguin, Harmondsworth, 1977, p. 145.

34 Nayantara Sahgal, *Storm in Chandigarh*, Orient Paperbacks, Delhi, 1970, pp. 184–185.

35 Amrita Pritam, *Selected Poems*, pp. 149–155.

36 Amrita Pritam, 'Stench of Kerosene', in Ranjana Ash, ed., *Short Stories from India, Pakistan and Bangladesh*, Harrap, London, 1980, pp. 90–95.

37 Anita Desai, *Voices in the City*, pp. 235–247.

38 Nayantara Sahgal, *Storm In Chandigarh*, pp. 216–217.

39 Anita Desai, *Where Shall We Go This Summer*, Orient Paperbacks, Delhi, 1982, pp. 34–35.

40 Anita Desai, *ibid.* pp. 148–155.

41 Shashi Deshpande, 'The Death of a Child', in *The Legacy and other Stories*, Writers Workshop, Calcutta, 1978, pp. 86–95.

42   Shashi Deshpande, *That Long Silence*, Virago, London, 1988, pp. 130–131.

43   See AK Ramanujan's superb translations of classical Tamil love poetry in *The Interior Landscape*, Unesco Collection, Clarion Books, Delhi, 1971.

44   See the tenth anniversary issue of *Manushi* (1989) which is on women *bhakta* poets.

45   Amrita Pritam, 'Knot', 'Talk' in *Black Rose*, pp. 29 and 10. Also 'Nagpanchami', in *Selected Poems*, p. 35.

46   Rashmi and Nita in *This Time of Morning* choose to have brief relations with a Danish architect and a politician respectively; Simrit in *The Day in Shadow* liberates herself from the shadow of a vindictive divorce by letting herself develop what might become a long-term loving relationship with a Christian political idealist. Devi finds renewing an old love affair with a British journalist a way of recovering herself in *A Situation in New Delhi*, London Magazine Editions, 1977.

47   Shashi Deshpande *Roots and Shadows*, pp. 188–189.

48   Shashi Deshpande, *That Long Silence*, pp. 192–193.

49   Kamala Das, *The Old Playhouse and Other Poems*, pp. 17 and 32.

50   Anita Desai, *Clear Light of Day*, p. 182.

51   Nayantara Sahgal, *Rich Like Us*, p. 234.

Helen Kanitkar

'Heaven Lies beneath her Feet'? Mother Figures in Selected Indo-Anglian Novels

Indian women writing in English hold a unique position in the interpretation of the traditions and beliefs of South Asian culture, especially in so far as women are concerned. They are marginal writers, who shrewdly observe and record, yet sympathetically understand, the values and motivations of Indian society, while maintaining an awareness of sources of misunderstanding and incomprehension among western readers. Their readership is likely to be mainly western, so some explanation of incidents and terminology may be called for, though this should not obtrude to the extent of boring, or, worse, irritating western readers with a knowledge of India, or Indian readers of that elite group which enjoys literature in English while remaining fully versed in tra-ditional Indian life, culture and social norms. These Indian women authors tread delicately in order to avoid mere fasci-nation with the exoticisms of arranged marriage, fearsome mothers-in-law, the ghostly memories of *sati*, or the tensions of the joint family, and yet all these cannot be ignored, as they are part of the discourse of South Asian life. Such mat-ters should rather form the background of traditional influence to daily existence, in the forefront of which real flesh and blood characters act out their worries, ambitions, loves and hatreds, while involving readers in universals of concern rather than the limitations of communal microcosms.

The literary marginality of Indian writers in English makes them interpreters of cultural patterns familiar to them, in a language which is often considered alien to the concepts recorded. Such a judgment may not take account fully of the place held by English in India's linguistic eclecticism. English is a language of India now; to some Indians it is their mother-tongue, spoken in the home, while others are so strongly influenced by its literature that the ideals and attitudes of the society portrayed therein become as, if not more, real and effectual than the social setting surrounding them, as in the childhood of Bim and Raja in Anita Desai's *Clear Light of Day*.[1] KR Srinivasa Iyengar has summed up the situation neatly: ' . . . Indian writing in English is but one of the voices in which India speaks. It is a new voice, no doubt, but it is as much Indian as the others.'[2] Since English is also a medium of international communication it opens up a wide readership for the Indo-Anglian writer, who may be thought of as an 'insider–outsider', one who uses available means of communication to reveal to those outside the mother-culture what are the innermost motivations of those within it, which have, gradually and imperceptibly from birth, influenced individual attitudes, judgment, ambitions and desires. Let Shashi Deshpande give a writer's viewpoint: ' . . . everyone has a right to choose a language . . . What's important is not the language in which one thinks, but how good the literature is.'[3]

For present purposes in this paper the term 'mother-culture' implies those internalised values and the resulting expectations of social interaction and response built up through each individual's constantly extending experience of her society's norms throughout childhood and adolescence. The language through which these are meaningfully expressed and effectively learned from babyhood is the mother-tongue.

In this paper three novels by two major modern writers

have been chosen for primary analysis: *That Long Silence*⁴ by Shashi Deshpande, and Anita Desai's *The Village by the Sea*⁵ and *Clear Light of Day*. The authors delve into the deep 'self-places' of very different Indian women; they use differing styles of writing, of narrative, of imagery, in their revealing and discovery of selfhood, and in their perceptions of the mother's role in the family. Those Indian women writers who have chosen English as their medium of expression can, through their experience of their mother-culture, reveal to their readership those social and cultural parameters which define the Indian wife and mother, and the processes which are utilised to mould the individual into a traditionally acceptable conformity. Their sensitivity to the way in which processes of change are beginning to stir in this area of Indian family life can alert us to the reality of the sometimes painful experience of decision-making and the responsibilities this brings to twentieth-century Indian women.

Jaya, in *That Long Silence*, begins to learn how unused she is to deciding upon even trivial matters of daily life; her husband, Mohan, is the one who always knows best what the family should have, while Jaya simply 'went along with him': 'But I cannot blame Mohan, for even if he had asked me – what do you want? – I would have found it hard to give him a reply . . . To know what you want – I have been denied that.'⁶ When Mohan leaves home, bemused and angered by what he believes to be Jaya laughing at him, she cannot even bring herself to move, since her source of direction has gone. She expresses her feelings through the rituals of a childhood game; like a child, she needs to be told what to do, but the teller is gone:

Simon says kneel down, the order came, and we knelt. Simon says clap your hands and we clapped our hands. An order without Simon's name tagged on to it had been no order at all in that childhood game of ours and we had stood rock still, unmoving. It was like that for me now –

the mysterious, all-powerful Simon, the Simon who had brooked no rival had disappeared.
And I could do nothing. I was overcome by a paralysis of will and sat staring at my slipper dangling from my toes, unable to move.[7]

The limitations to decision-making by women are set by the family structure, by the system of status and rank within it, and by those who wield the economic muscle. What use is it to make decisions, when there is no power to implement them? Jaya thinks of her maternal uncle's wife:

Perhaps the truth was that Vanitamami had never known what it was to choose. Since the day she got married she, like the rest of Ai's family, was dominated and ruled by that ghoul, her mother-in-law . . . Even Vanitamami's saris were chosen for her by the old woman.[8]

Vanitamami had suffered the terrible curse of childlessness, so she never enjoyed a mother-in-law's doctrinaire privileges in her own home, in her turn. Motherhood it is that reveals a route towards the exercise of authority for women, at least within the family, and the way in which they choose to exert that authority, to maximise their influence, is dependent on their arts of manipulation, the strength of their affective ties, especially with sons, and the intensity of their need for, and ability to achieve, self-expression and self-assertion. Some, consciously, or unconsciously, are seen to manipulate that internalised concept of *dharma*, personal duty, that Indian husbands/sons may be guided by; Jaya sees her father as the victim of the conflicting needs of his mother (*ajji*) and wife (Ai): 'Appa cycling three miles into town to see *ajji* and three miles back home to Ai again, cycling between the two women, up and down the undulating roads, his heart pumping furiously. Yes, that's right, they are responsible for his death, those two women.'[9] Each aspect of this cycle ride symbolises a wearying necessity of Appa's life; his mother and his wife have an unbridgeable distance between them,

which he must somehow try to span; 'up and down' go his
emotions as he moves from one to the other; his heart, as
traditionally the organ of affection, pumps 'furiously' as it
tries to cope with the pressures of these differing, incompatible demands. Yet the two women did not *kill* Appa; their
demands on him, both physical and emotional, did not have
that as their motive. Mother and wife merely accepted,
expected, what it was the husband/son's duty to give, and
thus shared the responsibility for his eventual collapse from
a strain which he, nevertheless, would not have presumed to
question. There is a suggestion here that the burden of family
responsibility resting on its male members is a consequence
of social norms which determine women's spheres of action,
restricting them to the home or to such work outside the
home which is acceptable to male relations. What *is* acceptable, of course, it is the responsibility of those males to
decide.

Mohan is proud to tell his friends that his wife Jaya is a
writer; in fact, his pride in her is limited to her magazine
articles – her self-revelatory stories are an embarrassment to
him, and she relinquishes that side of her work because of
this.

The traditional Indian wifely ideal is that of a woman
trained for marriage and the efficient performance of domestic tasks for the benefit of husband and children, regardless
of what work she may undertake outside the home. This
selfless lifestyle deifies yet subordinates women; the divinity
is as unattainable as the degrees of sacrifice necessary to obtain
it. Not for nothing is the mother goddess a powerful force
– perhaps even *the* most powerful force – in the Hindu pan-
theon; she is seen as the beneficent Parvati; Lakshmi, the
fortunate one; Durga, the fearsome destroyer of evil; or Kali,
the dread, merciless oppressor. All these are personifications
of personality traits; all can be found in one and the same
person at different times, though one will be dominant, forming that person's 'character'.

In Hinduism Maha Devi, the Great Goddess, shows all

these attributes in her various manifestations; but above them all is her character as Mother, as Shakti, the main creative force which stimulates the male deity, Shiva, to rouse himself to the dance of regeneration. The continuance of life – the motivation of conception, nurturing, nourishing, healing, educating, protecting – all this lies in the Mother's power; such an aweful power is the focus of both devotion and dread, possessing as it does the possibilities of both creation and dissolution.

The goddess Kali represents the uncontrolled destructive force of the Maha Devi. It is interesting that, mythologically, her lust to kill can be controlled only by her consort Shiva, either feigning death on the battlefield, so that, by dancing on the corpse of her husband, Kali's rage is calmed; or by his appearance as a crying baby – Kali's motherly instincts are aroused by this child/husband, she is distracted from slaughter, and the world restored to normality.

Durga, the warrior aspect of the Great Goddess, whose origins probably pre–date Hinduism, activates her destructive powers at the behest of the male deities, from whom she is said to have sprung; a mythological illustration of the control of female potential, so characteristic of Indian society. The arrival of the warlike male Vedic deities at the time of the Aryan conquest of northern India, thus altered worshippers' perception of Maha Devi, but could not destroy it. The Goddess, like woman, is essential to society, but her power, her potential, like that of woman, has to be controlled – by man, of course – if society is to retain its male-dominated stability. The Indian family, the focus of social activity in the sub-continent, is created and maintained by the fecundity of its female members, but, entering it as outsiders as they do, their potential for disruption is great and, without the extended family's controlling united male dominance, partition of property and dissolution of the family unit as a result of the machinations of these Kaliesque figures may ensue.

The structure of a mythology not only *arises* from the society within which it is meaningful; it also *functions* as a mechanism for safeguarding and codifying, as well as sanctioning, accepted values and beliefs, and validating them in practice. B Malinowski has summed up its sociological significance thus: 'The function of myth, briefly, is to strengthen tradition and endow it with a greater value and prestige by tracing it back to a higher, better, more supernatural reality of initial events.'[10]

I suggest, therefore, that the mythological encapsulation of Hindu understanding of the Great Goddess not only reinforces the nurturing function of womanhood, but also challenges the popular passive role of women in Indian society through the active Durga/Kali images, even though their activity is usually viewed as destructive; although, in the case of the disciplined Durga, such destruction is 'all in a good cause'.

Thus, the women of a family can inspire fear *or* devotion, constitute threat *or* blessing: for the Indian mother, Parvati is held as the ideal, though, as a new wife entering her husband's home, she is viewed as Lakshmi, bringer of good luck and wealth (literally, in the form of dowry). This 'Lakshmi' usually finds that to be perceived as the ideal, 'Parvati', demands not so much a denial of self and what is owed to the self in terms of development of potential (for denial implies making a decision, which is not a new bride's responsibility), as a blotting-out, a withering, of self-wish, self-ambition, self-fulfilment, and utter identification with the desires, aims and welfare of the husband and his family.[11] It is this household goddess whose image has given meaning to the popular saying 'Heaven lies beneath your mother's feet', implying that even the polluted earth is made pure, holy, full of divine bliss, by contact with a mother's humblest part. Even Jaya's maternal uncle's wife's sister, always referred to as 'our poor Venu' when alive, pitied because of constant child-bearing and lack of home comforts, nevertheless achieved, after her death, the veneration due to a mother, and the envy of other women of the family because of the continuing devotion shown by her son: a large photograph of his mother hangs in the hall, a garland of fresh flowers festooning it. "'He gets fresh flowers every day, however expensive they are,'' Vanitamami had whispered to me admiringly, wistfully, envying, it seemed her dead sister who had been "our poor Venu" when alive.'[12]

But we have been thinking only of the ideal; no real woman can achieve this kind of sainthood under the demands of everyday life. Women are given such a far-distant mark to aim at that they are foredoomed to failure; they carry this inherent, culturally determined shortfall which can result in a destructive negative self-image if pressed to an extreme. Important, though, is this over-ambitious perfection set before women, and perhaps even more potently, before men, since it represents an ideal of service, of suffering, of silence, necessitating a restraining of personal ambition, assertion of will and expression of selfhood, which has led to a 'long silence' only now being effectively broken, especially in the revelatory, analytical and challenging novels of the women writers who are our theme.

In *That Long Silence* Deshpande gives centre stage to an educated, urban wife and mother, Jaya (the meaning of which name, 'Victory', is repeatedly emphasised to give an ironic twist to the tale). Suspicion of professional malpractice and threatened unemployment creep ever closer to her husband; Jaya has to face this challenge and readjust to a humbler, more inconvenient lifestyle, which she thought she had left behind her. Gradually the return to her maternal uncle's small flat, and the memories it evokes of the influences of her childhood and teenage years, result in a questioning of her own purposes in life, and an examination of the 'self' that has been bound and unexpressed in her since marriage. This, she discovers, is 'a cruel process'[13] and, forced to sift out what she considers irrelevancies in her life, she is left with: 'I was born. My father died when I was fifteen. I got married to Mohan. I have two children and I did not let a third live.'[14] These important incidents, we note, are centred round: father, husband, children – pivots of a woman's existence.

That Long Silence shows Jaya crawling painfully towards, first, a realisation of her non-functioning as an individual in her own right; second, the dawning of the irrationality of this; and third, an awareness of her potential through an acknowledgment that the multitude of experiences she has been through, unique to herself in their implications and influence, have made her what she is, her own person: 'I'm Mohan's wife, I had thought, and cut off the bits of me that had refused to be Mohan's wife. Now I know that kind of a fragmentation is not possible. The child, hands in pockets, has been with me through the years. She is with me still.'[15] Jaya finally rejects the image of herself and her husband yoked together like bullocks, moving involuntarily, choiceless and in unison, with which she began her story, but to reach this stage she has remembered and analysed a whole series of meaningful flashbacks, incidents of her childhood and early married life, which have coerced her into acquiescence and silent acceptance. This handing over of responsibility for what happens, for what she does or fails to do, also enables her, in her own mind, to escape any blame for failure: she can blame her father; Ai her mother; her brothers; Mohan her husband – anyone but herself, until the end of the book, when she is led to the assumption of responsibility, and the courage to bear blame.

Two traumatic experiences bring her to full realisation of herself. Firstly, throughout their stay in Jaya's maternal uncle's flat, Mohan, in his anxiety about his job and possible legal proceedings, which have caused the temporary abandonment of their home, has more and more depended upon her as a mother: 'Jaya', he calls repeatedly when she is not near, 'Jaya!' He spends most of his time lying on the bed, sleeping or pondering his misfortunes. Hardly can he stir himself to have a wash. He does not explain in detail the reasons for his worry, and Jaya does not probe. She observes, but maintains her silence, mindful of the shock Mohan received when, early in their marriage, she had lost her temper:

. . . 'How could you? I never thought my wife could say such things to me. You're my wife . . . ' he had kept repeating . . . But what had really shaken me that day had been the distaste I'd seen on Mohan's face when I'd got into a temper. He had looked at me as if my emotions had made me ugly, as if I'd got bloated with them. Later, when I knew him better, I realised that to him anger made a woman 'unwomanly'. 'My mother never raised her voice against my father, however badly he behaved to her,' he had said to me once. I had learnt to control my anger after that . . . [16]

This repression of feelings, angry or otherwise, leads to a growing lack of communication between the couple. 'The vocabulary of love . . . had passed us by; so too had the vocabulary of anger', discovers Jaya; the heights of married life were not part of experience, neither were the depths. A monotony bore them onward, unrelieved even by the mechanics of sex, also silent. When crisis strikes, they are unable to talk things through, and Jaya is unable even to express concern for her husband, though she feels his need, even as she would feel that of a child. Even so, the parallel she draws is that of an unresponsive mother who has to be forced into caring, while the child is deformed, unable to move, to do anything for itself except clutch at its mother:

For some reason, on hearing him call out to me, I suddenly remembered Ramukaka's and Shantakaki's youngest, a hydrocephalic. I thought of him lying on the ground, patiently still, that pathetic, monstrously large head unmoving. His eyes were the only thing in that body that moved in frantic search of his mother, and only when she came into the room were they at peace. When she sat near him, he clutched at her sari, and if she moved away, he whimpered, the eyes making desperate attempts, it seemed, to follow her. But Shantakaki kept away from him as much as possible, she came to him only when *ajji*, a stern mother-in-law, shamed her into doing so. [17]

Jaya, like the many women she remembers in her family circle, has become adept at assessing her husband's moods; and tailoring her responses, or, more often, lack of them, to his comments. When Mohan bemoans his family responsibilities her instinct is to point out how he has encouraged dependency in the past, in order to demonstrate his prosperity and position: 'But the words remained unsaid. I knew his mood was best met with silence. And I was right. By the time we sat down to dinner, he was in a more agreeable mood.'[18] So many occasions of crisis experienced and observed by Jaya have been met by women's silences, and, though really against her nature, her response has been to conform to what is acceptable, right, womanly. A man is heard beating his wife; to his shouted questions her only answers are tears, and, poignantly enough, the moan 'Ai, Ai' – 'Mother, mother'. Mohan's own drunken father comes home late, demands chillies with his meal, throws the food against the wall and stalks out. His wife merely cleans the mess, gets chillies from a neighbour and re-cooks the meal, waiting for her husband's return before eating herself:

> [Mohan] saw strength in the woman sitting silently in front of the fire, but I saw despair. I saw a despair so great that it would not voice itself. I saw a struggle so bitter that silence was the only weapon. Silence and surrender.[19]

When Mohan finally explodes from the tension of his anxieties and the boredom of life in the small Bombay flat which they have made their temporary home, Jaya finds she has lost the art of reply. He blames her for apparent unconcern, for trying to avoid him and his problems by seeking others' company, for the way he has been driven into business malpractice in order to win promotion so as to afford a better life for her and their children. The tangles of their life together begin to unravel before Jaya, but not with constructive discussion, only destructive anger. Deshpande's vocabulary becomes sharp and threatening: 'I was under attack'; 'I cringed under his anger'; 'He had armed himself with an anger . . . My own feeble defences had no chance before this fierce onslaught'; 'real bitterness clawed its way through this self-mockery'; 'I was . . . chained to his dream'; ' . . . nothing could stop him. It was like a deluge'. Mohan's accusations, some fair, some not so, are received with incredulity, but to him they represent his incomprehension of all women, all women summed up in the figure of his wife before him. To Jaya, his disappointment in the change he has perceived in her since coming to the flat suddenly recalls her baby son, and the hysteria evoked by the trauma of Mohan's anger and desolation refuses control: 'Mohan's face, now what did it remind me of? Yes, Rahul. Rahul had looked like this when I had pulled my nipple or the bottle out of his mouth. Poor Rahul, poor Mohan deprived of the nipple . . . '[20] After this, the silence is complete, for Mohan walks away.

The directionless Jaya receives the practical help of her women neighbours, who accept her explanation of Mohan's absence; they know she must wait, it is not she who can walk away: ' . . . ever since I got married, I had done nothing but wait. Waiting for Mohan to come home, waiting for the children to be born, for them to start school, waiting for them to come home, waiting for the milk, the servant, the local carrier-man . . . '[21] A wife should not put her marriage at risk, for above all it is her husband who gives her a place in society, who ensures her role as a social being. He it is who gives her the sons who will dignify her later. 'A husband is like a sheltering tree,' Jaya's aunt tells her, and no matter how he treats his wife his presence is the most precious thing she has. Even Jaya's servant is heard to remind her complaining daughter-in-law: 'Don't forget he keeps the *kum-kum*[22] on your forehead. What is a woman, without that?'

What indeed? Jaya's nelgect of her needs, her appearance, her household work after Mohan leaves is almost that of a widow. Indeed, she almost persuades herself that Mohan is dead. She rouses herself to seek him in their family house, but he is not there; waiting for her is a second traumatic shock – their son has run away from the friends who have taken him on holiday – run away, but not run home to his parents, to his mother, but, as she eventually discovers, to his paternal uncle, with whom he is able to be himself. Through their mutual affinity they can relax as friends, disregarding kin duties and intergenerational respect. Seeing them at ease together, Jaya's new appreciation of her individuality is confirmed, and it is interesting that, in this book which introduces snippets of the Hindu faith only as asides, and sometimes scornfully, Jaya finds justification for her newly discovered selfhood in the *Bhagavadgita*, in Krishna's last words to Prince Arjuna. These words she finds written in her beloved father's diary; it is as if he is passing on advice to her: 'Krishna confers humanness on Arjuna. "I have given you knowledge. Now you make the choice. The choice is yours. Do as you desire."'

To achieve this humanness, this perception of selfhood, Jaya has suffered the two traumatic shocks of loss of husband and of son, both of whom return by the end of the book, though we are left to decide for ourselves, to make our own choices, as Jaya is, as to how the family will cope with the new base for its relationships. 'We don't change overnight . . . But we can always hope. Without that, life would be impossible. And if there is anything I know now it is this: life has always to be made possible.' Jaya has traced and re-incorporated into herself the meaningful incidents of her youth that have made her what she is; she has held to her given name, Jaya, Victory, and found meaningless her married name, Suhasini, her husband's choice, which is again ironic, since it means 'sweet-smiling', which betrays what Mohan had hoped for, but did not find in his thoughtful, introspective wife. For Jaya, highly literate, capable of more than is being asked of her by husband and family, India offers opportunities, but she has to build up an image of her own self-worth by facing and emerging from challenges to the life-style she has accepted as marked out for her. She does not instigate these challenges herself; they are triggered by the actions of other family members, like boulders thrown in her way which she has to negotiate. Through this experience she finds the path to herself. Perhaps, as the Maha Devi of Hinduism possesses both stability and chaos, creation and destruction within the wholeness of her Self, so the mother goddess of the household, too, has to come to terms with these processes. Jaya returns to the house wherein all she had valued had found its being, only to find an empty, lifeless shell; the dead flowers, the unadorned deities, the loud-cawing crow, bird of carrion, that will not go away, the drowned ants in a jug of water, clinging to each other still – even in death, symbols of those who had lived in the house, all these speak only of an ending. Deepest despair she comes to know in this setting, until a new hope begins to enliven the old, stale relationships. Writing of the Goddess as found in witchcraft beliefs, Luhrmann sums up the experience thus: 'The notion of the Goddess within the practical literature [of magic] is a vision of continuity between chaos and order, destruction and creativity, in which the way to personal empowerment and selfhood leads through the valley of dissolution.'[23] Will Jaya, with her new perception of herself as an individual, win through to her new role and build something from the debris of her former life?

Whatever happens, we can be sure that it will be her own choice, and that she will take responsibility for that choice, and take, too, any consequent blame. Somehow, life will be made possible.

Like Deshpande, Anita Desai, too, concerns herself with the painful problems of the individual faced with social and ideological change in modern India. Traditional values are challenged, and Indian women have to work out their own dignity and individual freedom within the surge towards emancipation. Shyam Asnani has pointed out that the new morality does not imply no-morality, but adaptation to new standards, new demands.[24]

Recognition of the need for this adaptation is the theme of Desai's sensitive novel of a fisher family's life in a coastal village of Western India. It is very close to actuality, although the author is inevitably an observer whose background and values differ widely from those of the actors in the tale. Principal among these are Hari, adolescent son of the family, and Lila, his eldest sister. Vividly shown are the ways in which family responsibilities devolve on these two as sickness incapacitates their mother, drunkenness their father. Hari, alarmed at the deterioration of his family's circumstances, leaves his village with a group of demonstrators who are going to Bombay to protest at a government plan to establish a chemical fertiliser plant in the village; this they see as a threat to their way of life. Hari, however, though almost overwhelmed by the noise, bustle, and traffic of Bombay, stays there to earn money for his family, firstly as an assistant in a roadside café, where he lives, works and eats; later as an apprentice to a watchmaker, who teaches him a trade useful in the modern world, which he perceives to be useful later, on his return to the village, when chemical engineers at the new factory will need their watches repaired. Hari, then, abandons his family in one sense, but with the aim of long-term betterment; Lila, his sister, is left to maintain continuity, to struggle to manufacture short-term solutions to the emergencies of desperate poverty, cope with her deteriorating drunken father, and nurse her weakening mother, while trying to maintain a near-normal daily routine for her two younger sisters.

Both experience a growing maturity, one which imposes on them at an early age the roles determined by traditional values and normative behaviour patterns, but their potential is widened by confrontation with the modern world outside their village, with all it offers economically, industrially, medically. What they achieve they could not have if they had stayed confined in the traditional milieu, and they learn more of what is possible for their generation than their parents ever contemplated.

Though scarcely figuring in the story's action, the sick mother throughout is a symbol, a barometer almost, of the family's plight. At the beginning she is bedridden, but able to speak, to take liquid nourishment, to offer instructions to Lila. Gradually she grows weaker, and the family's fortunes decline with her; she is, indeed, a Lakshmi who, as she fades, takes with her all that is fortunate. Help eventually comes from outside the community, in the shape of a wealthy businessman from Bombay who has a holiday home on the beach, and for whom Lila and her sisters work in order to get a little cash for their needs. Hearing of Lila's mother's illness, the De Silvas are alarmed, and take her to hospital, offering to pay all costs. Here Lila has to leave her, and this provokes her father, who comes home late, stinking of toddy, to a rage which only reflects the guilt he is feeling. Suddenly he explodes unexpectedly with the care for his wife that he has never shown before. 'How could you leave her alone? What if she needs something? What if she asks for me? . . . Cook some food quick – I will take it to her.'[25] When Lila goes to see her mother she finds him sitting outside the ward, chastened, humbled, sober: 'He looked so grey and old and bent that for the first time she felt sorry for him.'[26] Lila finds her mother's health improving – she had been seriously anaemic – and, as her mother begins to smile, the family's fortunes take an upward turn. The De Silvas provide money for medicines, as well as more stable employment for Lila; her father gives up his toddy, and, as Lila reaches home from hospital, a letter arrives from Hari in Bombay. Her mother – Lakshmi – is smiling again.

Hari is learning all the time in Bombay. His guru, the old watchmaker, encourages the boy: 'Learn, learn, learn – so that you can grow and change . . . You are young. You can change and learn and grow. Old people can't, but you can.'[27] Hari returns to his village with his earnings; their old hut looks the same, 'dark and dismal', he thinks, 'its earthen walls crumbling, its palm-leaf thatch hanging crooked and tattered over the eaves.'[28] But the welcome of his sisters makes him part of his home again; no longer does he view it with the critical eyes of a Bombay-wallah. He felt grateful for it, just as it was, and stood breathing in its air silently.[29]

It is significant that the children's mother returns home at Diwali, feast of Lakshmi; as houses light lamps and open their doors to welcome the goddess, who will bring prosperity for the coming year, so the fisher family welcome their mother, fit and active again, to make their home complete.

> Bela and Kamal had garlands ready for their mother, made of jasmine, roses and marigolds, and they cried and laughed as they put them over her head. To their dismay it was their father who started crying weakly at the scene while their mother laughed with joy. She went straight to the small altar in a corner of the kitchen where there were small clay idols of Ganesh and the goddess Lakshmi standing amidst sticks of incense and piles of rose petals, and offered them the garland with a prayer of thanksgiving.[30]

The story is rounded out to its apt conclusion by a return to the three sacred rocks near the beach on which the fisher women leave their offerings every day to be received by the sea as the tide sweeps in. The tale begins with Lila, at sunrise, wading out to the cluster of rocks and offering there a selection of the flowers found around their hut. As her mother was bedridden, this was her task. The last scene of the story takes place on the beach, too, but now the children's world has righted itself, and again the figure of their mother is the appropriate symbol:

> After the races, when the crowds had thinned, Hari still stood on the dunes and saw a group of women coming down the path with small flat baskets on the palms of their hands. They were walking down the beach to the three rocks that stood in the sea. He watched them wade into the peacock blue and green sea, the foam breaking against their ankles, to scatter flower petals and coloured powder on the rocks as they prayed to the sea. He saw that his mother was amongst them.

'Lila, look!' he said. 'Look, Lila.'[31]

In *The Village by the Sea* the mother's role is a passive one; she is acted upon rather than acting, but Desai has made her the reflector and indicator of the family's fortunes. She is a Lakshmi rather than a Parvati; her physical wellbeing brings luck, her sickness takes it away, but the practical nurturing of the family members is taken over by her eldest daughter, whose development, through the decisions forced upon her by her parents' incapacities and her brother's departure for Bombay, is recorded step by step. The outside world, in the form of the De Silvas, their guest, Sayyid Ali, the Alibagh Hospital and its staff, the proposed chemical fertiliser plant, forces itself upon her, and demands a response. The Durga of this story is Lila; she faces the demons of her mother's illness, poverty, her father's alcoholism, and fights till they yield; but her strengths are not used till they are summoned, they are controlled by and directed towards family needs only. This Durga, then, has within herself the tenderness and care of Parvati, too.

Anita Desai shows us a village girl of a new generation, literate, courageous, capable, one who, though inhabiting a world entirely different from Jaya's, still finds the hope without which life would be impossible. She does not have the time for self-analysis, for seeking and defining her selfhood, but she demonstrates it; significantly it is she whom the doctor at Alibagh Hospital remembers, and lets Hari know this when he goes to collect his mother:

'I am her son, from – from Bombay,' Hari had to say . . . 'Oh, from Bombay? No one told me she had a son in Bombay,' said the doctor. 'I only saw the daughter, from Thul.'[32]

Clear Light of Day seeks to explain the psychological pressures which have moulded the development of the four children of an old and dignified house in Old Delhi; Tara, married to a diplomat; Raja, son-in-law to a wealthy Muslim; Baba, the youngest, mentally retarded; and Bim, the spinster sister who has her own career as a college lecturer. This may seem a strange book in which to seek an image of motherhood, but in fact it delves deeply into the affective ties which can bind children to the emotionally influential focus of their youth. There is no obvious mother-figure; the children's parents, dead at the time-setting of the novel, spend much of their time at the club, and their mother gives a home to a poor relation, Aunt Mira, who looks after the needs of the children. Although theirs is an affectionate relationship, it is not a maternal one, and Aunt Mira eventually degenerates into the shame of alcoholism. As the novel progresses through a series of flashbacks, rather as *That Long Silence* does, we begin to understand that it is not a sentient mother-figure that embraces the children of the family, even though they are now adult, but the house and grounds themselves, in all their neglect, their dullness, their dark, parched and dry state: ' . . . even the papaya and lemon trees, the bushes of hibiscus and oleander, the beds of canna lilies, seemed abandoned to dust and neglect, to struggle as they could against the heat and sun of summer.'[33]

Abandoned here too are Bim and Baba, still living in the family home, struggling to survive in the sun of modern, independent India. Bim's memories are still of a period when English and English literature were the essential knowledge of a cultivated elite, and she and her brother Raja read and recited together the works of Eliot, Tennyson, Byron, Swinburne, and let their imaginations feed on such verse. The cultural patternings of classical English Literature were more internalised than the immediacy of India. Though a lecturer, Bim's experience of the outside world of India does not even go as far as New Delhi: 'Old Delhi does not change. It only decays. My students tell me it is a great cemetery, every house a tomb. Nothing but sleeping graves. And *New* Delhi . . . That is where things happen . . . it sounds like a nest of fleas . . . I never go.'[34] The house and grounds in Old Delhi are a Kaliesque mother image, even to Bim, who sees herself trapped there, but who has made only spasmodic, indeterminate efforts to free herself. Desai's imagery echoes themes of entrapment, of death, of decay; when Bim is attacked, as a girl, by an angry swarm of bees, Tara sees her as 'locked into the hive, as if she were the chosen queen, made prisoner . . . It was a bees' festival, a celebration, Bim their appointed victim, the sacrificial victim on whom they had draped the ceremonial shawl, drawing it close about her neck . . . '[35] And Tara flees a similar entrapment, driven by a 'spider fear that lurked at the centre of the web-world.'[36] Tara does eventually escape the clinging threads of the family home, but by a traditional route; she marries and thus enters the constantly stirring world of diplomacy, settling permanently nowhere. Even out in the world she feels the pulls of home in Old Delhi, and she and her husband return to the old house: 'We *must* come,' she says, 'if we are not to lose touch, I with all of you, with home, and he with the country.'[37] But her coming is unsettling for Bim; it rakes up old memories, and Tara's example of breaking free makes her feel restless, too. Baba is upset as well; Tara tries to encourage him to get up, get dressed, stop listening to his interminable gramophone records ('White Christmas', 'Lili Marlene', and, ironically, 'Don't Fence Me In' among them), and eventually he does climb into some clothes and venture out through the gates, to an area he believes, and has experienced, to be full of noise, horror, terror. Again his fear is justified; horrorstruck, he sees a horse beaten to death by its driver, and flees back to the safety of his encapsulating protective, Durga-like house: 'Tara saw him as he came climbing up the steps on his knees . . . she uncovered his face and saw his eyes rolling in their sockets like a wild horse's, his lips drawn back from his teeth as if he were racing, and the blue-black shadows that always lay under his eyes spreading over his face like a bruise . . . '[38] This is the end of Baba's adventures; he returns to his existence within the womb-like safety of his crumbling, deathly mother-house: 'He wore a grey bush-shirt worn and washed almost to translucency. His face, too, was blanched, like a plant grown underground or in deepest shade, and his hair was quite white, giving his young, fine face a ghostly look that made people start whenever he appeared.'[39]

It is Raja, the elder son, who makes the boldest and most successful bid for freedom; he takes as his example their wealthy, cultured Muslim landlord, marries his daughter, and so ultimately comes round full circle to being the owner of his old, decaying home, as a son inherits the care of a widowed mother. He passes this to Bim, allowing her to remain in her old home, and at the same rent, an act which he considers generous, while Bim is overwhelmingly insulted, and refuses to see Raja, contact him, or attend his daughter's wedding, although, as children they were on very close and affectionate terms. So it is matters concerning the house which have destroyed another of Bim's chances to experience the world outside, just as it was concern for the house that occupied *her*, not Raja, after their father's death: 'That, and the rent to be paid on the house, and five, six, seven people to be fed every day, and Tara to be married off, and Baba to be taken care of for the rest of his life, and you to be got well again – and I don't know what else.'[40]

Gradually Bim becomes more and more identified with the house, and her chances to develop her own personality, and to express her own self dry up, until she begins to see in the womb-house the source of future development:

With her inner eye she saw how her own house and its particular history linked and combined her as well as her whole family with all their separate histories and experiences – not binding them within some dead and airless cell but giving them the soil in which to send down their roots, and food to make them grow and spread, reach out to new experiences and new lives, but always drawing from the same soil, the same secret darkness. That soil contained all time, past and future, in it. It was dark with time, rich with time. It was where her deepest self lived, and the deepest selves of her sister and brothers and all those who shared that time with her.[41]

Nevertheless, the self-sacrifice and effacement of a mother who exists only in and for her family loom for both Bim and her house, and seem presaged by the death of the family cow, again a mother symbol, when she fell into their well many years before. Significantly, it is the two girls who find this a threatening, terrible place:

> The water at the bottom was black, with an oily, green sheen. It was very still except where a small frog plopped in from a crack between the stones, making the girls start slightly. They narrowed their eyes and searched but no white and milky bone lifted out of it. The cow had never been hauled out. Although men had come with ropes and pulleys to help the gardener, it had proved impossible. She had been left to rot; that was what made the horror of it so dense and intolerable. The girls stared, scarcely breathing, till their eyes started out of their heads, but no ghostly ship of bones rode the still water. It must have sunk to the bottom and rooted itself in the mud, like a tree. There was nothing to see – neither hoof nor horn nor one staring, glittering eye. The water had stagnated and blackened, closing over the bones like a new skin. But even the new skin was black now and although it stank, it gave away nothing.[42]

The skeleton represents the innermost selfhood of a mother enclosed within her family; it is covered over, hidden, useless, hard, dead and still. Those around cannot draw it out; the children who approach run away, perhaps because they fear being drawn in to it, only to end like Baba, aimless, motiveless, protected, reliant, entombed. The skin covering it is black, like Kali, the black goddess of merciless destruction, the other face of Parvati, the beneficient. Well-water can drown, as well as give life. There is more than a suggestion that extreme self-sacrifice, self-effacement can come to demand so much commitment in return that it can only be destructive, and we are reminded again of Deshpande's Appa, cycling between the demands of mother and wife, until he is consumed. We may surmise that, whatever these writers suggest may lie beneath so deified a mother's feet, the word to describe it is not 'heaven'.

A selfhood denied, controlled, rendered inexpressive over centuries can erupt eventually, disruptive in its demands. The potential of the Mother Goddess is recognised in Hinduism, but the potential of wives and mothers is directed and circumscribed by family needs and circumstances.

A recent survey of women in Delhi shows that the welfare of the family is always a first priority for them: 'Motherhood demands full concentration and ties them to the home. Success in her domestic domain changes a woman's status in the public domain.'[43]

Education for daughters is secondary to that for sons, and the range of socially acceptable occupations is narrower. To continue studies to postgraduate level is exceptional for women; very high qualifications will make a suitable husband hard to find, since it is generally held that a wife should be less well qualified then her husband. Sometimes a wife's salary may go into the joint family purse, giving her no control over the way her earnings are utilised. Social values thus limit the opportunities for women that exist on paper in modern India; yet it is true that entry of women into the labour market does gradually instigate 'a dynamic of change' for future realisation.[44]

Indians are not alone in their perceptions of what can happen when this potential finds full expression, and the modern Indian woman's challenge to existing social norms has to be accommodated before it turns destructive, sweeping away the valuable with the dross. Let Jean Markale, writing of Celtic society, sound a final warning call:

We have seen her . . . behind the various faces, or rather the various masks, men have given her. Whatever name she is given, she remains unique, the primordial mother, the original goddess, the Great Queen of Beginnings.

Yet she is exposed, not only to men's sarcasm, but also to their will to power, their egoism, their sense of property. It is men who have invented the woman as object, tricked out in endless fineries, but a prisoner just the same. Some day this woman, the goddess, the Great Queen imprisoned in the shrine, is going to shake off her chains, and her rebellion will be terrible, for she is a direct threat to the society that men have built without her.[45]

Notes

1 Anita Desai, *Clear Light of Day* (CLD), Penguin Books, Harmondsworth, 1980. All references in the text are to this edition.

2 KR Srinivasa Iyengar, *Indian Writing in English*, Asia Publishing House, Bombay, 1973, p. 3.

3 Shashi Deshpande in an interview with Stanley Carvalho, *Sunday Observer* (Bombay), 11 February, 1990.

4 Shashi Deshpande, *That Long Silence* (TLS), Virago, London, 1988. All references in the text are to this edition.

5 Anita Desai, *The Village by the Sea* (TVBTS), Penguin Books, Harmondsworth, 1987. All references in the text are to this edition.

6 Deshpande, TLS, p. 25.

7 *Ibid.*, p. 137.

8 *Ibid.*, p. 45.

9 *Ibid.*, p. 136.

10 B Malinowski, *Magic, Science and Religion*, Doubleday, New York, 1954, p. 146.

11 Shanka Acharya, 'Problems of the Self in the Novels of Anita Desai' in *Explorations in Modern Indo-English Fiction*, ed. RK Dhawan, Bahra Pubs Pvt Ltd, New Delhi, 1982, p. 239.

12 *Deshparde*, TLS, p. 23.

13 *Ibid.*, p. 1.

14 *Ibid.*, p. 2.

15 *Ibid.*, p. 191.

16 *Ibid.*, p. 83.

17 *Ibid.*, p. 29.

18 *Ibid.*, p. 78.

19   *Ibid.*, p. 36.

20   *Ibid.*, p. 122.

21   *Ibid.*, p. 30.

22   The dot of red powder worn on the forehead by married Hindu women whose husbands are alive.

23   TM Luhrmann, *Persuasions of the Witch's Craft*, Blackwell, Oxford, 1989, p. 87.

24   Shyam Asnani, 'New Morality in the Modern Indo-English Novel', in *Explorations in Modern Indo-English Fiction*, ed. RK Dhawan, Bahra Pubs Pvt Ltd, New Delhi, 1982, p. 59.

25   Desai, TVBTS, p. 100.

26   *Ibid.*, p. 101.

27   *Ibid.*, p. 129.

28   *Ibid.*, p. 136.

29   *Ibid.*, p. 136.

30   *Ibid.*, p. 148.

31   *Ibid.*, p. 157.

32   *Ibid.*, p. 147.

33   Desai, CLD, p. 1.

34   *Ibid.*, p. 5.

35   *Ibid.*, p. 135.

36   *Ibid.*, p. 134.

37   *Ibid.*, p. 5.

38   *Ibid.*, pp. 16–17.

39   *Ibid.*, p. 8.

40   *Ibid.*, p. 67.

41   *Ibid.*, p. 182.

42   *Ibid.*, p. 118.

43   Renuka Singh, 'The Modern Matriarchs?', *Times of India*, 4 March 1990.

44   Hilary Standing, 'Resources, Wages and Power: the Impact of Women's Employment on the Urban Bengali Household', in *Women, Work and Ideology in the Third World*, ed. Haleh Afshar, Tavistock Pubs, London, 1985, p. 49.

45   Jean Markale, *Women of the Celts*, Inner Traditions Int. Ltd, Rochester, Vermont, 1986, p. 146.

Jane Bryce-Okunlola

Motherhood as a Metaphor for Creativity in Three African Women's Novels: Flora Nwapa, Rebeka Njau and Bessie Head

To bear (children) and nurse them is best
To bear and have (not lose) is best
Keep me alive,
Let yams be plentiful
Let births come!
(Prayer of married women of the village of Umeke, eastern
Nigeria, as recorded by Emefie Ikenga-Metuh)[1]

Mommy
tough times mommy
tough
to enjoy a moment's pleasure
to bear a child
who is a load on your back
stuck there
like an awkward piece of clay
thrown by a childish hand . . .
(from 'Mama & child' by Mongane Wally Serote)[2]

The preoccupation with having or not having children,
amounting at times to an obsession, in certain novels by

African women writers, is more than a culturally induced insecurity. For some writers, most explicitly Flora Nwapa, it is a metaphor for the creative process itself, and points to the source of their creativity in the communal story-telling tradition of their foremothers. The privileges accorded motherhood within traditional society are counterbalanced by the penalties for childlessness, the failure to marry or simply to conform to social expectations. For a writer, who by the very act of writing challenges the patriarchal appropriation of power over the Word, motherhood becomes a site of struggle. Its literary representation is, explicitly or implicitly, an exploration by women of the last uncolonised territory, an integral part of a woman's identity as writer. The longing for a child on the part of fictional women who will be discussed here, such as Efuru and Selina, is a paradigm for feminine desire itself, the longing for what is *absent* from their lives. The writing of that desire by the author is a demonstration that, childless or husbandless, a woman *can* fulfil herself: through writing, the re-creation of her story in her own image, rather than that projected for her by her society.

The two fragments of poetry which form the epigraph, however, point to an important recognition, that of *difference* between the writers under discussion. The ontological security of the traditional outlook of a West African village society, the notion of motherhood as desirable and a cause for celebration, expressed in the Igbo women's song, contrasts sharply with the poet's observation of a South African township mother and child. The work of three writers, Flora Nwapa, Rebeka Njau and Bessie Head, is similarly marked by difference, arising from the specific social and political contexts they inhabit; but they also converge on one point, the centrality of the image of motherhood to their concept of identity, continuity and creativity.

This is not, however, the male-defined notion of the Mother as eternal, unchanging paradigm of all that is good in traditional society, as opposed to the modern, 'selfish', 'strident' woman of Femi Ojo-Ade's projection:

> Little does the bra-less female realise that her African counterpart has never been shackled by any means. For, in spite of the borrowed theorisations and totally baseless ranting of the alienated intellectual from Africa in support of the foreign organised movement, African woman has long held a position of power in society; she has been an integral part of the struggle for survival; she has ruled millions of people successfully. She is respected for her qualities and treated as a human being. She is the mother, she from whom all life emanates; she is indeed the one most important element of survival and continuity.[3]

While some of the aspects of motherhood on which Ojo-Ade touches are undeniable, particularly those of survival and continuity, this is a highly romanticised account which unnecessarily denigrates the changes African women are making in their own perception of their role. Most damaging of all is the accusation of foreign influence and alienation, when in fact African women have been careful to insist on the specifically African contours of their own feminism. Mineke Schipper quotes Mariama Bâ, in an essay entitled 'Mother Africa on a Pedestal', as refuting the Ojo-Ade image:

> As women, we must work for our own future, we must overthrow the status quo which honors us and we must no longer submit to it. Like men, we must use literature as a non-violent but effective weapon. We no longer accept the nostalgic praise to the African Mother, who, in his anxiety, man confuses with Mother Africa. Within African literature, room must be made for women . . . room we will fight for with all our might.[4]

This statement by Mariama Bâ crystallises the informing principle of this essay, that writing by African women offers the most explicit challenge to the idealistic, nostalgic concept of the woman's role, and, as 'a non-violent but effective weapon', is engaged not only in formulating an alternative, but in accurately recording what is, in fact, already there.

Novels by Flora Nwapa, such as *Efuru*, *Idu* and *One is Enough*, demonstrate the ability of women to transform both motherhood and childlessness into positive, self-defined and powerful experiences.[5] Rebeka Njau's *Ripples in the Pool* is a study of the destructive effects of social expectations on a woman who has broken with convention, and of her attempt to compensate herself for her childlessness by projecting her needs on to a younger female relative of her husband.[6]

The distortion in relationships, brought about by the moral confusion that has arisen in Kenyan society, is explored through Selina's subjective experience. Bessie Head's novels, *When Rainclouds Gather*, *Maru* and *A Question of Power*, problematise motherhood further, in reflecting the alienation and internal exile of motherlessness.[7]

The conflation of text and child is foreign to the western writer, who has traditionally seen writing and childbearing as mutually exclusive. Alice Walker, struck by Buchi Emecheta's dedication of *Second Class Citizen*, 'To my dear children . . . without whose sweet background noises this book would not have been written', comments:

> The notion that this is remotely possible causes a rethinking of traditional Western ideas about how art is produced. Our culture separates the duties of raising children from those of creative work.[8]

In this respect, Flora Nwapa's concern with motherhood may be seen less as the inability to raise her sights beyond the domestic and personal, for which she has been trivialised and marginalised, than as a re-examination of her identity through the role that is seen to define her. In her essay, 'Motherhood in the Works of Male and Female Igbo Writers', the critic Carole Boyce Davies quotes Filomena Steady to the effect that:

> The most important factor with regard to the woman in

traditional society is her role as *mother* and the centrality of this role as a whole . . . The importance of motherhood and the evaluation of the childbearing capacity by African women is probably the most fundamental difference between the African woman and her western counterpart in their common struggle to end discrimination against women.[9]

Considering that *Efuru* is not only a first novel, but *the* first novel to be published by an African woman, it is all the more remarkable that it so completely sets its heroine outside the norm. Nwapa's later novels show women forsaking marriages and men, but none of them makes such a strong case for a childless woman as does her first. Yet, Nwapa refutes the notion that Efuru is the creation of her individual imagination, and traces the genesis of the novel to conversations overheard in her mother's sewing shop:

'I happened to have known this particular woman. Efuru is so many women in one. I loved listening to stories. My mother would make clothes and . . . many women came while she sewed. I think it must have been from there that I got the idea of how these women behave.'[10]

Rather than a single, representative consciousness, therefore, her heroines are composites, invariably part of a network of women existing as an adjunct and alternative to the dominant world of men. After *Idu* (1970), her terrain shifts from the traditional, rural world, to the contemporary, urban one, but, like Efuru, nearly all her women end up alone, many of them from choice. But where a husband can be dispensed with, children cannot. Nwapa is concerned to explore the options for women in a changed, post-colonial society, which offers them, for the first time, social as well as economic and emotional independence. What the novel, *One is Enough*, shows, however, is that this is only achievable in a context of feminine supportiveness and solidarity, including the heroine's mother, sister and friends.

The novel begins with Amaka, the heroine, being informed by her mother-in-law that her inability to have children has driven her husband to have two sons outside the marriage. Her shock at this news is not, as Katherine Frank would have it, at 'the intolerable prospect of polygamy', since with characteristic Igbo pragmatism, she had already encouraged her husband to try for a child elsewhere. Her outrage arises from her husband's failure to inform her, which flouts the sense of self-worth instilled in her by her mother, with its 'emphasis on self-determination and mother-hood' (p. 23), rather than on marriage per se. Of her child-lessness she wonders:

> Was that really the end of the world? Was she useless to society if she were not a mother? Was she useless to the world if she were unmarried? Surely not? (p. 20)

And, in pursuit of this conviction, Amaka goes to Lagos, makes good, gets rich, acquires a priest as a lover, who gives her twin boys, and finally refuses to marry him – 'One is Enough'.

The main preoccupations of the novel are not so far from those of *Efuru* – a woman in the process of formulating her own identity, in the midst of a network of women who support, encourage and occasionally obstruct her. More pro-nounced than in *Efuru* is the concern with changing values, especially the hankering after and idealisation of marriage, brought about by missionary education, and firmly undercut by traditional pragmatism, as represented by Amaka's mother and aunt, and, indeed her mother-in-law. Her mother's response to her leaving Obiora is typically ener-getic:

> 'You fool,' she said to me. 'You are not my daughter. I told you to leave that husband of yours years ago if he was unable to make you pregnant . . . But you refused to take my advice. You were being a good wife, chastity,

faithfulness my foot. You can go ahead and eat virtue'.
(p. 32)

Amaka surprises her mother by her success in business,
which quickly brings her a new prestige and sense of self-
esteem, but her mother is caught out when her daughter
discovers that she actually prefers to remain without a husband. The husband who offers himself, Father McLaid or
Izu, leaves the priesthood for Amaka, and becomes a powerful figure in the new regime. Amaka's mother deploys all
her resources to persuade or force Amaka to marry him, but
she refuses. Ayo, Amaka's sister, sees what their mother is
doing:

> Just as their mother was fighting tooth and nail to have
> Amaka marry Izu, so were all mothers who knew Izu
> fighting tooth and nail to marry their daughters to him if
> they could. It was a matter of competition. Their mother
> was the first to realise this fact. (p. 144)

As she tells Amaka, as the wife of a federal commissioner,
she would be in a position to get contracts and make even
more money. It is here that Amaka's sense of self, of her
individual identity as a woman, asserts itself. Just as she
earlier vehemently refuted the possibility of prostitution to
her husband, she equally forcibly rejects marriage now. Of
Izu she says:

> 'I don't want him. I don't want to be his wife . . . I don't
> want to be a wife any more, a mistress yes, with a lover,
> yes of course, but not a wife. There is something in that
> word that does not suit me. As a wife, I am never free. I
> am a shadow of myself. As a wife I am almost impotent.
> I am in prison, unable to advance in body and soul . . . '
> (p. 127)

One should pause for a moment over this declaration,
because it can be all too easily misconstrued, as I think it is
by the American feminist critic, Katherine Frank. In her

essay, 'Women Without Men: The Feminist Novel in Africa', she seeks to show that recent African women's fiction, including *One is Enough*, have embraced the alternative of radical separatism – a life without men.[11] Her projection of white American feminist values on to the novel leads her to several mis-apprehensions. Specifically, she is bemused by what she sees as a contradiction in Amaka's character, between her independence and the means she uses to achieve it – kick-backs, inflated contracts and 'bottom power', which Frank calls 'really just a shrewd kind of prostitution . . . she is being exploited in the most fundamental and time-honoured way' (p. 21). By allowing herself to be exploited, choosing her 'oppressors . . . carefully, to maximise the benefits she gains from her sexual services' (p. 22), Amaka succeeds in moving 'out from the shadows and in so doing [losing] the feminine impotence or powerlessness of the traditional African woman she was at the start of the book' (p. 22).

I contend that this is a serious misreading of the novel, and an example of the dangers of ethnocentric, universalist assumptions in feminist, as in all other forms of criticism. For, in her own terms, Amaka was neither a traditional woman at the beginning nor did she set out to 'liberate' herself into a life without men. On the contrary, in the last lines of the novel, she makes her priorities perfectly clear when she tells the nun, who has come to inform her of Izu's return to the church, that, 'I shall forever remain grateful to him for proving to the world that I am a mother as well as a woman' (p. 154). What we have here is pragmatism rooted in the conventional values attaching to motherhood, combined with a recognition and acceptance of social change. In the subversion of the conventional happy ending, the union of man and woman, Flora Nwapa expresses her philosophy. However unacceptably materialist it may appear, it is a response to the empirical conditions of women's lives in Nigeria, an insistence on what *is*, not what ought to be. Its most significant aspect is its retention of the centrality of motherhood combined with the decentering of the role of wife, so rewriting the script of Nigerian middle-class values with its emphasis on the supportive 'good woman'.

Where Flora Nwapa's older women, or mother figures, function as the bearers of traditional wisdom and pragmatism, the touchstone whereby the younger protagonists are able to define their differences, the absence of a mother is a crucial factor in the neurotic behaviour of Selina, heroine of Rebeka Njau's *Ripples in the Pool*. This novel and Bessie Head's *A Question of Power* exemplify the *difference* already alluded to, in terms of both the psychological and social significance they attach to motherhood. As products of a particular cultural milieu, they reflect its disturbances and contradictions and the resulting alienation. *Ripples in the Pool* is a profoundly significant novel within the Kenyan literary context, which is entirely dominated by the worldwide reputation and extraordinary achievement of Ngugi wa Thiong'o. There is no doubt that Ngugi has created some of African literature's most memorable female characters, from Muthoni in *The River Between*, to Wanja and Nyakinyua in *Petals of Blood*, Wariinga in *Devil on the Cross* and Guthera in *Matigari*. Ngugi places exemplary emphasis on the role of women in the struggle for national self-determination against neo-colonialism. Charles A Nama in 'Daughters of Moombi' shows how Ngugi's women also 'conform with specific conventions of traditional aesthetics, and . . . consequently play crucial roles as defenders of traditional cultural values'.[12] It is by no means certain that Ngugi's resolutely materialist analysis of contemporary Kenyan society, informed by his Marxist political convictions, would concur with Nama's description of his work as 'attempting to retrieve the glorious age of Gikuyu greatness', for which purpose he 'portrays his heroines in conformity with the traditional, original role assigned to them in Gikuyu mythology . . . the embodiment of traditional values . . . ' (p. 149). It must, however, be acknowledged that Ngugi's women are powerful precisely because they are archetypes. The deliberately positive projections of a male author, become, in the case of Wariinga, almost a self-parody. It is noticeable, too, that where Nama's praise for the others is unqualified, he expresses reservations about Wanja, the prostitute and beer-brewer of *Petals of Blood*. She is still a 'strong' Gikuyu woman, but 'her dissolute life and her acceptance of brazen western materialism are all anathema to the traditional values of Ilmorog' (p. 143). For Ngugi's ex-colleague and co-writer, Micere Mugo, the problem with Wanja is that she teeters dangerously on the brink of 'stereotype, caricature and manhandling', for 'even in a great socialist realist novel such as *Petals of Blood*, the militant Wanja, to an extent, becomes crippled by the feminine biological desire to bear and mother a child', and she 'urges the expansion of female horizons so that they extend beyond motherhood'.[13]

The significance of Rebeka Njau's *Ripples in the Pool* lies in her attempt, not only to confront the objective realities of the social situation in Kenya, but to portray the subjective responses of all those affected by it. While, in Marxist terms, she fails to point to an alternative vision or indicate a route to change, concluding on a mystical note with the renewal of the sacred fig tree by the pool, she does make an important contribution to the characterisation of women in Kenyan fiction. In *Matigari*, his latest novel, Ngugi allows another prostitute, Guthera, to tell her own story, one of individual heroism in the face of impossible choices. Prostitution is presented as a pragmatic solution to the problem of survival and of taking responsibility for the survival of others. By making Guthera, 'the pure and the resurrected', sleep with a prison guard in order to effect the 'miracle' of Matigari's escape from prison, Ngugi powerfully undercuts the stereotype of feminine 'goodness' and chastity. Njau's heroine Selina is also, to some extent, a prostitute, a city woman who uses her sexuality to wield power over men and gain from them financially. The difference between Njau's treatment and Ngugi's is that Njau chooses to explore the communal neurosis of Kenyan society through the psyche of one woman, and through the perversion of all relationships in which she is involved. The reader is invited, not just to sympathise with Selina through being made to understand the conditions which have shaped her choices, but actually to identify with her. This involves sharing the painful process of her disintegration without the palliative of being able to see her as a victim. Since she is seen as making deliberate choices and refusing others, she cannot be absolved of responsibility. Yet, as Njau clearly shows, Selina is only the most extreme manifestation of the malaise infecting every aspect of life in Kenya. This malaise is diagnosed through the imagery of the perversion of motherhood, leading to infertility, madness and destruction.

Jean F O'Barr, discussing 'Feminist Issues in the Fiction of Kenya's Women Writers', including Njau, observes:

> Kenyan women are experiencing social situations fraught with contradictions. Novelists show women responding to these conflicts with a mixture of initiative and passivity . . . document the fact that structural constraints on the exercise of options by women is severe and that the individual solutions that women seek can be no more than temporary mechanisms allowing them to cope with the situations they face.[14]

The situation faced by Selina as a young girl is presented both by her mother-in-law and by herself. Her mother-in-law, remonstrating with her son Gikere for marrying a woman whose background he does not know, asks:

> 'Do you know that her own mother had fits? Do you know that the woman you say you love used to suffer from fits during her childhood and was once raped as she lay unconscious by the roadside?' (p. 8)

Selina, explaining to Gikere why she cannot forgive him for beating her, describes the life she led at the age of nine, after her mother died and her father said she was illegitimate: 'I was a daring little brat. I wasn't scared at all to be among a gang of rough and thievish boys. I dressed in tattered shorts and I feared no human being even at that age' (p. 52). She describes how she ran away after her father stripped her, tied her to the bedstead, doused her with cold salt water and thrashed her. The solution she found was to run to the city, where she survived, and eventually succeeded in training as a nurse. The conditions of life in the city and the effects of urbanisation on women in particular have been documented both by Kenneth Little and the Kenyan writer Miriam Were.[15] Selina is a fictional product of those empirical conditions. Her view of life and her wish to get married are expressed early in the novel to her friend Sophia:

> 'Men do not know what kind of woman they want. If you are a "yes" woman, they soon get tired of you; if you are intelligent and know your own mind, they don't have enough guts to deal with that! . . . I want a real companion myself, a real friend who will not desert me when I'm old and full of wrinkles on my face!' (p. 3)

It is this desire which leads Selina to marry Gikere and go to live with him in the village, where she is viewed as a city woman, synonymous with prostitute, who should be blamed for the misfortunes of her early life. The attempt to reverse the rural–urban transition brings all its inherent conflicts into sharp focus. Judged by the values of the rural community she enters, Selina is a failure because she cannot have children. As her mother-in-law says, 'women *like her* are sterile' (p. 12) and, to her face: 'You are not a woman. That is what is wrong with you. You will never bear him children' (p. 36). She in turn perceives the mother–son relationship as a threat and blames her mother-in-law for her repeated miscarriages, calling her a witch.

Selina's predicament, however, is not just personal. Njau gives it a tragic dimension by her emphasis on destiny, which means that the text of Selina's life is already written, she is already a sacrifice to the process of modernisation which is eroding the old values. Like her relative, Karuga, whose life is forfeit in expiation of his mother's crimes, Selina has to pay the debt of her past. This is a society in which motherlessness has become a crime and motherhood itself is perverted. Selina's desperate need for 'someone' is depicted as her attempt to compensate for the loss of her mother, whose suicide she blames on her father. When Gikere fails her, she projects this need on to his sister Gaciru, in a sort of perversion of the longing for a child, which here becomes an obsessive possessiveness which leads her to kill her out of jealousy. 'I am your mother, your sister, your friend, your everything', she tells Gaciru. 'You cannot break away from my world. I have power . . . and it is this power that binds you to me' (p. 111). Yet because this power is perverted, it destroys her, and through her, her husband, Gaciru and Karuga.

The powerful symbolism of Njau's narrative suggests that Selina's neurosis is Kenya's, and arises from the society's alienation from its roots, from traditional morality with its healing power. No one is exempt from this process of psychic disintegration, equated with motherlessness and the inability to bear children. Unlike the 'mad double' documented by Gilbert and Gubar in nineteenth-century women's fiction, the madwoman here is not the heroine's double, but the heroine herself, making the experience of madness central, rather than marginal. As Gilbert and Gubar suggest, 'Much of the poetry and fiction written by women conjures up this mad creature so that female authors can come to terms with their own uniquely female feelings of fragmentation, their own keen sense of the discrepancies between what they are and what they are supposed to be.'[16]

These same feelings of fragmentation and discrepancy, with their correlative of motherlessness, are at the root of Elizabeth's neurosis in Bessie Head's *A Question of Power*. This neurosis, actually an account of Bessie Head's own nervous breakdown, has been fully analysed by Elizabeth N Evasdaughter and Margaret E Tucker, and this essay will not attempt to add to their findings.[17]

Elizabeth Evasdaughter rehearses the by now well-known facts of Bessie Head's birth and upbringing: born in mental hospital to a white mother who had been confined there for becoming pregnant to a black employee, she was married for a year before her husband's promiscuity caused her, as she herself puts it, to 'pick up the small boy' (her son) and 'walk out of the house, never to return' (p. 19). She answered an advertisement for teachers in Botswana and became an exile there. All her three novels are set in Botswana, and behind all three of them is the strongly felt pain of displacement, alienation both from her country of origin and her country of adoption, and the stigma attached to being 'coloured' (not black or white) in a country where the only people resembling her are the Masarwa, or Bushmen, who are universally despised. But for Elizabeth, Bessie Head's fictional double, the most fundamental source of instability is the circumstances of her birth, which simultaneously divided her identity so she could claim neither white privilege nor black solidarity, and deprived her of the primary relationship with her mother. The illness which arises from this ontological insecurity, according to Evasdaughter, 'meets the criteria set forth in the Desk Reference to the Diagnostic Criteria . . . for paranoid schizophrenia' (p. 1).

While motherhood is not an explicit theme, nor does it occupy a central place in Head's writing, it is part of the fabric of her fiction and generally presented as problematic. Margaret Tucker uses French feminist theorist Hélène Cixous' definition of writing as 'precisely the possibility of change' to explicate *A Question of Power*, suggesting that it is the novel itself which redeems both Elizabeth, its protagonist, and Bessie Head, its author, from the mental anguish it seeks to explore (p. 171). This novel, therefore, exemplifies the feminist notion of the indivisibility of the personal and political, or, in psychoanalytic terms, the body and the text. In the act of writing, the woman writer recreates herself, her text the site of her resistance from within her captivity to the patriarchal symbolic order. In the words of Julia Kristeva, she forsakes the Law-of-the-Father to enter on a new terrain:

> Territory of the mother. What I am saying to you is that if this heterogeneous body, this risky text provide meaning, identity and jouissance, they do so in a completely different way than a 'Name-of-the-Father'. Not that they do not operate under the shield of a tyrannical, despotic Name-of-the-Father. I understand that, and we could engage in endless forensic contests. But it is only a question of power; the important thing is to see what exceeds it.[18]

And what exceeds it is the small, everyday events and interactions which Bessie Head has referred to as her 'philosophy of the ordinary'. Foremost among these in *A Question of Power* is her character's relationship with her son.

Referred to throughout the text as 'the small boy' or 'Shorty', Elizabeth's son appears almost incidentally, but at certain crucial moments, to drag her back from her world of nightmare delusions to his world of self-absorption and discovery. Motherhood is the site where conflicting emotions of anger, frustration, guilt, caring, responsibility and ultimately joyful release coalesce. Just as Elizabeth's lack of a mother (mother-figure, mother-country, mother-tongue) is a major factor in her unsettled sense of identity, so is her own mother-role the route to her regeneration. Repeatedly, and especially at the end of the novel, her son is the catalyst for the revelation which releases her from her neurosis. When her tormentor, Dan, prophesies that she will commit suicide, 'She nearly did, except that her small boy had asked her to buy him a football and he came down the road with a gang of eager friends' (p. 13). After one particularly tortured night, she succumbs to irritation at the child's need of her, and says, 'You'd like to be slaughtered, hey? Shut your mouth, you damn little nuisance' (p. 49). When she bursts into tears, his response, 'I can show you I know how to dress myself', makes her think:

> People who had mothers like he had were lost if they did
> not know how to care for themselves. She looked at him
> in a sort of agony and thought: 'Journeys into the soul are
> not for women with children, not all that dark heaving
> turmoil.' (p. 50)

Yet he punctuates her journey and rescues her simply by the
fact of his existence. He is her link with the villagers and ex-
patriate workers, one means by which people can demonstrate their concern without intruding. The boy relates to
Kenosi, Elizabeth's garden co-worker, in a direct, untram-
melled way which she feels excludes her (p. 88). The small
rituals of her life, 'making tea, cooking food for a small boy,
eating, washing, working', or the lighting of her cigarette
which is his special task (p. 91), are meaningful because
shared. He is the silent witness of her struggles, as when she
wakes up to find herself on the floor and him 'lying on the
floor beside her and peering into her face' (p. 93). He
shadows her moods, mimics her words and, she realises,
tracks her foot-steps. When she decides to kill them both,
'the trust he showed, the way he quietly walked back to his
own bed, feverishly swerved her mind away from killing
him, then herself' (p. 174). Near the end of the illness, when
Dan has pushed her to the brink, again, of suicide, 'the
cunning little bugger', her son, asking for a football, recalls
her to herself: 'The heavy weight of blankness shifted a little.
So she was his mother, was she?' (p. 193) Finally, as she
recovers enough to write what has happened to her, Shorty's
poem demonstrates how closely he has been following her
progress: 'She had to read it through several times in dis-
belief. It seemed impossible that he had really travelled the
journey alongside her. He seemed to summarise all her obser-
vations' (p. 205).

While Elizabeth's approach to her son is severely unsenti-
mental, her relationship with him partakes of the occasionally
experienced moments of transcendent love which she uses to
offset the brutality of Dan and the rest of her demons. She

has a similar, understated relationship with the volunteer Tom, who was 'exactly like the small boy' (p. 112), except that he says 'I don't need mothers' (p. 121). In hospital she even tells the nurse, 'He's my son' (p. 183), and he, Shorty, Kenosi and the vegetable garden are her markers of sanity. Margaret Tucker argues convincingly for Elizabeth's alienation from farming as 'alienation from any sort of reproduction', which she associates with sex, and therefore with evil, power, exploitation and violence. Her success as a gardner and the extraordinary growth of the Cape Gooseberry she plants may be seen as her coming to terms with a power in herself which she chooses to ignore. She repeatedly denies her sexuality and says at one point of her vagina, 'it was not such a pleasant part of the body to concentrate on' (p. 44). Yet her instinct towards nurturing of plants and mothering of 'small boys' is linked to her own reproductive powers, and ultimately to her power of self-expression as a writer. The 'question of power' and what exceeds it is answered by the novel in terms of the various revelations Elizabeth has of the meaning of love. Talking to Birgitte, a young Danish volunteer, she says:

> 'Here I am secure. Here I am safe. I have a peculiar sensation of sleeping with a whole lot of people in my arms, like a great and eternal mother.' (p. 86)

And the novel concludes with a gesture which is quintessentially maternal and protective: 'As she fell asleep, she placed one soft hand over her land. It was a gesture of belonging' (p. 206). This gesture, or its mirror image, is evident in the works of the three writers who are the subject of this essay. In their different ways they all reflect the centrality of motherhood to their sense of themselves as writers who are women and write from within an African cultural milieu. Motherhood is the signifier of something fundamental to their identity, which these writers have made into a metaphor for creativity itself.

Notes

1 Emefie Ikenga-Metuh, *Research in African Literatures* vol. 16, no. 3, 1985.

2 Mongane Wally Serote.

3 Femi Ojo-Ade, 'Bessie Head's Alienated Heroine, Victim or Villain', in *Ba Shiru* vol. 3, no. 2, 1977.

4 Mineke Schipper, 'Mother Africa on a Pedestal: The Male Heritage in African Literature and Criticism', in *Ngambika*, Africa World Press, Inc., New Jersey, 1986, p. 47.

5 Flora Nwapa, *Efuru*, Heinemann, London, 1966; *Idu*, Heinemann, London, 1970; *One is Enough*, Tana Press, Enugu, Nigeria, 1981 (reprinted 1984). All references to *One is Enough* in the text are to the second edition.

6 Rebeka Njau, *Ripples in the Pool*, Heinemann, London, 1975. All references in the text are to this edition.

7 Bessie Head, *When Rainclouds Gather*, Heinemann, London, 1972; *Maru*, Heinemann, London, 1971; *A Question of Power*, Heinemann, London, 1974. All references in the text are to these editions.

8 Alice Walker, 'A Writer Because of, Not in Spite of, Her Children', in *In Search of Our Mothers' Gardens*, The Women's Press, London, 1983, pp. 69–70.

9 Carole Boyce Davies, 'Motherhood in the Works of Male and Female Igbo Writers: Achebe, Emecheta, Nwapa and Nzekwu', in *Ngambika*, p. 243.

10 Interview with Jane Bryce-Okunlola in Harare, 31 July 1985.

11 Katherine Frank, 'Women Without Men: The Feminist Novel in Africa', *African Literature Today* no. 15, James Currey, London, 1987, pp. 14–34.

12 Charles A Nama, 'Daughters of Moombi: Ngugi's Heroines and Traditional Gikuyu Aesthetics', in *Ngambika*, p. 139.

13 Micere Mugo, 'Women Writers', keynote address at the New Writing in Africa Conference, Commonwealth Institute, London, November 1984, p. 170.

14 Jean F O'Barr, 'Feminist Issues in the Fiction of Kenya's Women Writers', *African Literature Today* no. 15, p. 57.

15 Kenneth Little, *The Sociology of Urban Women's Image in African Literature*, Macmillan, London, 1980; Miriam Were, co-author of chapter on changes facing Kenyan women as urbanisation alters their roles, in *Women in Africa and the African Diaspora*, eds. Rosalyn

Terborg–Penn, Sharon Healey, Andrea Rushing. Howard University Press, Washington DC, 1987.

16 Sandra M Gilbert and Susan Gubar, *The Madwoman in the Attic*, Yale University Press, New Haven & London, 1979, p. 78.

17 Elizabeth N Evasdaughter, 'Bessie Head's *A Question of Power* Read as a Mariner's Guide to Paranoia', *Research in African Literatures* vol. 20, no. 1, Spring 1989; Margaret E Tucker, 'A "Nice-Time Girl" Strikes Back: An Essay on Bessie Head's *A Question of Power' Research in African Literatures* vol. 19, no. 2, Summer 1988.

18 Julia Kristeva, 'The Novel as Polylogue' in *Desire in Language*, Oxford University Press, Oxford, 1980, p. 16.

Ann R Morris and Margaret M Dunn

'The Bloodstream of Our Inheritance': Female Identity and the Caribbean Mothers'-Land

Historically, England has been the 'motherland' to the peoples of the West Indies and, even in a post-colonial era, England is occasionally referred to in West Indian writing as the 'motherland' or 'mother country'. Such a reference is usually ironic, however. As the fiction and poetry of West Indian writers makes clear, it is Dominica or Jamaica or Barbados or Antigua that is truly the homeland, the motherland.

For the Caribbean woman, the notion of a motherland is especially complex, encompassing in its connotations her island home and its unique culture as well as the body of tropes, talismans and female bonding that is a woman's heritage through her own and other mothers. The land and one's mothers, then, are co-joined. If a woman is able to claim a connection to both, she is well prepared for the journey toward self-identity and fulfilment. But if she has been denied a developmental bond with her own mother, then the 'mothers' land' itself may provide a surrogate. This motherland concept, in all its variety and complexity, is explored in four contemporary West Indian novels: *Annie John* by Jamaica

Kincaid, *Wide Sargasso Sea* by Jean Rhys, *The Chosen Place, the Timeless People* by Paule Marshall and *No Telephone to Heaven* by Michelle Cliff.

The well-known feminist theorists Nancy Chodorow, Carol Gilligan and Jean Baker Miller agree that the mother-daughter bond is of primary importance in the development and mature realisation of female identity. Unlike male identity, which develops through early *separation from* the mother, female identity develops through early and continued *connection with* the mother. The female paradigm is thus one of relationship with others. Chodorow develops her ideas from a sociological perspective, emphasising the important place that connection and affiliation play in a woman's life. In Chodorow's words, 'Because of their mothering by women, girls come to experience themselves as less separate than boys, as having more permeable ego boundaries. Girls come to define themselves more in relation to others'.[1] According to Chodorow, then, female maturity develops through connectedness with, rather than separation from, one another. Gilligan extends Chodorow's ideas to the arena of moral development, postulating a female ethos of relationship and concern for the empowerment of others. In such an ethos, says Gilligan, 'identity is defined in a context of relationship and judged by a standard of responsibility and care'.[2] Miller, in a work whose two editions both pre-date and post-date the works of Chodorow and Gilligan, describes her own study as centering on 'the nature of "relational contexts" and "relational modes" which foster psychological development'.[3]

The theories of Chodorow, Gilligan and Miller are multi-dimensional, and they are in some respects controversial.[4] Yet it does seem clear that the female developmental paradigm is relational and that a mother-daughter connection is crucial, as some critics and commentators agree. Laura Niesen de Abruna's comment in this regard is typical: 'Unlike the young male self, the young female self is defined not through independence from the mother but through bonding and identification with her. [Thus] the nature of adult female identity arises specifically from the daughter's relationship with her mother . . ."[5] It follows, then, that if a daughter's relationship with her mother is unnaturally severed, for whatever reason, the daughter will seek a necessary replacement. If she has 'felt unmothered', in the words of Adrienne Rich, she 'may seek mothers all her life'.[6] Until she finds a mother, she will develop neither a secure sense of her own individually nor the concomitant ability to form connections with others. But what kind of replacement or surrogate must this be? Who or what can take the place of one's natural, biological mother? In various ways, Jamaica Kincaid, Jean Rhys, Paule Marshall and Michelle Cliff propose, for women of the Caribbean, an answer to this question. Each writer begins by stressing the importance of a developmental mother-bond. Kincaid does this by describing a strongly bonded mother-daughter relationship, while Rhys, Marshall and Cliff do so by exploring the pain that a woman experiences if she has been denied a mother's nurturance. Further, each writer demonstrates the complex connections that exist, for a Caribbean woman, between mother, culture and place. Climate, topography, foods, customs and memories forged in 'the word-shop of the kitchen', as Paule Marshall puts it,[7] combine in a melange that nurtures and sustains. Finally, all four writers suggest that a woman who plumbs and values her connection to the 'mother's land' itself may, even in the absence of a crucial developmental bond with her own or a surrogate mother, thereby find the means of achieving self-realisation.

Annie John,[8] Jamaica Kincaid's acclaimed West Indian novel, tells the first-person story of the young Annie John as she grows up in Antigua. This is not a startling story, nor even an especially dramatic one. In the first chapter the ten-year-old girl meditates about death, having encountered a first-hand knowledge of it when a schoolmate (but not a close friend) and then an elderly neighbour die. In the second chapter Annie, now twelve years old, tells various details of daily life with her family – a mother and father who obviously love her very much. The third chapter, entitled 'Gwen', describes Annie's infatuation with a brand-new friend and her (Annie's) rise to intense and much-savoured popularity at her new school. The five remaining chapters follow Annie through various adolescent rebellions at school and at home, culminating with her departure for England, at the age of 18, to enter training as a student nurse.

No work of fiction, it might appear, could be more straightforward in focusing on a young woman's development through childhood and adolescence. Yet one's strong impression after finishing the novel is that the story is really about Annie's mother, or at least as much about Annie's mother as about Annie herself. In the first chapter, for example, while Annie's first-person voice describes her own thoughts about death and the events connected with the deaths of a schoolfriend and a neighbour, she does so by describing her mother's actions and experiences. When a small girl named Nalda dies, she does so in the arms of Annie's mother, and the elderly neighbour collapses and dies while having a conversation with Annie's mother. Then Annie shuns a friend whose own mother had died: 'She seemed such a shameful thing, a girl whose mother had died and left her alone in the world' (p. 8).

In the next chapter, a compilation of episodes and anecdotes about daily life with her family, Annie's mother again figures prominently. Mother and daughter go to the grocery store together, cook and 'taste' together, do laundry together, often bathe together. 'How important I felt to be with my mother', the young Annie says at one point. 'When my eyes rested on my father, I didn't think very much of the way he looked. But when my eyes rested on my mother, I found her beautiful' (pp. 15, 18). By the end of this chapter Annie has become angry at her mother and the two quarrel, but in the next chapter that deals with Annie's 'successes' at school and with her new friend Gwen, the major portion is devoted to an 'autobiographical essay' that Annie writes in school. Lyrical, dreamlike, the essay first describes a mother-daughter picnic at the beach during which Annie becomes separated from her mother. Her mother comes back, of course, but then many times after that Annie has a nightmare in which her mother does not come back. The essay ends with Annie's telling her mother about the dream: 'My mother became instantly distressed; tears came to her eyes, and, taking me in her arms, she told me all the same things she had told me on the day at the sea, and this time the memory of the dark time when I felt I would never see her again did not come back to haunt me' (pp. 44–45).

Subsequent chapters continue in like vein. Even when Annie and her mother are quarrelling or estranged, the emphasis is on both of them, on their relationship. In fact, this relationship worsens as Annie grows older; she hates, then loves, then hates her mother: 'Suddenly I had never loved anyone so or hated anyone so.' Yet the bond between mother and daughter is so intense that Annie has difficulty in seeing her mother apart from herself: 'If my mother died, what would become of me? I couldn't imagine my life without her. Worse than that, if my mother died I would have to die, too, and even less than I could imagine my mother dead could I imagine myself dead' (p. 88).

Nevertheless, Annie rebels against family restrictions to the point that she chooses to leave Antigua and go to England where she will enroll in nursing school – even though she already dislikes England and the thought of being a nurse. Annie thinks that her mother is happy to be getting rid of her, but their leavetaking reveals the bond between them: 'Big tears streamed down her face, and it must have been that – for I could not bear to see my mother cry – which started me crying, too. She then tightened her arms around me and held me to her close, so that I felt that I couldn't breathe' (p. 147). Again, as throughout the novel, the focus is on the two of them rather than on Annie alone, and as the ship sails, Annie stands at the rail and waves a red handkerchief wildly until her eyes can no longer distinguish her mother from others in the crowd of people left behind.

Has Annie John's mother no name? Indeed she has. Her name, too, is 'Annie John'. The fact that mother and daughter share the same name is mentioned casually just a few times in the novel, yet the name duplication is significant. By the time one finishes the novel, it is clear that the title refers to both women, that Annie John the daughter is in fact telling the story of *two* Annie Johns and the crucial mother-daughter bond that joins them.[9] Stressing this bond, and indicating the significance of the shared names, the narrator near the end of the novel says, 'She was my mother, Annie; I was her daughter, Annie' (p. 105). Also crucial is the island culture in which they live; thus the young Annie John's memories and perceptions of her cultural roots are tied to memories and perceptions of her mother. Annie's mother, for example, would often worry about portents and then consult with 'her obeah woman, and with her mother and a trusted friend'. The young Annie remembers specifically the results of one such consultation when these various mother-women mandated 'a special bath in which the barks and flowers of many different trees, together with all sorts of oils, were boiled in the same large cauldron. We would then sit in this bath in a darkened room with a strange-smelling candle burning away' (p. 14).

Food, of course, is always connected with mother. Annie recalls her mother cooking the 'special kind of fish that each of us liked' (p. 12). Her mouth watering, she meditates upon 'pumpkin soup with droppers, banana fritters with salt fish stewed in antroba and tomatoes, fungie with salt fish stewed in antroba and tomatoes, or pepper pot' (p. 17).

When Annie is sick her mother makes a poultice 'of ground camphor and eucalyptus leaves' for her chest (p. 87). During another, more serious illness, Annie's mother calls in an obeah woman from Dominica named Ma Jolie, and then they call in Annie's grandmother, Ma Chess. Both women nurse Annie, but 'whatever Ma Jolie knew, my grandmother knew at least ten times more' (p. 123). Significantly, obeah on the island is handed down through the female line. Whether or not the young Annie will follow obeah in her own life, it is clearly an important element in the mother-lines that bind her to her island home.

All these facets of island culture are described lovingly, as are the sounds of calypso music and the buttery soft island patois. In sharp contrast are comments about anything English. Annie's description of her headmistress, Miss Moore, is an example: 'I knew right away that she had come to Antigua from England, for she looked like a prune left out of its jar a long time and she sounded as if she had borrowed her voice from an owl' (p. 36). Continuing with her impressions of Miss Moore, Annie mentions her peculiar 'English' odour, and she recalls a comment of her mother's about the English: 'Have you ever noticed how they smell as if they had been bottled up in a fish?' (p. 36) Then there is poor Ruth, a yellow-haired schoolmate of Annie's who is obviously out of place on Antigua: 'Perhaps she wanted to be in England, where no one would remind her constantly of the terrible things her ancestors had done . . . her ancestors had been the masters, while ours had been the slaves' (p. 76).

It is highly ironic, then, that the younger Annie John chooses to leave her family and go to England, the place that has held for her only unpleasant connotations. Yet the final word in the novel is claimed by the older Annie John, as she clasps her daughter in a final embrace: 'She said, in a voice that raked across my skin, "It doesn't matter what you do or where you go, I'll always be your mother and this will always be your home"' (p. 147). Annie John may indeed travel far, but her 'home' will always be that island of many mothers, the place where mother and culture and land are one.

Jamaica Kincaid's *Annie John* is a very positive work. Though it ends with the young woman's departure for an alien world, the implication is not just that she will be able to return to the land of her mothers but in addition that she herself knows this, that she has in effect been empowered in her search for self-identity. If Kincaid's Annie John illustrates the positive effect of a developmental mother-bond, Jean Rhys' Antoinette Cosway in *Wide Sargasso Sea*[10] illustrates the devastating results when the mother-bond is denied. Unlike Kincaid's young protagonist who knows a biological mother's love in her early years, Antoinette Cosway is deprived of it. Born to a white Creole family on the island of Dominica, Antoinette's childhood is far from happy. The family estate 'Coulibri' is poor and dilapidated, Antoinette's father having squandered his fortune before he died. Her mother, a young widow with two children, is distant and depressed. One of Antoinette's earliest memories is of a frown that has creased itself permanently in her mother's face, as if 'cut with a knife'. When Antoinette touches her mother's face, shyly and tentatively, trying to smooth out the frown, her mother shoves her away: 'She pushed me away, not roughly but calmly, coldly, without a word, as if she had decided once and for all that I was useless to her . . . "Oh, let me alone," she would say, "let me alone"' (p. 20).

At this point in her life, Antoinette believes that things could not be much worse. But when her mother marries again, things become much worse indeed. Formerly Annette Cosway had taken no interest in her daughter, not caring where she went and what she did, in effect permitting her to 'go native' and neglect her English ways and manners. But now Annette becomes critical and disapproving, and meanwhile the black islanders focus and vent their hatred on Annette's family, the 'white cockroaches' who symbolise slavery and exploitation. When a mob burns the family estate, both mother and daughter escape. But Annette is by this time insane and is sent to a private home to be cared for, and when Antoinette goes to see her, she receives a final, devastating rebuke. In Antoinette's words, the rebuke is thus: '"I am here," I said, and she said, "No," quietly. Then "No no no" very loudly and flung me from her. I fell against the partition and hurt myself' (p. 48).

Deprived of a bond with her biological mother, Antoinette reaches out to possible surrogates, but there are few to be had. Antoinette's Aunt Cora (her mother's sister) takes Antoinette into her home in Jamaica after Coulibri is destroyed, but before long Cora leaves again for England and makes arrangements for Antoinette to stay in a convent. Cora obviously cares for Antoinette and tries to be helpful to her, especially when, with all the force she can muster, she opposes the marriage that Antoinette's stepfather wants to arrange. Yet Cora is ultimately too old and too much concerned with her own life to give Antoinette the nurturing that she needs.

Another surrogate, the ambiguous servant Christophine from Martinique, has been a part of Antoinette's life for as long as she can remember. Antoinette's mother never really trusted Christophine, yet the black woman feels a genuine, sorrowful affection for the Cosway women even though she often scolds, even reviles them. When all other servants leave, Christophine stays with the family until it is split by the destruction of Coulibri. Later, at Atntoinette's mother's funeral, Christophine is the only mourner to shed tears. And still later, after Antoinette marries the man chosen by her stepfather, Christophine returns as a house servant to help Antoinette. The term 'house servant', though, does not begin to describe the function of Christophine in Antoinette's life. Over the years the black woman is confidante, adviser, nurse, mentor and obeah woman. Most importantly, Christophine is a part of island culture in a way that Cora, English from her head to her toes, can never be. When Antoinette becomes desperate to keep her husband's interest, she rides her horse through the hills to Christophine's house: 'I had seen her so often standing knee deep in the river at Coulibri, her long skirt hitched up, washing her dresses and her white shifts, then beating them against the stones. Sometimes there would be other women all bringing their washing down on the stones again and again, a gay busy noise . . . She smelled too, of their smell, so warm and comforting to me (p. 108).

Ultimately, if Antoinette finds a surrogate mother-bond at all, she finds one in some complex way that encompasses

Christophine and the islands themselves. Thus even though Antoinette's childhood experiences with people are almost uniformly negative, the lush tropical setting provides an antidote to human rejections and cruelties. When still a child she spends her days with an island friend named Tia at a bathing pool in an Edenic setting: 'The pool [was] deep and dark green under the trees, brown-green if it had rained, but a bright sparkling green in the sun' (p. 23). Even Coulibri itself, though it falls into disrepair and decay, is for Antoinette a magical place of 'the golden ferns and the silver ferns, the orchids, the ginger lilies and the roses, the rocking-chairs and the blue sofa, the jasmine and the honeysuckle' (p. 45). In first talking to her husband about her early life, Antoinette says that 'all the flowers in the world were in our garden' and that '[my mother and I] were alone in the most beautiful place in the world, it is not possible that there can be anywhere else so beautiful as Coulibri' (pp. 130–131).

The convent school, too, where Antoinette lives as a teenager, is a place that she remembers with affection. Located in Spanish Town on the island of Jamaica, the convent grounds and buildings are sun-drenched yet full of cool nooks and crannies. In describing it, Antoinette remembers 'the blazing colours of the flowers in the garden', and she says unequivocally, 'This convent was my refuge' (pp. 56–57).

When Antoinette is married, she and her husband move to Granbois, an old house in the mountains that Antoinette owns and one in which she spent happy childhood hours and days. The setting is primitive, even wild. To Antoinette's English husband, 'Everything is too much . . . Too much blue, too much purple, too much green. The flowers too red, the mountains too high, the hills too near' (p. 70). In fact, he will never learn to abide the tropical colour and abundance. Yet this is the place that Antoinette loves even more than she loved Coulibri: 'I love [Granbois] more than anywhere in the world. As if it were a person. More than a person' (p. 89). Through a barely conscious act of anthropomorphic transference, Antoinette finds sustenance through her connection with the land. Always sensitive to its beauty, she drenches herself in the colours of the place, saying, 'The sky was dark blue through the dark green mango leaves, and I thought, "This is my place and this is where I belong and this is where I wish to stay"' (p. 108).

The island and its native culture, then, are something that Antoinette cannot afford to lose. Her own mother may have rejected her, but the land and the black woman Christophine do not. In fact, Antoinette's own retreat from reality is not complete and irrevocable until her connection with the islands is severed and she is taken, against her will, to England. Certainly Jean Rhys herself experienced such severance. As Cheryl ML Dash says of Rhys and her protagonist, 'For the creolised white England can never be real, never be as alive and as vibrant as the West Indies which has formed their psyche.'[11] (206). Throughout the novel Rhys makes this clear, giving to Christophine the assessment of England that is perhaps the most succinct: 'I hear it cold to freeze your bones and they thief your money, clever like the devil' (p. 112).

At the novel's end, Antoinette has become a madwoman, living in the attic of her husband's estate in England. Yet her past has not deserted her, for she has a recurrent dream:

> I saw the orchids and the stephanotis and the jasmine and the tree of life in flames. I saw the chandelier and the red carpet downstairs and the bamboos and the tree ferns, the gold ferns and the silver, and the soft green velvet of the moss on the garden wall . . . when I looked over the edge I saw the pool at Coulibri. Tia was there. She beckoned to me . . . (pp. 189–190)

From the attic window of an English mansion she leaps to her death, believing in her madness that she is regaining her mothers' land.

Antoinette Cosway, as just discussed, was tragically rejected by her mother. But Merle Kimbona, the central character in Paule Marshall's *The Chosen Place, the Timeless*

People,[12] cannot even remember her mother who, in an incident that was never explained or solved, was murdered when Merle was only two years old. For Merle, as a child, there were no surrogates. Her mother had been her father's mistress, not his wife, and after her mother's death Merle was bounced from the home of one relative after another. Then, when her father's wife died childless, Merle's father acknowledged her and sent the thirteen-year-old girl to fashionable schools on the island. This acknowledgment, however, meant nothing to Merle because no affection, no relationship prompted it or grew out of it. In fact, Merle's primary attachment while she attended her fashionable school on the island was to an old woman with whom she boarded. This island woman, whom Merle calls 'Aunt Tie', is the one person in all the world to whom Merle remains close. As Merle says, 'She was Mother and Father to me' (p. 357).

Merle, however, is not like Antoinette who seemed always to know the importance of her island roots. Merle Kimbona rejected her birthplace (called 'Bourne Island' in the novel) and spent 15 years away, in England. Her father had sent her there to university, and Merle herself chose to stay. She lived wild and she lived high, until she met the man she would love and marry. For two years, during which time the couple's daughter was born, Merle felt that she had indeed achieved the essential 'connection' that had been missing from her life. Her marriage ended disastrously, however, with Merle's husband taking their daughter and leaving. So broken and distraught that she is subject to severe depressions and periodic breakdowns, Merle returned to Bourne Island. But she makes it clear that she did so reluctantly: 'I don't know why I came back to the damn depressing place! . . . God knows I never intended to. I tried to plan things while I was in England so I'd never have to set foot on this island again' (p. 228). Indeed, even though Merle is accepted in all strata of Bourne Island society, even though she knows everyone and moves easily from city to village and back again, she finds no peace. Instead, she seems engaged in a never-ending war with herself, fighting 'the struggle for coherence, the hope and desire for reconciliation of her conflicting parts, the longing to truly know and accept herself' (p. 401).

As Merle finally acknowledges, to accept herself is to accept her homeland and culture. And to accept these is to forge the bond, to find the means of connecting with others, that she has sought all along. She has always had compassion for the island's poor and dispossessed while despising and resenting the very real economic power wielded by white colonials. But she has also felt shame and rage at her people's backwardness while enjoying, herself, some accoutrements of European culture. Torn by the conflicts of compassion and shame, Merle, in support of her own people, had seemed capable only of intermittent tirades that accomplished nothing and embarrassed everyone. Gradually, however, Merle works her way toward a sense of self which, for her, is a sense of unity with her people and her land. She says, 'It's almost, you know, as if I was destined to come back here, so that no matter how hard I tried, there was no avoiding it' (p. 226).

Commenting about her novel, Paule Marshall stresses the thematic importance of 'truly confronting the past, both in personal and historical terms'.[13] For Merle, this confrontation results in a mighty, symbolic gesture as she sheds all the remnants of her earlier life: her father's estate furniture, her battered English Bentley and the heavy silver earrings that represented to her the wasted years in England. Even more important, she stops using the talcum powder that 'she was forever dabbing on her face and throat as though to mute her darkness'. Further, 'her hair, which she normally kept straightened flat with the iron-toothed comb . . . now stood in a small rough forest around her face, framing it' (p. 463).

At the end of the novel, Merle leaves for Africa to find and reclaim her daughter. But there is no doubt that she will return to her island as, very simply, she says, 'I'll be coming back to Bournehills. This is home' (p. 468). Much earlier, another character had said of Merle, 'I don't think she'll ever leave here again, not for any length of time anyway. She's become too much a part of the place. In a way I can't explain, she somehow *is* Bournehills' (p. 118). In this context, it is significant that Merle's route to Africa is not the usual 'European' one of flying fom the islands to New York and then to London. Instead she will fly south to Trinidad, to Recife in Brazil, and from Recife to Dakar. Merle Kimbona will go on, the novel implies, to strive mightily in the political arena, with her most difficult struggle over because she has found, in her island roots, herself.

Like Merle Kimbona, Clare Savage wanders in a disconnected state for many years. Clare is clearly the protagonist of Michelle Cliff's 1987 novel *No Telephone to Heaven*,[14] yet a large early section of the book focuses equally on Clare's mother Kitty who is Jamaica-born and never wants to live anywhere else. While still in Jamaica, Kitty marries Boy Savage and has two daughters. But then Kitty's mother, Miss Mattie, dies, and Boy seizes the opportunity to move his family to New York. For Kitty, the new life is a living death. She misses the climate, the foods, the music and patois, the customs and traditions of Jamaica. With no warning and no explanation, Kitty moves back to the islands, taking Clare's dark-skinned sister with her but leaving Clare and her father, both of whom can presumably make lives for themselves because they can 'pass for white'.

For Clare, however, Kitty's abrupt rejection is traumatic. She is left unmothered, while still a child, 'not feeling much of anything, except a vague dread that she belongs nowhere' (p. 91). Between Clare and her father a gulf exists that only widens with time, Boy Savage having embraced his adopted country when he arrived in Brooklyn and completing his rejection of all things Jamaican by eventually marrying a white New Yorker of Italian descent. After Kitty dies, Clare's sister comes to visit in New York. But there is no bond between the two young women, and Clare is unable to find out from her sister why their mother took one of them and left the other, Clare, without so much as a word of farewell or explanation. Feeling rootless and alone, Clare begins an odyssey that takes her from New York to London and eventually across Europe, with intermittent returns to Jamaica. As Cliff writes about her protagonist, 'There are many bits and pieces to her, for she is composed of fragments. In this journey, she hopes, is her restoration' (p. 87).

During her brief trips to Jamaica, Clare stays with relatives on her father's side of the family. These relatives are in fact quite proud of her when she moves to London and enrolls in university there, and they always encourage her to make the best of this wonderful opportunity. Clare, though, thinks sardonically of her motives: 'Choosing London with the logic of a creole. This was the mother-country. The country by whose grace her people existed in the first place' (p. 109). At the same time Clare's only close friend in Jamaica, a transvestite who calls himself Harry/Harriet, tries urgently to persuade Clare that she must return permanently to Jamaica, her true home. She resists Harry/Harriet's urging, yet she finds London no more hospitable than New York: 'I feel like a shadow', she says, 'like I could float through my days without ever touching . . . anyone' (p. 111). Still resisting a return to Jamaica, Clare becomes involved with a black man from Alabama, a Vietnam veteran who carries a leg wound that will never heal. Together, both of them fleeing demons that they can hardly name, they embark on a cross-European journey. As might be expected, they are unable to succour each other. After a miscarriage, and seriously ill from a resulting infection and fever, Clare returns to Jamaica for good. At this time, she is 36 years old.

The Jamaica to which Clare returns is ravaged by poverty, crime and civil insurrection. Yet in the midst of all this, Clare begins to find her roots. She finds the way to her grandmother's house, now in ruins but now also belonging to Clare. Nearby is a river where, as a child, she watched washerwomen at work, slapping the clothes on rocks worn as smooth as silk. Here, too, she often swam, and in remembrance she does so again: 'The importance of this water came back to her. Sweet on an island surrounded by salt. She shut her eyes and let the cool of it wash over her naked body, reaching up into her as she opened her legs. Rebaptism' (p. 172).

This was not, though, a place where Clare came alone as a child. Thus she remembers that this river-place was where her mother, Kitty, 'was alive, came alive', and Clare thinks, 'I was fortunate I knew her here.' But then she stops, corrects herself: 'No, I was blessed to have her here. Her passion of place. Her sense of the people. Here is her; leave it at that' (pp. 173–74).

Indeed, 'here is her' for Clare Savage. In returning to her mother's land, Clare finds her mother. Equally important, she finds herself. At one point an old island woman thinks that Clare *is* Kitty, and this seems to Clare an appropriate sign that the years and miles separating mother and daughter are diminished. In response to a question as to why she returned, Clare says, 'I returned to this island to mend . . . to bury . . . my mother . . . I returned to this island because there was nowhere else . . . I could live no longer in bor- rowed countries, on borrowed time' (pp. 192–93: the ellipses are in the original). Having found her mother and herself, Clare goes on to make a personal and political commitment to Jamaica and its people. For the first time since leaving Kingston many years ago, Clare has found the place where she belongs.

In various ways, then, the lives of Annie John, Antoinette Cosway, Merle Kimbona and Clare Savage illustrate the complex relationship of a Caribbean woman to the land and culture of her mothers. Annie John bonds with her own mother and, through her, with their island home of Antigua. Antoinette Cosway, cruelly rejected by her own Creole mother, compensates by developing a bond with the black island woman Christophine and with the mother-islands of Dominica and Jamaica, where Coulibri and Granbois are located. Merle Kimbona, left un-mothered at the age of two, wanders for years until in middle age she reforges a long-severed bond with her island home and culture. And Clare Savage, also a wanderer until middle age, then finds the mother whom she had lost as she is literally rebaptised in the waters of her mother's land. All these women experience exile, described by Edward Said as 'fundamentally a discontinuous state of being. Exiles are cut off from their roots, their land, their past.'[15] Yet only Antoinette is destroyed by exile, because she alone is unable to return. The others are able to claim and connect with their island homes, and by doing so they truly find themselves. 'The question of a Caribbean identity', as one recent critic puts it, is 'the pre-emptive concern' of all West Indian literature.[16] This is true for individuals as well as for the region as a whole. And for women in particular, it appears that achieving such an identity depends upon a bond with and through many mothers, to one's island home itself.

A strong woman, declares Adrienne Rich, is one who has experienced the supportive empowering of another woman: 'I am talking here about a kind of strength which can only be one woman's gift to another, the bloodstream of our inheritance. Until a strong line of love, confirmation, and example stretches from mother to daughter, from woman to woman across the generations, women will still be wandering in the wilderness.' [17] Rich's words are particularly applicable to daughters of the Caribbean, for whom 'mother' and 'land' are inextricably related. Indeed, the 'bloodstream of their inheritance' flows through the islands. For it carries, in essence, a collective experience that encompasses language, laughter and love across the generations in the mothers' land.

Notes

1 Nancy Chodorow, *The Reproduction of Mothering: Psychoanalysis and the Sociology of Gender*, University of California Press, Berkeley, 1978, p. 93.

2 Carol Gilligan, *In a Different Voice: Psychological Theory and*

Women's Development, Harvard University Press, Cambridge, USA, 1982, p. 160.

3 Jean Baker Miller, *Toward a New Psychology of Women* (second edition), Beacon Press, Boston, 1986, p. xxiii.

4 The work of Chodorow and Gilligan in particular is considered controversial by many feminists, primarily because both writers ground their arguments in contemporary object relations theory which can in turn be traced to its roots in Freudian psychoanalytic theory. In essence, Chodorow and Gilligan work with a male 'separation paradigm' and a female 'connection-paradigm', both of which were developed by Freud. But Freud characterised the male separation-paradigm as superior and the female connection-paradigm as inferior (his theories about 'penis envy' and the 'castration complex', so offensive to feminists, are a logical extension of the male-centred perspective). Chodorow and Gilligan *reverse* this perspective, asserting that the female connection-paradigm is superior while the male separation-paradigm is destructive. Still, some critics contend that the Chodorow-Gilligan argument is a bad one because it perpetuates and legitimises a view of women as essentially different from men. See, e.g., Anne Hockmeyer, 'Object Relations Theory and Feminism: Strange Bedfellows', in *Frontiers* 10 (Autumn 1988), pp. 21–28. and Coppelia Kahn, 'The Hand That Rocks the Cradle: Recent Gender Theories and their Implications', *The (M)other Tongue: Essays in Feminist Psychoanalytic Interpretation*, eds. Shirley Nelson Garner, Claire Kahane and Madelon Sprengnether, Cornell University Press, Ithaca, New York, 1985, pp. 72–88.

5 Laura Niesen de Abruna, 'Twentieth-Century Women Writers from the English-Speaking Caribbean', *Modern Fiction Studies* 34 (Spring 1988), p. 87 and pp. 85–96.

6 Adrienne Rich, *Of Woman Born: Motherhood as Experience and Institution*, Norton, New York, 1976, p. 242.

7 Barbara Christian, 'Paule Marshall', in *Afro-American Fiction Writers After 1955*, eds. Thadious M Davis and Trudier Harris, vol. 33 of *The Dictionary of Literary Biography*, Gale Research, Detroit, 1984, p. 161 and pp. 161–170.

8 Jamaica Kincaid, *Annie John*, Farrar Straus Giroux, New York, 1983. All page references in the text are to this edition.

9 Bryant Mangum (in 'Jamaica Kincaid', *Fifty Caribbean Writers: A Bio-Bibliographical Critical Sourcebook*, ed. Daryl Cumberdance, Greenwood, New York, 1985, pp. 255–263) discusses this dual

focus in *Annie John*, but his argument moves in the other direction, stressing the separation of mother and daughter instead of their connection. The daughter, writes Mangum, must escape 'the pull of the world of prenatal union and harmony'. In effect, Mangum in such statements echoes the Freudian perspective that the male paradigm of separation is superior. Thus Mangum can say that 'every detail in [Annie's] life is important because it underlines the inevitability of her separation from her mother' (pp. 260–261). Taking instead the Chodorow-Gilligan perspective that the female paradigm of connection is superior, one might simply change the slant of Mangum's contention and say that 'every detail in Annie's life is important because it underlines the immutability of her connection with her mother'. Or, in refuting Mangum, one might cite this statement by Jean Baker Miller: 'Our theories of development seem to rest at bottom on a notion of development as a process of separating from others. I believe this notion stems from an illusion, a fiction which men, but not women, are encouraged to pursue.' (p. xxi)

10 Jean Rhys, *Wide Sargasso Sea* (first published in 1966), Norton, New York, 1982. All page references in the text are to this edition.
11 Cheryl ML Dash, 'Jean Rhys', in *West Indian Literature*, ed. Bruce King, Archon, Hamden, Connecticut, 1979, p. 206.
12 Paule Marshall, *The Chosen Place, the Timeless People* (first published in 1969), Random-Vintage, New York, 1984. All page references in the text are to this edition.
13 Quoted in Barbara Christian, p. 167.
14 Michelle Cliff, *No Telephone to Heaven*, EP Dutton, New York, 1987. All page references in the text are to this edition.
15 Quoted in Lucy Wilson, 'European or Caribbean: Jean Rhys and the Language of Exile', *Frontiers* 10, no. 3, 1989, pp. 68–72.
16 Erika J Smilowitz, 'Tales of the Caribbean', *The Women's Review of Books*, November 1987, pp. 13–14.
17 Adrienne Rich, p. 246.

Velma Pollard

Mothertongue Voices in the Writing of Olive Senior and Lorna Goodison

Jean D'Costa, Jamaican linguist and foremost Caribbean writer of children's novels, contends that the West Indian writer who wishes to satisfy himself, his local audience and his foreign audience, must evolve a 'literary dialect' which not only satisfies both these audiences but also is an authentic representation of the 'language culture' of his community.[1] And Garth St Omer, one of the better known of the West Indian novelists, comments on the dilemma of the post-colonial writer who must not only represent the society honestly but must be understood by all in the society.[2] Both these writers are addressing a situation that is the context of this discussion on Mothertongue. The tension between the ability to use a number of overlapping codes and the necessity to be understood not only within the society but by the reader outside of it is a constant part of the Caribbean writer's reality as s/he creates in prose or in poetry.

This essay looks at the language of the prose of Olive Senior and the poetry of Lorna Goodison to see how this, and other linguistic tensions are resolved in the writing of these two women who have achieved national and international recognition. It notes how they use the complex language situation to their advantage in the act of creating, particularly in terms of character identification.

A brief description of what D'Costa refers to as a 'polydialectal continuum with a creole base', is in order. The official language of Jamaica is Standard Jamaican English (SJE), a dialect of English as accessible to English speakers the world over as Standard American or Standard Australian English. It is the language of the school and of all the official organisations of the society. The majority of Jamaicans, however, speak Jamaican Creole (JC), a Creole of English lexicon which everyone in the speech community understands. Because of the lexical relationship between the two languages most Creole speakers regard themselves as English speakers. There is, in addition, a code introduced by the Rastafari, a socioreligious group, and adopted by other speakers, particularly the young. This code, Dread Talk (DT), has been described as an example of lexical expansion within a Creole system,[3] in this case Jamaican Creole. The grammatical structures of the code are, with few exceptions, the same as those of JC. The lexical items, however, taken originally from English, the source of most Jamaican words, have been subjected to a number of word-making processes drastic enough to give some words new sounds and others new meanings.

Most educated speakers in the society switch from one to the other of the codes described above, with no difficulty at all, as the discourse situation demands. Uneducated speakers tend to speak JC regularly and to attempt to switch to SJE only when they perceive the social situation to require it.

Because language and social class, in the stereotypical descriptions of these, are closely aligned, creative writers are able to use the codes to identify prototypical characters and attitudes. This is not to suggest a particular self-consciousness in the production of literary writing, for I believe that what we will look at is a reproduction of natural speech. What the artists have done is to select to write about situations requiring the use of the different codes available to speakers. It is precisely because the natural language of the people in the community is reproduced, that we are able to discuss language as it functions within the speech community, using as evidence texts from the writing we are about to examine.

Olive Senior

While all the stories in Olive Senior's two collections[4] might serve as a kind of laboratory for examining Jamaican speech, it might be useful to examine the speech behaviour of the characters presented in one story in detail, and then flesh out the comments possible with references from others. We will look at 'Real Old Time T'ing' from the earlier collection, largely because the content of the tale forces the author to have characters switch from one code to the next, thus offering us good examples of how the language operates in the real-life situation.

An ageing father, recently made a widower, finds himself up against a social-climbing daughter who wants him to build a new house bigger than the one in which he had raised their family of nine. Patricia, the nouveau riche, is introduced by the narrator who obviously does not intend this character to be a favourite with the reader. Examine the tone of the lines which begin the piece and introduce Patricia to the reader: 'Is the one name Patricia did start up bout how Papa Sterling need a new house . . . '

When Patricia eventually enters the stage her language is immediately perceived to be different from the narrator's. JC is the language of the teller of the tale. Patricia attempts to speak SJE:

> But hear the one Patricia she – this one Sunday she did drive down with the pickney dem. The husband didnt come:
>
> 'Poppa, this place really just too bad. The children shame to come here. We have to do something about it.'

The JC plural 'pickney dem' in the narrator's language is replaced in Patricia's by the SJE translation: 'the children'.

Note also the JC past tense 'did drive down' (not to be confused with the emphatic 'did' possible to SJE) where English would prefer 'drove' or 'had driven'. The attitude to Patricia is made clear in the idiomatic 'the one Patricia she' a turn of phrase reserved for deep disdain.

Patricia considers herself a speaker of SJE but her English retains the tell-tale signs of late or incomplete acquisition, its style typical of the speech of someone newly arrived at her current station in life. One expects 'the children are ashamed to come here', for example, where Patricia uses the JC 'the children shame . . . '

The father in the story is a JC speaker who controls SJE well enough to use it for effect. He pretends confusion when his daughter makes the suggestion that his house is too small:

> Too small? How yu mean gal? Doan is seven of you raise in this house. Plus yu mother alive then and me make nine. Nine of we live here. And now yu all gone and yu mother dead leaving me one and you telling me this house that I build with my very hands too small. Child you are speaking to me in parables. (p. 55)

Note that the last of the sentences in the extract above is in English and is in distinct contrast to what comes before. Papa has switched to English to allow the daughter to see the ridiculousness of her suggestion. He is being sarcastic. What his daughter says is quite clear. It is no parable but it is so illogical that there must be something not immediately obvious to him.

The JC used in the passages above is not pure or broad Creole which is, in any case, an abstraction for analysis by linguists. In terms of D'Costa's description, it lies somewhere along a continuum between JC and SJE. The non-JC speaker, while rare in the Jamaican community, is not shut out: and the foreign reader who understands English can make sense of it.

Let us look at the grammatical features of that part of the discourse, not found in English: The verb 'to be' does not always appear in JC where SJE would expect it, as in the chunk: 'now you—all gone and you mother—dead'. The verbs are not always marked to indicate past time where this is the time of the activity. See, for example, in ' . . . this house that I BUILD with my very hands . . . '. The subject pronoun 'we' is used in the object position as in ' . . . Nine of we live here . . . '.

The language with all its nuances, is clear to the Jamaican reader, and the essential sense can be gleaned by the foreign reader even if some of the finer points might be missed.

Miss Myrtella, who aspires to Papa's hand, is a caricature of someone who knows the virtue of English as a status marker. She talks with her mouth 'curl round the words', and is afflicted with an exaggerated case of the added 'H'. Note the following report:

'Ho Cousin Orris,' she call out. Horace is Papa Sterling first name. 'Oi dont know wot to do hit his so howful to be ha woman holl holone hin this worl Cousin Orris.'

While the dropping and adding of 'H' (as in '[H]am and [H]eggs') is common in Jamaican speech, the sustained adding exemplified in the excerpt above signals the speaker's intention to produce fine English.

Miss Myrtella has other attributes of the class Patricia wants to belong to. She wears good clothes; she knows about (green) tea (as 'opposed perhaps to folk drinks like mint and fever grass) and she sticks out her little finger while drinking from a cup. The two women are competitors. Miss Myrtella's arrival challenges Patricia's monopoly on these things. Patricia says maliciously that Miss Myrtella has no class and, among other things, 'can't speak properly', where 'properly' signifies English. The reader knows that Patricia herself has some difficulty with the language, although she has fewer problems than Miss Myrtella. But their competition serves only to underscore the point made earlier, that many Jamaicans who perceive themselves to be speakers of English are not.

While the use of language to identify character is most highly developed in this story, perhaps because its themes are class and society, it is also carefully matched with character in all the other stories. In the story 'Ascot', in the same collection, the written rather than the spoken word helps the reader note the development of the hero. Compare the following letters sent home to his mother from America as Ascot moves up in the world:

> Dear Ma wel i am her in New York is big plase and they have plenty car I am going to get one yr loving son Ascot.
>
> Dear mother wel here I am in Connecticut. Connecticut is Big plais. I driveing car two year now but is not wite yr loving son Ascot.
>
> Dear Mother Chicago is Big plais I drivein wite car for a wite man but he don make me where wite is blak unform so I mite leave yr loving son Ascot.

With each letter the language is more grammatically close to English, the sentences longer. (The amount of money sent home also increases with each letter.) When Ascot actually returns home on a visit, we note the change in his oral expression as well. The last record of his speech before migration runs: 'Laaad Mass Jackie is nuh me do it sah', as he defends himself from the charge of banana theft. When we meet him again he greets everybody and introduces his wife, ' . . . this is my wife Anthea', language being only one of the markers of this man's social development.

Constantly language marks off territory in an unobtrusive but precise way. This continues in Senior's second collection of short stories, although the language is consistently closer to English as the characters are closer to the middle and upper levels of the society. Note, however, the broad JC used as the maid in 'See the Tiki-Tiki Scatter' rejects the grand-daughter of the house with these words: 'No, no white people back yaso . . . Go weh. Back to yu big house' (p. 85). The word 'yaso', which translates as 'here' or more precisely 'in this place', signals a purer, broader level of JC than Senior commonly uses. The language of the helper in a household is likely to be far from English. People in the Big House speak English. People in all the big houses in the stories speak English.

In another story from that collection, 'Two Grandmothers', the narrator, their granddaughter in common, interacts with two women from different social worlds. Language is one of the measures of identification of these worlds. The narrator, recently back from holidaying with her father's mother, reports to her own mother:

> Mummy can you believe that everyone in church remembered me? And they said: 'WAT-A-WAY-YU-GROW' and 'HOW IS YU DAADIE?' and 'HOW IS YU MAAMIE?' till I was tired.

Her personal and instructive comment is:

> Mummy, that is the way they talk, you know, just like Richie and the gardener next door. 'WAT-A-WAY-YU-GROW.' They dont speak properly the way we do, you know. (p. 70)

The narrative voice in Senior's stories depends entirely on the identity of the narrator. In those instances, however, where the language is a version of JC, it is the turn of phrase, the idiom, more than the differences in grammar or lexicon, which signal its use. The non-JC speaker is unlikely to have difficulty understanding the words. Note the opening gambit of perhaps the most popular story of the collection *Summer Lightning*, 'Do Angels Wear Brassières?':

> Beccka down on her knees ending her goodnight prayers and Cherry telling her softly, 'And ask God to bless Auntie Mary.' Beccka vex that anybody could interrupt her private conversation with God so, say loud loud, 'no. Not praying for nobody that tek weh mi best glassy eye marble.' (p. 67)

or the righteous indignation of Aunt Mary at the kind of question Beccka chooses to ask her, whether she knew 'how worms reproduce':

> 'Yes, please. That is what the child ask me. Lightning come strike me dead if is lie I lie. In my own house. My own sister pickney. So help me I was so frighten that pickney could so impertinent that right away a headache strike me like autoclaps . . . ' (p. 69)

Mothertongue, certainly for a writer like Senior, is a number of speech codes: the broad JC of the maid in 'See the Tiki-Tiki Scatter', the English of the middle and upper classes, the hyper-corrected forms sometimes used by the aspirants to competence in English, the barely non-standard forms which make up the relaxed speech of many educated Jamaicans or the mixture of all these as the educated speaker switches from one code to the other, responding to situation or trying for effect. Because she is true to the characters she creates, and because she creates characters across the social boundaries, Senior exposes the reader to a very wide range of possibilities within the continuum between JC and SJE. Any study of this artist's language must take account of this range.

Concerning voice in her work, Senior, in an interview with Anna Rutherford, makes the following revealing statement:

> To me the sound of the voice is extremely important. I try to utilize the voice a great deal in my work and more and more find that what is happening is that the voice is taking over. In other words I am more and more concerned that my characters should speak directly to the reader and therefore I am dealing almost purely in narrative, in letting people tell their own story.[5]

They tell it each in her/his own mothertongue.

Lorna Goodison

Although poetry and good prose share many features, there are several differences, not the least of which is the terseness of the poetic form. An examination of mothertongue in poetry, in this case Lorna Goodison's poetry, is qualitatively different from the exercise just performed on Senior's prose.

Pamela Mordecai and Edward Baugh have both commented on Goodison's ability to slide from one to the other code of the Jamaican speech community. Mordecai notes the significance of the effective use of code-sliding as part of the 'mix-up' that is Jamaican culture.[6] Baugh's more detailed description praises her skill at, *inter alia*, 'interweaving erudite literary allusion with the earthiness of traditional speech'.[7] The idea of interweaving runs close to the present description which uses the term 'overlapping' to describe one feature of Goodison's style.

Two related features are here identified: one grammatical, the other lexical. In the one, two or three codes are made to overlap within the same line or poem: in the other the occasional JC item is woven into a poem whose fabric is undoubtedly SJE. The fact that all the codes in the Jamaican speech community are English-related facilitates the effectiveness of Goodison's strategies. If one of the codes were French-related, as is the situation in St Lucia, for example, the procedure would not be possible.

Baugh, in his study, looks at the poem 'Poui' from the second collection *I am Becoming My Mother*[8] and shows how, by using JC verb forms in the first and last lines ('She don't put out for just anyone/ . . . and she don't even notice'), the poet gives a JC flavour to a poem written almost entirely in SJE. In Goodison's hand the occasional JC item is like yeast in its effect on the mass of the poem. The content is accessible to JC and non-JC speaker alike, the language can be claimed by both.

Another poem from the series in which 'Poui' appears, 'Shame Mi Lady', furnishes a good example of both grammatical and lexical overlap operating within the same three lines. In order to receive the force of the strategy the reader has to be able not only to recognise but to produce JC because intonation is important. Let us examine the lines. The poet compares herself with the shrub whose name is the title of the poem:

> now, if I can find favour (me with my bold face)
> you bashful you shy you innocent lady
> must/bound to find absolution/grace (p. 14)

The 'you' of the second line is emphatic in English and is opposed to 'I' in the line above. But another reading is possible. The 'you' can be pronounced with a short 'u' in which case it becomes a JC pronoun with the accompanying predicate adjective 'bashful'. The utterance 'yu bashful' thus translates to English 'you are bashful'. The line then contains three sentences describing the lady and the sense must wait on the next line. That next line admits both JC and SJE, giving the reader the choice between the JC 'must (and) bound' of emphatic obligation, and the English 'must'. There are lexical sleights which depend only partly on intonation for their point. 'Bold face', for example, can be one Creole term, with the stress on 'bold', meaning 'fearless' bordering on rude, or two English words with equal stress, the one qualifying the other. In the same line a pun on 'favour' is also hinted at. The SJE meaning is dominant but lurking behind it is the kind of JC sentence, 'you face favour . . .', for which the listener is expected to supply some animal considered daring in folk parlance, 'favour' being in JC a verb meaning 'resemble'.

The poem 'My Will' has 46 lines. Among them there is only one instance of linguistic overlap. But the single word does have the effect of including JC among the vehicles of expression. The poet is leaving in her will a number of positive attributes and behaviours she wishes on her son. Included is the following: 'May you never know hungry' (p. 19). The uninitiated may well pass that over as an error and replace 'hungry' with the English 'hunger'. But what it is, is the JC predicate adjective 'hungry' in a sentence that might read 'may you never hungry' and might translate to SJE 'may you never be hungry'.

Later in the same poem Goodison, wishing for the boy none of the dangerous commodity, gold, translates the Creole 'bold face' explained above, to English ' . . . its face is too bold'. The initiated will immediately hear 'it too bold face'. And so here again JC and SJE are interwoven or overlap in the same utterance, this time only by inference. At this level the notions depend entirely on the listener's knowledge. The national community may hear two voices, the international community, one.

The rendering of complex behaviours and the sound of complex voices in a single statement by the deft manipulation of lexicon and syntax of the different codes is, I believe, Goodison's major contribution to Caribbean literature.

Perhaps the most daring use of this strategy is in the poem 'Ocho Rios II' from the earliest collection *Tamarind Season*.[9] In this poem it is necessary to express emotions felt by all Jamaicans. Speakers of JC, SJE and of the code of Rastafari are represented. The scene is set in Ocho Rios, the second largest tourist city of Jamaica. The poem begins with discourse by a Rastafarian who enters the stage soliloquising: 'Today I again I forward to the sea'. The form 'again' recognises both the habit of the Rasta man and the existence of an ealier poem 'Ocho Rios I', analysed in detail by Mordecai in the study cited above. The first person pronoun used initially might be either JC or Dread Talk (DT), but its repetition in the sentence with overtones of the first person alternative, 'I and I', available only to DT, identifies the speaker as a Rasta man. The choice of verb reinforces this interpretation. For while 'forward' adequately describes the act of walking, it is not used in this way in SJE or in JC. It is, however, a commonplace in DT. The first movement of the poem continues:

. . . to the build–up beach where a faithful few

lie rigid, submit to the smite of the sun.

Today I bless you from the sore chambers of my temples.

These lines are written in SJE except for one area of possible grammatical overlap with DT. The reader may now recognise it in the last line. The first person pronoun 'I', because of the repetition performed in the first line, may be identified as either DT or SJE. The presence of the Rasta man is maintainted by the use of DT. SJE indicates that the sentiment expressed is shared by the larger Jamaica.

An examination of an additional stanza, one again involving the sentiments of all Jamaica, serves to reinforce the point. It is the third movement of the poem in which Jamaica blesses the tourist and apologises to him for inclement weather:

> Bless you with a benediction of green rain, no feel no way
> its not that the land of the sea and the sun has failed,
> > is so rain stay.
> You see man need rain for food to grow
> so if is your tan, or my yam fi grow? is just so.
>
> P.S thanks for coming anyway. (p. 53)

In the first of these lines the double negative introduces the aside which marks the switch from English to JC, 'no feel no way'. In the next line the explanation 'is so rain stay' is JC. It is the voice of the peasant farmer for whom 'green rain' which ruins the tourist's tan is a blessing. It brings green lushness and productivity to the plants which are his source of income. He apologises for what might seem to the tourist to be a selfish preference; rain over sun. Note that JC used here can be understood (I believe) by the English-speaking foreigner who might himself have rendered it 'that is how rain is'.

All the speakers identify with the sentiments of the next two lines but it is the voice of the Rasta man that articulates it. What seems to be the impersonal 'man' in SJE is in fact the multifunctional pronoun of DT sometimes represented by its variants, 'the man', 'I-man', 'the I'. It is followed by the unmarked verb of JC and of DT. The next line continues with the voice of the peasant farmer in JC, to be followed by the polished English of the tourist board representative thanking the disappointed tourist for choosing Jamaica for his holiday. In each case it is language that identifies the different actors in this dramatic piece; and the voices of characters identify their place in the society, the sectors of the society they represent, enhancing the word pictures which they accompany. It is in this example that Goodison's use of the languages of the society in poetry resembles most Senior's use of it in prose.

Dread Talk, the code of Rastafari, features very strongly in the poem above. Elsewhere in Goodison the Rasta man, through his words, is constantly acknowledged as part of the Jamaican manscape. Sometimes it is necessary to repeat an idea already expressed in SJE, to accommodate this code. The repetition, however, is not obtrusive because the words are different. Note for example the following from 'Ceremony for the Banishment of the King of Swords' from the collection *Heartease*:[10] ' . . . go through this again so you can penetrate it . . . ' (p. 53) To 'penetrate' in SJE means to go through in a very literal sense. In DT, however, it means to 'understand'. The sentence really means 'go through that again so you can understand it'. What is important for the purposes of this paper is the extent to which Goodison seems to have internalised the multilingual nature of the speech community.

Another example is found in 'A Rosary of Your Names' from this same collection. God is worshipped here in a litany of fine words:

Your names are infinity
light and possibility
and right
and blessed
and upfull (p. 58)

'Upfull' is a DT word whose meaning includes both 'right' and 'blessed'. And, although it is not an English word, its sound is so much in accord with the words around it that the ear accustomed to English does not reject it.

The final example of this use is the last stanza of the poem 'Heartease I', in which the poet puns on the sound of the pronoun 'I' and so includes one strong symbol from the Rastafarian belief system articulated in the words of the code: the sound which is shared by the first person pronoun mentioned before, and the organ of sight:

> Believe, believe
> and believe this
> the eye know how far
> Heartease is (p. 33)

'The-I' is an alternative to 'I-man' and 'I-and-I'. It is the Rastafarian sound of the 'ego'. It is also the sound which describes the organ of sight. 'Seeing' is very important to the Rastafari, its opposite 'blindness' is a hallmark of non-believers. Again one might easily think Goodison is employing non-standard English and needs to correct the verb to 'knows'. But the sentence is: 'I know how far Heartease is'. Choosing to write 'eye' instead of 'I' concedes that the reader will take the former for granted but needs to be pointed to the latter. Goodison is generalising a sentiment. The narrator knows how far away from the present reality Heartease is, as do we all, especially the Rasta man who is particularly far from ease in the society in which he is the oppressed (downpressed). Here is clever artistry that goes beyond the simple pun and describes a multiple consciousness in what seems on the surface to be a single mode of expression.

One challenge Goodison has more than adequately met is the representation of the complex Jamaican language situation within the terse form that is poetry.

Conclusion

Mothertongue as it is traditionally defined, is one-dimensional. It is that one language the individual first acquires and learns to use in communicating with other people. To operate effectively in the Jamaican situation however, and in situations similar to it, is to master at least two codes. Mothertongue in the Jamaican situation might usefully be thought of as 'language' rather than 'a language'. Indeed, recent research into Caribbean language has certainly begun to consider acquisition in these terms.[11]

This brief incursion into the use of language by two creative writers points to the intricacy of the patterns people in the Jamaican and similar speech situations continually make. The exercise also responds in part to the concerns articulated by D'Costa and St Omer and referred to at the beginning of this essay. Both local and foreign readers are accommodated by these two artists; although admittedly, one group, for whom this complexity of codes is Mothertongue, responds to each text on more levels than the other.

Notes

1   Jean D'Costa, 'The West Indian Novelist and Language: a Search for a Literary Medium' In *Studies in Caribbean Language*, ed. Lawrence Carrington et al., University of the West Indies, St Augustine 1983.

2   Garth St Omer, *The Colonial Novel*, a Ph.D. dissertation, Princeton University, 1975: published by University Microfilms, Ann Arbor, Michigan.

3   For a description of this speech see Velma Pollard, 'Dread Talk: the Speech of the Rastafari of Jamaica', *Caribbean Quarterly* vol. 26, no. 4, 1982.

4   Olive Senior, *Summer Lightning and Other Stories*, Longman, Harlow, 1986; and *Arrival of the Snake Woman and Other Stories*, Longman, Harlow, 1989. All page references in the text are to these editions.

5 Anna Rutherford, 'Olive Senior Interview' In *Kunapipi* vol. viii, no. 2, 1986.

6 Pamela Mordecai, 'Wooing with Words: Some Comments on the Poetry of Lorna Goodison', *Jamaica Journal* no. 45, 1981, pp. 38–40.

7 Edward Baugh, 'Goodison on the Road to Heartease', *Journal of West Indian Literature* vol. 1, no. 1, 1986, p. 20.

8 Lorna Goodison, '*I Am Becoming My Mother*, New Beacon Books, London, 1986.

9 Lorna Goodison, *Tamarind Season*, The Institute of Jamaica, Kingston 1980.

10 Lorna Goodison, *Heartease*, New Beacon Books London, 1988.

11 See Lawrence D Carrington, 'Acquiring Language In a Creole Setting', *Papers and Reports on Child Language Development*, no. 28, Stanford University, California, 1989.

Absent and Adopted Mother(land)s

Laura Niesen de Abruna

Family Connections: Mother and Mother Country in the Fiction of Jean Rhys and Jamaica Kincaid

For the generation of Caribbean women writing in the 1980s and into the 1990s, literary foremothers are such writers as Phyllis Shand Allfrey and Jean Rhys, the latter the better writer of the two. This essay will explore the notion of the 'colonial motherland' in terms of literary inheritance, particularly the influence of one of the pioneer writers, Jean Rhys, on one of the fine contemporary writers, Jamaica Kincaid. Rhys is a foremother in the sense that her presentation of the full range of women's experience is rarely found in the writing of male or female writers, even in the Caribbean, with its predominately matrifocal family. Full female experience, or even the different perspectives provided by women characters, has begun to be presented only in the work of a very few women writers. In the Caribbean, Jean Rhys is one of the first and one of the best of these authors, both in terms of the formal aesthetic merits of the fiction and the exquisiteness of psychological portrayal. Rhys is the literary mother to the next generation of women writers because she was the first Caribbean woman to create texts dealing with the complex mother-daughter matrix. She was also the first writer to employ modernist narrative devices, such as dreams and associative thinking, as the narrator's strategies of resistance to the dominant culture.

The formal qualities of such texts as *Wide Sargasso Sea*, her best work, are poetic compression, orality and metaphor, as well as interior monologues and the importance of dreams and association as representational forms. The primacy of the dream vision ending that novel and the continual use of dreams in *Voyage in the Dark* draw attention to Rhys' modernist use of dreams and to the greater acceptance of dreams as a respected type of reality in the work of women writers.[1] In *Voyage in the Dark* dreams and reveries give the novel its structural principle since the narrator uses these means to return to her past whenever something threatening occurs in her present. The blurring of past and present was a deliberate strategy. In a 1934 letter to Evelyn Scott, Rhys pointed out her desire to make *Voyage in the Dark* a conflation of the present and the past. The novel would show, through the use of dreamlike narrative, that the past and the present exist side by side[2]: 'I tried to do it by making the past (the West Indies) very vivid – the present dreamlike downward career of a girl'.[3] Rhys' great contribution to full presentation of female life is her exploration of the mother–daughter bond, and specifically the effects of the loss of maternal matrix.[4] The alienation from the mother becomes a metaphor for the white Creole girl's alienation from the mother culture, England.

An emphasis on the personal area of experience is characteristic of women's writing in many cultural contexts. In their recent anthology entitled *Her True-True Name*, Betty Wilson and Pamela Mordecai testify to a flowering in the 1980s of women's writing dealing with such concerns as surviving sexism, negotiating mother–daughter relationships and an interest in relational interaction, or 'bonding'.[5] Most of this literature is concerned, as Evelyn O'Callaghan points out, with bringing the 'personal (private, emotional issues) into the public arena (literature)' (p. 147). In her and Merle

Collins' anthology of black women writers, *Watchers & Seekers: Creative Writing by Black Women*, Rhonda Cobham argues for the centrality of either bonding or the absence of bonding in the texts of Caribbean women writers, especially in the literary focus on emotional inter-dependence of mothers and daughters, granddaughters and grandmothers, friends and sisters:

> Their perspectives may be critical, nostalgic or celebratory, sentimental or distanced. But repeatedly there emerges a sense of sisterly solidarity with mother figures, whose strengths and frailties assume new significance for daughters now faced with the challenge of raising children and/or achieving artistic recognition in an environment hostile to the idea of female self-fulfillment. (p. 6)

These are the very issues that Rhys was the first to explore in her fiction, so that every Caribbean writer is in this sense the literary descendant of Rhys.

Suggesting a literary mother-daughter link between Rhys' and Kincaid is problematic because there are major differences between the two in terms of race and class interests in their work. Although critics have recognised the aesthetic merits of her fiction, Rhys has not been fully accepted as a West Indian writer because she was a white Creole whose family came from the planter class. Yet a rejection of the formal beauty and the power of the female Creole voice in Rhys' fiction is unwise and untenable. Rhys is a major voice in West Indian writing and has exerted much influence on the younger generation of women writers.

Rhys functions as a literary mother to Kincaid because both authors focus so intensely on the relationship between mothers and daughters and the consequences of the lack of this relationship. In both authors' works, there is a correlation between the political difficulties afflicting the island-'mother' country relationship and the problems affecting the mother-daughter family relationship. In both cases, the characters' separation from the mother or the 'mother' country evokes

extreme anxiety that appears as cultural and psychic alienation. In Rhys' writing, especially her novels *Voyage in the
Dark* and *Wide Sargasso Sea*, it is the absence of an affirming
mother or an affirming 'mother' country that causes dislocation and alienation, and ultimately speaks to the importance
of such bonds.[6] A later writer like Jamaica Kincaid uses the
mother-daughter relationship as her major focus, and also
the daughter culture-mother culture bond in a much more
direct way (in *Annie John* for example), because Rhys had
already prepared the way through her fiction.

To demonstrate this indebtedness of child to mother text,
I propose to look at Jean Rhys' first novel, *Voyage in the Dark*
(1934), and Jamaica Kincaid's first novel *Annie John* (1983).
Both novels concern a young woman's struggle to achieve
an identity based on the West Indian cultural experience.
Both Anna (*Voyage in the Dark*) and Annie (*Annie John*)
experience great tensions in their relationships with their
mothers: Annie because of the early intensity of the bond,
and Anna because of the complete severance of that bond. In
both novels, the importance of female bonding is central and
centred in the character's relationship with her mother. In
both texts, the character's personal alienation is explored
directly and then as a metaphor for the alienation of the
daughter-island from the mother-country. The metaphorical
exploration offers a criticism of the neo-colonial attitudes that
inhibit the lives of both Annie and Anna. Both women are
victims of their environments since Anna experiences real or
near-death in the abortion scene at the end of the novel,
and Annie experiences a long mental breakdown just before
deciding to leave for England.[7] Both Anna and Annie are
forced by family circumstances to leave their islands and
attempt to find new lives. At the end of *Annie John*, Annie
can find her own identity, signalled through her calling on
her own name.[8] She is able to do this through her identification with her mother and her grandmother, Ma Chess,
who fills the maternal role when Annie's mother can no
longer cope with her illness. In *Voyage in the Dark*, in con-

trast, Anna's slide towards prostitution and then into a botched abortion and death (at least in the original manuscript) testifies to her inability to find that speaking self, that identified self Annie is able to locate. Anna's complete alienation and destruction may be due to her amorphous status as a white Creole attempting to negotiate an identity in England. Not having been accepted in either the black community in her own island, or the white British community in England, Anna really has no identity except as alien. Annie, on the other hand, will probably survive the trip to England because she is less divided in both her cultural and her personal identity. While it is the literary daughter character Annie who is more successful than the older character Anna, the significance of the first character cannot be underestimated. The story of divisions in self-concept and in cultural identity as experienced by West Indian women was told first by Jean Rhys. In particular, Rhys' first novel *Voyage in the Dark* creates a clear space for the concerns of another specific novel, Jamaica Kincaid's *Annie John*.

Jean Rhys' fiction is often autobiographical in inspiration. While the female narrators of *Voyage in the Dark*, Anna Morgan, and *Wide Sargasso Sea*, Antoinette Cosway, are clearly not Rhys herself, the ruptures in mother-daughter bonds suffered by Anna and Antoinette are similar to the personal experiences of Rhys as a young woman. Rhys has provided evidence in both her letters, collected by Francis Wyndam and Diana Melly, and in her unfinished autobiography *Smile Please*,[9] that her link with her mother was strained and eventually severed after Rhys moved to England. Rhys' mother, Minna Lockhart Williams, was apparently a reserved woman who neglected her daughter and completely ignored her after Jean reached puberty.[10] Teresa O'Connor quotes a section of Rhys' unpublished journal, known as the 'Black Exercise Book', that indicates maternal abuse: 'My mother beat me ["whipped me severely" is inserted above the line] I was fond of her but somewhere in my heart I despised her' (f. 12). (Quoted in O'Connor,

p. 22.) In fact, O'Connor argues that the unresolved nature of Rhys' relationship with her mother was the force drawing her back to the island of Dominica, or the myth of Dominica, throughout her life and explains why her final and best work takes place in the Caribbean (p. 10).

The facts of Anna Morgan's life parallel those of Jean Rhys' own life. In 1907, at the age of seventeen, Ella Gwendolen Rees, later to be known as Jean Rhys, left Dominica and emigrated to England. After two years spent in school and on stage she met a considerably older man and stopped working. After the end of the affair, she was left alone to cope with an unwanted pregnancy and a botched abortion. Rhys almost died, but when she recovered she began writing compulsively about the affair in an exercise notebook, later called the 'Black Exercise Book'. The original indicates that the first title of *Voyage in the Dark* was 'Two Tunes', which indicates the shifts of the novel from Anna Morgan's present life in England in 1914 to her past life on an island that is clearly Dominica. As in *Wide Sargasso Sea*, there is in *Voyage in the Dark* a prominent role given to dreams and their ability to carry meaning. For Rhys the dream-like feeling of the novel is a way of conflating the past and the present. Although it was not published until two decades after it was written, Rhys later claimed often that it was her favourite novel (quoted in O'Connor, p. 7), probably because it delved into the same intense layer of autobiography as did *Wide Sargasso Sea* but did so earlier and in a less mediated form.

Deprivation of the mother and emigration to England are also the fate of Anna Morgan, whose life is similar to that of Rhys. Anna leaves Dominica to attend school in England, under the guardianship of her stepmother. After her father's death Anna leaves school and joins a chorus group. She meets Walter Jeffries, a considerably older man, and falls into a sexual liaison that is destructively based on her dependence and his dominance and exploitation.

Critics and readers have been puzzled about the breakdown that Anna experiences after Walter Jeffries leaves her. Even more important is the paralysis that she has suffered because of inadequate strength of ego, which is related to inadequate mothering. When she realises that she has been abandoned she is consumed with a fear that is out of proportion to the event:

> And I saw that all my life I had known that this was going to happen, and that I'd been afraid for a long time, I'd been afraid for a long time. There's fear, of course, with everybody. But now it had grown, it had grown gigantic; it filled me and it filled the whole world.[11]

After their meeting she decides to tell him that she does not want money but simply to see him again: 'You think I want more than I do. I only want to see you sometimes, but if I never see you again I'll die. I'm dying now really, and I'm too young to die' (p. 97). This feeling is linked immediately to the death of her mother, since her subsequent and impulsive reverie is about a funeral in Dominica, with voices murmuring that the deceased was too young to die (p. 97). When begging Jeffries does no good, Anna imagines herself as being drowned, a figure looking out from underneath the water, her face like a mask.

After Jeffries abandons her, Anna drifts into prostitution and becomes pregnant. She tries to arrange for an abortion, but is caught in a typical 1914 situation – no one but a hack is willing to perform such an operation. The novel's original ending shows Anna dying as a doctor attempts to remedy the botched, illegal abortion she has endured. When Rhys submitted the novel to her publishers, Constable, the editors disapproved of ending the novel with Anna's abortion and death. They insisted that she rewrite it. Under constraint, Rhys complied so that in the published version, the version that is still in print, the doctor and Anna's friend Laurie are laughing as he is attending Anna. Anna's words are:

> When their voices stopped the ray of light came in again under the door like the last thrust of remembering before

everything is blotted out. I lay and watched it and thought about starting all over again. And about being new and fresh. And about mornings, and misty days, when anything might happen. And about starting all over again, all over again . . . (pp. 187–88)

The original version of the manuscript indicates that Anna dies during this last scene. The final paragraph of the manuscript reads:

And the concertina-music stopped and it was so still, so still and lovely like just before you go to sleep and it stopped and there was the ray of light along the floor like the last thrust of remembering before everything is blotted out and blackness comes. (Quoted in O'Connor, p. 129.)

The original ending indicates that Rhys intended that Anna be a young woman without maternal support, exploited by men, who dies in a hostile country.[12] Rhys' own sense of the correctness of her ending is reinforced by the logic of the narrative. The narrative demands Anna's death since only this logically follows Rhys' attempt to make the maternal and colonial deprivations parallel. Anna is killed by the absence of a nurturing mother and of nurturing 'mother' country. Anna drifts into death when her consciousness is 'blotted out', and her voyage from Dominica to England is a voyage into the darkness of death. This voyage into the dark, and out of the light, suggests the way the colonial is treated in the mother country – a coercive and oppressive relationship that is followed by an attempt to control the minds and bodies of those colonised.[13]

This coercion of the colonised, a colonisation of their bodies, is clear during Anna's pregnancy when she compares her situation to being on a ship and then being thrown overboard. When Anna becomes pregnant it appears to be accidental. Almost immediately, she thinks of having an abortion as a way of controlling her situation. Her reveries of what she should do are punctuated with memories of being forced away from her island. She dreams that she is on a ship and:

> From the deck you could see small island – dolls of islands – and the ship was sailing in a dolls' sea, transparent as glass.
>
> Somebody said in my ear, 'That's your island that you talk such a lot about.'
>
> And the ship was sailing very close to an island, which was home except that the trees were all wrong. These were English trees, their leaves trailing in the water. I tried to catch hold of a branch and step ashore, but the deck of the ship expanded. Somebody had fallen overboard. (p. 165)

The heaving of the boat wakes her up and becomes the heaving of her stomach as she suffers nausea. She is the person who has fallen overboard in an alien ocean. The ship has taken her from Dominica to England, the place where the trees are all different. Having been forced away from her island, it has assumed an air of unreality and triviality, like a doll island rather than a human homeland. The social and economic powerlessness she feels in England, the desperate feeling of being trapped by changes in her body, and the deprivation of the maternal matrix represented by the island, are all embodied in this dream.

In *Voyage in the Dark*, as in Rhys' later novels, there is a woman narrator who is deprived of parental nurturing and suffers from this lack of support. Anna's mother has died before the opening of the novel, and her father dies soon after her arrival in England. Her situation is exacerbated because of her political status as a white Creole and her subsequent alienation as a colonial in England. There she becomes a marginal woman living on the money received in exchange for sex. This is a pattern not only in *Voyage in the Dark* but also in all of her novels, in each of which the female character is rejected first by their mothers and then by a male lover, or series of lovers. It appears in all of these novels that the men in positions of power and wealth are the enemy, but the problems of identity and self-esteem for the women characters stem from their inadequate bonding with their mothers. Unable to form a positive self-identity, they are vulnerable to exploitation by men and other women.

The narrative pattern in *Voyage in the Dark* is therefore one of maternal loss and attempted compensation through memory. In these memories, Anna attempts to recapture the island itself, symbol of the mother. Although the memories seem to be reveries out of Anna's control, they form a pattern. Each time Anna suffers loss or humiliation, she returns to thoughts of the island as an unconscious way of deflecting despair through imaginative attachment to the mother. While the projection of such comfort is an admirable strategy against complete dominance by the colonial power, it is inadequate to save Anna, and we must wait for Antoinette Cosway to find a character capable of turning dream compensation into adequate resistance.

Anna's emigration to England was a watershed for her, the breaking off of all possibility of finding connection with the maternal or the maternal island. To indicate this frequent break of past from present, Rhys uses the image of a curtain falling. The novel's first words concern the alienation Anna felt upon arriving in England: 'It was as if a curtain had fallen, hiding everything I had ever known. It was almost like being born again' (p. 7). Here England acts as a negative substitute for the parents, and especially the mother, that Anna has lost in coming to the 'mother' country. In being born again she has lost connection with her biological mother and has re-emerged as a child without parents, as an orphaned consciousness unable to ground itself.

Anna searches for mother substitutes throughout the novel, and her search is represented in terms of images of the island. In the first chapter Anna thinks to herself that an older woman in the chorus, Laurie Gaynor, is the only woman on stage who shows her affection. (And it is Laurie who takes Anna into her home when she needs an abortion.)

This act of mother substitution is followed immediately by a memory about Dominica:

> Lying between 15° 10' and 15° 40' N. and 61° 14' and 61° 30' W. 'A goodly island and something highland, but all overgrown with woods,' that book said. And all crumpled into hills and mountains as you would crumple a piece of paper in your hand – rounded green hills and sharply-cut mountains.
>
> A curtain fell and then I was here. (p. 17)

Anna never adjusts to life in a different country because her problems with her mother are unresolved. She longs for the 'rounded green hills' of the goodly island, a maternal image that reinforces the traditional association of the land and of nature with the female. A falling curtain points to the impossibility of the desired pre-oedipal merging with the mother. A falling curtain also indicates the end of a theatrical presentation, like the one in which Anna is currently engaged, and marks an end rather than a beginning. Coming to England does not indicate the opening of the curtains but their closing, the end of something. The novel does not move forward in time, just as Anna's life does not progress but stagnates in its own despair. Her sexual liaison with Walter Jeffries is not romance but a symptom of stagnation, an attempt to destroy reality: 'You shut the door and you pull the curtain over the windows and then it's as long as a thousand years and yet so soon ended' (p. 79). And, when she closets herself in a new room after the affair and writes about it, she remarks 'I kept the curtains drawn all the time' (p. 104).

A further image associated with the falling curtain is impending blindness, the falling curtain being the image suffered by someone whose retina has become detached by a hard blow to the head. The image is repeated later in the novel to describe the condition of people in marginal positions. The preacher at Marble Arch, dismissed by Maudie as insane, attracts Anna because she respects his understanding, 'because his eyes had a blind look, like a dog when it sniffs something' (p. 48). The image of blindness is also linked with darkness, and darkness with death, leading to the true ending of the novel. In formal terms, the narrative is aborted by the closing of a curtain on the future.

Because there is no future to anticipate, Anna is tempted to compress the past and the present into a dreamlike state that adumbrates the death scene at the end of the novel: 'Sometimes it was as if I were back there and as if England were a dream. At other times England was the real thing and out there was the dream, but I could never fit them together' (p. 8). This confusion of dream and reality is also one of the formal experiments of the novel. Anna is suspended in a static, dreamlike state because she cannot fit past and present together. As she remarks about her experience with Jeffries: 'I got that feeling of a dream, of two things that I couldn't fit together' (pp. 77–78). Because she cannot fit past and present together, there is no possible future for her. Rhys shifts the narrative from straightforward progression to dreamlike sequences throughout the novel to reinforce the idea that Anna is caught in a nightmare state of unreality imposed by her psychological stress.

Throughout the novel Anna meets a series of unforgiving, negative mother figures. Many of them are landlandies, whom Anna regards as surrogate mothers. The first in this series is the landlady who reproves Anna and Maudie for coming downstairs in their nightgowns and robes. Maudie acknowledges the link between reproving landlady and mother directly: ' "It's all right, ma," Maudie said. "I'm going up to get dressed in a minute" ' (p. 9). Later, when Maudie and Anna bring home Walter Jeffries and his companion, she 'glares' at them, speechless in her disapproval. At her flat in London, Anna's landlady dislikes her receiving flowers and money from a man and tells her to leave: ' "I don't want no tarts in my house, so now you know" ' (p. 30). Anna describes all of her landladies in detail, but focuses on their reactions to her, thereby giving them judgmental power. After her affair with Jeffries has ended, Anna's new landlady is monstrous: 'This one had bulging eyes, dark blobs in a long, pink face, like a prawn' (p. 103).

Images of the critical mother–landlady are juxtaposed with compensatory dreams of the island. The image of Anna's second landlady is followed by reminiscences of the good mother substitute, Francine, her black nurse in Dominica, who once saved her from a great fear of cockroaches: 'I was happy because Francine was there, and I watched her hand waving the fan backwards and forwards and the beads of sweat that rolled from underneath her handkerchief' (p. 31). In *Smile Please* Rhys speaks of a black woman, Francine, whom she admired and who told stories beginning with a ritual invocation to the obeah god Boissêche. Francine's positive role is carried through into that of Anna's nurse Francine in *Voyage*. Interestingly, Rhys identified her own nurse as a woman named Meta, whom she disliked and feared. According to the account in *Smile Please*, Meta told Rhys enough stories about zombies, soucriants and loup-garous (werewolves) that she claims to have remained marked by fear throughout her life: 'Meta had shown me a world of fear and distrust, and I am still in that world' (p. 24).

Through her identification with Francine, Anna fantasises that she herself is mulatta and attempts to link herself imaginatively with others who have been cast out by the British. She identifies with one of the slaves on her family's old estate, a house servant named Maillotte Boyd, listed in the records as 18 years old, Anna's present age. Anna returns to this identification when she realises that Jeffries considers her a disposable purchase. Then she remembers Maillotte again: '*Maillotte Boyd, aged 18. Maillotte Boyd, aged 18 . . . But I like it like this. I don't want it any other way but this*' (p. 56). She recognises the link between Maillotte and herself since both are women whose bodies are owned by men who can sell them, or buy them off in Anna's case, when they grow tired of them. Anna cannot find any comfort through identification with Francine because the racial barrier prevented a bond that would have been continually nurturing. Despite their good communication, Francine, here more like Rhys' Meta, is ultimately suspicious of Anna because she is white: 'But I knew that of course she disliked me too because I was white; and that I would never be able to explain to her that I hated being white' (p. 72). For the same reason, Maillotte cannot really be a sister substitute.

Despite these problems of identification with oppressed peoples, Anna has some strategies for resistance. Among them is that of aligning poor white women with the black women whose bodies were bartered for money. Writing, too, is a strategy of resistance, as she re-creates her experience of emotional and financial bondage in her room, in her words, and from her perspective rather than from the male power base represented by Walter Jeffries. Writing allows her to find a connection between herself and the Carib Indians who were never conquered by the Europeans who sought to subdue Dominica: '"The Caribs indigenous to this island were a warlike tribe, and their resistance to white domination, though spasmodic, was fierce . . . " They are now practically exterminated' (p. 105).

Anna's stepmother Hester is the worst of the rejecting mothers, a woman who represents all the pettiness and hostility of all of the landladies and shopkeepers. Without consulting Anna, she had written to Anna's Uncle Ramsay telling him that she should really go back home. Hester has suspected how Anna lives without any visible source of income and eschews responsibility for her behaviour. She writes to her uncle insisting that he pay for half Anna's fare back to Dominica. Ramsay states that Hester has cheated Anna out of the inheritance of the estate since Hester sold it and moved to England without giving Anna any money from the sale. Hester's response to this letter evidences a resentment of the island, her husband, the isolation, weather and the people, about whom she shows a real racism. She turns around the conversation by accusing Anna of whoring: 'Because don't imagine that I don't guess how you're going on. Only some things must be ignored some things I refuse to be mixed up with I refuse to think about even' (p. 63). Hester clearly regards everyone who grew up in Dominica mulatto or black and feels free to reject Anna on that basis alone. She never writes again to Anna, and that is her last communication with the woman who is supposed to be her stepmother. Instead of fighting with her, Anna concedes defeat and hopes that she can live on Jeffries' money.

Ethel Matthews is the final negative mother image in the novel. A victim of British respectability yet unable to support herself, Ethel walks the line between masseuse and madame. She expects Anna to behave in the same way, but Anna does not know British hypocrisy games, nor does she really care enough about her reputation to indulge in duplicity. As if in a strangled mother-daughter dyad, Ethel feels that she both hates Anna, asking her to leave at one time, and also needs her desperately because she is getting old and wants company. At one point she reveals some of her genuine feelings: 'Look here, I'll tell you something. You can clear out. You're no good; I don't want you here' (p. 144). Yet she also begs Anna's forgiveness because she needs her company. When Anna becomes pregnant, Ethel turns sour and writes to Laurie trying to get money, saying that Anna owes two weeks' rent. Ethel had thrown Anna out when she discovered the pregnancy and leaves her to find lodgings with Laurie. Ethel believes that Anna has crossed the line from respectability to tramping:

> It is one thing for a girl to have a friend or two but it is quite another for it to be anybody who she picks up in the street and without with your leave or by your leave and never a word to me. (p. 166)

She ends the complaint by saying that Anna is not someone who will do anything for herself. The unwillingness to privilege self-interest is for Ethel the ultimate obscenity to commit in British culture.

The end of the novel represents Anna's farewell to the

mother, the flesh and the island as she prepares to die while dreaming of Carnival. The word 'carnival' derives, of course, from the Latin *carne vale*, meaning farewell to the flesh. Throughout the novel Anna has associated the behaviour of the English with that of the masked carnival players who became inhuman ants or animals in Dominica, where masks were worn by the blacks in order to satirise their white masters. Anna feels that she is the victim of both black and white hatred that is signalled by the mask. The British wear masks without effort or irony; they know how to mask their feelings, how to use one another to 'get on', as Vincent and Walter Jeffries say. The blacks in Dominica use masks once a year to poke fun at the whites, just as Meta did to Anna:

> But most of all I was afraid of the people passing because I was dying; and, just because I was dying, any one of them, any minute, might stop and approach me and knock me down, or put their tongues out as far as they would go. Like that time at home with Meta, when it was Masquerade and she came to see me and put out her tongue at me through the slit in the mask. (p. 178)

At the end of the novel, Rhys introduces a new character, Meta, whom Anna says came specifically to her house, masked, to tease her. It is surprising to see Meta's name where one would have expected Francine's without explanation of this new character who shares a name with Rhys' nurse. Interestingly, Anna mentions Meta here for the first and only time. (In *Smile Please* Meta is, of course, the name of Rhys' nurse, who seems to have been transformed in *Voyage in the Dark* into Francine.) As the emotions intensify for Anna, Rhys seems to revert back to the prototype of the nurse and abandons the name Francine for Meta. Although this may have been an authorial slip, Meta still acts as the final negative mother figure who literally sticks her tongue out at Anna as she is dying.

Meta acts for all Dominican blacks in resenting and then mocking the more powerful whites. The laughing masks and the concertina music are brought together, in synchrony, as Anna is dying. This image leads to the scene in which Anna haemorrhages while the doctor's laughter at her, the scornful mask of the British and the concertina music, played by a black man, announce her death. The death scene also gives the image of a final ray of light that comes into Anna's consciousness, linking this to the idea of blindness and of the curtain falling. In the final scene, Anna is the victim of two things that she cannot put together – her emotional vulnerability caused by a lack of adequate mothering and her victimisation by the 'mother' country.

The mask is a symbol for the text's strategies of resistance. Anna does fight back through telling people what she thinks, through running away from the insensitive Walter Jeffries and, most of all, through her refusal to evaluate all human relationships, especially sexual relationships, in terms of money. Echoing the masked Meta, she even sticks out her tongue at Jeffries when she jams a cigarette on his hand. The text represents her other strategies of resistance through her continual use of dreams to subvert the economic and sexual relationships she is forced into in England. Anna can defy her family and the British, although she is surely also the victim of maternal abuse and the abuse of the 'mother' country. Yet, as the text passes into the hand of the readers, it assumes another mother role. In aligning the reader's sympathies with Anna the text sticks its tongue out at the 'mother' country and unmasks its hostility and anger at the lost maternal matrix and the irresponsible and bigoted behaviour of the imperialistic power. This juxtaposition of the unmasking and taunting of mother and 'mother' country is the centre of the daughter text of *Voyage in the Dark*, Jamaica Kincaid's *Annie John*.

We have known for some time that Jamaica Kincaid writes with a double vision. From one point of view, her early fiction and sketches in *The New Yorker*, her collection of dream visions, *At the Bottom of the River* (1978), and her novel *Annie John* (1983) all concern the coming-of-age narrative of a young woman in Antigua. Much of Kincaid's fiction, especially the intensely lyrical prose poetry of *At the Bottom of the River* and the autobiographical novel *Annie John*, focuses on the relationship between mother and daughter and the painful separation that occurs between them. Careful examination of the psychoanalytical implications of these relationships will surely open up the meanings of these texts. A psychoanalytic analysis from a feminist perspective, one examining mother-daughter bonding, would point out that the narrators in Kincaid's fiction resist separation from the mother as a way of denying their intense fear of death. The fear of separation is further complicated in *Annie John* because the narrator leaves the island for Britain with the clear intention of making a break with her environment. Both she and her mother, who is also named Annie, have left their respective mothers and their own homes to seek a more comfortable life elsewhere. The process of Annie's leaving her mother is mirrored in the process of leaving the island. Displacement from an initial intimacy with her mother's realm is reflected in a growing away from the environment until, at the end of the novel, Annie can only dream of leaving her own home for England.

Along with a psychoanalytic-feminist perspective, however, other views must be taken of Kincaid's fiction. *Annie John*, for example, is not just the story about a young woman's involvement with her mother and her home. There is a story behind this story of how and why these conflicts are situated in a West Indian island recently liberated from British rule. The novel is not the story of a white, bourgeois mother and daughter but of an African-Caribbean mother from Dominica and her daughter living in a nine-by-twelve mile island that is drought- and poverty-stricken and far removed from the privileges of middle-class life in Europe or the United States.

That Kincaid thought about these differences when writing her fiction is clear from a 'Talk of the Town' article for *The New Yorker* which appeared in 1977. Kincaid, who rejected her British name Richardson, recalled that most of the African-Caribbean people of Antigua worked as carpenters, masons, servants in private homes, seamstresses, fishermen or dockworkers. She added that, 'A few grew crops and a very small number worked in offices and banks.'[14] When Kincaid was seven she was herself apprenticed to a seamstress for two afternoons a week. People who worked in offices and banks were white, and the most wealthy ran a country club called the Mill Reef Club. The whites owned the banks and the offices and reserved most of the island's pleasant beaches for themselves. This historical and political context is central to Kincaid's fiction.

Much of Kincaid's distrust of the post-colonial environment went unnoticed by the reviewers of *Annie John*. The novel was received as simply a book about mothers and daughters, a popular topic in feminist literary criticism, especially during the late 1970s when Nancy Chodorow and Carole Gilligan each published influential studies.[15] Female bonding is the novel's subject and receives the most narrative attention, whereas within the novel there are only two explicit statements of resentment made about the political or social situations. One is a comment the narrator makes while observing a classmate, Ruth, who is the child of British missionaries:

> Perhaps she wanted to be in England, where no one would remind her constantly of the terrible things her ancestors had done; perhaps she had felt even worse when her father was a missionary in Africa. I could see how Ruth felt from looking at her face. Her ancestors had been the masters, while ours had been the slaves. She had a lot to be ashamed of . . . I am quite sure that if the tables had been turned we would have acted differently.[16]

Earlier in the novel, while Annie and her friend the Red Girl watch a cruise ship with wealthy passengers go by, she fantasises that they throw them confusing signals and crash the ship: 'How we laughed as their cries of joy turned to cries of sorrow' (p. 71).

Any doubts that there is implicit criticism of the post-colonial Antigua in *Annie John* were erased by the publication of *A Small Place* in 1988. This series of essays externalises Kincaid's resentment of the British upper class and forces us to look at *Annie John* from a different angle. Emphasis shifts to the way Annie constantly rebels against the cultural norms imposed by the British slave owners and the wealthy, like the members of the Mill Reef Country Club. Viewed from the perspective of *A Small Place*, the fantasy of Annie and the Red Girl becomes not a minor incident but the tip of a mass of repressed feelings. The Red Girl allows Annie to explore her true feelings precisely because the Red Girl – and this is her major attraction for Annie – does not participate in any of the 'young lady' or 'proper person' rituals that are imposed on Annie by her school and her mother. The Red Girl refuses to behave in stereotyped roles, especially gender roles, and avoids all the rules and rituals associated with being a 'young lady'.

Resentment of British influence is even clearer in *A Small Place*. There she recites an elegy for an Antigua that no longer exists. The British have ruined much of the island:

> And so everywhere they went they turned it into England; and everybody they met they turned English. But no place could ever really be England, and nobody who did not look exactly like them would ever be English, so you can imagine the destruction of people and land that came from that. The English hate each other and they hate England, and the reason is they have no place else to go and nobody else to feel better than.[17]

At the age of seven Kincaid remembers waiting for hours in the hot sun to see a 'putty-faced princess' from England disappear behind the walls of the governor's house. Later she found out that the princess was sent to Antigua to recover from an affair with a married man. In both the schools and libraries, the British found opportunities to distort and erase Antiguan history and to glorify British history in its place. One of the crimes of the colonial era was the violation of the colonised peoples' languages: 'For isn't it odd that the only language I have in which to speak of this crime is the language of the criminal who committed the crime?' (*A Small Place*, p. 31).

The thematic connection between *Annie John* and *A Small Place* became clearer in an interview with Selwyn Cudjoe appearing in *Callaloo*. Kincaid discussed her ideas in *A Small Place*, particularly her dislike of colonialism which she developed by the age of nine:

> When I was nine, I refused to stand up at the refrain of 'God Save Our King'. I hated 'Rule Britannia'; and I used to say that we weren't Britons, we were slaves. I never had any idea why. I just thought that there was no sense to it – 'Rule Britannia, Britannia rules the waves, Britons never shall be slaves.' I thought that we weren't Britons and that we were slaves. (p. 397)

Elsewhere in the interview Kincaid indicates an instinctive rebellion she felt concerning England, despite the validation of British culture: ' . . . for us England (and I think this was true for VS Naipaul, too) and its glory was at its most theatrical, its most oppressive. Everything seemed divine and good only if it was English' (p. 398). Although Kincaid eschews an overtly political allegiance, there is a close connection between Kincaid's anti-colonialist essays in *A Small Place* and the feeling ascribed to the young narrator of *Annie John*. The attitudes expressed explicitly in *A Small Place* are implicit in *Annie John*.

Thus, when we talk about the women characters in Kincaid's fiction, especially *Annie John*, we must talk not only about the autobiographical experiences, but also about the life of a young and brilliant African-Caribbean woman from an impoverished neighbourhood on an island that won independence from the 'mother' country. A feminist perspective will remind us that it is absurd to pretend that a novel written by a woman about women will not differ from a novel written by a man about men. However, one must be careful to examine the appropriateness of white, middle-class feminist theory to the texts produced by Caribbean women. Ketu Katrak, among others, has criticised famous literary theorists like Frederic Jameson for their appropriation of post-colonial texts as 'raw material' for the production of literary theories consumed in western academies.[18] Also, as Evelyn O'Callaghan states in an article on the application of feminist theory to Caribbean literature, 'Cross-cultural self-conceptions of men and women appear to be more dramatic than contrasts between those who share the same socio-cultural system' (p. 148). In other words, cultural differences might be as salient as gender difference in interpretation of literary texts. Particularly important is O'Callaghan's suggestion that there are problems for Caribbean women's writing when an over-rigid concept of feminist theory is applied. However, she is in favour of a 'crossroads' model which situates each work at a point of intersection of other concerns with race, class, or Creole cultural forms unique to the region (p. 160). Women's stories will relate the female perspective on these experiences and reflect on any sexist strategies that persist in post-colonial societies.

The critic must take issues of race, post-colonial history, class and gender into consideration as they come up in the literary work. The feminist critic should be careful not to use prescriptive models in interpreting West Indian women's texts. This being the case, we must conclude that Kincaid is writing not with a double vision but a vision that has four perspectives. To look at all of them is beyond the scope of this essay, so I propose to offer a new reading of the ways in which *Annie John* combines the narrator's dissatisfaction with her personal relationships with a dissatisfaction with her post-colonial environment.

In particular, it should be pointed out that in Antigua, and elsewhere, there was much cultural violence directed toward women based on popular attitudes toward their sexuality and their bodies. These attitudes were a combination of Victorian ideology and regressive religious views. Such attitudes spread through the educational system and were widely adopted, sometimes even by the women who were denigrated by these ideologies (Katrak, p. 171). The same system of British education that erased and colonised indigenous history also attempted to erase female sexuality and to control the female body. Attempted colonisation of the female body is one of the points of contention between Annie and her mother because Annie constantly rebels against those aspects of her society that have been imposed by the British. Some of these norms have been absorbed by Annie's neighbours, her school and, especially and unfortunately, by her beautiful, loving and well-intentioned mother. She is not presented negatively but sympathetically as a victim of post-colonial strategies to erase her identity and to substitute European ideology in its place. In *A Small Place* Kincaid calls her mother someone who is suffering from her 'innocence' of white racism (p. 29). There is not a conscious understanding of this on the character Annie's part but simply an uneasy feeling about authority figures.

In *Annie John* the narrator's personal displacement is reflected in a growing away from the environment. The first chapter, in a novel ostensibly about coming of age, ironically concerns death. This is Kincaid's deliberate strategy since the novel is not about a beginning but about the end of the narrator's intimacy with her mother and her island. During a period when she was ten years old, the narrator becomes obsessed with attending funerals. The displacement and boredom she experienced – she had nothing to do and spoke only to her parents – led her to focus on the only source of activity in the neighbourhood, the cemetery where she would see 'stick-like', three-dimensional figures. After Annie's mother says that these people were attending a funeral, and that children died, Annie became afraid of death. For the first time, the separation of death is connected with her mother:

'My mother knew of many people who had died in such a way. My mother knew of many people who had died, including her own brother' (p. 4). Later, when a neighbour girl dies in her mother's arms, Annie begins to connect her mother's circling arm with death, as if the mother were both the place of protection and the instrument of destruction.

To reinforce this sense of separation, there is a series of lost parental figures. Annie's father was left in Antigua by parents who went to Latin America, leaving him with a grandmother who died when he was 18. When Annie cries at this story, her mother comforts her: 'She said that I needn't worry about such a thing as her sailing off or dying and leaving me all alone in the world' (p. 24). Yet, Annie's mother had also lost her father when she was quite young and was constrained to set out on her own. She was an independent woman who, at 16, after quarrelling with her father, packed a trunk and left home. When Annie was young the trunk contained things that had belonged to her, starting from just before she was born. Her mother would lift up each object and tell her the story connected with it – a tremendous pleasure for Annie: 'No small part of my life was so unimportant that she hadn't made a note of it, and now she would tell it to me over and over again' (p. 22). Despite the closeness that Annie experiences with both her father and her mother, they consider her old enough to leave the house at 17 or even 16 – the age they were when they set out on their own. After this age Annie is not completely welcome in the house.

The most dramatic changes occur for Annie when she turns 12, the summer she reaches puberty and a watershed in her relationship with her mother. She refuses to cut a dress for herself and for Annie from the same material: 'You cannot go around the rest of your life looking like a little me' (p. 26). Annie is devastated: 'It wasn't just what she said, it was the way she said it' (p. 24). Annie feels bitterness and hatred, not for her mother, but for 'life in general' (p. 26), as if realising that her mother could not be blamed for the process of growing into an adult.

Complying with expectations for a proper British lady, Annie's mother abandons the values represented by the trunk and appropriates those of the culture she sees around her. There are many lessons to teach Annie how to behave as a 'young lady'. Annie takes lessons in manners but is sent home because she cannot resist making farting noises when practising her curtsy. Likewise, the piano teacher dismisses her because Annie cannot resist eating from a bowl of plums that is on the table. To Annie, the teacher is 'a shriveled-up old spinster from Lancashire, England' (p. 28). Although Annie may be thwarting the lessons because her mother is planning their separation, she is also responding to the tyranny of the lessons themselves and to the cultural values implicit in them.

The problem that definitively sours their intimacy is the older woman's attitudes toward sexuality and the body. Rushing home from Sunday school, Annie returns to the house to hear sounds coming from the bedroom. She focuses on her mother's hand that she sees circling her father's back: 'It was white and bony, as if it had long been dead and had been left out in the elements' (p. 30). The hand signals death to Annie, and here it is the death of her love for her mother. There is also something new in her mother's tone toward her: 'She said in a voice that was sort of cross and sort of something else, "Are you going to just stand there doing nothing all day?"' (p. 31) A few days after this Annie meets a young girl, Gwen, and 'falls in love' with her as a way of compensating for the love she felt had been withdrawn.

Her mother believes that a woman's body is the property of the respectable male who will marry her. Until that time, strict vigilance must be practised so that one does not appear loose or vulgar. Annie's mother is extremely regressive on this issue, accepting a Victorian ideology that includes the colonisation of the female body. In the story 'Girl' from *At the Bottom of the River* the mother recites a litany of sexual warnings at her daughter:

> On Sundays try to walk like a lady and not like the slut
> you are so bent on becoming . . . this is how to hem a
> dress when you see the hem coming down and so to
> prevent youself from looking like the slut I know you are
> so bent on becoming . . . this is how to behave in the
> presence of men who don't know you very well, and
> this way they won't recognise immediately the slut I have
> warned you against becoming. (p. 4)

The mother's obsessive refrain of hostility indicates her belief
in the necessity of guarding one's sexual virtue if one is to
be an unspoiled commodity on the marriage market. In *Annie
John* the major explosion between the two women comes
from the daughter's sexual coming of age. When she is 15
Annie is looking in the shop windows on Market Street,
alone, when she becomes aware of a group of boys laughing
at her: 'I knew instantly that it was malicious and that I had
done nothing to deserve it other than standing here all alone'
(p. 95). She recognises one of the young men and attempts
to speak to him, but he and his friends laugh slyly and
refuse to treat her as someone worthy of conversation. She
remembers playing with this boy when they were younger.
Feeling his cruelty on this occasion brings a sharp memory
of another incident, the day he persuaded her to take off her
clothes and sit beneath a tree where there were many red
ants.

Annie's mother sees the conversation with the young men
and instantly accuses her daughter of behaving as a 'slut':

> The word 'slut' (in patois) was repeated over and over,
> until suddenly I felt as if I were drowning in a well but
> instead of the well being filled with water it was filled with
> the word 'slut', and it was pouring in through my eyes,
> my ears, my nostrils, my mouth. (p. 102)

To save herself, Annie is rude to her mother, who replies
'Until this moment, in my whole life I knew without a doubt
that, without any exception, I loved you best' (p. 103). There

is no going back because this incident strips Annie of her belief in herself and initiates a long mental breakdown. To the extent that Annie's mother accepts bourgeois attitudes toward women's bodies, she will never appreciate her daughter in an uncorrupted way. Like the young boys, she treats Annie as if she were merely a body to be controlled or possessed.

In other parts of the novel Annie's comments and dissatisfactions are responses to the British education that was forced on her, with her mother's approval. In Annie's new classroom, for instance, while the students write autobiographical essays, Miss Nelson reads from an 'elaborately illustrated edition of *The Tempest*' (p. 39), Kincaid's signal that the classroom is another occasion for the imperialist, prosperous Prosperos to force their language and traditions on the indigenous Calibans of the island. During the history lesson recounted in the chapter 'Columbus in Chains', the class reads *The History of the West Indies*, an account written only from the British point of view. A picture of the dejected and miserable Columbus, who was brought back to Spain after his third voyage fettered in chains, sparks Annie's interest: 'What just deserts, I thought, for I did not like Columbus' (p. 77). She is reminded of her own grandfather. He had forced her mother from their home and from Dominica because she wanted to live alone, and he insisted that unmarried women should live with their fathers. On hearing that the old man needed a cane to walk, her mother had exclaimed: 'So the great man can no longer just get up and go' (p. 78), a phrase that Annie musingly associates not only with the patriarchal figure in her family but also with the patriarchal figure in her schoolbook. She writes the phrase under the picture of Columbus.

The grandfather's attempt to control the body of his daughter is similar to the colonials' attempts to own women's bodies. In fact, her grandfather's assumption of control outlasted the coloniser's control of the island as well as any strategies of decolonisation. Annie is punished for her impertinence and disrespect: 'I had gone too far this time, defaming one of the great men in history, Christopher Columbus, discoverer of the island that was my home' (p. 82). As a discipline, she must copy books I and II of *Paradise Lost*, a work that evokes the biblical imagery of a lost Eden in the novel and is suggestive of the snake as coloniser whose poison is circulating through the system.

During one of Miss Nelson's classes the students are asked to write an autobiographical essay. One student discusses an aunt living in England, and her dream of one day moving in with her; another girl told of a brother studying medicine in Canada; someone else had taken tea with Lady Baden-Powell. Annie's composition, the prototype of the novel itself, dealt with her mother: 'What I had written was heartfelt, and, except for the very end, it was all too true' (p. 41). In the essay she tells of the swimming lessons during which she was afraid of the water and would only go into the sea on her mother's back. When she cannot find her mother one day, 'A huge black space then opened up in front of me and I fell inside it' (p. 43). Her mother finds her and tells her that she will never leave her: 'And though she said it over and over again, and though I felt better, I could not wipe out of my mind the feeling I had had when I couldn't find her' (p. 44). The other girls concoct stories that reflect the corruption of their desires and dreams. They want to go to England, Canada or, at least, have tea with a noblewoman from Britain. Annie, on the other hand, feels the gulf that separates her from the others, specifically her mother, and tells of falling into a black depression.

Her final fantasy, her mother telling her that no separation will occur, is incorrect in two ways. Annie's mother is assiduously preparing her daughter for the separation that will assuredly occur since her parents want the grown Annie to create her own household. In addition, Annie will always feel a gulf separating her from her own island. The classroom scenes suggest that the island's inappropriate education provides one of the worst forms of alienation. Yet, her mother completely approves of this British cultural imperialism. Annie's mother is well intentioned and watches out for her child, hoping to give her opportunities she did not have. But she is also carrying within her a type of poison that distracts and threatens Annie.

This tension is conveyed through several images. The mother used to accompany her father into the mountains to gather food. Once, walking down the mountain with a bunch of green figs on her head, she was startled by a huge snake that had hidden itself in the fruit. The snake is the obvious symbol of evil carried in or on the head of the mother. One also thinks of Medusa whose head of snakes turned people to stone, but the connection in Kincaid's mind was more likely through *Paradise Lost*. The poison that Milton presents is conformity of Creole life to British expectations.

The gap separating Annie from her mother and home becomes an ugly depression when she is 15: 'My unhappiness was something deep inside me, and when I closed my eyes I could even see it . . . it took the shape of a small black ball all wrapped in cobwebs' (p. 84). This depression is completely defined in Annie's mind by her relationship with her mother: 'Something I could not name just came over us, and suddenly I had never loved anyone or hated anyone so' (p. 80). For three months the rains pelted Antigua and during that time Annie fell into a breakdown taking the form of complete lassitude. She stayed in bed and watched as the room and the house became distorted. The British doctor could find nothing wrong with her except that she was run-down. Annie's problem is clearly psychological. She feels that her parents have stripped her of any identity, and she has sunk into confusion in order to try to save a precarious sense of self. This is symbolised in her erasure of all of the people in the family pictures, even herself, except for the shoes that she had bought despite her mother's protests (p. 120). Finally, Ma Chess appears one day when the steamer was not due and brings with her a knowledge of obeah, something the British doctor could not understand.

Ma Chess had fought her own battle when her son John died.
When he was sick, Ma Chess was sure that a western medical
doctor was the last thing he needed; Pa Chess was sure that
this was the one thing he did need. The old man had his
way, and his son died. After her arrival in Antigua, the
grandmother settled on the floor at the foot of Annie's bed,
eating and sleeping there, so that Annie was soon able to
count on her. Ma Chess is the positive woman Annie has
sought. The grandmother shows Annie the importance of
her life and is willing to eat and sleep in the same room and
even share the same bed with her, something her mother
seemed unable to do since the girl was now sexually mature
and a covert threat. Annie recovers immediately and thinks
of leaving. It is significant that it is not the British medicine
that made Annie well but the old ways of obeah.

After enduring a type of psychic death, the experience that
Annie had so feared, she is ready to leave her family. The
first words that come to her on the day she leaves are, 'My
name is Annie John' (p. 130), signifying that she has recovered her identity, although only as distinct from other family
members. Since Annie has survived psychic death, she can
now suffer the separation that was the symbol of it. She
realises that her father is 35 years older than her mother, and
that he is now an old man, with some children older than
his wife: 'I plan not only never to marry an old man but
certainly never to marry at all' (p. 132). She sees perhaps
why her mother could no longer be her first love after she
had married a man so much older than herself, a teenager
while he was middle-aged. On the walk to the jetty Annie
remembers the first time her mother had sent her to the store
alone: 'If I had just conquered Persia, she couldn't have been
more proud of me' (p. 140). She sees this as a cruel betrayal,
the first of many lessons on how to leave home. The only
place she feels real pity about leaving is the library, the place
where she learned to love words. Yet her mother's last words
to her are prophetic: ' "It doesn't matter what you do or
where you go, I'll always be your mother and this will always

be your home" ' (p. 147). The novel tells the sad story of the woman in exile who feels that dreams of leaving are not as sweet as the time of loving, and that the mother country is never as welcoming as the mother.

Notes

1 See the foreword to the US edition of *Watchers & Seekers: Creative Writing by Black Women*, Rhonda Cobham and Merle Collins, eds., Bedrick, New York, 1988), p. 1. (First published in 1987 by The Women's Press, London.) Two of the concerns of these writers, as noted by the editors in their foreword, are the use of dreams and visions and the struggle against oppression.

2 Mary Lou Emery, 'The Politics of Form: Jean Rhys' Social Vision in *Voyage in the Dark* and *Wide Sargasso Sea*', *Twentieth Century Literature* 28 (1982), p. 425. In an excellent and early analysis of the narrative strategies in Rhys' two novels, Emery shows that, in each case, the form of *Voyage in the Dark* and *Wide Sargasso Sea* is subversive of the dominant culture. The ending of *Wide Sargasso Sea* shows the dream of Antoinette Cosway triumphant over the reality of Rochester's control. Emery suggests that the dream provides the structure for the entire novel: 'This dream model of association, condensation, and displacement structures the text of the entire novel' (p. 425).

3 Jean Rhys, *Letters 1931–1966*, André Deutsch, London, 1984, p. 24.

4 Ronnie Scharfman, 'Mirroring and Mothering in Simone Schwarz-Bart's *Pluie et vent sur Télumée Miracle* and Jean Rhys' *Wide Sargasso Sea*', *Yale French Studies* 62 (1981), pp. 88–106.

5 Pamela Mordecai and Betty Wilson, eds., *Her True-True Name: An Anthology of Women's Writing from the Caribbean*, Heinemann, London, 1989. This anthology brings together the work of Anglophone, Hispanophone and Francophone women writers.

6 Very useful and insightful work on the mother-daughter question in Rhys' fiction has been accomplished by two recent critical works: Teresa F O'Connor's *Jean Rhys: The West Indian Novels*, New York University Press, New York, 1986; and Deborah Kelly Kloepfer's *The Unspeakable Mother: Forbidden Discourse in Jean Rhys and HD*, Cornell University Press, Ithaca and London, 1989.

7   The 'Black Exercise Book', which is part of the Jean Rhys Collection at McFarlin Library at the University of Tulsa, indicates major differences between the ending Rhys intended for the novel and the ending that her publishers, Constable, forced her to use in the published version. The major difference, which is discussed later in this essay, is that the original manuscript ending indicates that Anna dies after an illegal abortion whereas the published version hints that she could live to 'start all over again' (*Voyage*, p. 188).

8   Unlike Anna, Annie is able to find an identity for herself after she leaves her mother. On the day that Annie plans to leave her island home, Antigua, and her parents, she points to her own name: "'My name is Annie John'" (p. 130). Anna loses her sense of self at the end of *Voyage*, but Annie's stronger bond with her mother allows for separation without complete psychological dislocation.

9   Jean Rhys, *Smile Please: An Unfinished Autobiography*, André Deutsch, London, 1979.

10   In *Smile Please* Rhys describes her mother as 'lonely, patient and resigned' (p. 36) to what must have been an unhappy life. Rhys felt that her mother disliked or ignored her: 'Even after the new baby was born there must have been an interval before she seemed to find me a nuisance and I grew to dread her. Another interval and she was middle-aged and plump and uninterested in me' (p. 33).

11   Jean Rhys, *Voyage in the Dark*, Norton, New York, 1982, p. 96. (First published in Great Britain by Constable in 1934.) All references in the text are to this edition of the novel.

12   Although Rhys never attempted to restore the original ending of *Voyage in the Dark*, evidence from her letters indicates that she never accepted the validity of the revised ending. In a 1963 letter to Selma Vas Dias, in which she and Rhys discussed a proposed dramatisation of *Voyage*, Rhys regrets her choice:

A dead girl? . . . Certainly a dying girl. Perhaps you see no difference between the two versions and I agree that an abortion gone wrong is not a pretty sight and impossible on the stage or even in a book or radio. All the same I think it better – and more what I wanted. This girl is an innocent. Really without guile or slyness. Why should she live to be done in over and over again? (*Letters*, p. 237)

13   Helen Tiffin, 'Mirror and Mask: Colonial Motifs in the Novels of Jean Rhys', *World Literature Written in English* 17 (April 1978),

pp. 328–341. Tiffin points out the parallels between destructive male-female relationships and the imperialist power-colonial victim dyad (p. 329). Tiffin says: 'The pattern of her life mirrors her own Caribbean history of European conquest, flirtation, and desertion, and the resultant dependence of the colonial on the colonizer' (p. 334).

14 Daryl Cumber-Dance, ed., *Fifty Caribbean Writers*, Greenwood, New York, 1986, p. 255.

15 Nancy Chodorow's *Reproduction of Mothering*, University of California Press, Berkeley, 1978, is the standard reference in feminist psychoanalytic object-relations theory about gender formation. Carol Gilligan's *In a Different Voice: Psychological Theory and Women's Development*, Harvard University Press, Cambridge, 1982, examines differences in ego formation in young men and women.

16 Jamaica Kincaid, *Annie John*, New American Library, New York, 1983, reprinted 1985, p. 76. All references in the text are to this edition of the novel. (Published in Great Britain by Picador in 1985.)

17 Jamaica Kincaid, *A Small Place*, Farrar, Straus & Giroux, Inc., New York, 1988, p. 24. All references in the text are to this edition of the essays. (Published in Great Britain by Virago in 1988.)

18 Ketu H Katrak, 'Decolonizing Culture: Toward a Theory for Postcolonial Women's Texts', *Modern Fiction Studies* 35 (1989), pp. 157–179. Katrak's essay asks what theoretical models would be appropriate for discussion of women writers from the Third World. She proposes an historically situated method of approaching the work of women writers. Katrak points out that regressive aspects of culture, particularly those aimed at women, persist and sometimes intensify during attempts at decolonisation (pp. 161–162).

Isabel Carrera Suárez

**Absent Mother(Land)s:
Joan Riley's Fiction**

Out of our acrid neighbourhoods springs this rioting literature. It is not art for art's sake; its vibrance and immediacy
are intended to forge unity and wrench a new identity.

Lauretta Ngcobo, *Let It Be Told*[1]

In a brief introductory note to *Waiting in the Twilight* (1987),
Joan Riley explains that the book was written 'for the sake
of putting at least a small part of the record straight where
the West Indian woman in Britain is concerned', thus describing a purpose in her writing which is also applicable to her
other two novels, *The Unbelonging* (1985) and *Romance*
(1988),[2] and stating in no uncertain terms the direct relationship between her fiction and the collective from which it
springs. Riley's work combines the recovering of a history
(often re-writing it, against official versions) with the task of
inscribing a specific group of people into literature: the West
Indian community in Britain, and specifically its women.
The author is contributing to the collective text written by
so many other West Indian/African writers of the diaspora,
through whose art a history of oppression is being recorded.

To speak of Riley's fiction without reference to the context in which it is produced would be unthinkable – in fact, the painstaking detail in which the social, political and psychological circumstances are described in her narratives has the effect of providing the reader with the context itself; indeed, it could be argued that the context *becomes* her text, such is the wealth of factual information and analysis embedded in it.

This contextual explicitness extends to detail of place (London areas, streets, institutions) and time (dates, public figures, events), thus facilitating recognition on the part of the community which the novels attempt to inscribe. It is this 'shock of recognition', this sense of 'being talked about' experienced by readers hereto unrepresented in literature, that is one of the attractions of Riley's fiction. For her work has an undisguised didactic/subversive aim. It is indeed 'a rioting literature', or, in words also applied to Amryl Johnson's writing, 'a scream of rage'[3]; and with it all, an effort to heal through representation.

In the three novels published so far, Joan Riley deals with the recent period of immigration from the West Indies to Britain, seen through the eyes of its women. Adella, the elderly protagonist of *Waiting in the Twilight*, joins her husband in London after the Second World War, leaving several children behind in Jamaica; we see her life (through flashbacks) from the perspective of her old age. Hyacinth, in *The Unbelonging*, is called to England by her immigrant father when she is 11, and lives her adolescence in London in the 1970s. Verona and Desiree are young women living in Croydon in the late 1980s, having arrived in the country as children. In all three cases, they are suffereing blatant racism from a society that does little to disguise the fact, let alone correct it; in each case, their problem is aggravated by gender oppression. These women are, in many repects, paradigmatic of the experience of West Indian immigrant women in England. If any reader were to doubt the recurrence of the instances of racial harassment, social and economic discrimination, and the specific types of hardship shown in Riley's novels, it would be enough to read *The Heart of the Race*[4] and compare the accounts given by the many women who contributed their testimony to this collective document: the book reads almost as a parallel text to Riley's novels, showing the fine line that separates fiction and reality. Both emphasise the by now undisputed fact that race, gender and class converge to produce the oppression of racial minority women, in Britain as elsewhere. To these we may add, as suggested by Lauretta Ngcobo, 'the burden of history' (*Let It Be Told*, p. 1), powerfully specific in the Caribbean context, where slavery and colonisation have deeply affected family relationships. But, however paradigmatic some of their traits, the protagonists of Riley's books also become highly individual people, with their own choices and responses to general situations. Her portraits are careful psychological studies, where the social and the personal interact to create character, but where stereotyping and over-generalisation are avoided. The tension between the collective subject and the individual subject lies at the core of Riley's literature.

Riley's novels are women-centred texts. Some of her men are tactfully portrayed, but in general they remain functional characters; her protagonists are women and the world described in any detail is the female world – its physical, domestic, emotional and social reality; its personal, economic and political dimension. Her women suffer a pervading racism outside their homes; but they also suffer, within their own family or community, an often brutal sexism. The crises that shape their lives frequently originate in instances of gender oppression. Hyacinth, the young girl in *The Unbelonging*, suffers dramatically from fear of her schoolmates and teachers, but also from the tyranny of her violent father; her response to sexuality is forever marred by her father's assault. The irreversible change produced in Stanton, Adella's formerly caring husband in *Waiting in the Twilight*, is brought about by her supposed failure in having only female children by him; earlier, in Jamaica, Adella had lost all chance of earning a living successfully when she had become pregnant by Beresford, her lover, and the middle-class ladies, echoing his hypocrisy, had cancelled their demand for her sewing skills. As to Verona, in *Romance*, her sexual trauma derives from her rape by her sister's boyfriend when she is a teenager, which leads to her disastrous relationship with (white) Steve and her status as a single parent. Desiree herself suffers constant oppression from her husband and has to face alone the traumatic loss of her womb at 33.

All these are turning points in the women's lives, but racism permeates their existence with equal force, both directly and through their husbands' and children's lives. Women and men alike must suffer racist redundancy and promotion policies, negative expectations for their studies and their behaviour, barriers to buying property, and ubiquitous verbal and physical harassment, all this from institutions and individuals alike. The immediate consequence of social barriers is the inescapable entrapment of practically all characters in what Ngcobo calls 'the Black-working-class' (*Let It Be Told*, p. 18), the only category below that of the (white) working class. The interlacing of all these factors in Riley's novels expose the functioning of the structures of power, oppression and enforced silence. The frustration or sheer hatred of whites is discharged on black men, who then discharge their own on black women. This chain is continued, in *The Unbelonging*, by the woman against the stepdaughter Hyacinth, and even by an exploited child-Hyacinth on her younger stepbrothers.

That the understanding of the chain does not imply justifying this transmission of oppression is explicitly stated by several female characters. While making excuses for their men, the women fight a constant, though painfully slow, battle for the admission on the part of their husbands of the fact that racism affects both sexes. Only one of them, Desiree, seems to succeed in any significant degree. For the main part, the women remain the easy way out for the men's frustration and violence, the necessary 'other':

The reduction of a 'person' to a 'nobody' to the position of 'other' – the inexorable plot of racism. There has to be some 'other' – no master without a slave, no economico-political power without exploitation, no dominant class without cattle under the yoke, no 'Frenchman' without wogs, no Nazis without Jews, no property without exclusion – an exclusion that has its limits and is part of the dialectic. If there were no other, one would invent it.[5]

The quotation is from Hélène Cixous, primarily known as a 'French' feminist, but whose experience of exile, colonialism and racism (as an Algerian-born Jew) produces an awareness of the hierarchy of oppression reflected in this construction of an 'other' to measure (an 'other' who, Cixous interestingly observes, becomes 'invisible' to its oppressor). In her own search for *self* (race, language, nationality), Cixous eventually comes against the problem of discovering herself to be a woman, and the insoluble contradiction that 'the friend is also the enemy . . . "We" struggle together, yes, but who is this "we"?' (p. 574). In Riley's *Romance* a very similar question is asked with respect to women and the struggle at BUF, although class and race are more central to the questioning. Cixous' analysis eventually centres on women, but the quotation is interesting as it contains the elements of race, class, colonialism and, as a condition to it all, *the reduction of a 'person' to a 'nobody'*. This is the ultimate tool of oppression. It is suffered by the men of Riley's fiction at the hands of colonialism/racism (England takes away their 'pride'), and by her women, doubly, with the addition of sexism. For where blacks are constructed as that necessary 'other' by white society, black women are left as the only available 'other' to black men. What has been described as *double jeopardy* by Afro-American writers, is here defined as a double *non-entity*: black women are doubly 'nobody'.

Another writer of the diaspora, Canadian-Trinidadian Claire Harris (in an essay that shows the many parallels between the situation of the West Indian woman writer in

Canada and in Britain) expresses the need to overcome this loss: ' . . . to reclaim sensibility black women have to disco-ver/define two aspects of the self: the authentic female self and the authentic black self.'[6] This is the urgent need of Riley's characters, and it is this double reconstruction of the self that her writing builds up to, even if her protagonists cannot always succeed in the task.

Riley's fiction presents more clearly the loss and absences in her characters' world than the reparation of that loss. Her writing is hopeful in the hints of other possibilities – minor characters whose luck has changed, whose life is happier; the optimistic ending of *Romance* – but it concentrates on the representation of that fragmented self and the disruption of lives and hopes that the racist, post-colonial setting is respon-sible for. In this literature of loss and absence, there is a literal and metaphorical absence that shapes the books: the absence of a mother, a mothertongue, a motherland. The self – female and black – can only be reconstructed when this gap is bridged.

The 'authentic black self' is buried so deep in some of Riley's characters that their own perception of themselves amounts to self-hatred. This is truer the more isolated the character is from her community. Hyacinth, who goes through her early years in England estranged from her people, hates being different, as that difference means insults and cruelty towards her. She internalises the values of white society and, as the obvious marker of race is physical, begins by hating her body: 'How much she hated her brittle hair, the thickness of her lips' (*Unb* p. 78). Hair is a recurrent theme in these novels, for its symbolic importance is great. It is, with colour, a visible racial difference, but also a powerful sexual symbol, which complicates the issue for women. Hya-cinth straightens her hair and awaits the reaction of (black) Colin Matthews. Beauty has been defined for both of them by white society (in a more grotesque example, page three in *The Sun* shamefully appeals to black men in *Romance*). Eleven-year-old Hyacinth feels ashamed of her plaited hair even on arrival at the airport in England, and later is afraid to use hair oil 'in case they thought her primitive' (*Unb*, p. 78). Her reading of romance novels allows her to imagine herself the heroine, her hair 'blonde and flowing', in exact anticipation of what Verona, in Riley's third novel, will do systematically to escape the reality of her body.

Gradations of colour are also an issue in all three novels, showing the internalised racism: Hyacinth admires Manley's 'pass for white' colour, while she thinks one of the students at the college 'would have looked quite nice if he wasn't so black' (*Unb*, p. 81). Beresford's wife, in *Waiting in the Twilight*, who is responsible for his middle-class job, has 'light skin'. The mixed-race child in Hyacinth's school, adopted by white people, is the most aggressive towards her; being even one step further away from her community than Hyacinth, her need to separate herself in other people's minds mirrors that of Hyacinth at college, where she associates with Indians and shuns blacks.

But the physical estrangement from oneself, crucial as it is, constitutes only one part of the alienation. For the concept of 'black' that Hyacinth rejects is far more complex: it is a *construct*, partly her own, mostly social, based on whites' definition and conditioning. 'Black', to Hyacinth, has become associated with violence, aggressiveness, dirt, lack of education, drink, poverty. Partly this is due to her own experience of black men, embodied in her father's violence and frustration, but even she, at a certain point, must place her father's house in the context of class and race in British society. Hyacinth, furthermore, has absorbed the concept of 'civilisation' as applicable to European society: 'she found the idea of Africans having civilisations too far-fetched to believe' (*Unb*, p. 113). She has absorbed a snobbery which makes her feel secure with Charles, 'in the knowledge that she was West Indian, he a mere African' (*Unb*, p. 125). For Africa is, in her view, uncivilised and tribal; and her black self remains wholly undiscovered.

Hyacinth's extreme rejection of her own race and history,

is treated more subtly in the characterisation of Verona (*Rom*) who reads romance to escape, goes out with white men and shows little interest in her own Guyanese past. Interestingly, it is Adella, in *Waiting in the Twilight*, the earlier immigrant, who is the toughest resister of this definition of her black self by the society that surrounds her. The enforced silence of her cleaning job does not prevent her from muttering her thoughts about white rudeness, her West Indian values are upheld till the end, and she refuses to be intimidated by white society, even while her own husband defers to the estate agent man in their visit to the house they are to buy. In Adella's case, the female self is more battered than the black self.

Acceptance of the female body can become as difficult as that of blackness when its femaleness seems only a source of pain. Once again, it is the perception of the female body by others (in this case males, mostly black) that produces that rejection. The early experience of both Hyacinth and Verona is that their body was there to be violated by men, the father or the sister's boyfriend, and Adella's first sexual encounter is far from being pleasurable, while its consequences are disastrous. Hyacinth bathes in her father's presence, conscious of (though only half-understanding yet) 'the lump in his trousers', and her feelings come as no surprise to the reader: 'She hated her body, felt shame at the wisps of black hair that had started to grow in her pubic area and the fact that her breasts had started to swell' (*Unb*, p. 52). The negative associations of womanhood produce the rejection of becoming an adult, what Annis Pratt has termed the 'growing-up-grotesque [literary] archetype',[7] induced by fear of the female sexual/social role. Verona, the victim of a similar association of sexuality and violence, seeks refuge behind a fat body, which she is ashamed of, but by which she feels protected. One of the dramatic losses of all of Riley's protagonists is their sexual self. There is no evidence of pleasure experienced by any of the women. Beresford extracts sexual favours as his 'right' from a disgusted (but economically dependent)

Adella, pregnant after their first night together. Her sexual activity is always associated with 'mistakes': pregnancy, like a curse, also follows what appears to be her only decision for pleasure, her brief encounter on the ship from Jamaica, on her way to join her husband. Verona's secret affairs with old white men are, as well as an unsatisfactory substitute of equal sex, a protest against the apparent impossibility of obtaining precisely this. Ironically, of course, she chooses the road most likely to confirm her fears, culminating in young, blond Steve's brutal reaction to her pregnancy. Her sister Desiree's sexual life, which we presume (like Adella's with Stanton) was once satisfactory, is now reduced to being available for her husband's Wednesday nights, 'nights of recreation: a few jars with the boys, then home for some sex to round the evening off' (*Rom*, p. 103). Riley thus presents a bleak view of a sexuality poisoned by gender roles which preclude a happy exchange.

But like the definition of 'black', that of 'woman' goes beyond physical (sexual) traits. These women have femaleness defined for them by their society and their men. Adella and Desiree, whose sexual trauma has not been as shocking as Hyacinth's or Verona's, have nevertheless allowed themselves to be defined by others. Adella's shame at being abandoned by her husband never disappears, and her disappointment in some of her children (two of whom repeat her own history of unwanted pregnancy) has as much to do with the community's gossip as with her own feelings. She is a victim of the double standard that allows her husband to change women but condemns her for relationships that she had to maintain in order to feed her children. She alone has struggled to bring them up, but she still perceives herself as a failure. As to Desiree, it takes her much pain and time (and the help of her friend Mara) to stop believing that '[her] whole life was wrapped up in that womb' (*Rom*, p. 226), to realise that she is something else apart from wife and mother.

The social construction of woman as primarily wife and mother, with no desires of her own, constrains Riley's protagonists, who feel guilty for any deviation from the norm. Study is shown to be superfluous or to imply inattention to children, when what the argument really hides is a fear of competition on the part of the men, a fear of their wives having a better salary or a better education, as is clear in John and Winston in *Romance*. The men do not hesitate to use pseudo-arguments such as 'the role of African women' or the children's need for a mother (*Rom*, p. 23) to thwart their attempts at acquiring education. For the man's role is that of provider, and women should not meddle with it, even when the man does not fulfil it, as in the case of Stanton. If he does, it becomes 'a talisman' (*Rom*, p. 25) that excuses all other failings, as does their suffering at the hands of the whites, which wives must patiently make up for: 'I have a duty to support John, [Desiree] admonished herself. If he don't get loyalty from me, where he supposed to get it?' (*Rom*, p. 10)

The problem of defining the *self* is not, for these women, merely that of any individual of the human species, the quest for that ultimately unattainable unified self. Their own quest begins with a negative definition which they must overcome. It has as a starting point a double ontological insecurity which, beyond a merely split self, produces a fragmented personality, torn between multiple demands, suffering multiple absences. For, to the absence of an authentic black and female self, we must add the absence of place, of belonging, the absence of an authentic motherland. It is worth noting, before we turn to this crucial point, how Riley's characters dream of escaping the negative reality they cannot face, and what part(s) of their self their dreams refer to. For Hyacinth, the fantasy is of Jamaica and of Aunt Joyce, of warmth and, above all, of belonging. Adella dreams of her husband's return, a return that would correct her failure as wife. Verona dreams of romantic love, but in white colours. All are impossible expectations. Jamaica is idealised beyond recognition, Stanton is evidently not worth waiting for and Verona will not become blonde or find a mysterious stranger. But the dreams compensate for that part of self that is bruised most strongly: in Hyacinth, her sense of community; in Adella, her wifely pride; in Verona, self-worth in sexual terms. Their actions in real life are failed attempts to reverse their losses, a failure closely related to their inadequacy in the 'motherland' they inhabit.

While all of Riley's protagonists are made to feel unwelcome by British society, their attitude to the 'Motherland' is not identical. For Hyacinth, despite her unconscious absorption of values, Britain is never a home. She has not chosen to come, has been deeply unhappy there, and constantly dreams of finishing her education to return to Jamaica, where she believes she belongs. Adella, thoroughly disillusioned in her old age, had nevertheless emigrated to the 'Motherland' – a term that is used several times in the book, with obvious irony – with great expectations. The legend of streets paved with gold had moved her husband Stanton to the adventure of the voyage, hoping to make money in a few years and return to Jamaica. In contrast, Verona and Desiree, having lived in Britain with their parents from childhood, have no plans for moving back. It cannot be said, however, that any of them considers Britain a 'Motherland'. In Hyacinth's eyes, until the very end, the motherland is Jamaica, desired with the intensity of the absent. To Adella also, Jamaica will seem, in retrospect, the real motherland, but it has become unattainable, for her shame will never allow her to return to her village. Verona and Desiree are hardly aware of their native Guyana until the grandparents from Jamaica arrive, but England can hardly be seen for them as the hospitable place that the term implies. The absence in their case is a less perceptible pain, but lies at the root of their displacement. In all cases, the irony is the exchange of a homeland for a supposed 'Motherland' in the hope of improving a life made difficult in great part by the exploitation of that 'Motherland' itself, only to find the utter rejection and ill-will of the newly adopted country. In the need for integration, in the abrupt separation from the home community, the culture is lost, the self disintegrates.

One way in which this abrupt break, with its tragic loss, is represented in Riley's work is the absence of the physical mother. Hyacinth is raised by her aunt from birth. We know nothing of her mother. Verona and Desiree lose their mother in the first decade of their lives. Adella does have a mother, but she is mentioned only briefly and in ambiguous terms: 'Her mother never showed emotions, was never unhappy, or happy either. Everybody called her strange, whispered that she had an evil eye' (*WT*, p. 37). This absence of the mother figure contrasts with the strength of the mother-daughter relationship in other female West Indian narratives, notably *Annie John* by Jamaica Kincaid. While one has to be careful of applying Western psychological theory to cultures in which the extended family is the norm, Riley's work displays this lack in a way that can hardly be seen as coincidental. It is not merely the absence of the mother that recurs: more importantly, the strong matrilineal line is abruptly interrupted in all cases. Mothers, grandmothers, aunts, do not accompany the protagonists when they move away. The bond is severed, with grave consequences for the child/woman.

Psychologically, the separation from the female members of the family leaves the young girls with an incomplete process of mirroring and individuation, without a model to learn from, without the security of a 'mother figure' and of positive, practical help. 'If only Mama had been alive, she would have known what to do', Desiree laments (*Rom*, p. 11). When Adella has her first baby in Kingston, Granny Dee's visit provides invaluable moral and practical support. The break with these women deprives them also of physical warmth and sexual knowledge. For Hyacinth in England, bodily contact is related only to violence, the only positive image given in the book being the memory of Aunt Joyce's warm embrace. She is totally ignorant of what menstruation means, as well as of any sexuality except the association of her father's 'lump' with anger and violence. Warmth in physical contact is scarce in Riley's writing, even in *Romance*, where women and children have a close relationship.

There is another aspect in which the mother has been deemed transcendental by many West Indian writers: the telling of stories, the transmission of a language and an oral culture. Paule Marshall has repeatedly referred to how the powerful language and story-telling of immigrant Bajan women, and in particular her mother, resulted in her own creative power. From the language of their kitchen meetings, she learned not only black culture and their 'poet's skills', but also their confidence:

> All that free-wheeling talk together with the sometimes bawdy jokes and the laughter which often swept the kitchen, was, at its deepest level, an affirmation of their own worth; it said that they could not be demeaned or defeated by the daily trip out to Flatbush. It declared that they had retained and always would a strong sense of their special and unique Black identity.[8]

Riley's characters are deprived of this atmosphere, of this intimate female world. They are not the 'verbal communicators' that Ngcobo talks about (*Let It Be Told*, p. 2), precisely because the connective, intimate 'mothertongue' has been lost. Her characters generally have difficulty in expressing themselves. Those brought to Britain in their childhood are also ignorant of their own culture and history. In *Romance*, it is only the visit of Granny Ruby and Grandpa Clifford from Jamaica that gives back to their great-grand-children the stories and traditions of black West Indian culture, from Anansi to the Maroons, from crochet to West Indian language.

The figures of (absent, remembered) grandmothers, aunts and great-aunts are crucial in all three of Riley's novels. Aunt Joyce is Hyacinth's only refuge. Adella's Granny Dee, together with the aunts, are the female models from whom she can choose, as well as the protection of her childhood.

Mada Beck, the matriarchal figure of the village, is Adella's model for old age, and the general respect she received is sadly compared with Adella's own situation in Britain. Granny Ruby (aided by Grandpa Clifford) transforms the Croydon household with her energy, plain language, stories, and herbal remedies – not to forget her symbolic crochet. It is as if the women need to skip a generation back to find their firm grounding, in a parallel to their quest for black identity, where Africa is, after the West Indies, the ultimate goal.

Where is the resolution of these absences and fragmentations of character in Riley's novels? *The Unbelonging* leaves us with Hyacinth's desperate encounter with the real Jamaica that she had denied herself in her memories: 'She had run back where black people ruled, only to find that it was all a dream. They were all still slaves, still poor, still trodden down' (*Unb*, p. 143). We are presented with her tragedy and her mistakes, not her reconstruction. Adella's death is also tragic in the measure that her final triumph is only an illusion: in her last vision, Stanton comes back and she has the respect of all her children. *Romance* is the first novel to allow room for optimism about the future of the protagonists, for they have, to a great extent, understood what their own selves are about, and have begun to fight for them. The model here has been crucial: Mara, the free woman, devoted friend, who has gained a confident black and female self, and who 'mothers' Verona and Desiree into their new personality. The elements of Mara's own transformation must be noticed. She has changed from being her husband's doormat to leaving him, finishing her education, getting a new job, and understanding in depth her rights as a woman and her culture as a person of African descent. She is practical, and anything but a victim.

The steps of Mara's liberation, a permanent example for Desiree and Verona, are shown as the counterpart of the other two women, in the coupling of opposites that Riley frequently uses in her work. Hyacinth's mental alienation had been made more evident by Perlene's political conscience, Lisa's practicality repeatedly saves Adella while also showing her blindness to Stanton's abuses. Mara, now strong and independent, is a symbol that goes further than these. She has the courage to live her own life as a woman, as a single parent, and to oppose the false political arguments of her own men, speaking to them directly without being intimidated. She is that figure of the 'free woman', the 'free virgin' (again to use Annis Pratt's term) whose independence is resented by men, envied by women and admired (more or less openly) by both. But her influence extends beyond the female model. She is also a confident upholder of black identity, having taken the time and effort to learn about her culture and her roots: 'Desiree glanced at the Africa map clock above the fridge and suddenly it seemed to symbolise all the change Mara had achieved in her life' (*Rom*, p. 218). Mara's full integration in the black community, her friend Olu, her readings, are the opposite end of Verona's dreams of white men, just as her decision in refusing to be stepped on by males is contrasted with Desiree's hesitation. She is the living proof of the truth of Granny Ruby's words 'There's nobody to liberate yourself from but yourself.' As Desiree puts it, looking back, '"Don't you see, V? When me and Mara spend all our time on the way we get treat, we never have time to think about our own self."' (*Rom*, p. 226). Interestingly, Riley's portraits are of victims for whom one feels sympathy, but the only hopeful conclusion in her three novels is this resolution of both sisters, each in their own way, to be their own selves, this conscious abandoning of their role of victims to take their life in their hands.

The resolution of these women's conflicts comes, therefore, through a new kind of mothering: their mothering of each other as friends, sisters, relatives, as a community helping one another to regain a confident self; and ultimately, through their mothering themselves into a new life of their own. In a parallel process, the search back into their history for origins takes them to the West Indies first, then to Africa

'An Africa mythologized as the "mother", source of authenticity, wholeness and original innocence' (Harris, 'Poets in Limbo', p. 122) – an authentic 'Motherland', whose culture will provide its daughters (and sons) in the diaspora with the sense of community and identity needed for survival.

The structure of Riley's novels, as well as the struggle of her characters, is susceptible to wider interpretations, particularly those that encompass the collective struggle of a whole people. Lauretta Ngcobo has suggested that Hyacinth's fate in *The Unbelonging* can be seen as a metaphor for her whole people's fate, for the black experience in Britain, a schizophrenic existence created by the rejection of the host society and the estrangement from the homeland. Paule Marshall has compared her own struggle to break away from her mother with the larger struggle of black people: 'that need to break away, to move away from domination, to prove your own worth'.[9] The need to free themselves from domination is evident in Riley's characters, and ranges from the tyranny of the father in Hyacinth's case, to the loving but patronising influence of the sister, in Verona's. The first easily leads to parallels of slavery and colonialism, the second is more open-ended, but can point to the more subtle ways in which a culture can be silenced or canalised imperceptively – even from the inside.

Riley's exhaustive accounts of black experience in Britain are careful not to romanticise its reality in any way. The failings of certain collective organisations are exposed mercilessly, the miserable existence that extreme poverty allows in parts of Jamaica is not embellished, the oppression of a close rural community and the racism and hypocrisy that is encountered among a certain section of the urban population are evident in Adella's lifestory. Her characters' failings are displayed in understanding, though also in an impacable critique. Her literature is no romance. In this respect, the central motif of her third novel, Verona's compulsive reading of romance books, functions as a 'text within a text', or a contrastive element similar to that of Riley's opposed characters.

The narrator's and characters' comments often amount to a criticism of a literary genre, and a literary manifesto through negation. For this reason, it is worth analysing how the dreams of romance literature fit into the structure of the novel.

Each of Riley's protagonists has a different dream: Jamaica, the return of the husband, or that of romance literature. Each of these dreams represents a legitimate desire of fulfilment, and the mistake of the dreamers lies not in their wishes, but in their inability to distinguish dream and reality. Verona's reading has all the stereotypes of romance as described by studies of the genre: the foreign setting, the mysterious stranger, the virginal heroine, the detailed description of an inevitable attraction between them, the happy ending which never goes beyond a certain (early) point in the relationship. Verona is the classic reader of such fiction: escaping a reality in which she feels inadequate, though knowing that what she reads is only a fantasy of change. But as Alison Light has pointed out, both texts and readers of romance are more complex than the usual explanation of escapism, for romance is a literature in which the woman is subject, and which offers a dream of equality in sexual relationships, while giving women 'uncomplicated access to a subjectivity that is unified and coherent *and* still operating within the field of pleasure'.[10] When Verona wishes, in the middle of Steve's egotistical and rough sexual fumbling, for the gentleness described in her romance books, it is not the fantasy that is at fault, but her inability to demand at least an approximation of it rather than pretend to herself that what is taking place is great. While her desire to be a blonde heroine is obviously misplaced, the more subtle one of being loved and treated as a person is not. Her greatest mistake, of course, is to have mixed reality and fantasy in a deeper sense: associating her hero with whites (aided by her memory of a black man's assault), she has chosen precisely the wrong object for her ideal love. It is also evident, however, that Verona had little alternative reading that could provide her with fantasies not harmful to her. Verona's reading can be seen as a double (if useless) rebellion: a protest against the lack of equality in love, and a demand for a pleasurable literature that would have *her* (black, female) as a positive subject.

In *The Unbelonging*, Charles tells Hyacinth of his own romanticising of his country: 'There is no harm in it, so long as I know the reality,' he says (*Unb*, p. 121). This is the normal reaction to fantasy, and the way that much non-realist literature works. It allows for hope, it works towards utopia, it believes in change. Fantasy is not necessarily limited to escape, but often contains elements of transgression, at times of subversion. Mara's historical and political reading is not incompatible with literature that fulfils fantasies, although the fantasies must be more appropriate than those of traditional, predictable, white romance. Just as many white women writers in the world, after describing in detail the discrimination of women, felt the need to create strong, active, or care-free women to counteract the overwhelming feeling of the inescapable role of the victim, other black writers have opted for the humorous or transgressive model (Grace Nichols is a good example). Riley, in her own work, has chosen mainly to counteract the lies of romance, of boarding-school stories, and presumably of much of the literature available, first and foremost through an uncompromising realism. As a consequence, most of her characters are inevitably victims. However, *Romance* contains, in Mara and in the two sisters' change and hopes for the future, the beginnings of a life, and a literature, which breaks away from victimisation and presents a course of action. It seems an area that the author might explore in her future writing.

Having set out to inscribe into literature the reality of 'the forgotten or unglamorous section of [her] people',[11] Riley's work could not but be on the opposite extreme of romance. Its aim is not the pleasurable model of fantasy literature. It does, however, have the healing quality of allowing recognition in the reader, of contributing to the construction of aspects of selfhood which had become silenced in her community. The fragmentation and absences which she describes in her characters become one with her writing, which is also poised in the schizophrenic world of her fiction. Set between a lost Caribbean past and an English drabness poignantly symbolised in Adella's pail of dirty water, it works towards the recovery/re-creation of a history, a culture, a language. It lacks precise literary precedents but is building, gradually, a more confident expression. It is, once again, a mothering of oneself into writing, shared with other women writers in Britain, and a mothering of each other into a solid literary community which discovers/defines itself in its art.

Notes

1   Lauretta Ngcobo, ed., *Let It Be Told: Black Women Writers in Britain* (First published by Pluto Press in 1987), Virago, London, 1988.

2   All three books are published by The Women's Press, London. The following abbreviations are used: *Unb* (*The Unbelonging*), *WT* (*Waiting in the Twilight*) and *Rom* (*Romance*).

3   In *Let It Be Told*, p. 36, Amryl Johnson quotes a publisher as saying to her: 'I would like to take on your work, but how do I market it? It is like a scream of rage. How do I publish a scream of rage?'

4   Beverley Bryan, Stella Dadzie and Suzanne Scafe, *The Heart of the Race: Black Women's Lives in Britain*, Virago, London, 1985.

5   Hélène Cixous, 'Sorties: Out and Out: Attacks/Ways Out/Forays', from *The Newly Born Woman*, translated by Betsy Wing, English translation published by Minnesota University Press, Minnesota, 1986. French edition, *La Jeune Née*, with Catherine Clément, published by Union Général d'Editions, 1975. This essay was reprinted in *Contemporary Critical Theory*, Dan Latimer, ed., Harcourt, San Diego, 1989, p. 569.

6   Claire Harris, 'Poets in Limbo', in *A Mazing Space*, Shirley Neuman and Smaro Kamboureli, eds., Longspoon/NeWest, Edmonton, 1986, p. 120.

7   Annis Pratt, *Archetypal Patterns in Women's Fiction*, Harvester, Brighton, 1982.

8   Paule Marshall, in an interview with Mary Helen Washington, in *Writing Lives: Conversations between Women Writers*, Mary Chamberlain, ed., Virago, London, 1988, p. 164.

9   Chamberlain, p. 166.

10   Alison Light, '"Returning to Manderley" – Romantic Fiction, Female Sexuality and Class', in *Feminist Literary Theory: A Reader*, Mary Eagleton, ed., Blackwell, Oxford, 1986, p. 142.

11   Introductory notes to *The Unbelonging*, The Women's Press, London, 1985.

Valerie Kibera

Adopted Motherlands: The Novels of Marjorie Macgoye and Bessie Head

Born within a decade of each other on two different continents, Marjorie Macgoye and Bessie Head chose to work out their personal and artistic destiny in adopted African motherlands (Kenya and Botswana respectively) which provide the setting and substance of their fiction. Macgoye and Head differed in their reasons for moving from their natal to their adopted countries and, consequently, in some of the issues they deal with in their novels. What they share is their gender, their vocation as writers and their commitment to their adopted motherlands. This essay explores how these various factors contribute in shaping the fictive world of their novels.

Macgoye, a white woman, was born in England in 1928, went to Kenya as a lay missionary in 1954. Six years later she married a Kenyan and settled permanently in the country where she has worked for most of her life in the book trade. She has published five novels (only two of which, *Coming to Birth* (1986), and *The Present Moment* (1987), will be the subject of this paper,[1] a collection of poetry, *Song of Nyarloka and Other Poems* (1977), and two historical works, *The Story of Kenya: A Nation in the Making* (1986) and *Rebmann* (forthcoming).

Bessie Head was born in South Africa, an illegitimate child of mixed parentage. For breaching the taboo of race – her black father worked as a stablehand for her maternal family – Head's mother was placed in an asylum where Bessie was born in 1937. She was fostered by a Coloured family until she was 13 and then sent to a missionary boarding school; here Bessie was traumatised when informed simultaneously of her mother's recent death and the circumstances of her own birth. Head worked as a teacher and as a journalist in South Africa but, after a brief marriage and her involvement in the legal trial of a friend, she left and went with her young son into permanent exile in Botswana in 1964. Her precarious plight as a 'stateless' person ended in 1979 when she was granted Botswanan citizenship. She died in 1986 at the untimely age of 49. Head published three novels, *When Rain Clouds Gather* (1968), *Maru* (1971) and *A Question of Power* (1974), a collection of short stories, *The Collector of Treasures* (1977) and a historical account of the Tswana village where she lived for a decade *Serowe: Village of the Rain Wind* (1981).

As is evident from *Coming to Birth*, *The Present Moment* and her two historical works, Macgoye's imagination is fired by modern Kenyan history, an era of rapid social change during which the country was founded, colonised, achieved political independence and now confronts the issues of national identity, democracy, justice and development. Macgoye's two central and linked themes – the gradual process of female emancipation and the creation of a nation – are reflected in the constant interplay in her novels between individual and national growth. Paulina, the protagonist of *Coming to Birth* begins her journey to autonomy in the Emergency-racked capital city at precisely the time her colonised motherland is actively engaged in a quest for political independence. Decisive changes in Paulina's life (a failing marriage, an extramarital relationship, her son's death, her growing freedom) are paralleled by landmark national events (the freedom struggle, the achievement of self-government, the major crises of post-colonial Kenya). The early years of the main character in *The Present Moment* coincide with the country's beginnings. When she is barely 17, Wairimu leaves the ridges of home to follow her beckoning rainbow to Nairobi, the city enveloped in the 'golden haze'[2] of her dreams of expanded opportunity and experience. She is in on the new life from the beginning: labouring for a wage in Nairobi and on the coffee farms, participating in the budding African resistance to colonial rule, travelling across the country, learning Swahili, learning to read.

Macgoye's novels, almost exclusively focused on women, present a kind of Kenyan 'herstory' in which private necessity or inclination mesh with widening public opportunities to afford women the means of controlling their lives. The historical changes wrought in female expectations are conveyed in Wairimu's powerfully suggestive metaphor of expanding choice:

> He [Waitoto] had opened a door through which one could see picture after picture . . . and try oneself out on each, accepting or rejecting. Before there had been pictures – Wairimu, girl – Wairimu, bride – Wairimu, mother – Wairimu, elder's wife – Wairimu, grandmother – but nothing to choose between them, only to be chosen. And if one was not chosen to have a child then the pictures became very few indeed.[3]

Unmarried and childless, Wairimu does not yearn for traditional female roles, valuing herself rather for the new knowledge and experience she acquires. Constantly, she reiterates her desire to be 'like a man',[4] 'a chooser and a doer'.[5]

Paulina, a rural 16-year-old beginning her married life in the bewildering big city of Nairobi, meekly accepts the prescribed roles of wife and prospective mother. But, under the pressure of prolonged childlessness, she is forced to seek alternative routes to self-definition, recognising that women cannot view themselves, any more than men do, solely in terms of marriage and parenthood. Before she can accomplish the biological task of birthing a baby, she must engage in the uniquely human one of creating and giving birth to her own identity. She succeeds. Aided by changing times and mores, Paulina is able to equip herself with marketable skills, eventually creating her own ordered, modestly self-sufficient world. The distance she has travelled is apparent in her relationship with her husband. From marriage being 'a whole history of getting used to things',[6] she is at last able to assert the validity of her own perceptions and decisions: 'And in insisting so, Paulina for the first time set up her will against Martin's . . . It was no longer obvious that decisions had been made for her.'[7]

While alive to its communal strengths, Macgoye refuses to idealise traditional society. She holds, as does Achebe in *Things Fall Apart*, that, apart from the colonisers' superior firepower, the traditional African society carried within itself the seeds of its own destruction:

> We have lived, traditionally, a very eventful life as regards plagues, famines, migrations, raiding parties. I don't think any of these ladies grew up in the expectation . . . of a calm course of life . . . We had the picture of that kind of life, but it wasn't one to take for granted. If it had been, perhaps people would have resisted the changes the colonialists brought more strongly.[8]

In Macgoye's novels, history intervenes as both opportunity and tragedy. Kenyan society is depicted as, for the most part, eagerly adapting itself to the new in the shape of material goods, Christianity, modern medicine, transport and formal education. Women step out of predestined fates into a more complex world of dilemma and choice. The underbelly of this new world in formation will bear little scrutiny: there are the slums, prostitutes and abandoned children; the impoverished elderly who end up institutionalised; the demented, like Vitalis, appropriately decked out in the bits and bobs of the new order. However, Macgoye and her female characters throw their weight on the side of the new because it represents widening horizons and a potentially better life. Even when the 'golden haze over the city turns black and smoky',[9] Wairimu, for example, rejects the notion of returning to the ridges of home because they could not 'satisfy even the narrowest part of her dream'.[10]

The modern world which enables individuals to move from provincial inwardness towards a larger life, simultaneously encourages the growth of a national consciousness. The roads and railways which aid Wairimu in her quest for experience also open up the country and unify the fledgling nation. Emerging institutions and modern communications – the army, newspapers, workers, education – engender a community of action and resistance to colonial rule: '. . . what was happening was Nairobi drawing together, becoming, on the African side, a community . . . The ground was ready and the community began to grow.'[11]

Macgoye's heroines start off on their journeys of self-discovery from rural homes but their destination is the city. Here their relations with individuals from other Kenyan ethnic groups account in part for their own individual growth and enlarged consciousness. Paulina's shift from her initial absorption in personal concerns to a wider socio-political engagement is made possible by her encounter in Nairobi with the parking boys and with Mrs M the politician's wife who kindles her interest in the imprisoned female MP. Wairimu learns Swahili in order 'to enter a wider world than the Kikuyu world'.[12] The main characters in *The Present Moment* are from different ethnic groups – Kikuyu, Luo, Luhya, Seychellois, Swahili. Besides forming a community of shared suffering, they are also structurally linked together, often unknown to themselves, in a thicket of social and blood relationships.

However, the search for a national identity and for a genuine nationhood is as problematic as is the modern African world itself. In both Macgoye's novels, the people's hopes for equity, freedom and unity leak away in disillusion, over-taken by a now familiar litany of evils: political assassination, repression, corruption, the growing gulf between a rich elite and the poor majority. The country's post-colonial rulers manipulate ethnic rivalries for the same reason the colonisers did: to further their own interests, to extend and consolidate their power. The Kikuyu who buys the settler's farm where Wairimu works symbolises at one stroke the disillusionment of the post-colonial era and the temporary defeat of African nationalism: not only do his workers' material conditions remain unchanged but soon the workers themselves are replaced by their employer's 'clansmen'.[13] The Pan African ideal of the 1950s, even the already existing East African community, shrink back in the 1970s and 1980s to narrow and fearful isolationism. The current divisions within and between African countries cut deep.

Bessie Head's novels are largely autobiographical, born of her personal history of suffering and exclusion. They explore various facets of her own condition as a Coloured woman, refugee, single parent and artist. Head sought to construct in her fiction her vision of the ideal human society – tolerant, accepting, nurturing. For her this was a serious, even desper-ate enterprise because for most of her life she had suffered the pain of being an 'outsider' even, and perhaps most especially, in the country of her birth. Like Elizabeth in *A Question of Power*, Head, too, 'felt that some of the answers lay in her experiences in Botswana.'[14] Militating against her vision of a harmonious society, typified by human love, generosity and solidarity between men and women, between people of different classes and races, were prejudices rooted in colour, race, class and gender.

South Africa's institutionalised racism was the reason for Head's move to Botswana. She was orphaned twice over: literally at birth and metaphorically when she was forced to choose exile from her native land. As a victim of apartheid, South Africa and the vicious consequences of racism loom large in Head's fiction. In two of her three novels, the main characters, closely modelled on Head herself, are South African refugees living in Botswana. Makhaya, the protagonist of her first novel, escapes to Botswana from South Africa where 'black men were called "boy" and "dog" and "kaffir" . . . '[15] His constant restlessness and turbulent emotional life are a consequence of his bitter experiences in his motherland. Makhaya's thoughts turn incessantly to the exclusion and degradation imposed on blacks at home, to the egotism and vainglory of white arrogance: 'We are this way because we have white skins . . . We don's smell like Black Dogs do and we are also very clever. We invented machinery. We, we, we.'[16] Similarly, Elizabeth, the main character in *A Question of Power*, constantly recalls her past in South Africa: 'It was like living with permanent nervous tension because you did not know why white people there had to go out of their way to hate you or loathe you.'[17]

Her own experiences made Head especially sensitive to and unselective in denouncing bigotry wherever she found it. In *Maru*, the Masarwa (Bushman) Margaret Cadmore is tormented by her Tswana schoolmates as she is despised by their elders. Maru, the Tswana chief who falls in love with Margaret, marvels: 'How universal was the language of oppression! They had said of the Masarwa what every white man had said of every black man: "They can't think for themselves. They don't know anything."'[18]

Gender, another visible form of human difference, also calls forth warped cultural attitudes. Head held that traditional African societies, with their rigidly defined, stereotyped sex roles, encouraged the sexes to objectify and manipulate each other. Makhaya retreats, 'repelled'[19] by what passes for marriage among his poeple, the Zulu: the woman values a man only for his stud services while at the same time internalising her own culturally defined inferiority. In Botswana the relations between the sexes are similarly fraught and distorted. Soon after he crosses the border into Botswana, an old woman offers Makhaya her 10-year-old grandaughter's sexual services for a fee. In Golema Mmidi, where Makhaya settled, the women 'pretended to be inferior' to their 'wilting, effeminate shadows of men who really feared women . . . It was as though a whole society had connived at producing a race of degenerate men by stressing their superiority in the law and overlooking how it affected them as individuals.'[20] Maru, the eponymous hero of Head's second novel, is bitterly disappointed in his numerous relationships with women whom he dismisses as scheming social climbers. In *A Question of Power*, a major part of Elizabeth's inner struggle is directed against her feminine dependency, her fear and disgust of her own sexuality. Both Makhaya and Maru seek out and marry women with whom they can enjoy a relationship characterised by mutual respect and nurturing support. Head's ideal of sexual love is defined thus: it is 'two people mutually feeding each other, not one living on the soul of another, like a ghoul.'[21]

Against all the evils besetting both her natal and adopted societies, Head's moral idealism projects itself in the metaphor of the agricultural co-operative which has a central place in her first and third novels. The co-operative in Golema Mmidi, in *When Rain Clouds Gather*, is 'a unique place' consisting of 'individuals who had fled there to escape the tragedies of life'[22] while the one in *A Question of Power* is located on the edge of the Kalahari desert at Motabeng, 'the place of sand'.[23] Significantly, both communities are composed of, inspired and run by refugees from dead, stultifying worlds – South African, Tswana and English.

For Head, the co-operative operates not just on a technical level, designed to triumph over practical problems, whether archaic land tenure and food production systems or Botswana's inhospitable climate, but on a more vitally human plane. It constitutes a community given over to purposeful, productive work and undergirded by human solidarity. For Head, who had in South Africa 'lived most of [her] life in shattered little bits', it was as a new refugee in Botswana, on the Bamangwato Development Farm, that 'somehow, here the shattered bits began to grow together. There was a sense of wovenness, a wholeness in life here . . . [24] In a similar way, Makhaya in Golema Mmidi 'found his own kind of transformation in this enchanting world' and worked towards 'a putting together of the scattered fragments of his life into a coherent and disciplined whole'.[25] So, too, Elizabeth's work with Kenosi on their experimental vegetable plot helps her to recover her sanity. Elizabeth is like the Cape Gooseberry which she cultivates: it was 'a complete stranger' to Botswana but, in time, the plant 'settled down and became a part of the village life of Motabeng'.[26] Eventually, Elizabeth too roots herself in her adopted country. The novel closes on a note of acceptance: 'As she fell asleep, she placed one soft hand over her land. It was a gesture of belonging.'[27]

Macgoye and Head's fictive worlds share as much in common as the writers themselves do as women and as transplanted individuals. Their novels evince a deep commitment to their adopted societies. In Macgoye's case this is made especially clear in the contrast between her work and that of two white female writers of the colonial period in Kenya. Karen Blixen and Elspeth Huxley wrote primarily for a foreign European audience. While Huxley was an apologist for colonialism, Blixen was intent on cultivating her own fine sensibility in semi-feudal surroundings. For them, Africans were a quaint form of lesser life, exasperating or amusing by turns, 'like children' (an analogy frequently used by colonial writers and settlers). Both authors lavish more space and tenderness on Kenya's flora and fauna than on their 'natives' who are mere bit players in the colonial drama.

Far from being the movers and shakers of society, Macgoye's characters are people of humble origin; yet each individual, whether beggar, parking boy, prostitute or lunatic, is accorded his/her human honour. The old, institutionalised women in *The Present Moment* are not 'problem cases', they are 'people with problems'.[28] Macgoye reveals lives of extraordinary courage, enterprise and resilience lurking behind the most unpromising human facades:

> The stories we learned when we were children were all about big people – braver, stronger, fiercer, cleverer, even wickeder, than anyone we knew. The ordinary people got passed off as hares or hyenas or birds. But if we knew the secrets of those little people, or the littleness of the big people . . . then there would be the true story of our people.[29]

In *Coming to Birth* the writer even stakes a place for herself in her fictional world among the heroine's female network of associations. She is the assistant to Ahoya the missionary, 'the younger one with glasses'[30] present when Ahoya offers refuge to Paulina who gets lost as a newcomer to the big city. Seven years later, at the independence celebrations in Kisumu, 'Paulina spotted the little white girl . . . with two children now and a black husband.'[31] The writer's hopes for and anxieties about her own children are evident in the novel when Paulina ponders the place of mixed-race youngsters in Kenya. One of Macgoye's major themes is the forging of a national consciousness that will enfold Kenyans of all races and ethnic backgrounds.

All Head's novels are markedly autobiographical. The predicament of the main characters in her novels – Makhaya, Margaret, Elizabeth – closely resemble Head's own situation as a refugee or outsider in Botswana. This is most poignantly true of the author's namesake, Elizabeth, in *A Question of Power*, Head's last novel. Elizabeth, like the author, is an orphan, a South African Coloured refugee living with her young son in Botswana, insecure in her new society, afflicted by constant mental breakdowns and engaged in the struggle to understand herself as she searches for her place in her adopted society. For much of the novel Elizabeth remains mentally unhoused by her inner demons. Before she can knit together her divided psyche, she must, over four extended years of mental collapse and anguish, confront and acknowledge her shadow side including her latent racism and her insecurity about her mixed racial identity in a black country. Botswana is the country where the protagonists of her novels, like Head herself, sought – and found – a chance for new beginnings, community and a place to call home.

Also significant for two writers who came as strangers and settled down in a foreign country is the emphasis in both Macgoye and Head's fiction on connectedness, generosity and hospitality. Human beneficence redeems the desolate background in which their novels are set and the trials their characters experience – the slums of Kenya, the harsh climate and beautiful but bleak landscape of Botswana, the class-stratified society in both countries. Makhaya, commenting on the extended drought in Golema Mmidi when, 'Even the trees were dying, from the roots upward', asks Maria, 'does everything die like this?' Her reply is:

> No . . . You may see no rivers on the ground but we keep the rivers inside us. That is why all good things and all good people are called rain. Sometimes we see the rain clouds gather even though not a cloud apears in the sky. It is all in our heart.[32]

Hard pressed as they often are, Macgoye's and Head's characters never lack human solicitude. In *The Present Moment*, Priscilla explains her courtesy towards the mentally unhinged Vitalis in this way: 'My madam . . . would never have turned anyone away from the house roughly. She used to say that in one place or another we were all strangers and pilgrims.'[33] Mma-Millipede, whose wisdom and compassion 'relieves' Makhaya's heart of 'much of its ashes, frustration, and grief',[34] explains to him why she sees 'good in everything': 'It is because of the great burden of life . . . You must learn only one thing. You must never, never put anyone away from you as not your brother.' To Makhaya's query 'Who is my brother, Mama?' she states emphatically: 'It is each person who is alive on the earth.'[35]

An important and revealing aspect of the fiction of both

Macgoye and Head is the recurring image in their novels of the artist figure, emblematic of their own work as constructors of imagined worlds. When Macgoye's parking boys tell Paulina their tales of woe or the old women in *The Present Moment* narrate the story of their lives, we recognise this as part of the author's own storytelling art at work. With great verve, Paulina tells her young charges in the M's household 'one of Amina's Swahili tales'[36]; as she relates it, Paulina 'felt herself hot with the sweat of sympathy',[37] very much how the author herself depicts her characters and the reader responds to them.

Head's novels, a fictional telling and re-telling of the story of her own life, plumb her South African past as a clue to how her present and future in Botswana can be, must be different. In the agricultural co-operative Head creates the kind of environment and nurturing community she herself longed for 'to escape the tragedies of [her own] life'.[38]

In Head's novels, too, we see art's various powers – of consolation, creation, exorcism, revelation, illumination – at work. Art's liberating possibilities, a reflection, perhaps, of how it served in the author's own life, are made clear. The animal carvings of the child-artist Isaac in *When Rain Clouds Gather* outlive his own brief, lonely, impoverished existence and celebrate his memory. In *Maru*, Margaret Cadmore senior, through her art, confers dignity and meaning on the despised Masarwa woman whose corpse she sketches. Elizabeth in *A Question of Power*, like Paulina in *Coming to Birth*, is also an artist: both women refashion their own being; through struggle, suffering and imagination, they create new selves and therefore new destinies. Significantly, when they are well on their way to achieving their new identity, Paulina begins to tell stories while Elizabeth starts writing poetry.

Head's most fully developed artist character is Margaret Cadmore junior in *Maru*. Independent-minded and serene, the girl inherits not just her adoptive mother's limited artistic abilities but the wonderful art of her own people, the Bushmen. Margaret's art is prophetic; her paintings anticipate her

marriage to Maru, bearer of 'a vision of a new world'.[39]
Margaret's paintings speak to Maru of the moral superiority
and the impulse to freedom of the despised of the earth, who
are Margaret's oppressed people just as they are also the
enslaved black majority of Head's own native motherland:

> Thus the message of the pictures went even deeper to his
> heart. 'You see, it is I and my tribe who possess the true
> vitality of this country. You lost it when you sat down
> and let us clean your floors and rear your children and
> cattle. Now we want to be free of you and be busy with
> our own affairs.'[40]

The union of the artist Margaret and the visionary idealist
Maru establishes a version of truth, echoing Plato's Parable
fo the Cave. The novel closes with the Masarwa of Dilepe
energised for freedom by news of Margaret's marriage to the
chief:

> . . . a door silently opened on the small, dark airless room
> in which their souls had been shut for a long time. The
> wind of freedom . . . turned and flowed into the room . . .
> They started to run out into the sunlight, then they turned
> and looked at the dark, small room. They said: 'We are
> not going back there.'[41]

Macgoye and Head are delineators of new societies in the
making where social relations, notably those between the
sexes, are in flux. Both authors focus on the loosening grip
of tradition on women's lives and on the resulting ambivalence in female attitudes to men, marriage and children.
This ambivalence is explained by the very real uncertainty
and confusion women, including the authors themselves,
experience in confronting shifting gender roles in modern
Kenya and Botswana.

Head's characters' concept of egalitarian marriage is undermined by inconsistencies. The leading figures in her first two
novels are men and women in search of a spouse in an equal
marital relationship. The women – Maria, Paulina, Margaret

– are strong, independent-minded individuals; the men –
Gilbert, Makhaya, Maru – are enlightened and sensitive. Yet,
before and after marriage, they all fall back, part of the time
at least, on the old gender roles of female docility and male
mastery. Paulina, we are told, 'always knew where she was
going and what she wanted'.[42] So her startled reaction to her
suitor's offering to make himself a cup of tea is comically
stereotyped: '"Goodness!" she cried in alarm . . . "Don't
touch the fire. It is woman's work."' On this occasion
Makhaya's response is reassuringly progressive: '"It is time
you learned that men live on this earth too. If I want to make
tea, I'll make it, and if I want to sweep the floor, I'll sweep
it."'[43] Less reassuring is a later scene at the cattlepost where
they discover Paulina's son has perished during the long
drought. Refusing to let her see her son's remains, Makhaya
becomes patronisingly protective and possessive: '"Can't you
see I'm here to bear all your burdens? Come on." And he
walked towards the car knowing she would meekly follow
him.'[44]

Something similar occurs in the Maria–Gilbert relationship.
Maria is . . . 'a busy, preoccupied, self-absorbed woman',[45]
Gilbert a forward-looking liberal. But marriage alters them
to fit their conventional roles. When she emphatically rejects
ever wanting to live with him in his mother country,
Gilbert's aggressive reaction is as disturbing as Maria's timid
capitulation:

'You're not Dinorego's daughter any more,' he said to
Maria, in a quiet threatening voice. 'You're my wife now
and you have to do as I say. If I go back to England, you
go there too.'

The woman of common sense retreated rapidly before the
threat, and the other woman softly contradicted her, 'I did
not say I won't obey you, Gilbert. I only wanted to find
out what was on your mind.'[46]

Maru, too, for all his idealism, his denunciation of antiquated social forms and the exploitative relations between the sexes in his society, is himself manipulative, unscrupulous and overbearing. He uses his adoring sister, Dikiledi, as bait to steal Margaret away from his rival, Moleka, the man Margaret loves. Maru then proceeds to claim Margaret in marriage, bundling her off to some faraway isolated place. In none of these plans, which affect her so intimately, does he consult her, still less ask her consent.

Given all these examples of marital inequality, one sympathises with Elizabeth's rejection of marriage in *A Question of Power*. Her well-meaning American friend, Tom, advises her to find herself a husband as a 'defence' against her loneliness and mental suffering. Elizabeth, who is nearly at the end of her long, successful battle with her own female dependency and with 'Dan', her inner demon and symbol of domineering, brute male energy, replies:

> 'It's not a part of my calculations, Tom . . . I don't care to be shoved out of the scheme of things. I want to live the way I am without anyone dictating to me. Maybe in some other life I'll just be a woman cooking food and having babies, but just now Shylock is demanding his pound of flesh. I have to attend the trial . . . '[47]

Macgoye, for her part, 'solves' the problem largely by avoiding it or alluding to it indirectly. She concerns herself almost entirely with women in both her novels. In recalling the men in their past, the motley band of old women in *The Present Moment* hark back to dismal memories of limited happiness, pain, death, loss and betrayal. The only male character rendered in some depth is Paulina's husband, Martin, in *Coming to Birth*. Though he bullies his wife, he is treated sympathetically; we are made to understand that his insecurity is caused by the systematic undermining of his illusions. Yet, in the last analysis, he is weak and inadequate. As his wife's life opens to varied possibilities, his own closes in on his dwindling aspirations.

Macgoye's and Head's fiction reveals an ambiguous

attitude towards children, too. Except for Paulina Sebeso's son and daughter and Elizabeth's neglected young boy, children are peripheral to the lives of the leading female characters as they are not in African society. Childlessness almost seems a necessary qualification for women desiring or even being capable of living a full life. In *The Present Moment*, the old women who are the least crushed and have experienced the most interestingly varied lives are precisely the independent, childless ones such as Wairimu and the ex-prostitute, Nekesa. Much of the anguish of their companions (Bessie, Sophia, Mama Chungu, Rahel) is directly connected with their living or dead children and grandchildren. In *Coming to Birth*, Paulina's childlessness constitutes the very reason she must and can undertake her odysssey in search of an identity. As Elizabeth, a single parent, ruefully puts it in *A Question of Power*: "'Journeys into the soul are not for women with children . . . They are for men.'"[48]

As writers about adopted motherlands, Macgoye and Head have a unique but double-edged perspective: their vantage point allows them, simultaneously, an outsider's clear sightedness, an insider's intimacy and the very real risk of misinterpreting what they see. For all the affinities they share as individuals and as artists, they differ in important ways too. The seeming paradox of their fiction is this: Macgoye seems more in harmony with her adopted society, 4000 miles away from her natal home, than is Head in Botswana right across the border from the country of her birth. The paradox is, however, accounted for by what fundamentally distinguished them as transplanted writers: while Macgoye came out and eventually settled voluntarily in Kenya; Head, like many of her compatriots, was forced into exile by what she regarded as her intolerable existence as a non-white person in South Africa.

Apart from her Christian liberalism, there is little direct evidence of Macgoye's English past in her fiction. She integrated remarkably well into her new community. While well aware of its shortcomings, Macgoye is hopeful about Kenyan society. She can, occasionally, be tartly ironic in deflating the pretensions of the powerful but, generally, hers is a compassionate, optimistic view of human beings. Her style is economical and her dialogue captures faithfully the rhythms of Kenyan speech. So authentic is her portrayal of the lives of African women in colonial and post-colonial times that someone unaware of her race and country of origin would readily assume her novels were written by a native-born Kenyan.

As opposed to Macgoye, there is a scant sense in Head's novels of the larger political world of her adopted country. She is more interested in personal relationships. Her fiction makes very clear that she carried her personal and social traumas with her, determined to resolve them in exile. Her fiction is the record of her personal history and of her efforts to gather together the 'shattered little bits'[49] of her life. In her first novel, Head tells her own story in the guise of a male hero. But the pathos and power of her last novel is that it is so transparently autobiographical: the naked pain and vulnerability of Elizabeth, her namesake and *alter ego*, was Head's condition too; as was Elizabeth's determination to win through to a larger, more adequate conception of her own humanity.

It is against this background that Elizabeth's profound ambivalence to traditional African society becomes comprehensible. She judges it harshly for its narrowness, superstition and male chauvinism; she also lauds its warm hospitality and concern with human relations. Being racially rootless herself, excluded from the village life of Botswana as she once was from family and community in her native South Africa, she wants the kind of community where she could have her niche – the multiracial agricultural co-operative of Motabeng. The co-operative is Head's antidote to the exclusions of tribe, race, class and gender that operate in Southern Africa. More positively, it represents her vision of a transcending brotherhood of humankind.

As one who had been an 'outsider' from birth, Head's main target in her fiction is exclusion of all kinds. Her villains (Matenge, Joas, Seth, Morafi, Pete, Camilla, the chauvinistic male) are drawn in broad, satirical, melodramatic strokes; they are small-minded individuals who seek to delimit and degrade others because of their race, colour, gender or class. The characters of whom Head approves (Mma-Millipede, Gilbert, Makhaya, Maru, Eugene, Margaret Cadmore senior, Birgette) are imbued with generosity of spirit, animated by a love of their fellows and the impulse to draw all within their orbit into a community of interdependent equals.

The work of Macgoye and Head represents an impressive achievement. Their novels, short stories, poetry and non-fiction comprise a substantial body of work. Both women belong to that small band of female writers in Africa who, between the 1960s and the 1980s, grappled with and succeeded at the task of depicting societies in transition and giving voice to the female dimension of experience. Most of all, however, Macgoye's and Head's special achievement lies in their authentic portrayal of motherlands they adopted in adulthood.

Notes

1 Of her five published novels, two are slight works (*Murder in Majengo*, 1968 and *Street Life*, 1987) and one (*Growing up at Lira School*, 1968) is a children's book.

2 Marjorie Macgoye, *The Present Moment*, Heinemann, Kenya, 1987, p. 17.

3 *Ibid.*, p. 54.

4 *Ibid.*, pp. 18, 54, 56.

5 *Ibid.*, p. 18.

6 Marjorie Macgoye, *Coming to Birth*, Heinemann, Kenya, 1986, p. 6.

7 *Ibid.*, pp. 113–114.

8 *The Present Moment*, p. 37.

9 *Ibid.*, p. 49.

10 *Ibid.*, p. 50.
11 *Ibid.*, p. 46.
12 *Ibid.*, p. 54.
13 *Ibid.*, p. 113.
14 Bessie Head, *A Question of Power*, Heinemann, African Writers Series, London, 1968, p. 19.
15 *When Rain Clouds Gather*, Heinemann, New Windmill Series, London, 1968, p. 16.
16 *Ibid.*, p. 133.
17 *A Question of Power*, p. 19.
18 Bessie Head, *Maru*, Heinemann, African Writers Series, London, 1972, p. 109.
19 *When Rain Clouds Gather*, p. 126.
20 *Ibid.*, p. 93.
21 *A Question of Power*, pp. 13 and 197.
22 *When Rain Clouds Gather*, p. 22.
23 *A Question of Power*, p. 19.
24 *Serowe: Village of the Rain Wind*, Heinemann, African Writers Series, London, 1981, p. x.
25 *When Rain Clouds Gather*, p. 122.
26 *A Question of Power, p. 153.*
27 *Ibid.*, p. 206.
28 *The Present Moment*, pp. 36–37.
29 *Ibid.*, p. 88.
30 *Coming to Birth*, p. 20.
31 *Ibid.*, p. 52.
32 *When Rain Clouds Gather*, p. 168.
33 *The Present Moment*, p. 65.
34 *When Rain Clouds Gather*, p. 126.
35 *Ibid.*, p. 130.
36 *Coming to Birth*, p. 103.
37 *Ibid.*, p. 104.
38 *When Rain Clouds Gather*, p. 22.
39 *Maru*, p. 7.
40 *Ibid.*, p. 109.
41 *Ibid.*, p. 126–127.
42 *When Rain Clouds Gather*, p. 77.
43 *Ibid.*, p. 139.
44 *Ibid.*, p. 162.
45 *Ibid.*, p. 28.

46   *Ibid.*, p. 103.
47   *A Question of Power*, p. 192.
48   *Ibid.*, p. 50.
49   *Serowe*, p. x.

Elaine Savory Fido

Mother/lands: Self and Separation in the Work of Buchi Emecheta, Bessie Head and Jean Rhys

Words said that she died not blessing me. That hurt, it did hurt and for twenty years I carried the hurt.

Buchi Emecheta[1]

At a certain moment for the person who has lost every-thing, whether that means, moreover, a being or a country, language is what becomes the country.

Hélène Cixous[2]

No language can sing unless it confronts the Phallic Mother.

Julia Kristeva[3]

Mother. Mother who is the first country, the first known territory which lies outside. Mother, from whom we leave and to whom we return, the one who is the starting point of all journeys and the point of reference for all destinations, even when the relation between mother and daughter is dis-turbed. In a sense, we know that there is no homecoming unless mother is at the end of it. It is through our relations with our mothers that we, daughters, discover who we are and, moreover, whether or not who we are is acceptable. Let there be a break in nurturing support which must come from the one we most resemble, and there is a danger of a self-rejection or self-doubt which can cripple the confidence and dispose a young woman to risky ventures in order to escape. The damage is serious whether our mother dies, is absent or disapproves of us.

Thus I take a woman's relation to her motherland to mean, simultaneously, a number of things. Firstly, there is mother's body which is the first land. This, after we are born and grown to adolescence is the one we watch as we first encounter the mysteries and cycles of being adult and female. Mother belongs to a culture and a country, which becomes ours, and gives us our first social identity. But should the mother's approval be withdrawn from us, or should she leave us in some traumatic way, perhaps we might be willing to perform that fundamental act of betrayal, that of loving someone, somewhere, else. We might seek, in other words, not only a substitute relation with another woman, an adoptive mother, a substitute, but also an adoptive country, a place where we might hope to lose the sense of pain and inadequacy which stems from the difficulties in our relation with our source of self-image. But what if we are, moreover, workers with words, women who seek to ease the inner conflicts by making the world over as text? Then, if we discover our words at the deepest source, we must also discover our loss and our attempts at replacement.

Our interest here is in three women who create a textual relation with the world, who add to the experience of living an experience of making texts, sometimes so tightly woven into their living that one and the other are hard to separate. Buchi Emecheta, Jean Rhys and Bessie Head all write auto-biographically, creating of themselves a fictional self, a space in the world contained by their own words. We know that even when the writer uses the classic construct 'I' that there is still little difference between autobiography and fiction in the sense that both are created versions of the world, shaped and ordered, and merely employing different forms. As Sidonie Smith says:

> The autobiographical text becomes a narrative artifice, privileging a presence, or identity, that does not exist outside language.[4]

Thus the autobiographical account, once text, becomes another kind of artistic enterprise and the reader can read the life between fiction and autobiography with ease. This is particularly important when, as in the case of Jean Rhys and Buchi Emecheta, an autobiography exists which fills out the fictional versions of the life. Rhys and Emecheta both write several versions of the same life stories (as mother or daughter), and the cumulative texts of their lives may be read through both autobiography and fiction. Bessie Head's fiction also contains much autobiographical material, although she is more elusive in this respect, and there is no formal autobiography. But in the case of Rhys, the autobiography does provide a dimension which the fiction omits, that of the artistic woman, the writing woman.

These three writers come from very different backgrounds. Jean Rhys was born in 1890[5] in Dominica, of a white Creole mother of Scottish ancestry and a Welsh father. Bessie Head was born in 1937 in South Africa, of an African father and a white mother. Her mother was incarcerated in an asylum because of her pregnancy, and that is where Bessie was born. Buchi Emecheta was born in 1944 of Igbo parents, in Nigeria. But there are powerful circumstances which link them and make it possible to read their work as comparable, despite differences of style, form and cultural identity.

Most importantly, all three compose not only the stories of a created self or selves, each one a reading of experience by the creative resources of the author, but they also chronicle the missing mother, the one who is not there, whose absence creates an unbridgeable chasm between the homeland and the heart. However we turn, the mother stands behind them and stands in front of us, the readers. But what is marked and ever present in works by all three writers is that the discerning reader has to seek for her. She is absent, silent, yearned after and mourned. She is not there in physical shape, but she affects the very words which we read, and to forget her means that the reading of the text is deeply distorted.

We do not have to seek far to explain this. All three of these women left their mother's land, and in important ways, their mother's tongue, to go and live in exile, after which they became writers. Bessie Head suffered the most traumatic loss of all, since her mother was denied her firstly by reason of her incarceration in the asylum and secondly because of the difference in race between mother and daughter in divided South Africa. It was not some kind of distance or conflict which grew out of the relation between mother and daughter which divided her from her mother, but the simple and undeniable fact of race and the fact of race being used as a social and political divider. Bessie Head's own existence was a subversion of existing laws which tried to exert absolute control over human social contact. She grew up with a foster mother until puberty and was then sent to a mission school and trained as a teacher. Some years later, she left South Africa and went to Botswana, where she lived until she died.

Buchi Emecheta left Nigeria with her husband, as a result of their marriage, but the marriage itself had caused a distance between her and her mother. It failed, and by that time she had five young children and a strong will to try to be a writer. Rather than think of going home, she set about surviving poverty, racism and self-doubt. The result was not only a number of books, but the achievement of the children's well-being and the ownership of a house in London. Finally, after 20 years in England, she came to realise that her mother had loved her, and to think of her memory more fondly and closely than before. But she still felt that her mother 'never understood the short, silent, mystery daughter she had'.[6] It is significant that her own mother's exile from traditional culture (Ibusa, in Eastern Nigeria) to colonial culture (Lagos), preceded Emecheta's own kind of exile.

Jean Rhys left Dominica to study drama in London as a young woman. Her father died a year later and the most likely course for her to take was obviously to return home to her mother in Dominica. But she refused, and instead began to struggle to survive on her own, finding the relatives she had in England too difficult, and soon discovering the poverty and uncertainty of making a life as a music-hall dancer. Eventually, she began to write, after a traumatic love affair which did her a great deal of emotional damage. She returned home only once, many years later, for a few weeks, and it was not a success. Even after her mother moved to England, Rhys did not contact her.

Losing the mother means losing the mother-tongue, that almost private language within language which is a mother's gift to her children. A child who is gifted with words understands this particularly well. When Emecheta says of English that it is not her mother-tongue, she not only suggests something which is common to all writers in post-colonial societies, the knowledge that language is multi-layered, and that a foreign tongue for the heart can still be put to use by becoming a channel of communication for ideas, and an expression of political reality, but she also suggests something deeper even than that, to do with her own personal distance from her mother's reality. The language of the heart is the closest to the mother. When a woman writes her alienation from her mother, she might adopt many different voices, but none will carry that proximity to the mother's culture which marks daughter and mother as two different modulations of the same voice.

I resist the judgment which Judith Kegan Gardner makes in her essay on Jean Rhys, Doris Lessing and Christina Stead, in which she says of Rhys, as well as the others:

> . . . the white colonial woman has no secure place of origin. Their birth nation is not the home of their culture; England is not the home of their birth . . . [7]

In relation to Rhys, this is misleading. Whereas some sense

of displacement no doubt does come from the accident of birth, Rhys can sound the Creole voice of her mother, as well as British English.

Rhys' different voice textures cut across each other. Sometimes male and female interact, as in the double narrative of *Wide Sargasso Sea*,[8] and here the English voice contains and isolates the Creole. Sometimes the Creole becomes an African language, often spoken by an alternative mother like Francine in *Voyage in the Dark*[9] or Christophine in *Wide Sargasso Sea*. In this way, Rhys writes her distance from her mother-island-home into the voices of every text.

In a more complex way, Bessie Head's idiosyncratic English style, which is full of abstractions and moral terms, seems both mission-school and close to the spirit of African traditions of moral teaching through words. Once more this language writes both the separation from the mother, as defiant writer of her own moral code, apart from communal values from and union with her, as one who suffered for her refusal to acknowledge difference between the races. Each of these styles represents a different mode of dealing with the divorce of the tongue from the heart which accompanies the division of mother from daughter.

Also, and this is important, the fact of the British Empire, with its spurious notion of England as a motherland for all who lived within the Empire, gave these writers the resource of exile within an English-speaking, multi-national world. Despite the fact that England was often emotionally and physically cold, racist, excluding, both Rhys and Emecheta found an audience there for their works and enough encouragement for them to persevere with writing at times when they needed that support. For Bessie Head, Botswana was a refuge.

I suggest then that they were willing to be cross-cultural, in their lives as in their writings, because of that early severance from the first powerful loyalty to mother and culture which we have discussed. There is no more important denominator of culture than language, and, as Hélène Cixous observes, language becomes the land of those who are dispossessed of everything else.

Furthermore, each of these writers is differently, but comparably, involved in the business of depicting the growth of the female self, in each case a self which grows to maturity in a strange land and without the assistance and guidance of a mother. One aspect of this experience which has dramatic consequences for the development of a woman's life, and which is prevalent in the works of all three writers, is the often disastrous dependency on male-female relations to advance the young woman's sense of self. The isolated young women in the novels of Rhys, Emecheta and Head turns to men, even whilst the experience is often destructive and disorientating. Mary Daly defines this syndrome well:

> Pathologically re-enacting against her own endogenous powers of resistance to invasion, she sides with her invaders, her possessors. Her false self blends with the Possessor who sedates his Beloved prey.[10]

This serves to explain Buchi Emecheta's bewildered comment on her own behaviour:

> Why, oh, why do I always trust men, look up to them more than to people of my own sex, even though I was brought up by women? I suddenly realised that all this was due to the relationship I had with my mother.[11]

When a daughter loses a mother, she loses lines of communication with other women as well. One solution to distrusting other women is to turn to men, but in the attempt to please them, a false self may be created. Demaris S Wehr writes about the need to destroy this facade:

> Women, too, need to 'die' to something before a new self can be born . . . Perhaps women . . . need to die to the false self system that patriarchy has imposed on them, whatever form it has taken. This is not the same thing as the annihilation of the ego but dying to the false self would

necessarily precede the birth of the true self. The result of this 'death' could be, as with men, a capacity for true relationality.[12]

But the 'false self' is not only the result of patriarchy, but the result of trauma between mother and daughter.

There is a powerful example of this in the accounts which Jean Rhys gives in her autobiography of her mother's preference for black babies as prettier than white ones, and of her own self-rejection as palest of the family and the one called Gwendolyn (white in Welsh). We can see the source of this in the child's reaction to a fair doll she had been sent from England: asked by her mother to give up a similar doll which had dark hair to her sister, Gwendolyn took the pale one into the garden and smashed its face with a rock. This is the clearest declaration of refusal to accept the real self. If the mother does not accept that self, another can be created either in exile or in fiction. It is this self which can confront Kristeva's powerful 'Phallic Mother'.

In addition, as Teresa O'Connor has shown, Rhys' relations with her mother were strained because of her mother's emotional distance. O'Connor quotes from Rhys' Black Exercise Book a passage describing the way in which Rhys remembered her mother coming to her after a nightmare. The passage ends with an acceptance of isolation:

> Yes, I said because when she took her arms away I knew no-one would save me and that I must do it.[13]

There has been much more work on Rhys' connection with her mother and the relation of this to her fiction than in the case of Emecheta or Head. O'Connor recognises that Rhys' heroines are 'singularly motherless; they live without nurture or sustenance, though they seek both endlessly'.[14] Deborah Kelly Kloepfer argues that textualisation becomes the key in Rhys for coming to terms with the image of the mother,[15] and Nancy Harrison, in *Jean Rhys and the Novel as Women's Text*,[16] establishes the idea that there is a 'mother-text' in Rhys' work. She also discusses the important image contained in Rhys' autobiography *Smile Please* of two books, God (the father) as the larger book, and her mother's needle-case as the smaller one,[17] but this evident intertwining of mother and creativity nevertheless confines the mother to the domestic sphere. Susan Rubin Suleiman cites Kristeva in support of her argument that the relation between writing and motherhood has to be explored.[18] Rhys said she was not a good mother herself. That the role of mothering did not attract her perhaps indicates in another way a rejection or judgment of the mother figure who was her first role model.

Woman can then become a riddle, a double layer of sig-nification. She is both outer self and inner self, both false and true, conventional and an outlaw. Even for the woman whose relationship with her mother is good and supportive, there comes a time for individuation, about which Adrienne Rich is perceptive:

> Matrophobia can be seen as a womanly splitting of the self, in the desire to become purged once and for all of our mother's bondage, to become individuated and free. The mother stands for the victim in ourselves, the unfree woman, the martyr. Our personalities seem dangerously to blur and overlap with our mothers'; and, in a desperate attempt to know where mother ends and daughter begins, we perform radical surgery.[19]

Rich defines matrophobia as the fear of *becoming* one's mother, rather than the fear of one's mother.

The most important aspect of the woman writer for us, however, remains that she writes – whatever the superficial aspects of the victim in her life and self, there is a deeper reality, of the controlling creator. We can see this layering of the self in *In the Ditch*,[20] one of Emecheta's early proto-novels, in the character of Adah, in whom the superficial selves of mother, wife and worker become less important than the developing writer.

In Rhys' autobiography, there is also a strong sense that

the writing self is the viable self, and makes the difference between success and failure for the whole life. In her fiction, there is no artist/woman, only the story, told over and over again in different ways, of the hidden self, female, imprisoned, dependent. This culminates in Antoinette's final bid for escape and freedom in *Wide Sargasso Sea*, an escape which is immediately preceded by memory of home, of the island, and of the whole, painful reality of childhood, represented most vividly by Tia, for whom there had been genuine feeling.

Another layering of the self in this novel symbolically relates to real and assumed names, as when Antoinette suffers the name Bertha to be attached to her in her confined and suppressed state. When Antoinette is told that she attacked her visitor, she simply says, 'If I had been wearing my red dress, Richard would have known me': the real identity would have been seen.

Bessie Head gives her major women characters an immensely strong sense of alienation and isolation and depicts their struggles for selfhood. In *Maru*,[21] Margaret Cadmore is faced with a world which tries to stereotype her because of her racial identity. She is honest about her Masarwa background, despite the opportunity to deny it and pretend to be of mixed race which would be less controversial in her circumstances. Her inner self emerges only through the development of her artistic ability, which is in fictional terms the parallel to Head's own capacity to use her writing skill to explore her life and society, as well as to survive the trauma of her childhood.

Very often in the fiction of Emecheta, Head and Rhys, there is a link between a woman's loss of mother and home and problems with her sense of identity. In Emecheta's *In the Ditch*, which is, like *Second-Class Citizen*,[22] an autobiographical proto-novel, the major character Adah suffers from lack of self-confidence. As a mother herself, she desires to give her children 'a good home background with warmth to cushion them through life'.[23] Adah's mother is dead, but she dreams of chatting to her mother while she is ill. At another time, she blames her lack of confidence on having had no real childhood. More explicitly, in *Second-Class Citizen*, Adah says:

> She thought that it was these experiences with Ma so early in life that had given her such a very low opinion of her own sex. Somebody had said somewhere that our characters are usually formed early in life. Yes, that somebody was right. Women still made Adah nervous. They had a way of sapping her self-confidence.[23]

Clearly, for such a woman, going home after a bad experience would be futile, for home presents only more alienation of a much more hurtful kind than exile. Instead, there is an alliance with the foreign society, foreign attitudes and customs. Emecheta has been rightly identified as having perpetuated and reinforced certain negative stereotypes about Igbo culture and Africans in her writing. This is perhaps the symbolic equivalent of the false self, an attitude which both revenges hurt feelings about the mother through attacking her culture and makes peace with the new and alien environment. In *The Slave Girl*[24] Ojebeta asks, after her mother's death, 'Why did she leave me behind with no one to look after me?' She is sold into domestic servitude by her brother (a story which Emecheta identifies as her own mother's in *Head Above Water*), and there follows the story of her growth to maturity in the household of 'Ma' Palagada. There are many times when the mother-role becomes a crucial element in relations between Ojebeta and the world: from the opening question of Okoline at Ma Palagada's market stall, 'Where is your mother?', to the promise of Ojebeta's husband-to-be, to be father to her as she will be mother to him. As a result of the shift from one home to another, because of her mother's death and the selling, Ojebeta must 'learn to be somebody else'.[26] The false self is created for the false mother, to hide the real self which can no longer grow in harmonious relation to the real mother.

In *The Joys of Motherhood*,[27] which is dedicated to all mothers, Nnu Ego is deprived of her own independent-minded mother through death. Once again, the young woman must make her way in life without a mother's experience and without that close bond, that deepest of all intimacies, which comes from the similarity between mother and daughter. Nnu Ego has a loving father, but he lacks the sensitivity to recognise her needs.

Though the novel is structured more around the failings of men and the impact of colonialism on male-female relationships, clearly Nnu Ego's relationship with her dead mother is an implicit level of meaning, a sub-text. For the most important aspect of Ona, Nnu's mother, and perhaps the reason why her husband adores her so much, is that she is her own woman. She is forbidden to marry by her father, but even after her father's death, she will not marry the man she loves, Nnu Ego's father. By contrast, Nnu Ego is a traditionalist who tries to live by all the conventions of wifely and motherly propriety, even in the relative exile of colonial Lagos, where such conventions are breaking down. Lacking her strong and original-minded mother, she searches in vain for happiness. In her turn, she has no close relations with her daughters, and dies deserted, 'with no child to hold her hand'. The question arises, then, as to whether this domesticated, exploited woman is not living a false life, a life which denies the identity once given her because of her looks, that of 'Mammy Water'. The legendary 'Mammy Water' figure is not only beautiful, however, but also an ideal of the independent, talented woman who has difficulty submitting to the confines of conventional marriage and motherhood.

Yet even in her success in submitting to the demands of wifehood and motherhood, Nnu Ego feels trapped and asks 'When will I be free?'[28] She regards herself as a 'prisoner of my own flesh and blood'.[29] Although part of Nnu Ego's unhappiness in Lagos is that she must contend with a rapidly modernising city in which she has no firm place and context as she might at home, Emecheta shows the alienation which occurred in the village. Carole Boyce Davies comments, in her essay on motherhood as depicted by Igbo writers, that it was a pity that Emecheta killed Ona, instead of allowing such a powerful figure to develop in the novel.[30] But Ona's death makes the condition of mother-loss the crucial factor in Nnu Ego's difficult life, and thus is Emecheta's own estrangement from her mother also re-enacted.

In *A Question of Power*,[31] Bessie Head depicts the mental agony of a woman undergoing a breakdown. Near the beginning of the novel there is an important sentence which indicates the disruption of the mother-daughter relationship: speaking of her capacity to blend the normal and abnormal in her mind, Elizabeth says that this was 'manageable to a certain point' because of her background and 'the freedom and flexibility with which she had brought herself up'.[32] This upbringing had been achieved despite a foster mother. Elizabeth's real mother (like Antoinette's in Rhys' *Wide Sargasso Sea*), has been certified insane by society, and the daughter is reminded of this in a cruel and destructive way. In this kind of circumstance, the daughter has to try to choose another pathway, for to yearn after similarity to the absent mother is to yearn after destruction. Obviously this pathway must be pursued alone, and the lack of a mother increases the possibility that the daughter will choose badly, perhaps trying on another self to divert her from the real inner self, who might too much resemble the dangerously needed absent mother. Elizabeth's mother is even described as asking for the latter identification to be made:

'Now you know. Do you think I can bear the stigma of insanity alone? Share it with me.'[33]

An important aspect of the separation between mother and daughter is that they are of different races, the mother being white and Elizabeth both white and African. This difference would not have an important meaning if their family closeness daily overcame it, especially in a culture which tolerated or accepted it. But in the divisive world in which Elizabeth lives, she can only reflect the stresses of separation in nightmare and dislocated feeling. She would, for example, 'fly into a rage and start shouting about not being an African'.[34] She is used to isolation, but it is clearly a factor in her illness, and her isolation, as a refugee, is clearly an extension of her separation from her mother. There is no passionate attachment to country of birth, because there is alienation from that first country, mother herself.

Elizabeth finally recovers and, as part of her recovery, feels she has been taught 'an alertness for falsehoods within'. There is a sense of newness, a rebirth of self, at the end of the novel. Most importantly, she makes a 'gesture of belonging', and that is the last moment that we see her, on the novel's final page. The breakdown, which has really been an important crisis of racial and gender identity, is finally at an end.

In *Maru*, Margaret Cadmore bears the same name as her adoptive mother, the white missionary's wife who is also a talented artist. This is an interesting combination, and Head makes an original character by indicating the dangers of the missionary stance towards people, as well as showing how the artist has a finely tuned unconventional morality. Margaret Cadmore the elder sketches the dead mother of the younger Margaret and gives her dignity by harassing the nurses to wash her body and lay it out for burial. She writes under one sketch, 'She looks like a Goddess.'[35] After the woman is buried, Margaret Cadmore adopts the daughter, names her after herself, but tries to raise her to belong to her own people, the Masarwa. In other words, she tries to prevent a false sense of belonging to develop in the child towards herself, and when the time comes that the young Margaret is trained and able to start her adult life as a teacher, the older woman gives her money and a new handbag, and leaves for England. That handbag is a good symbol of English maternal and female concern. But there is a curious detachment, which develops more out of a rational sense of right and wrong than a heartfelt love for the young woman, and inevitably is damaging for her. There are several hints that the adoption was a kind of experiment for the older Margaret, and whatever we think of her sending her adopted daughter back to her people, we realise that this action exposes the younger woman to dangers and hurts, and effectively leaves her motherless. Instead of rising above the fact of racial difference, because of motherly love for the girl, Margaret Cadmore reinforces it. The symbolism of the goats, the white mother (the Queen of Sheba) and the black kid (the Windscreen-wiper), is an alternative system of relationship: their different colours signify no division in the animal world, and their relations are the normal ones of mother and child. But in the human environment, love is thwarted by material differences.

A woman may also, as part of her rebellion, seek to avoid the reproduction of her mother's experience. Antoinette, for example, in *Wide Sargasso Sea*, like Elizabeth in *A Question of Power*, moves to action rather than replicating her own mother's rather passive insanity. In this she is different from her mother, just as Elizabeth is different from her mother, in her fight to rid herself of hurtful dependence on men, protect her own son and recover a sense of herself. Elizabeth's mother stayed in the asylum, unable to guide and develop her daughter directly.

All three writers also indicate textually a very clear connection between loss of the mother and the risk of exploitation by men. In *After Leaving Mr Mackenzie*,[36] Julia's estrangement from her family is expressed by her mode of relationship to her dying mother and to her sister, who has become caretaker for the mother. In her careful attempts to dress with style and colour, her evident need for money and support and her desire to be in the world, she reminds Nora of her own self-abnegation, and provokes resentment. As in all of Rhys' novels, the real mother is unable to reach the daughter, and so Julia encounters her sister trapped in a superficial persona which seems shallow, vain and unfeeling, and which encourages the kind of relations with men which are inevitably going to lead to Julia's abandonment.

In *Voyage in the Dark*, Anna Morgan is asked by the man who will seduce her and leave her whether Hester Morgan is her mother: she replies, 'No, Hester's my stepmother.' There is then no reason for him to hesitate in his desire to 'fix it up', so that they can meet again. Anna is alone, without the protection and the guidance of a mother. As so often happens in Rhys' writing, the surrogate or substitute mother figures, like Ethel, are exploitative and unable to penetrate the protective outer surface of the central character. Anna is imprisoned by her own facade of indifference, which quickly turns into a prison as men relate to and desire only what they see. The absent mother and the absent island become associated with one another, but neither is close enough to distract Anna for long from her 'exiled' selfhood, her actions which seem divorced from feeling, and directed towards self-hurt. Only once or twice does Anna find that her dead mother returns, in the form of a warning voice. She takes a taxi to Walter Jeffries' house to discuss the letter she has received from his cousin Vincent, and suddenly thinks of dying, her mind returning to her mother's death and the funeral. The mother's presence is seen through the smell of stephanotis, and the candles seem to be crying 'wax tears'. In this short passage there is real feeling, and then the shutter closes once again and Anna adopts her pleading, passive persona, and suffers deep hurt at Walter's hands.

In *Wide Sargasso Sea*, Antoinette's husband knows from the beginning that she is reluctant to marry him. Yet, as she begins to soften towards him, he still thinks of her as well as of the island, that 'What I see is nothing – I want what it *hides* – that is not nothing.'[37] At this point, he can only sense the inner self which Antoinette hides. However, he still desires this, at least until he is manipulated into suspicion and cruelty by Daniel Cosway. But he is always afraid of the intensity and the passion which the vivid landscape suggests to him, and as she becomes more alive, less the 'pale silent creature' he has married, he is more and more aware of his own fear and dread.

In Bessie Head's *A Question of Power*, male figures both torment and help to heal Elizabeth. In *Maru*, both Maru himself and Moleka have important relationships with Margaret. In Emecheta's work, although male figures are characterised with an unrelenting inadequacy, they nevertheless remain important for her central characters. A woman like Adaku in *The Joys of Motherhood*, who refuses to depend on men, or Ona, who loves a man but is not a wife, are more marginal figures. This is ironical in the light of the fact that Buchi Emecheta has lived a life of independence herself. The other side of the separation from the mother is that the father – text, the male principle – becomes both more important and more mistrusted.

In this short paper there is little space to explore these connections fully, but they clearly form a powerful sub-text within the fictional world of the three writers. Exile, then, becomes a space in which hurt can be explored and contained within the creation of fictions, stories which circle the mother's absence and are, at the same time, circled by it. Paula Grace Anderson speaks of Antoinette in *Wide Sargasso Sea* as living in a 'physical and psychic ambivalence', in a 'natural dualistic state',[38] a state which could equally describe the condition of characters in the fiction of both Bessie Head and Buchi Emecheta as well.

I am concerned here with a certain kind of cross-cultural writing. It is possible to live in a foreign country, as an exile, without ever breaking the tie to the birth country. But truly cross-cultural living requires a need to break out of the circle of childhood experience and accept what is foreign and strange as one's own, despite the fact that there are no assurances that the foreign culture will appreciate or reward this. This paper tries to suggest that loss of a mother can cause a woman writer to write culture within fiction in a particularly complex way. Sometimes Rhys, Head and Emecheta are perceived to occupy a somewhat difficult, conflicted place within the canons of literature to which they most obviously belong – West Indian and African literatures. Emecheta clearly absorbed some important influences from Britain in a manner which marks her out as different from other African writers. Rhys has finally been accepted as a Caribbean writer but not without long debate and not without some caution as regards some of her work. Head is sometimes regarded as too idealistic, with the inference that she remains removed from the concrete realities of Southern African life.

However, if we begin to regard such writers as belonging at least as much together, as a group of women whose displacement has to do with the dislocation of a primary relation between mother and daughter, then perhaps we can begin to see the 'true self' of their work emerging best. Head's image of Africa as a 'bewitched crossroads'[39] is perhaps apposite to describe her work, as well as that of Rhys and Emecheta. A place where a number of roads meet and strangely, powerfully, deeply intersect. These writers come from different backgrounds, and their differences are important and should not be ignored. Identity rests upon particularity. But also, and this is very important, they share the difficulty of belonging to spaces in between, to the intersections of cultures.

Notes

1 Buchi Emecheta, *Head Above Water*, Ogwugwu Afo, London and Nigeria, 1986, p. 3.

2 Hélène Cixous, 'From the Scene of the Unconscious to the Scene of History', *The Future of Literary Theory*, ed. Ralph Cohen, Routledge, London and New York, 1989, p. 5.

3 Julia Kristeva, *Desire in Language*, Columbia University Press, New York, 1980, p. 191. Kristeva also says that 'the image of the Mother, for women' is 'a paradise lost, but seemingly close at hand' (DIL, p. 240), focusing again on the notion of a lost country.

4 Sidonie Smith, *A Poetics of Women's Autobiography*, Indiana University Press, Bloomington and Indianapolis, 1987.

5 Jean Rhys is variously said to have been born in 1890 or 1894. The year of her birth was 1890.

6 *Head Above Water*, p. 9.

7 Judith Kegan Gardner, 'The Exhilaration of Exile: Rhys, Stead

and Lessing', in *Women's Writing in Exile*, eds. Mary Lynn Broe and Angela Ingram, University of North Carolina Press, Chapel Hill and London, 1989, p. 141.

8   Jean Rhys, *Wide Sargasso Sea*, Penguin, Harmondsworth, 1966.

9   Jean Rhys, *Voyage in the Dark*, Penguin, Harmondsworth, 1967.

10   Mary Daly, *Gyn/Ecology*, The Women's Press, London, 1979, p. 337.

11   *Head Above Water*, p. 3.

12   Demaris S Wehr, *Jung and Feminism: Liberating Archetypes*, Beacon Press, Boston, 1987, p. 103.

13   Theresa O'Connor, *Jean Rhys: The West Indian Novels*, New York University Press, New York, 1986, p. 24.

14   *Ibid.*, p. 27.

15   Deborah Kelly Kloepfer, *The Unspeakable Mother*, Cornell University Press, Ithaca and London, 1989.

16   Nancy R Harrison, *Jean Rhys and the Novel as Women's Text*, University of North Carolina Press, Chapel Hill and London, 1988.

17   Jean Rhys, *Smile Please*, Donald Ellis, Berkeley, 1979. p. 20.

18   Susan Rubin Suleiman, 'Writing and Motherhood' in *The M/Other Tongue*, eds. Garner, Kahane and Sprengnetter, Cornell University Press, Ithaca, 1985, pp. 352–377.

19   Adrienne Rich, *Of Woman Born*, WW Norton and Company, New York, 1976, p. 236.

20   Buchi Emecheta, *In the Ditch*, Allison & Busby, London, 1979 (revised edition).

21   Bessie Head, *Maru*, Heinemann, London, 1971.

22   Buchi Emecheta, *Second-Class Citizen*, Fontana, London, 1977.

23   *In the Ditch*, p. 82.

24   *Second-Class Citizen*, p. 12.

25   Buchi Emecheta, *The Slave Girl*, Fontana, London, 1979, p 29.

26   Ibid, p. 74.

27   Buchi Emecheta, *The Joys of Motherhood*, Heinemann, London, 1979.

28   Ibid., p. 187.

29   Idem.

30   Carole Boyce Davies, 'Motherhood in the Works of Male and Female Igbo Writers: Achebe, Emecheta, Nwapa and Nzekwu', in *Ngambika: Studies of Women in African Literature*, eds. Carole Boyce Davies and Ann Adams Graves, Africa World Press, Trenton, New Jersey, 1986, p. 253.

31   Bessie Head, *A Question of Power*, Heinemann, London, 1974.
32   *Ibid.*, p. 15.
33   *Ibid.*, p. 17.
34   *Ibid.*, p. 183.
35   *Maru* p. 15.
36   Jean Rhys, *After Leaving Mr Mackenzie*, André Deutsch, London, 1969.
37   *Wide Sargasso Sea*, p. 73.
38   Paula Grace Anderson, 'Jean Rhys' Wide Sargasso Sea: The Other Side/Both Sides Now', a paper presented to the Department of English, University of the West Indies, Mona, Jamaica, May 1981 (unpublished typescript), p. 9.
39   Bessie Head, *A Bewitched Crossroad: An African Saga*, Paragon, New York, 1986.

Notes on Contributors

Laura Niesen de Abruna is associate professor of English at Ithaca College, New York. She has been working on women writers from the Caribbean for the past four years and has delivered several research papers on the subject; she has recently been awarded a Fulbright scholarship to come to Europe and complete her book, entitled *Twentieth Century Women Writers From the English-Speaking Caribbean*.

Ranjana Ash is an extra-mural literature tutor at the University of London, specialising in South Asian literature. She has published several articles and is the editor of *Short Stories from India, Pakistan and Bangladesh*, Nelson, Walton-on-Thames, 1980. She is currently attached to the Centre for Multicultural Education at the Institute of Education as a visiting fellow.

Elleke Boehmer lives in Oxford and is a lecturer in English at the University of Leeds. Her first novel, *Screens Against the Sky*, was published by Bloomsbury, London, in 1990.

Jane Bryce-Okunlola was born and brought up in Tanzania. She is now a freelance writer and editor who has written extensively on African, Afro-American and Black-British literature. She completed a doctoral thesis on Nigerian women's writing at Obafemi Awolowo University in 1989. While in Nigeria, she wrote for the *Guardian* and *This Week*.

Abena Busia is associate professor of English at Rutgers University. She has published articles on discourse and on black-women's writing. A volume of her poems *Testimony of Exiles* has just been published.

Shirley Chew studied at Singapore University and Oxford, and is senior lecturer in English at the University of Leeds. She has published on English and Commonwealth authors, and is the editor of *Arthur Hugh Clough: Selected Poems* (Carcanet, 1987) and *Re-visions of Canadian Literature* (University of Leeds, 1985). At the moment she is collaborating on a critical study of new writing in English from Commonwealth countries.

Carolyn Cooper teaches literature at the University of the West Indies, Mona, Jamaica. She has written and published widely on the subject of Caribbean women's writing and has been the recipient of several research awards for her work. She is one of the contributors to *Out of the Kumbla: Women and Caribbean Literature* (1990), edited by Carole Boyce Davies and Elaine Savory Fido, Africa World Press, Trenton, New Jersey.

Margaret M Dunn is co-ordinator of English and Humanities at Rollins College, Florida. Her particular specialisation is Modern British and American literature; she has published several articles on women writers including H D, Ursula Le Guin, Kate Chopin and Gertrude Stein.

Elaine Savory Fido is a senior lecturer in African, Caribbean and American literature at the University of the West Indies, Barbados. She is presently visiting scholar at Brown University, United States of America. Her published work has been mainly on African and Caribbean writers and theatre. She is co-editor, with Carole Boyce Davies, of *Out of the Kumbla:*

Women and Caribbean Literature, Africa World Press, Trenton, New Jersey, 1990, and is working at the moment on a study of cross-cultural writing by women.

C L Innes is senior lecturer in English at the University of Kent, where she teaches African and Caribbean literature. Recently published books include *Chinua Achebe* Cambridge University Press, Cambridge, (1990) and *The Devil's Own Mirror: The Irishman and the African in Modern Literature*, Three Continents Press, Washington DC, USA, 1990. Dr Innes has also written a number of articles and research papers on African women's writing.

Helen Kanitkar is lector in the Department of Anthropology, School of Oriental and African Studies, University of London. She edits the *Anthropological Bibliography of South Asia* and the *Bulletin of the Vrindaban Research Institute*. Her publications include *Hindus in Britain*, a pamphlet written with R Jackson and published by the School of Oriental and African Studies, London, 1982; her main research interests are South Asian communities in Britain and the Indo–Anglian novel.

Valerie Kibera was born in Kenya and is a lecturer in the Literature Department of Kenyatta University, Nairobi. She is currently on study leave at Teacher's College, Columbia University, working for a doctorate in Education. She is the editor of *An Anthology of East African Short Stories*, Longman, Harlow, 1988.

Ann R. Morris is Director of Graduate Studies in English at Stetson University, Florida. She is a specialist in twentieth century literature and has published a variety of articles on women writers including Kate Chopin, Zora Neale Hurston, Gloria Naylor and Alice Walker.

Judie Newman was educated at the universities of Edinburgh and Cambridge. She is the author of *Saul Bellow and History*, Macmillan, London, 1984, *John Updike*, Macmillan, London,

1988 and *Nadine Gordimer*, Routledge, London, 1988. She is currently a lecturer in English literature at the University of Newcastle-upon-Tyne.

Marlene Nourbese Philip is a Trinidadian novelist, short story writer and poet. She lives in Canada. Her first novel, *Harriet's Daughter* (William Heinemann Ltd, London, 1989), was recently published, as well as a collection of poems, *She Tries her Tongue*, Ragweed Press, Canada, 1989.

Velma Pollard is a lecturer in Education at the University of the West Indies, Jamaica. She is also a short story writer and poet and has recently published a collection of short stories, entitled *Considering Woman*, The Women's Press, London, 1989, and a collection of poetry, *Crown Paint and Other Poems*, Peepal Tree Press, 1988.

Caroline Rooney was born in Zimbabwe and is a tutor in African literature and Women's Writing at Oxford University. She is also assistant editor of the *Southern African Review of Books* as well as the author of several essays on African Women's Writing.

Isabel Carrera Suárez is a lecturer at the University of Oviedo, Spain, where she teaches new literatures in English. Her research interests centre on contemporary writing and literary theory, with special emphasis on feminist criticism and post-colonial literatures. She wrote her doctoral thesis on the short story by women writers in English, and has published essays on Jean Rhys, Margaret Atwood, Doris Lessing and Olga Masters.

Select Critical Bibliography

Berrian, Brenda, *Bibliography of Women Writers From the Caribbean*, Three Continents Press, Washington, 1989.
   Bibliography of African Women Writers and Journalists, Three Continents Press, Washington, 1985.

Brown, Lloyd, *Women Writers in Black Africa*, Greenwood, Connecticut, 1981.

Bruner, Charlotte, *Unwinding Threads: Writing By Women in Africa*, Heinemann, London, 1985.

Christian, Barbara, ed., *Black Feminist Criticism*, Pergamon, New York, 1986.

Cudjoe, Selwyn, ed., *Caribbean Women Writers*, Callaloux, Massachussetts, 1991.

Davies, Carole Boyce and Graves, Anne Adams, eds., *Ngambika: Studies of Women in African Literature*, Africa World Press, Trenton, New Jersey, 1986.

Davies, Carole Boyce and Fido, Elaine, eds., *Out of the Kumbla: Caribbean Women and Literature*, Africa World Press, Trenton, New Jersey, 1990.

Evans, Mari, ed., *Black Women Writers: Arguments and Interviews*, Pluto Publishing, London, 1985.

Ferrier, Carole, ed., *Gender, Politics and Fiction*, University of Queensland Press, London and New York, 1985.

Gates, Henry Louis, ed., *Black Literature and Literary Theory*, Methuen, London and New York, 1985.

    ed., *Race, Writing and Difference*, University of Chicago Press, Chicago, 1986.

Gooneratne, Yasmine, *Silence, Exile and Cunning: The Fiction of Ruth Prawer Jhabwala*, Longman Orient, New Delhi, 1983.

Grewal, S, et al., *Charting the Journey: Writings by Black and Third World Women*, Sheba, London, 1988.

Gunew, Sneja, ed., *Feminist Knowledge: Critique and Construct*, Routledge, London, 1990.

Jain, Jasbir, *Stairs to the Attic: The Novels of Anita Desai*, Printwell, Jaipur, 1987.

    Nayantara Sahgal, Arnold-Heinemann, New Delhi, 1978.

Jones, Eldred and Marjorie, and Palmer, Eustace, eds., *Women Writers in African Literature Today*, Currey, London, 1987.

Jump, Harriet, Devine, *Diverse Voices: Essays on Twentieth Century Women Writers in English*, Harvester, London, 1991.

Kirpal, Viney, ed., *The New Indian Novel in English: A Study of the 1980s*, Allied Publishers, Bombay, 1990.

Kloepfer, Deborah Kelly, *The Unspeakable Mother*, Cornell University Press, Ithaca and London, 1989.

Minh-ha, Trinh, *Woman, Native, Other*, Indiana University Press, Bloomington, 1989.

Moi, Toril, *Sexual/Textual Politics*, Methuen, London, 1985.

Mukherjee, Meenakshi, *The Twice Born Fiction: Themes and Techniques of the Indian Novel in English*, Heinemann, New Delhi, 1971.

Ngcobo, Lauretta, *Let it Be Told: Black Women's Writing in Britain*, Virago, London, 1987.

Rich, Adrienne, *Of Woman Born*, W W Norton, New York, 1976.

Russell, Sandi, *Render Me My Song: African-American Women Writers from Slavery to the Present*, Pandora, London, 1990.

Schipper, Mineke, *Unheard Words*, Allison & Busby, London, 1985.

Showalter, E, ed., *The New Feminist Criticism*, Virago, London, 1986.

Smith, Sidonie, *A Poetics of Women's Autobiography*, Indiana University Press, Bloomington, 1987.

Spivak, Gayatri, *In Other Worlds*, Routledge, London, 1988.
    The Postcolonial Critic, ed. S Harasym, Routledge, London, 1990.

Taiwo, Oladele, *Female Novelists of Modern Africa*, Macmillan, Basingstoke, 1984.

Walker, Alice, *In Search of Our Mothers' Gardens*, The Women's Press, London, 1984.

Wall, Cheryl, ed., *Changing our own Words: Essays on Criticism, Theory and Writing by Black Women*, Routledge, London, 1989.

This is a selected critical bibliography; other useful material can be found in articles in journals such as *Kunapipi, Journal of Commonwealth Literature, Wasafiri, Signs, World Literature Written in English* and many others. Readers should also refer to the notes of individual essays.

Index